Cases and Materials on
Social Security Law

A

AUSTRALIA
The Law Book Company Ltd.
Sydney: Melbourne: Brisbane

CANADA AND U.S.A.
The Carswell Company Ltd.
Agincourt, Ontario

INDIA
N. M. Tripathi Private Ltd.
Bombay
and
Eastern Law House (Private) Ltd.
Calcutta
M.P.P. House
Bangalore

ISRAEL
Steimatzky's Agency Ltd.
Jerusalem: Tel Aviv: Haifa

MALAYSIA: SINGAPORE: BRUNEI
Malayan Law Journal (Pte.) Ltd.
Singapore

NEW ZEALAND
Sweet & Maxwell (N.Z.) Ltd.
Auckland

PAKISTAN
Pakistan Law House
Karachi

Cases and Materials
on
Social Security Law

by

Harry Calvert, LL.M.

Professor of Law and Dean of the Faculty of Law,
University College Cardiff

LONDON
SWEET & MAXWELL
1979

Published in 1979 by
Sweet & Maxwell Limited of
11 New Fetter Lane, London
and printed in Great Britain by
Page Bros. (Norwich) Ltd.

ISBN 0 421 24380 5

PREFACE

MANY of the basic source materials of social security law have long been out of print and some are virtually unobtainable. Particularly for teaching purposes, it is hard to obtain copies in sufficient numbers to ensure ease of access for students and this problem will only be aggravated by their increasing numbers. The aim of this collection is, therefore, the very modest one of making available at a reasonable price (and, therefore, within a limited compass) a personal, portable library.

Obviously, the coverage cannot be comprehensive; indeed, many sources which are admittedly important in one sense or another have been omitted. The book is certainly not a "course-book" (although it can be used as such if properly supplemented) and it should not be assumed that a sufficient familiarity with its contents amounts to a sufficient knowledge of social security law. In particular, the legislative sources of social security law are vast; but they are also readily accessible and obtainable and I have therefore preferred to devote little space to them.

The cases here reproduced are not even, necessarily, "leading cases" in the sense in which that term is normally used. "Leading cases," by definition, receive considerable attention in "following cases" and their sense and purport may appear to some extent in a subsequent report which is more fruitful for pedagogic purposes. I have tried to aim at a general coverage offering breadth of illustration; a less significant decision, if the only one on a minor benefit, will have been preferred to a more significant one on a major benefit already well covered. I have, further, preferred those decisions whose content is richer in its discussion of issues to those whose actual decisions may be more seminal, but whose argumentative content is thin. I may thus have preferred a Commissioner's decision to a High Court decision. All other things being equal, authority rules.

I have found discussions of the subject with my colleagues Alan Page, Antony Lewis and Richard Lewis helpful in compiling this collection. The latter's suggestions with regard to industrial injuries law were particularly valuable.

Blades   H.C.
June 5, 1979

ACKNOWLEDGMENTS are due to the Incorporated Council of Law Reporting and the proprietors of the All England Law Reports and Lloyd's Law Reports for permission to reproduce extracts from their reports.

CONTENTS

Contents

TABLE OF CASES

[Pages where extracts are reproduced are indicated in **bold** type.]

TABLE OF DECISIONS

*Note on Reported Decisions of the National Insurance
Commissioners in National Insurance and
Family Allowance cases*

Reported decisions of the Commissioners, cited frequently
throughout this book, are the chief source of doctrine in United
Kingdom social security law. They are published by HMSO indi-
vidually, as reported and in bound volumes, every four or five
years.

A standard method of citation has been used in all Great Britain
cases since 1950. All reported decisions bear the prefix "R." There
follows next, in brackets, the series symbol. Decisions are now
reported in six series. The original four series are indicated thus:

(G) indicates the general series (Maternity benefit, Widow's
    benefit, Guardian's allowance, child's special allowance
    and death grant);
(P) indicates the retirement pension series;
(S) indicates the sickness benefit series; and
(U) indicates the unemployment benefit series.
(F) indicates the family allowance series (since 1960); and
(A) indicates the recently-added attendance allowance series.

Within each series, reports are cited by reference to number and
year, thus; *R(U)* 7/62 indicates reported unemployment benefit
decision number 7 of 1962.

In Northern Ireland decisions, the same type of symbol is used
in different order. Thus: *R7/62 (UB)* indicates reported Northern
Ireland unemployment benefit decision number 7 of 1962. The
Northern Ireland series are:

D.G. Death Grant.
F.A. Family Allowances.
M.B. Maternity benefits.
  P. Retirement pensions, Widow's benefit, Guardian's
    allowance and child's special allowance.
S.B. Sickness Benefit.
U.B. Unemployment benefit.

Prior to 1951, various methods of citation were used in Great Britain. The prefix "R" did not come into use until 1951. The earliest decisions do not even bear a series indication but are cited solely by reference to case number and year, with the suffix "K" or "K.L.," thus: *652/48 (KL)*. Most decisions before 1951, do, however, bear a series indication, prefixed by "C," thus: *C.U. 19/48*, sometimes with the suffix "K" or "K.L." They are, however, reported in order of case number within each year. The only exception is in the case of Scottish and Welsh decisions, indicated by the symbols "S" or "W" in the prefix, thus: *C.S.U. 14/48 (K)*. These Scottish and Welsh series are separately numbered and appear at the end of the annual list within each series. Thus, in the unemployment benefit series for 1948, *C.U. 109/48 (KL)* is followed by *C.S.U. 14/48 (K)* which is followed in turn by *C.W.U. 6/48 (KL)*.

There is a complete set of reported Great Britain decisions in the custody of the clerk of each National Insurance Local Tribunal who should allow consultation by or on behalf of bona fide appellants at reasonable times.

The decisions referred to in this book are set out in the following pages.

TABLE OF DECISIONS

Pages where extracts are reproduced are indicated in **bold** type.

NORTHERN IRELAND DECISIONS

TABLE OF STATUTES

[Pages where extracts are reproduced are indicated in **bold** type.]

TABLE OF STATUTORY INSTRUMENTS

[Pages where extracts are reproduced are indicated in **bold** type].

CHAPTER 1

UNEMPLOYMENT BENEFIT

SOCIAL SECURITY ACT 1975, ss. 14–18

14—(1) . . . a person . . . shall be entitled—
  (a) to unemployment benefit in respect of any day of unem-
      ployment which forms part of a period of interruption
      of employment; and
  (b) to sickness benefit in respect of any day of incapacity for
      work which forms part of such a period.

. . . .

(3) A person shall not be entitled either to unemployment benefit
or to sickness benefit for the first 3 days of any period of interruption
of employment.
  (4) . . . unemployment or sickness benefit shall be payable—
  (a) at the higher rate specified in relation thereto in Schedule
      4, Part I, paragraph 1—
      (i) in the case of a married woman, during any period
          falling within subsection (5) below, and
     (ii) in the case of a person other than a married woman;
          and
  (b) at the lower rate so specified in the case of a married
      woman during any period not falling within that
      subsection.
  (5) The periods . . . are—
  (a) any period during which she is entitled to an increase of
      benefit in respect of her husband under section 44(2) of
      this Act (dependent husband incapable of self-support)[1];
      and
  (b) any period during which she is residing with[2] her husband
      and he is entitled to—
      (i) an invalidity pension . . . , or
     (ii) a Category A retirement pension . . . , or

[1] See *post*, pp. 310–312.
[2] See *ante*, pp. 301–303.

      (iii) a Category C or Category D retirement pension . . . ,
        or

      (iv) any unemployability supplement or allowance . . . ,
        and

    (*c*) any period during which she is not residing with her husband nor is he contributing to her maintenance at a weekly rate not less than the difference between the higher rate and the lower rate of benefit.—

. . . .

(7) Where a person is entitled to unemployment or sickness benefit, he shall also be entitled to earnings-related supplement of the benefit . . . for any day of unemployment or incapacity for work, being a day . . .

    (*b*) which forms part of a period of interruption of employment and is not earlier than the 13th day of that period; . . . .

. . . .

15. (1) Subject to the following provisions of this section, where in respect of any period of interruption of employment a person has been entitled to sickness benefit for 168 days . . . , then—

    (*a*) he shall cease to be entitled to that benefit for any subsequent day of incapacity for work falling within that period; and

    (*b*) he shall be entitled to an invalidity pension for any day of incapacity for work. . . .

16.—(1) If a person is more than 5 years below pensionable age . . . then, in respect of every day of that period . . . he shall also be entitled to an invalidity allowance . . . .

. . . .

17.—(1) . . . .

    (*a*) . . . a day shall not be treated . . .

      (i) as a day of unemployment unless on that day he is capable of work and he is, or is deemed in accordance with regulations to be, available to be employed . . . , or

      (ii) as a day of incapacity for work unless on that day he is, or is deemed in accordance with regulations to be, incapable of work by reason of some specific disease or bodily or mental disablement,

    ("work", in this paragraph, meaning work which the person can reasonably be expected to do);

    (*b*) where . . . employment . . . has not been terminated,

then . . . a day on which in the normal course that person would not work . . . shall not be treated as a day of unemployment unless each other day in that week . . . on which in the normal course he would so work is a day of interruption of employment;

(c) the expression "day of interruption of employment" means a day which is a day of unemployment or of incapacity for work;

(d) any two days of interruption of employment, whether consecutive or not, within a period of 6 consecutive days shall be treated as a period of interruption of employment and any two periods not separated by a period of more than 13 weeks ("week" for this purpose meaning any period of 7 days) shall be treated as one period of interruption of employment;

(e) Sunday or such other day in each week as may be prescribed shall not be treated as a day or unemployment or of incapacity for work and shall be disregarded in computing any period of consecutive days.

. . . .

(3) Subsections (1) and (2) [which authorises the making of regulations] shall, for the purposes of earnings-related supplement under section 14(7) . . . have effect—

(a) with the substitution for paragraph (b) of subsection (1) of the following paragraph—

"(b) where . . . employment has not been terminated but has been suspended by the employer, a day shall not be treated in relation to that person as a day of unemployment unless it is the 7th or a later day in a continuous period of days on which that suspension has lasted, there being disregarded for the purposes of determining the first 6 days of the period (but for no other purpose)—

(i) Sunday . . .

(ii) any day of . . . holiday . . .

(iii) such other day as may be prescribed;"

. . . .

18.—(1) A person who, in respect of any period of interruption of employment, has been entitled to unemployment benefit for 312 days shall not thereafter be entitled to that benefit for any day of unemployment . . . unless before that day he has requalified for benefit.

Proof

R3/61(UB)

. . . .

. . . the onus lies on the claimant to show that, during the period under consideration, he was unemployed. The claimant's solicitor submitted that, if there was any doubt, his client was entitled to be given the benefit thereof but I do not agree with that. I am not dealing with a criminal charge in which the claimant is the accused. I am concerned with a claim on the National Insurance Fund and the onus is on the claimant to substantiate his claim by proving his case, on the balance of probabilities, in the same way as a plaintif would have to do in a civil action.

. . . .

"Day of unemployment"

R(U)11/73 (T)

. . . .

3. There is no dispute as to the material facts which are as follows. The claimant was employed in Scotland as an aircraft electrician working a 40 hour basic week made up of shifts, separated by a mid day break, totalling 8 hours daily from Monday to Friday inclusive. His basic hourly wage rate (75p per hour) was laid down by a schedule which is in evidence before us. Different increases of this rate were payable for work in excess of 8 hours on any of those days or on Saturday or Sunday. The employers were not what is known as a federated firm, and there was in existence no guaranteed week or other form of guarantee of any kind.

4. By Friday 11th February 1972, as a result of the strike in the coal mining industry, a state of emergency had already been declared and the claimant's employers had been officially notified that no electric power would be available for their premises during the two weeks beginning on 14th February 1972 on any of the days in paragraph 1 above or on Saturday 26th February 1972. Since the employers' operations depended on such power, they on Friday 11th February 1972 notified all concerned that for those two weeks the premises would be closed and there would be no work.

5. On Monday 14th February the shop stewards approached the management and after discussion a verbal agreement, to which we will refer for brevity as the "Monday agreement", was reached

between them. Most of its terms are recorded in a letter from the employers to the manager of the local employment exchange dated 19th April 1972. The effect of the agreement was as follows: the premises would be open and some work would be done during the two weeks: in the first week on Tuesday 15th, Thursday 17th and Saturday 19th February; and in the second week on Tuesday 22nd, Thursday 24th and Friday 25th February. The hours of work would be 11 hours on each Tuesday and Thursday and 8¾ hours on the Saturday and the Friday. "The hourly rate of pay of each employee would be adjusted to ensure that he received the same basic rate of wages for 32.25 hours as he would have received for 40 hours" (the letter of 19th April). Anyone who worked less than 32.25 hours in either week would however receive payment only at his basic rate for the number of hours worked. All calculations would be made on the basic hourly rate, even though normally some of the wage would have been paid as overtime at a higher rate.

6. The claimant duly worked for the six days on which the premises were open during the fortnight. He obtained no other work on any other days during that fortnight. He claimed unemployment benefit for the five days at the head of this decision. He did not claim it for Saturday 26th February and accordingly no question relating to that day is before us.

7. There is no evidence that anything was agreed expressly on the question whether the employees were entitled, on days during the fortnight when the premises were not open, to obtain work elsewhere if they could nor whether on the other hand they were bound to hold themselves at the disposal of the employers. If any change in the arrangements had become necessary because the state of emergency did not last as long as was expected a fresh agreement between the shop stewards and the employers would have been necessary. The claimant himself understood that he was entitled to seek work elsewhere if he wished and that he was not at the disposal of the employers except on the six work days. . . .

15. . . . Unfortunately the word "unemployed" is ambiguous. Sometimes it is used to describe a person who on the day in question has no work or perhaps no work and no pay; sometimes to describe one who has no contract of employment or in whose case there is no subsisting relationship of employer and employee. If an hourly paid worker never works on Saturday, few people would on Saturday describe him in ordinary language as being "unemployed" on that day or his employment as having been terminated. But he may well be unemployed . . . though there may be several reasons why he is not entitled to unemployment

benefit: the day may be an isolated day[3] . . . or a "normal idle day"[4] . . . or the claim may be defeated by regulation 7(1)(f).[5] If however he was put on short time and then did not work on either Friday or Saturday, formerly he could have been entitled to unemployment benefit not merely for the Friday but for the Saturday also. It was for this very reason, as was explained in Tribunal Decision R(U) 11/72 paragraph 10 onwards, that section 4 of the National Insurance Act 1957 was enacted, now replaced by section 20(1)(b) of the Act.[6] That provision makes clear that a person whose employment has not been terminated can in certain circumstances be entitled to unemployment benefit. The first sentence of the local tribunal's reasons in this case was therefore very wide of the mark.

16. In this case there were three separate periods; firstly, the period when the claimant's normal terms of employment, which did not contain or incorporate any guarantee clause, applied before the Friday lay-off took effect; secondly, Monday 14th February, when the Friday lay-off governed the position; and thirdly, the remainder of the fortnight from Tuesday 15th February onwards, when the Monday agreement was in force.

17. In our judgment, none of the cases cited to us is indistinguishable from the present one. In U.D. 6084/24 and R(U) 21/53 the question was not what days were covered by a single payment. There were separate payments made, in the former case as "retaining fees" during a period of suspension, and in the latter case holiday pay. In the case the subject of Decision C.S.U. 2/73 there was no guarantee clause but it appears from the decision that a main purpose of the emergency agreement was that during the power cuts the employees should not suffer suspension or short time. In the present case the claimant was on Friday 11th February suspended and the Monday agreement laid him on again only on certain days. The principle laid down in Decision R(U) 21/56 paragraph 15 was based on the fact that in that case there was in force a guaranteed week clause which resulted in the claimant's being at his employers' disposal on every day. In Decision C.U. 3/73 the Commissioner, Mr. Lazarus, was dealing with a situation where the original agreement did contain a guarantee clause, which was subject to an express availability condition, but an emergency agreement was made to deal with the power cut period. The

---

[3] *i.e.* incapable of being linked with another day of interruption of employment so as to form part of a period of interruption of employment (see *post*, p. 70).
[4] See *post*, pp. 27–32.
[5] Now regulation 7(1)(e), see *post*, pp. 36–44.
[6] Now section 17(3), see *post*, pp. 55–57.

Commissioner felt able to hold on the evidence and the particular facts of the case that Decision R(U) 21/56, which was relied on behalf of the insurance officer, was distinguishable and the claim was allowed. The result was similar in Decision C.U. 4/73, decided also by Mr. Lazarus, but dealt with on the basis that there was no guarantee clause. In Decision C.U. 14/73 (not reported) there was a guaranteed week clause subject to an express availability condition. The claimant was laid off for two days in each week owing to a strike elsewhere in the autumn of 1972. But there was no supervening agreement modifying the guarantee clause. On the evidence and the facts of that case the same Commissioner, Mr. Lazarus, held that it was governed by Decision R(U) 21/56 and the claim failed. These different results in decisions by different Commissioners and even the same one all underline the fact that, since the matter is governed by the application of the general word "unemployed" in regulation 7(1)(a), there may well be different results in cases arising out of the same emergency or similar ones, because they depend on the differing contractual arrangements and other circumstances on the relevant days in the various cases. It therefore by no means follows that the Commissioner's decisions referred to are inconsistent.

18. Having carefully considered Mr. Nuttall's submissions we do not feel justified in accepting them.

19. On each of them an overwhelmingly important fact is that there never was any guarantee clause.[7]

20. As to the first submission (paragraph 13 above) we assume in Mr. Nuttall's favour that he was correct in arguing that Decision R(U) 21/56 gave *a* reason but not necessarily *the only* reason why the existence of a guarantee clause might defeat a claim, and that it might defeat it if its effect was that the claimant was being paid remuneration covering non-working days, even though its effect was not that the claimant was required to be at his employers' disposal on those days. Nevertheless we do not think that his analysis fits the facts. Eventually he was driven to argue that the wage rate had not been adjusted, though the letter of 19th April 1972 records that that was what was agreed and there is no evidence to the contrary. In our judgment the effect of the Monday agreement was that the employers would provide work on the three days in each week and would pay the claimant for the hours which he worked at his basic hourly rate with a small bonus if he worked 32.25 hours. It may well be that everyone hoped that those concerned would receive something approximating, though not exactly

[7] *Post*, p. 18.

B

equivalent, to what they had been earning without overtime in earlier weeks. But in our judgment the claimant was not being remunerated for any of the days during the fortnight which were not working days.

21. As to the second submission (paragraph 14 above), it was in our judgment clearly no part of the Monday agreement that the claimant should be at the employers' disposal on any of the days at the head of this decision or on Saturday 26th February 1972.

22. We think that great caution should be exercised in acceding to the argument which appealed to Mr. Reith that it would be a curious result if during the emergency the claimant received in the form of wages and benefit more than his normal earnings. National insurance law contains many anomalies, some of them in closely related fields: for example an employee whose terms of employment entitle him to wages during a period of sickness can be better off drawing wages and sickness benefit than when working and drawing wages only. The claimant in the present case would not be listened to if he argued that he should be paid because otherwise he would be worse off. Further, we think that Mr. Nuttall's "realistic" argument is a somewhat dangerous one. It has never at any stage been suggested that the Monday agreement was anything but a perfectly genuine one, and our duty is to decide the case on the evidence of what in fact was the agreement between those concerned rather than on any general ideas as to what is "realistic" on which opinions will almost certainly differ.

23. We fully recognise how unfortunate it is when there are different results in appeals, the circumstances of which appear to claimants to be similar. The test to be applied in deciding whether there is title to unemployment benefit may often result in fine distinctions, and one case may fall just on one side of a line, whilst another falls just on the other side. There are however substantial distinctions between the two cases now before us. In this case there was no guarantee clause; in the other[7a] there was: and such a clause is a package containing advantages and disadvantages, and the person concerned must accept the latter with the former. The existence of such a clause at any stage may well make it very difficult for the claimant to establish that the clause was not operative at the relevant time, and that during the period covered by any emergency arrangements he was not throughout at the disposal of the employers. Moreover in this case the Friday lay-off intervened; in the other case there was no such event.

. . . .

[7a] R(U)10/73.

R(U)6/77

. . . .

3. Although the claimant has alluded to other aspects of his entitlement to unemployment benefit, the issue in this appeal is a single narrow one. It is essentially whether the 64 days enumerated (or any of these) constituted days of unemployment (within the meaning of section 14(1) of the Social Security Act 1975), or can be treated as such by virtue of satisfying the conditions of regulation 7(1)(h) of the Social Security (Unemployment, Sickness and Invalidity Benefit) Regulations 1975 [S.I.1975 No. 564].

4. It is explicit in section 14(1) above-cited that a person is not entitled to unemployment benefit except in respect of days of "unemployment". The cardinal requirement of entitlement to benefit thus is that the claimant be unemployed. Confusingly, the words "employment" and "unemployment" are used in different senses, with different connotations, in different contexts in the Act and Regulations. And their effective meaning is, in different contexts, controlled by various positive and negative "deeming" provisions. Although the Social Security Act 1975, in Schedule 20, provides a "Glossary of Expressions", I do not find that very helpful in the present instance. When section 17(1) goes on to provide that "a day shall not be treated in relation to any person . . . as a day of unemployment unless on that day he is capable of work and he is, or is deemed in accordance with regulations to be, available to be employed in an employed earner's employment" it is not proposing an exhaustive definition of "a day of unemployment", it is in effect adjecting an *additional* requirement: namely that the person concerned be not only unemployed, but be capable of work and available (or deemed available). Section 17(1) in no way *relaxes* the cardinal requirement, that the claimant be unemployed. *Prima facie* at least, a day on which a person earns reward for services rendered is not a day of unemployment in his case. But regulation 7(1)(h) above-cited may provide some relaxation.

[Regulation 7(1)(*h*) is set out *post*, p. 65.]

. . . .

6. Although this regulation is couched in negative terms (". . . a day shall not be treated . . .") the statutory provisions which it replaces (with minor changes in terminology) have consistently been construed in a positive sense: as authorising a day which would *prima facie* be regarded as a day of employment to be treated as a day of unemployment by in effect disregarding the employment if it satisfies all 4 prescribed conditions.

7. The days in question were days on which the claimant attended meetings of a local authority as an elected member. In respect of his attendance he received an "attendance allowance" (not actually *paid* until later, but that is of no relevance; compare Decisions R(P) 5/53 and R(P) 1/70). The allowances are said to have been at the discretion of the authority, but the claimant in fact claimed them, in the justifiable expectation of getting them: and he did get them, amounting to £5 or £10 for each attendance, depending on its duration. The claimant has stated that his attendances consistently occupied over 21 hours a week, mainly, I understand, in the evening, so that he was devoting substantial time to council business. The local tribunal found that "As an elected member of a Council the claimant (in common with other Councillors was entitled to and did claim an attendance allowance on occasions when he attended meetings on Council business. Such allowances compensate the elected member". There is no suggestion that these payments were merely reimbursements of expenses.

8. In my judgment, on each of the days in question the claimant was engaged, to a significant extent, in employment, and was not unemployed. Nor can the employment on any of these days be disregarded under regulation 7(1)(h), because, in my judgment, the allowance for which he qualified in respect of each day of attendance, constituted "earnings derived from that employment, in respect of that day": and they exceeded 75 pence, which means that not all of the conditions of regulations 7(1)(h) can be satisfied. It is unnecessary, and inappropriate, that I express my opinion as to the other conditions. The days listed cannot be treated as days of unemployment. Unemployment benefit is not payable in respect of any of them.

R(U)4/71

2. It was agreed that New Year (paid) holidays at the claimant's place of employment be observed "from noon on Wednesday, 31st December 1969 to 12 noon on Saturday, 3rd January 1970". But owing, it is said to a decline in orders, the management found it necessary to close the mill "for the whole of the New Year Week", *i.e.* from closing time on Saturday 27th December 1969 until midnight on Sunday 4th January 1970. At the same time the management intimated—"The three holiday days will, of course, be paid for in the usual way at the appropriate rates".

3. The claimant was thus "idle" during the whole week from Monday, 29th December 1969 to Saturday 3rd January 1970, and claimed unemployment benefit. It was, I understand, accepted that

Monday 29th and Tuesday 30th December 1969 were days of interruption of employment. But a question arose as to whether Wednesday 31st December 1969 was a day of interruption of employment.

4. . . . it has long been recognised that "when in accordance with the terms of his employment an employee is entitled to receive, and does receive, from his employer part wages during periods when his actual services are not required, he continues during such periods to be in employment and is not unemployed"—see, for example, Decision R(U)21/53.

5. No doubt the arrangement between employer and employees whereby the three days holiday should run from noon, so that it was made up of two half days plus two whole days, was intended to suit the interests of all concerned, while at the same time involving an amount of pay equal to three days' pay. As between the employer and the employees, apparently, no difficulty arises from the fact that the three days were not three complete days.

6. But it does not follow, in relation to unemployment insurance, that only three days were affected. Generally speaking the National Insurance Acts are not concerned with parts of a day: the day (*i.e.* from midnight to midnight) is the minimum unit of computation. Where it is desired to take cognizance of parts of a day, special provision may be made. Thus in the case of night workers[7b], whose shift begins on one day and extends over midnight into the following day, special provision is made to declare which of the two days involved is to be treated as a day of interruption of employment, and which is not: . . . Similarly special provision had to be made, . . . to provide that a person who becomes incapable of work during the course of a day may, in the prescribed circumstances, be deemed to be incapable of work throughout that day.[7c]

7. No regulation has been made, so far as I am aware, to provide that if a person receives holiday pay for part of a day only he may be desired nevertheless to be unemployed on that day. In the absence of some such special provision, I am of opinion that since Wednesday 31st Decembr 1969 was a day in respect of which the claimant was entitled to receive, and doubtless did receive, part wages from his employers, he cannot be regarded as being "unemployed" on that day. That day does not count as a day of interruption of employment so as to qualify for unemployment benefit. In my judgment, the decision of the local insurance officer, unanimously affirmed by the local tribunal, was correct.

. . . .

[7b] See *post*, pp. 63–64.
[7c] See S.I. 1975 No. 564, reg. 3(2).

R(U)5/75

. . . .

4. It is a fundamental condition of entitlement to unemployment benefit that the claimant be "unemployed"—or, as it is technically put in the statute—that each day in respect of which unemployment benefit is claimed should be a day of interruption of employment. It is now made clear by the claimant himself that throughout the period in issue he was working under an unexpired contract of employment. In terms of this contract he was entitled to a salary of a stated amount payable at intervals of four weeks. Three such payments had been made, but thereafter there was default in payment. The claimant continued to carry out his duties under the contract, hoping no doubt that his salary would be paid up in due course. It never was: and the claimant then gave up his job, registered for employment and claimed unemployment benefit. The simple fact thus was that for the period in question in this appeal the claimant was working under a contract of service, but was not paid the salary due for that period.

5. The claimant ingeniously bases his appeal to the Commissioner on the contention "that unemployment benefit is designed to protect against loss of income, and not against loss of occupation and that one can be considered unemployed if working in expectation of reward which is eventually not forthcoming due to employers default". He asks for citation of precedent for a person in that position being denied unemployment benefit. I am afraid the claimant's contention represents an entire misconception. The contingency which unemployment insurance insures against is that of unemployment; not default of payment of salary or wages—which is quite a different matter, giving rise no doubt to other remedies or reliefs. This is a fundamental principle. Under the original Unemployment Insurance Acts, the highest appellate authority was the Umpire. In Case No. 8851 (24/11/1924) the Umpire said—"The first qualification for receipt of unemployment benefit is that the applicant is unemployed . . . I can find nothing in the Unemployment Insurance Acts to indicate that a person is to be deemed to be unemployed merely because he is not receiving remuneration for the services he renders to his employer . . .". In Case No. 610 26 (15/3/26) the Umpire dealt specifically with the case where non-payment was due to the default of the employer. He said ". . . I agree with the Chief Insurance Officer that the applicant was, in fact, employed from 17th September to 14th October. Unfortunately for him his employer was dishonest or impecunious, or both, and did not pay him any wages, but that does not alter the fact that he was employed by, and working for,

an employer . . .". In the context of the current National Insurance Acts, a Tribunal of Commissioners (in Decision R(U)18/64 at paragraph 18) reiterated that " . . . The main purpose of insurance against unemployment is to insure against a risk . . . of unemployment". There is no suggestion that default in payment of wages is to be treated as consituting unemployment. It is true that by a specific regulation . . . [8] in circumstances therein prescribed a person who receives payment is treated as not unemployed. But there is no corresponding provision which says that if he fails to receive due wages he shall be deemed to be unemployed. It is also true that certain limited forms of unpaid work (particularly certain forms of training) may in certain circumstances be held not to constitute "employment" so as to debar the person concerned from unemployment benefit—*see*, in particular, Decision R(U) 3/67.[8a] But even in that decision, at paragraph 7, the Commissioner observed ". . . The words 'employment' and 'employed' are not exhaustively defined but it is made clear that a person is gainfully occupied in an employment (and therefore employed) if he is employed under a contract of service . . .". And it is well settled that a person is "gainfully occupied" if he works in the hope or expectation of remuneration or profit, even if that hope or expectation is not, in the end of the day, fulfilled. In comment on the claimant's request to be referred to a precedent. I can only say that I am not aware of any precedent for a person being awarded unemployment benefit in respect of a period in which he fulfilled his part of the contract of employment but the employer failed to pay him his contracted wages or salary.

6. I am satisfied that during the period here in question the claimant was not "unemployed". The days constituting that period were not days of interruption of employment. For this basic reason unemployment benefit cannot be paid for them. It is unnecessary to consider other possible bars to payment, in particular the question whether the claimant was "available" for employment in the sense of the statute, or whether there was good cause for his delay in claiming benefit. I agree with the local tribunal that unemployment benefit is not payable, but my conclusion is arrived at on a different basis.

. . . .

---

[8] See, now; the Social Security (Unemployment, Sickness and Invalidity Benefit) Regulations 1975 (S.I. 1975 No. 564), reg. 7(1)(*d*), *post*, p. 44.
[8a] See *post*, pp. 17/18.

R(U) 33/56

. . . .

2. The claimant was employed as a clerical officer in a Government department from the 1st February, 1954 to the 25th November, 1955. On the latter date he was suspended from duty without pay and on the 28th November, 1955 he claimed unemployment benefit.

3. In reply to further inquiries made on the 19th December, 1955 and the 2nd January, 1956 the employers explained that the claimant was still suspended from duty without pay and was likely to remain so for some considerable time. They said that he was an established civil servant who was suspended for alleged misconduct, which had so far not been proved and which was now being investigated, and that he would be discharged or reinstated according to the outcome of these investigations which would take a long time to complete.

. . . .

7. In Umpire's Decision 137/10/32 (not reported) the Deputy Umpire took the same view of the problem here in question as was subsequently taken in Umpire's Decision 605/40 and the same view appears to be taken in Umpire's Decision 100/28. (It is however to be observed that none of these decisions of the Umpire was reported.) The *ratio decidendi* of Umpire's Decision 13710/32 (not reported) was that "the claimant was under the special rules governing his employment as a civil servant still regarded as being in the employment of the Welsh Board of Health, the board being in the position to direct him to return and perform his duties at any time and the claimant being under obligation so to do." I will assume that the claimant's employers had the right to give the claimant a similar direction.

8. In this case it is not disputed that the claimant was available for employment during the period for which the local insurance officer disallowed his claim for unemployment benefit and in my opinion the fact he might at some future time be obliged to resume his work as a civil servant does not prove that he was not unemployed when his claim for unemployment benefit was disallowed but only that he might cease to be unemployed at some future date.

9. It is true that on the assumption made above if the claimant were ultimately reinstated he would be paid his salary for the period for which he had received unemployment benefit and (since his good faith in obtaining the benefit is not in question) he could not be required to repay the benefit he had received. But the provisions of the National Insurance Act, 1946 which deal with

unemployment benefit constitute a scheme of insurance against the event of the loss of the insured person's means of livelihood. It would be contrary to the manifest object of such a scheme that when this event has occurred and the insured person has suffered the loss of his means of livelihood he should be denied benefit because of the possibility that he might receive a payment at some unknown future date.

. . . .

R(U) 4/63

. . . .

2. The claimant is a charge hand in a linoleum factory. A breakdown occurred in some of the factory plant, with the result that repairs had to be made, and meantime a calender was out of action. On the 10th May 1962, the employers issued a notice in the following terms. "Notice. Due to the fact that the jacket on No. 5 calender has to be changed immediately, the calender will be off until 6 a.m. on Tuesday morning. It is regretted, therefore, that there will be no work available for No. 5 calender and No. 3 Banbury Squads from 6 a.m. Friday, 11th May until 6 a.m. Tuesday 15th May, 1962. Employees should report to the labour exchange and claim benefit on Monday 14th May, 1962. . . .".

3. An official of the union to which many of the affected employees belonged approached the management in order to obtain, if possible, a mitigation of the hardship which the lay-off would cause to his members. The management agreed that workers who had been stood off would be paid a sum equal to half wages for the stand-off period. This sum was to be paid along with the wages earned, on the next pay-day. No express conditions were attached to the payment. The arrangement was made only in relation to the stand-off in question, which was expected to be of short duration, and it was not to be regarded as a precedent.

. . . .

9. It is necessary to come to a conclusion as to the nature of the payment in the present case. It was essentially gratuitous, for the employers were under no obligation to make it. I am satisfied, moreover, that no counter obligations were imposed as a condition of payment. The workpeople affected were not required to be at the disposal of the employers on the days in question. They were free, if they wished, to seek other employment. They were not, by reason of the payment, put under obligation to return to work after the stand-off. According to the trade union official concerned, it was not specifically stipulated that only those workpeople who returned should get the payment. No doubt, in view of the shortness

of the stoppage, it was assumed that virtually all would in fact return. In view of the fact that payment was to be made along with the earned wages on the next pay-day, it was probably an implied condition of payment that the employee should in fact return: but even if this was an implied condition, it does not follow in the least that the employees were put under any obligation to return. There is no evidence that the agreement to pay imposed any obligation on the workpeople either during the stand-off or at the end of the stand-off. No doubt, in agreeing to make the payment, the management were influenced to some extent by the desire to maintain good industrial relation. But the payment was none the less an act of grace, with no obligations attached.   10. Reference was made, in the course of the argument, to Decision R(U) 8/54, which related to a ship's musician who was paid half wages between voyages. In the circumstances of that case, he was held not to be unemployed between voyages. . . . .the fact that the payment was conditional on the claimant undertaking a continuing obligation was, I have no doubt, a very material factor in leading the Commissioner to his conclusion. That factor is not present in the present case.

11. I think the association's representative was right when he said that, but for the payment in question, there would have been no doubt as to the claimant's right to receive unemployment benefit. This is in accordance with what was said in Decision R(U) 11/60, at paragraph 5, where the Commissioner speaking of a factory worker whose employment was temporarily suspended owing to a shortage of orders, said—"In such a case the contract of service between employer and employee is not terminated but employment is suspended and it is understood by both sides that it will be resumed as soon as trade permits. In that case unemployment benefit is commonly paid during the period of suspension."

12. Taking the view, as I do, that the payment in the present case represented an act of grace by the employer, involving no obligation on the part of the employees, I see no reason why its receipt should deprive the claimant of unemployment benefit for the days in question, to which I understand he is admittedly otherwise entitled. I hold that the days in question were days of unemployment in the case of the claimant, and that he is entitled to receive unemployment benefit in respect of them.

. . . .

(See also, R(U)10/73, R(U)1/75, R(U)1/76, R(U)3/67, below.)

Training

R(U) 3/67

. . . .

. . . the claimant, whose home was in Bristol, was attending a selection and training course at . . . London. On the completion of the course he was accepted . . . for employment, and started work under a contract of service. He received no remuneration while attending the course, but his travelling expenses were reimbursed and he received a subsistence allowance.

. . . .

6. It is clear from paragraphs 6 and 8 of Decision R(U) 4/59 that the Commissioner's conclusion was based on his acceptance of certain observations of the Umpire . . . in relation to cases arising under the repealed Unemployment Insurance Acts. The particular observation which the Commissioner thought to be in point and applied was as follows:—"Where a person is required to undergo a course of training with an employer as a condition of future employment at wages, and has accepted training with a definite understanding (*sic*) that he will be employed for wages by the person giving the training when he becomes proficient, he is to be regarded as employed during the period of training."

7. It may be that this fairly expounded the law as it was under the Unemployment Insurance Acts. The language of those Acts however was in many important respects different from the language of the National Insurance Acts and with all respect to the learned author of Decision R(U) 4/59 I cannot regard the Umpire's observation as a reliable guide to the question I have to decide. There seem to me several reasons for a circumspect approach to the Umpire's views, but for the purpose of the present appeal I need only mention one. In the context of the . . . Acts and the Regulations made thereunder it seems to me clear that in principle—that is, except when a regulation specifically provides for exceptional treatment of a particular case—a person is employed if he is gainfully occupied in an employment, and that he is not employed (or is unemployed) if he is not so gainfully occupied. The words "employment" and "employed" are not exhaustively defined, but it is made clear that a person is gainfully occupied in an employment (and therefore employed) if he is employed under a contract of services, if he holds an office of profit, if he carries on a trade or business, or if he exercises a profession or vocation [See, now, the Social Security Act 1975, ss. 2 and 51 and Sched. 20].

8. I find nothing . . . which requires me to give the word "unemployed" a special meaning. I therefore conclude that the regulation requires a person claiming unemployment benefit for any day to prove that he was not gainfully occupied in employment on that day.

9. It is clear on the facts that in the week I am considering the claimant was not employed under a contract of service. He was therefore unemployed unless he was gainfully occupied in some other kind of employment . . . . I do not think . . . that attendance at the course can aptly be described as occupation in an employment. The true view is that while *a priori* unemployed the claimant was qualifying for employment under a contract of service. In any case he was not gainfully occupied. He received no remuneration; he was merely reimbursed his travelling expenses, and received a payment towards the cost of his living expenses while away from home.

  . . . .

Guarantee agreements

(See also, the Employment Protection (Consolidation) Act 1978, ss. 12–18).

R(U) 21/56T

  . . . .

13. The question of the effect of a guaranteed week agreement was dealt with recently in Decision C.U. 12/56. . . .[9] That decision was given by a single Commissioner. When it was learned that the present appeals were to be brought it was not known that the question whether the 1956 guarantee was effective might arise and it was thought desirable that a tribunal of three Commissioners should take the opportunity to consider whether the views expressed in Decision C.U. 12/56 required any modification.

  . . . .

15. In our opinion the burden of proof resting on the claimant in such cases was correctly stated in the following passage in Decision C.U. 12/56 (not reported). "The burden of proving that he was unemployed on the 6th March [the date there in question] rests upon the claimant. To discharge it he must show that he was under no obligation to place his services at the disposal of his employers on that day. Whether he can show this depends upon

[9] Decision C.U. 12/56 is reported as an appendix to R(U) 21/56. For later consideration of R(U)21/56, see R(U)10/73 and R(U)11/73, (*ante*, pp. 4–8.), R(U)1/75 and R(U)1/76.

whether the meaning of the guarantee agreement is that in consideration of the guaranteed payment of minimum earnings of [the
sum specified] the claimant will remain at the employers' disposal
for all the days of the working week (which is a 5-day week) or
only for [the guaranteed number] of those days." In other words
the ultimate question in these cases is not—what does the employer
guarantee? but—what does the employee undertake in consideration of the employer's guarantee? The agreement dealt with in
Decision C.U. 12/56 contained a provision which the Commissioner
interpreted in the light of its context as meaning that the employee
only undertook to be at the employer's disposal on 4 days in the
week in contrast to such agreements as that considered in Umpire's
Decision 958/41 which provided that the guarantee was conditional
on the claimant keeping himself available each day up to 2 p.m.
Where there is no such express provision the employee's obligation
may be inferred from the terms of the employer's guarantee. Thus
if the guarantee is expressed to be of a weekly payment and no
mention is made of any period of work the inference is that the
guarantee is offered and accepted on the terms that the employee's
services will be at the employer's disposal on every working day
of the week.

16. It follows from the view expressed above that if (as we hold)
the 1946 guarantee still applied to the claimant during the period
in question he was not unemployed during that period. That
guarantee was of wages equivalent to his inclusive hourly plain
time rate of 34 hours in any pay week provided that the claimant
was available for work during working hours. Under such agreement the claimant clearly undertakes that in consideration of the
guaranteed payment he will be at the disposal of the employers
for 34 hours which could be spread over the entire week.

. . . .

Exclusionary rules

Days which fall prima facie to be classified as days of unemployment by
the above criteria may nevertheless be excluded by, *e.g.* the "normal idle
day rule" (s. 17(1)(*b*), *ante*, p. 2), the suspension rule in the case of
earnings-related benefit only (s. 17(3), *ante*, p. 3) and various others
established by regulation and considered below. Many of these rules are
conditioned upon the employment having terminated.

Termination of employment

R(U) 7/68 (T)

. . . .

8. Under the National Insurance Act 1911 every workman who, having been employed in one of certain specified trades, was unemployed and fulfilled the statutory conditions was entitled to unemployment benefit (section 84 and the Sixth Schedule). The Act contained a trade dispute provision, which can be recognised as the forerunner of section 22(1) of the 1965 Act. There was however no specific provision for holidays or days on which the workman did not ordinarily work. So far as relevant to this appeal, the short question which had to be decided was whether the workman had been "continuously unemployed" (section 86(2)). In Umpire's Decision 228 (given in 1912) the Umpire said "As at present advised, I do not consider that a workman has been continuously unemployed when his non-employment is due to recognised annual holidays which form part of the accepted terms of his engagement, there being the intention on the part of the workman to resume work and on the part of the employer to accept the workman's services at the termination of such holidays in the ordinary course. Where such holidays are extended by mutual consent the extended period forms part of the regular holidays. Where the extension is to meet the employer's convenience alone, then during such extended period the workman has not been employed." Further decision under the 1911 Act are U.D. 301 and U.D. 393.

9. In the Unemployment Insurance Acts 1920 and 1935, the main Acts which replaced and extended the 1911 Act, the classes of persons who came within the scope of the insurance were defined somewhat differently. They no longer referred to a person who had been employed in a trade: "all persons . . . who are engaged in any of the employments specified" in a Schedule were insured. The Schedule referred mainly to employment under any contract of service. Under both these Acts therefore the insurance was directly related to the contract. Such provisions obviously give rise to a problem. If the only person insured is a person who is employed under a contract of service, how can he at the same time be unemployed? As to this it is necessary to say no more than that under both the present and past legislation it has always been accepted that a person may be unemployed even though his contract of service continues to run, *e.g.* a factory worker who is temporarily laid off for a few days but would be regarded as continuing in the employment of the occupiers of the factory.

Under the 1920 and 1935 Acts there was still a trade dispute disqualification but no specific reference to holidays nor any specific provision for any normal idle days. The question, so far as relevant to this case, still was whether the claimant had been continuously unemployed.

10. Under the 1920 Act the Umpires continued to develop the doctrine referred to in paragraph 8 above. See U.DD. 473, 535, 536, 614, 3599, 5819, 1331/26, 16930/31 and 18284/32. During this period the doctrine was extended to trade dispute cases and the "12 days rule"[9a] was evolved. The effect of this rule was that if a person's employment had been terminated (in the ordinary sense) before a period during which, if still subject to a contract of employment, he would have been disentitled to benefit, *e.g.* a holiday period or a period of a strike, benefit was disallowed unless at least 12 days before that period he had been discharged and there was no intention of resuming the relationship of employer and employee on the next available opportunity (U.D. 16930/31). By then the doctrine had become extremely elaborate, and in U.D. 18284/32 the Umpire laid down 21 main principles for dealing with holiday cases.

11. The 1965 Act divides insured persons for the purposes of the Act into three classes, employed persons, self-employed persons and non-employed persons. "Employed persons" are persons gainfully occupied in employment in Great Britain, being employment under a contract of service (section 1(2)).[10] It is clear from the definition of self-employed persons that a person can be gainfully occupied in employment in Great Britain but at the same time not be an "employed person". That phrase therefore has a special technical meaning. The interpretation section (section 114)[10] provides that, except where the context otherwise requires, "employed contributor's employment" means any employment by virtue of which an insured person is an employed person; and "employment" includes any trade, business, profession, office or vocation and "employed" shall be construed accordingly except in the expression "employed person". . . .

12. If we disregard certain provisions which never came into force owing to the outbreak of war (see paragraph 5 of Decision R(U) 1/62), the first express provision for holidays was contained in regulation 6(1)(c)(i) of the National Insurance (Unemployment and Sickness Benefit) Regulations 1948 [S.I. 1948 No. 1277]. This provided that for the purposes of unemployment and sickness

[9a] See now R(U)6/71, *post*, p. 84.
[10] See, now, Social Security Act 1975, ss. 2 and 51 and *sched.* 20, definition of "Employed earner."

benefit "a day shall not be treated as a day of unemployment if on that day a person does no work, and—(i) is on holiday; . . .". Regulation 6(2) qualified this provision and referred to indefinite suspension and termination of the employment; regulation 6(1)(d) also referred to termination.

13. The "normal idle day" rule was first enacted by section 4(1) of the National Insurance Act 1957, which provided that "where a person is employed in any employed contributor's employment which has not been terminated" certain legal consequences follow unless an additional condition is fulfilled. Section 4(2) enabled regulations to prescribe amongst other things circumstances in which an employed contributor's employment which had not been terminated might be treated as if it had been terminated. (We will refer to these as the 1957 Act and section 4.) Section 4 is reproduced in section 20(1)(b), as originally enacted, of the 1965 Act, which still applies and will apply until March 1969 (as the law stands at present) for the purposes of basic unemployment benefit. The new paragraph 20(1)(b), substituted by the 1966 Act, is in operation for the purposes of earnings-related supplement, but not yet for those of basic unemployment benefit. We therefore have the situation that two different statutory provisions at present operate concurrently for different parts of the same benefit claimed for the same day.[11] The new section 20(1)(b) provides that "where an employed contributor's employment has not been terminated but a person's employment therein has been suspended by the employer, a day shall not be treated in relation to that person as a day of unemployment unless it is the seventh or a later day in a continuous period of days on which that suspension has lasted," certain days being disregarded for that purpose. A new paragraph 20(2)(b) gives the Minister (now the Secretary of State) the widest powers to prescribe circumstances in which an employed contributor's employment may be treated as having been, or not having been, terminated or suspended for the purposes of the new section 20(1)(b).

14. Between 1948 and 1966 the Commissioner accepted that the Umpire's doctrine of termination of employment applied equally under the legislation in force during that period; see for example, Decision R(U) 20/57 in relation to the trade dispute provision, Decisions R(U) 16, 17 and 18/59 in relation to the normal idle day provision and Decisions R(U) 19/59, R(U) 1/62, R(U) 1/66 and R(U) 2/66 in relation to holidays. All these were decisions of Tribunals of Commissioners. In Decision C.S.U. 4/61 (not

---

[11] See, now, Social Security Act 1975, ss. 17(1) and (3), *ante*, p. 2.

reported) a Commissioner applied the same doctrine under regulation 6(1)(d).

15. The Umpire's doctrine of termination was stated in Decision R(U) 16/59 as follows:

> "8. The distinction between the "termination" and the "suspension" of employment was formulated by the Umpire in decisions under the Unemployment Insurance Acts. It may be well to point out that in these decisions the Umpire did not use the word termination in the sense of termination of the legal obligations of the contract of service . . . The Umpire used the word "terminated" as meaning "finally discharged without any intention of resuming the relationship of employer and employee on the next available opportunity". See Umpire's Decision 16930/31.
>
> 9. By the words "on the next available opportunity" the Umpire clearly meant an opportunity which would occur after an interval of unemployment which was not longer than the employee would normally be prepared to accept before taking employment elsewhere."

16. Regulation 6(1)(e)(i) was revoked as from 6th October, 1966 by the National Insurance (Unemployment and Sickness Benefit) Amendment Regulations 1966 (S.I. 1966 No. 1049], which substituted for it as regulation 6A a provision which is now in regulation 7(1)(j) of the (consolidating) regulations of 1967.[12] This provides that ". . . where in the case of any person an employed contributor's employment has not been terminated, a day shall not be treated as a day of unemployment if it is a day of recognised or customary holiday in connection with that employment, unless that person's employment therein has been indefinitely suspended and the day in question is the seventh or a later day, ascertained in accordance with the provisions of section 20(1)(b) of the Act, as substituted by section 3(1) of the 1966 Act, in a continuous period of days on which that suspension has lasted. . . ."

. . . .

19. The insurance officer's representative helpfully formulated his main propositions in writing in a document headed "General propositions". One of these was that if the employment of a claimant who regularly works intermittently for one employer in an industry at a place is regarded as suspended by his employer under the "finally discharged without any intention of resuming

---

[12] See, now, the Social Security (Unemployment, Sickness and Invalidity Benefit) Regulations 1975 (S.I. 1975 No. 564) reg. 7(1)(i), *post*, p. 51.

the employer/employee relationship at the next available opportunity" test, the employment of a claimant who regularly works intermittently for more than one employer in that industry at that place should similarly be regarded as suspended.

20. The 1965 Act was a consolidating Act, and the insurance officer did not seek to rely on the fact that section 20(1)(b) of the 1965 Act re-enacted words which had been interpreted by the Commissioner under section 4 of the 1957 Act. We think that his argument can be stated most strongly in relation to the enactment of the new section 20(1)(b) in 1966 containing those words which had since 1957 been construed in accordance with the Umpire's doctrine. The argument seems to us however to be much weakened by the mention in the section of suspension used in contrast to termination. The argument also seems to us far less strong where it is based on the reference to termination of employment in section 4 of the 1957 Act and the 1948 regulations. The Umpire's explanation of the meaning of termination was not an interpretation of that word appearing in any Act, but of the word used in phrases devised by him or his predecessor to explain words which were in the Act. In relation to holidays the interpretation was two stages removed from the Act. He explained "termination", which he used to explain what was meant by being on holiday, which was not in the Act but was itself an explanation of the meaning of the phrase "continuously unemployed", which did appear in the Act. We have of course not overlooked the further argument open to the insurance officer that the practice of a Tribunal of Commissioners has almost invariably been to follow earlier decisions of such a Tribunal, and any other course has been taken only in exceptional circumstances.

. . . .

22. In considering whether the Umpire's doctrine ought to be departed from we think it important to have in mind both the history of decisions by which it came to be accepted and the effects which have resulted and are likely to result from its adoption. Decision R(U) 11/53 was a decision on the meaning of "on holiday" in regulation 6(1)(e)(i), in which the Commissioner adopted in favour of the claimant the Umpire's limitation of the meaning of the words based on recognised or customary holiday, although no such words appeared in the regulations. In Decision R(U) 20/57 the Tribunal of Commissioners were concerned with the trade dispute section, which was a re-enactment of a similar provision in earlier legislation. In considering the question whether the claimant had lost employment by reason of a stoppage of work they adopted the Umpire's principle but held on the facts that the

employment had been terminated and the claimant was therefore not disqualified. Manifestly, if they had not adopted the Umpire's interpretation, the same conclusion would have been reached. Strictly speaking therefore their adoption of it was not necessary to the decision.

23. Decisions R(U) 16, 17 and 18/59 were decisions on section 4 of the 1957 Act. Here for the first time the Commissioners were concerned with a section which included the words "employed contributor's employment". If we write out section 4 or the original section 20(1)(b) in full in the light of the interpretation sections in the statutes it reads as follows:—

> ". . . where a person is employed in any employed contributor's employment, that is to say employment by virtue of which he is an "employed person", which means a person employed under a contract of service, which has not been terminated . . ."

24. Decisions R(U) 16 to 18/59 contain no reference to the definition of "employed contributor's employment" or an "employed person", and we venture to think that insufficient attention was paid to the question whether the Umpire's doctrine could be applicable under the 1946 or the 1957 Act. In considering whether a person had been continuously unemployed the Umpire was dealing with a period of time, and it may well be that a somewhat imprecise conception of employment was permissible. Under the 1946, as well as the 1965, legislation we are concerned with individual days of unemployment, each of which if necessary has to be considered separately. In our judgment where one is dealing with employment, on a particular day, under a contract of service, which has not been terminated, this involves precise concepts, where the Umpire's doctrine is wholly inappropriate. In our judgment the acceptance of that doctrine in the 1959 cases was erroneous.

25. This is confirmed if one considers what the results have been. The insurance officer's representative told us that paragraph 9 of Decision R(U) 16/59 does not represent anything which is to be found in any Umpire's decision. It is a gloss on them, designed to limit, in favour of the claimant, the severity of the Umpire's rule, and it was relied on for that purpose by the majority in Decisions R(U) 1/66 and R(U) 2/66. In Decision R(U) 19/59 the Umpire's doctrine was applied under the holiday regulation [see *post*, pp. 51–55] . . . and this was followed in Decision R(U) 1/62, a case where unfortunately the claimant was unrepresented, his argu-

ments were of little assistance, and he did not appear before either the local tribunal or the Commissioners.

26. The history of the holiday cases since 1962 is that of a stream of indignant appellants who could not understand how their employment could be said not to have terminated when their contract of employment no longer subsisted. Countless anomalies were disclosed, as can be seen from many decisions collected in Mr. Jenkins' Digest at page 533 and the following pages, and in even more numerous unreported decisions. In the present case the insurance officer admits that a group of employers cannot be regarded for any of the relevant purposes as 'the' employer. It seems to us that his proposition would produce further difficult problems in deciding the limits of an industry and a place. The present case illustrates the extreme difficulty of drawing the line. The Umpire's doctrine was applied in the 1959 decisions where there were several employers in one dockyard; here there are more numerous employers spread over different parts of London.

27. At the hearing a further anomaly was revealed between decisions of the Minister of Social Security (now the Secretary of State for Social Services) on contribution and credit questions and those of the statutory authorities. In answer to an enquiry from us the insurance officer's representative ascertained that where on a credit question the Minister is deciding whether employment has been terminated and the question would have been decided by the statutory authorities if the matter had come before them, the Minister applies the Umpire's doctrine in the same way as the statutory authorities would have done. If on the other hand the question is one for decision by the Minister in any event, then "termination" is interpreted according to its natural and ordinary meaning.

28. Our attention was drawn to a number of recent Commissioner's decisions, in which different views of these problems have been expressed. They included Decisions R(U) 4/67, C.U. 21/67, C.U. 1/68, C.U. 5/68 and C.S.U. 1/68 (the last four not reported).

29. Having given this matter anxious and careful consideration we have reached the clear conclusion that the Umpire's doctrine which we have discussed should not be applied in this case. In our judgment the phrase termination of employment in the old and new sections 20(1)(b) and in regulations 7(1)(j) and 7(1)(e) (which replaces 6(1)(d)) should be interpreted according to its natural and ordinary meaning with the result that as soon as the contract of service between the particular employer and the claimant is terminated the employment under it is terminated also and not merely suspended.

30. Applying this to the facts of the present case we have no doubt that at the end of his night's work with each employer the claimant's employment was terminated, and accordingly the new section 20(1)(b) did not operate to defeat his title to earnings-related supplement. This makes it unnecessary for us to consider the alternative arguments submitted by counsel on his behalf.

. . . .

Normal Idle Days

(See R(U)7/68, above). An ascertaining "normality", see R(U)14/60, *post*, p. 36).

R(U)15/60

. . . .

3. The claimant is a process worker in a rayon factory which operates continuously day in day out for 24 hours a day. In order to keep the factory going, an elaborate shift system has been devised. The shifts are from 6 a.m. to 2 p.m., 2 p.m. to 10 p.m. and 10 p.m. to 6 a.m. After having worked 5 morning shifts (6 a.m. to 2 p.m.) a worker has a break of 48 hours. He then works 5 afternoon shifts (2 p.m. to 10 p.m.) and has another break of 48 hours. He then works 5 night shifts (10 p.m. to 6 a.m.) and has a break of 72 hours. The effect of the 72-hour break after each three weeks is that the worker begins his next round of shifts one day earlier than the preceding round; thus, if he began the cycle at 6 a.m. on a Monday, his next three-week round would begin at 6 a.m. on Sunday. The full cycle takes 20 calendar weeks to complete. That is to say, if a worker began the cycle at 6 a.m. on Monday, he would not begin again at 6 a.m. on a Monday until after the lapse of 20 weeks. In the course of that 20 weeks, each set of 5 successive shifts differs from the preceding set of 5 successive shifts and a worker never exactly repeats the same set of shifts. On the other hand, he can foretell with perfect accuracy on what day and on what shift he will be working in the course of the 20-week cycle. This matter is relevant in considering whether "in any week" there is "a day on which in the normal course" the claimant "would not work" for the purposes of section 4 of the National Insurance Act, 1957, a point with which I deal later on.

4. In the normal course of the cycle the claimant was due to work as follows:—

Saturday 22nd March to
Wednesday 26th March 1958 } 2 p.m. to 10 p.m.
(5 days including Sunday 23rd March)

Friday 28th March 10 p.m. to ⎫
Wednesday 2nd April 6 a.m. ⎬   10 p.m. to 6 a.m.
(5 night shifts)   ⎭

5. He was however temporarily unemployed owing to slackness
of trade. He did not work on Saturday the 22nd March or on the
following Sunday, Monday, Tuesday or Wednesday. Thursday was
his free day. On Friday the 28th March 1958 he was due to start
work at 10 p.m. and in fact did so.

6. He claimed unemployment benefit for Saturday, Sunday,
Monday, Tuesday, Wednesday, the 22nd to the 26th March, and
also for Friday the 28th March. Unemployment benefit was paid
to him for 5 days Saturday the 22nd to Wednesday the 26th March
(including Sunday the 23rd March). Whether benefit is payable
for Friday the 28th March is the question now at issue.

7. The effect must first be considered of what is called the Night
Workers regulation, that is regulation 5 of the National Insurance
(Unemployment and Sickness Benefit) Regulations, 1948 [S.I. 1948
No. 1277] as amended by regulation 3 of the National Insurance
(Unemployment and Sickness Benefit) Amendment Regulations,
1957 [S.I. 1957 No. 1319].[13] The Night Workers regulation is set
out in its amended form (which is the form applicable to this case)
in the Schedule to the last-mentioned Regulations, as follows:—

> "5.—(1) The following provisions shall apply in relation to
> night workers for the purposes of unemployment sickness
> benefit:—
>
> (c) where a period of employment begun on any day extends
>   over midnight into the following day, the person
>   employed shall, in respect of such period—
>
> (i) be treated as having been employed on the first day
>   only, if the employment before midnight is of
>   longer duration than after midnight, and, in that
>   case, the first day shall not be treated as a day of
>   interruption of employment; or
>
> (ii) be treated as having been employed on the second
>   day only, if the employment after midnight is of
>   longer duration than that before midnight, or if
>   the employment before and after midnight is of
>   equal duration, and, in either of these cases, the

---

[13] See. now the Social Security (Unemployment, Sickness Invalidity Benefit) Regulations 1975 (S.I. 1975 No. 564), reg. 5, *post.* p. 63.

second day shall not be treated as a day of interruption of employment.

(3) Where a person—

(a) is, by virtue of the provisions of paragraph (1) of this
regulation, to be treated as having been employed
on one day only of two days; and,

(b) throughout that part of the other of those two days
during which that person is not employed, is, or is
deemed in accordance with regulations to be, available for employment in an employed contributor's
employment or incaplable of work by reason of
some specific disease or bodily or mental
disablement,

that person shall, for the purposes of unemployment or sickness benefit, be deemed to be so available for employment,
or, as the case may be, to be so incapable of work, throughout
that other of those two days."

8. Since the claimant was employed from 10 p.m. of Friday to
6 a.m. on Saturday, he is to be treated as having been employed
on the Saturday only, by virtue of regulation 5(1)(c)(ii), and also
as having been available for employment throughout the Friday,
by virtue of regulation 5(3). If the matter had rested there, the
claimant would no doubt have been entitled to unemployment
benefit for Friday the 28th March 1958.

9. However, it does not rest there, for on the 5th August 1957
(which is the day on which the amendment to the Night Workers
regulation [S.I. 1957 No. 1319] came into force) section 4(1) of
the National Insurance Act, 1957, also came into force and enacted
as follows:—

"4.—(1) For the purposes of the principal Act, where a
person is employed in any employed contributor's employment
which has not been terminated, then, in any week, a day on
which in the normal course that person would not work in
that in that or any other employed contributor's employment
shall not be treated as a day of unemployment unless each
other day in that week (other than Sunday) on which in the
normal course he would so work is a day of interruption of
employment."

Section 4(3) provides that, in sub-section (1), "the expression 'week' means a period of seven days commencing with
the midnight between Saturday and Sunday."

10. The first question which arises under section 4(1) is whether in the claimants case there is any "day on which in the normal course that person would not work," remembering that his pattern of employment changes from week to week and is never twice the same in 20 weeks. Can a person so employed be held to have any day on which "in the normal course" he would not work?

11. In my view, when the days on which a person is to be employed are governed by a rota, the question whether a day is one "on which in the normal course that person would not work" has to be determined by referring to and applying the rota. If, for example, it is clear from the operation of the rota that a person will not work on a particular Tuesday, that Tuesday becomes "a day on which in the normal course that person would not work" notwithstanding that on other Tuesdays before and after it he will be at work. It not infrequently happens in large establishments, where work goes on continuously from day to day without a break, that a worker's rest days, or "idle days" as they are sometimes called, vary in successive weeks according to a rota. In such a case, the only way of deciding which days are the worker's rest days, or in other words days " on which in the normal course that person would not work" is by referring to and applying the rota.

12. In the present case, in the normal course of the cycle of work, Thursday the 27th March 1958 was a normal rest day. In that week it was a day on which, in the normal course of events, the claimant would not work, and it therefore cannot be treated as a day of unemployment. The claimant evidently accepts that view, for he has not claimed unemployment benefit for Thursday.

13. In regard to Friday the 28th the question is whether Friday is "a day on which in the normal course" the claimant "would not work." The claimant relies on the fact that in the normal course of the cycle he actually did work on Friday, i.e. for 2 hours from 10 p.m. He contends therefore that section 4 of the 1957 Act, which applies only to days on which a person would not normally work, does not affect him, since normally he would work, and in fact did work, for 2 hours from 10 p.m. He then relies upon the Night Workers regulation which treats him as having been "employed" on Saturday only and as having been "available for employment" throughout Friday, and contends that he is thus entitled to unemployment benefit on Friday.

14. Such a contention is, in my view, fallacious. If the claimant relies upon his 2 hours work on Friday night so as to escape from section 4 of the 1957 Act, he cannot at the same time claim that Friday is a day of unemployment. On the other hand, if he claims that Friday is a day on which he was available for employment,

by virtue of the Night Workers regulation, then in my view Friday must be treated as a day on which he did not work, for the purposes of unemployment benefit, and, since whatever happened on Friday the 28th March 1958 happened in the normal course of the rota, Friday was a day on which in the normal course the claimant would not work.

15. The Night Workers regulation in its amended form (that is as set out in the Amendment Regulations [S.1. 1957 No. 1319]) and section 4 of the 1957 Act both come into operation on the same day, the 5th August 1957, and both these provisions have to be construed together. In my view, there is no material distinction between a day on which a person is not "employed" in the regulation and a day on which a person does not "work" in section 4(1) of the 1957 Act. The Night Workers regulation is expressed at its beginning to "apply in relation to night workers for the purposes of . . . unemployment benefit" and under the regulation the claimant is deemed to have been available for employment throughout Friday the 28th March 1958; the purpose of section 4(1) of the 1957 Act is also to treat certain days as, or as not, days of unemployment, and it appears to me that, in consistency, the claimant must also be regarded as not having worked on that Friday for the purposes of section 4(1) of the 1957 Act. In other words, the 2 hours work after 10 p.m. which he did in the normal course on the Friday night are transposed to Saturday for all purposes relating to unemployment benefit.

16. It follows, from these reasons, that Friday the 28th March 1958 was "a day on which in the normal course the claimant would not work." In that week each other day was *not* a day of interruption of employment for he was employed on Saturday the 29th March. Friday the 28th March is therefore not to be treated as a day of unemployment, by force of section 4(1) of the 1957 Act.

17. On the assumption that Friday the 28th March is a day on which the claimant in the normal course would not work, there is another reason why unemployment benefit is not payable for that day. Regulation 4 of the National Insurance (Unemployment and Sickness Benefit) Regulations, 1948 [S.I. 1948 No. 1277] which, in the form applicable to this case, is set out in regulation 2 of the National Insurance (Unemployment and Sickness Benefit) Regulations, 1957 [S.I. 1957 No. 1319], provides as follows:—

> "Special provisions relating to day substitued for Sunday
>
> 4—(1) In the case of a person who,—
>
> > (a) in any week in which, in the normal course, he would work as an employed person on not more than six

days including the Sunday, is unemployed on that Sunday; and

(b) claims unemployment benefit for that Sunday;

the day of that week on which, in the normal course, he would not work as an employed person, or (if that week contains more than one day on which in the normal course he would not so work) the later or last of those days, shall be substituted for that Sunday as a day which, by virtue of the provisions of paragraph (d) of subsection (2) of section 11 of the Act, is not to be treated as a day of unemployment or of incapacity for work for the purposes of any provision of the Act relating to unemployment or sickness benefit and, for those purposes, is to be disregarded in computing any period of consecutive days.

(2) In this regulation, the expression 'week' means a period of seven days commencing with the midnight between Saturday and Sunday."

18. The claimant was unemployed on Sunday the 23rd March, a day on which in the normal course he would have worked, and he claimed and was paid unemployment benefit for that Sunday. Under regulation 4 quoted above, the later or last of the days of that week on which, in the normal course, he would not work is to be substituted for Sunday as a day which is not to be treated as a day of unemployment. Since in my judgement Friday the 28th March 1958 was the last day of that week on which, in the normal course, the claimant would not work (in the special sense indicated above), that Friday has to be substituted for Sunday and thus cannot be treated as a day of unemployment for which unemployment benefit is payable.

. . . .

Regulation 16 of the Social Security (Unemployment, Sickness and Invalidity Benefit) Regulations 1975 (S.I. 1975 No. 564) sets out several important modifications of the normal idle day rule. One of these has the effect of excluding casual workers from the operation of the rule.

Casual Workers

R1/61 (UB)

. . . .

7. There are, indeed, two main issues arising in this case, and they are those already adverted to by the claimant's representative,

Mr. McT., none of the other main facts and circumstances of the case really being in dispute. Those issues are, in my opinion:

(1) Whether the employment—which showed a regular enough pattern of three nights per week—can truthfully or properly be said to have been terminated at the end of each night's engagement, whilst the apparent pattern of regular engagements continued; and

(2) If not, whether, *in relation to the claimant,* that employment can properly be said to be "casual" employment. If so, then the employment is, by the relevant regulations, to be treated as if it had been terminated.

In all the circumstances of the present case I think the balance of all the evidence is such as to suggest that the employment was not, in fact, on any interpretation of the work, "terminated" at the end of any night's engagement[14] and I will therefore proceed to consider the second issue . . . .

8. As to the second issue now arising I will confess immediately that my initial impression was that this employment was not "casual" in any true sense. I have, however, come to the conclusion on fuller examination of the relevant legislation and the authorities decided under it, that this may indeed be too superficial a view.

In considering what precisely is meant by "casual" employment in this context, it has to be remembered that paragraph (*a*) of Regulation 7A(3)[15] of the regulations can only have application where the employment has not been terminated. So that it may be inferred that the legislature did not intend that either the continuity of the relationship of employer and employee, or the recurrence of spells of actual work at intervals necessarily made such employment other than "casual" in relation to the claimant. And here it is interesting to note the remarks of the Tribunal of Commissioners at paragraph 11 of Decision R(U) 16/59, when they observed:

"It follows that the word 'casual' in regulation 7A(3)(*a*) can only mean casual to an extent which is consistent with the intention of both parties to resume the employment on the next available opportunity. On the other hand the employment must also be casual in relation to the particular claimant so

---

[14] See, now, R(U) 7/68 (T), *ante*, p. 20.
[15] See, now, regulation 16, *ante*.

that, if in his case the employment exhibits a degree of continuity or periodicity which is incompatible with any reasonable interpretation of the word 'casual', it will not avail him that the record of employment of other persons engaged in the same occupation shows that their employment is clearly casual".

And further helpful comment on the correct interpretation of "casual" in this context is made by the Commissioner—at paragraph 9 of Decision R(U) 13/59.

In addition to the factors already adverted to by the learned Great Britain Commissioners, a further factor appears to me to arise for consideration in the instant case in the interpretation of the phrase "casual employment . . . in relation to that person . . . ", and that is the substance, or the extent of the duration, of each engagement; this being a quite distinct question from that of the regularity of recurrence (or "periodicity") of the engagements. I do not think it is too wide a generalisation to suggest that as the spells of work diminish in duration so the probability of their being in a true and practical sense "casual" increases. The jobbing gardener who goes to the same house for a short period several times a week is likely to be regarded by most people as a casual worker, notwithstanding that he goes to the same employer with a high degree of regularity. The spells of work in the present case last for a maximum of four hours of the late evening and night on each occasion. And, if not directly relevant to the present issue, it is at least of general interest that the total of those hours represents a small fraction only of a working week; and that the claimant has on several occasions worked on ordinary employment during the day in addition to playing in this dance-band at night.

There is, indeed, no "continuity" of the actual employment in this case. In considering the degree of "periodicity", as it has been called, the shortness of the duration of each spell seems to me to point rather to the employment being "casual" than to the contrary, for the reasons I have indicated. And in considering the other relevant factors in the case in relation to this question, amongst the more important matters seems to me to be the fact that though, indeed, there might be an expectation on Monday of resumption of actual work later that week, and usually on Wednesdays and Saturdays, preference would be, and on several occasions actually was, given by the claimant to other employment. The claimant was paid, each evening he worked, at the end of the evening, and this was not always the same amount since identical hours were not always worked between the hours of 9 p.m. and 2 a.m. There were no terms or conditions of service, so far as I could discover, even of the most informal character extending beyond the individual evening's engagement, *e.g.*, there was no period of notice evisaged. Though the absence of notice is by no means a characteristic exclusive to casual employment, nevertheless it seems to me to be another circumstance tending to negative the concept of regular or permanent employment in the claimant's case. And having examined at the hearing the method of recruitment of these musicians by Mr. McS—sometimes by going round their houses, sometimes by their calling with him, but usually—if not, indeed, always—subsequent to the last prior evening of engagement—suffice to say that it suggest to me casual employment rather than otherwise. Nor do I consider, at all events on the evidence before me that the claimant had, in the words of Decision R(U) 16/59 "any assurance as to the date at which he would be resuming work": the distinction being one between a reasonable hope or expectation on the probabilities and an assurance. It follows that in my opinion this is employment which, under the said Regulation 7A(3) falls to be treated, in respect of each week during the period, as if it had been terminated immediately after its commencement.

9. This is, indeed, a very difficult case and one which has, I feel, been made more difficult for the Insurance Officer by the failure of the claimant to mention earlier that on an appreciable number of the evenings during the period May, 1959 to July, 1960, on which he was recorded as employed by Mr. McS., he was in fact working for other outside employers, including other named dance-bands from whom some corroboration is now forthcoming.

10. It will be deduced from my preceding remarks that the circumstances of each individual case need to be looked at to ascertain whether any claimant's employment is, indeed, casual employment in relation to him. Bearing in mind the factors which I have mentioned above, I think the facts of the present case are readily distinguishable from those of my own previous Decision 16/59 (U.B.) where the claimant's sole employment was for three full working days each week, where she had a complete assurance of continued employment (though with three different employers) on each of those days; and where the pattern was that of steady, continuous employment for three days a week, rather than that of relinquishment and uncertain resumption of employment of a claimant on a multiplicity of the same days in successive weeks.

. . . .

Full Extent Normal

Social Security (Unemployed, Sickness and Invalidity Benefit) Regulations 1975 (S.I. 1975 No. 564), reg. 7

(1)(*e*) . . . a day shall not be treated as a day of unemployment if on that day a person does not work and is a person who does not ordinarily work on every day in a week . . . but who is, in the week in which the said day occurs, employed to the full extent normal in his case, and in the application of this sub-paragraph to any person no account shall be taken, in determining either the number of days in a week on which he ordinarily works or the full extent of employment in a week which is normal in his case, of any period of short-time working due to adverse industrial conditions; . . .

(2) Paragraph (1)(*e*) shall not apply to a person unless—
  (a) there is a recognised or customary working week in connection with his employment; or
  (b) he regularly works for the same number of days in a week for the same employer or group of employers.

R(U) 14/60

. . . .

10. . . . In paragraph 11 of Decision C.U. 518/49 (reported) the Commissioner said "A claimant who has in fact worked only on some days of the week for a period of a year or more is 'a person who does not ordinarily work on every day in a week' unless there are some exceptional industrial circumstances relevant to his case". In paragraph 16 of Decision R(U) 14/59 however the Commissioner said that where "during the year ending with the day in question (or such other period as may provide a more suitable test in a particular case) a claimant has worked on less than 50 per cent. of the days of the week in question (excluding any day of incapacity for work or holiday and days on which he was unemployed because his employment had been terminated) that day should be held to be one on which in the normal course the claimant would not work. If the claimant has worked on as much as 50 per cent. of such days it should (in my view) be held that it has not been proved that in the normal course he would not have worked on the day in question". We think it well to point out that there may be other exceptional days which should be excluded as well as those referred to above. In the cases to which Decisions C.U. 518/49 (reported) and R(U) 28/58 related there was a period of a year during which the claimant *never* worked full-time. In the present case this was not so: occasionally throughout the year before the relevant week

the claimant did a full-time week; during two thirds of the weeks she worked on only three days . . . . In the course of the long history of the decisions under the regulation a number of different types of case have emerged. There are those in which a clear and regular pattern of days worked and days not worked can be seen: it may be a regular weekly pattern, or the period may be longer (as in the rota cases, *e.g.* Decision C.U. 518/49 (reported) itself); it may even be a season (as in the unreported case dealt with in Commissioner's file C.U. 160/59, where a toilet attendant worked six days weekly in a summer and four days weekly in winter, and was held (on the authority of Decision C.U. 272/50 (reported)) to be disentitled by the regulation to benefit for the other two week-days in winter). On the other hand, there are cases both under the regulation and under this section, where (under the regulation) the weeks in which some days are not worked or (under the section) the instances of the particular day not worked show no clear pattern. In such cases the only materials on which a decision can be given are the claimant's record over a period. In Decision C.U. 518/49 the Commissioner was dealing with a case which was a test case in the sense that all the men on the same rota as the claimant were affected by it. But he was not considering any question arising out of an irregular pattern or the lack of any pattern of employment, since no such question arose in the case before him: the rota in that case apparently produced a completely regular pattern. And if the whole decision is read and the sentence quoted above is taken in its context, it is clear that the Commissioner was not attempting to lay down a rule applicable to all cases. In particular, we are sure that he did not intend, by his reference to a person working only on some days of the week for a year, to imply that the converse was true. He could not have meant to imply that a person escaped the regulation if he had been employed for less than a year; in paragraph 16 he referred to Decision C.U. 151/49 (reported) which related to a case where the claimant had worked only fifteen weeks. Nor could he have meant to imply that a person would necessarily so escape if during a year's previous employment he had worked all the days of the week in some weeks of the year; the work "ordinarily" certainly means something less than "always". As the insurance officer's representative said, the opposite view would mean that any claimant could completely evade the regulation by working a week or two full-time each year at suitable intervals. In our judgment making full allowance for the differences between the regulations and the section, the idea conveyed by the words "ordinarily" and "normal" in the regulation and the phrase "in the normal course" in section 4(1) is the same.

One of the meanings of "ordinarily" according to a standard dictionary is "as is normal or usual". Accordingly we think that similar tests should be applied in both cases.

11. It follows, in our opinion, from Decisions C.U. 518/49 (reported) and R(U) 14/59 read together, that, in detemining the questions whether a claimant ordinarily works on every day in a week (Sundays being disregarded) and whether in the week in question he has been employed to the full exetent normal in his case, or whether a day is a day on which in the normal course he would not work in an employed contributor's employment, his employment history for a year before the week in question should be examined, unless for any reason *e.g.* owing to a change of employers or a change within his employment some other period would be more suitable in the particular case. How the problem of answering these questions should be approached is explained in paragraphs 16 and 17 of Decision R(U) 14/59, which must be read as being subject to the qualification, expressly stated in Decision C.U. 518/49, "unless there are some exceptional industrial circumstances relevant to his case".

. . . .

Change of Normality

R(U) 30/53

. . . .

3. The claimant was a groundsman for 25 years but he suffers from angina pectoris and had to give up that occupation. For two years to May 1951 he was employed as a porter liftman. He was sick from May, 1951 to April, 1952, and from April, 1952 to the 8th November, 1952 was employed as a park ranger. Each one of the foregoing employments was a full-time employment. From the 10th November, 1952 the claimant was required to work as a park ranger at week-ends only, *i.e.*, on Saturday and Sunday, and was not required to work on any other day of the week. The claimant was ready and willing to take full-time employment, but he is registered as a disabled person and is 57 years of age and, placed as he is, he finds it difficult to secure suitable employment.

4. The local tribunal evidently took the view that, when the claimant ceased to work full-time, he changed his normal occupation to one in which he worked only at week-ends and that as soon as he made the change he thereby became "a person who does not ordinarily work on every day in a week." I think that might be true of a man who of his own free will adopted a part-

time occupation with the intention of making that henceforth his normal occupation; it could truly be said of a man that, as soon as he had made the change, part-time employment had become his normal occupation as soon as he undertook it, and that he was thereafter "a person who does not ordinarily work on every day in a week."

5. It is different, however, when a man, who regularly all his life has worked thoughout the week, suddenly finds part-time work thrust upon him with no choice but to accept it or lose his employment altogether. I think it is wrong to say of such a man that he is "a person who does not ordinarily work on every day in a week" as soon as he accepts part-time employment. The claimant, in particular, had little prospect of obtaining other employment if he lost his work as park ranger. A man who has no practical alternative to accepting part-time employment in circumstances like the present must, I think, be allowed a certain time in which to take stock of his position and to decide whether it is worth his while to continue as a part-time employee. It was suggested in Decision C.U. 518/49 (reported) that if a claimant in fact had worked only on some days of the week for a year or more he could probably be regarded as "a person who does not ordinarily work on every day in a week."

6. I have no doubt that the claimant could not properly be so regarded on the 10th November, 1952. His ordinary employment was unquestionably full-time employment. It is true that long-continued part-time employment may show that, by force of circumstances, part-time employment has become a man's normal employment, but that stage had certainly not been reached in the present case. The claimant was well justified in temporarily accepting part-time employment as an expedient, in the hope that something better might turn up, as is shown by the fact that he was re-admitted to full-time employment as a park ranger on every day of the week on the 9th February, 1953. I hold that from the 10th November, 1952 on the 9th February, 1953 the claimant never ceased to be a person who *ordinarily* works on every day in a week but that, during the weeks in question, he was obliged *temporarily* to accept week-end employment only.

. . . .

"Adverse Industrial Conditions"

(See, also, in relation to the normal idle day rule, the Social Security (Unemployment, Sickness and Invalidity Benefit) Regulations 1975 (S.I. 1975 No. 564), reg. 16(3)(*d*)).

R(U) 21/60

. . . .

2. The claimant was employed as a crane driver in the engineering industry and his employers made castings for steam locomotives for British Railways, as well as to some extent for railways overseas. Until May 1958 it had been customary at his place of employment to work six or even seven days a week, time and a half being paid in respect of Saturday work and double time in respect of Sundays, although the working week agreed between the employers' federation and the trade unions concerned provided for a working week of 44 hours on five days. After May 1958, however, the hours of work were substantially reduced because the demand for castings for steam locomotives dropped considerably as the Transport Commission had decided that British Railways should change over to diesel engines. This coincided with the expiry of some long term overseas contracts. In order to meet this changed situation, the claimant's employers had to undertake re-tooling, and contemplated manufacturing castings for diesel engines in due course, as they had in the past manufactured castings for steam locomotives.

3. From May 1958 until May 1959 the days of work were reduced to five, that is to say, the working week contemplated by the agreement referred to above, but in May 1959 the days of work were further reduced to four days a week until the end of October 1959, when there was a reversion to five days a week. Subsequently a further improvement in demand led to the resumption of some Saturday work.

4. When the claimant had his days of work reduced to four days a week, he sought to claim unemployment benefit on the two days of the week on which he did not work, one of which was a Saturday. The local insurance officer decided that he was not entitled to unemployment benefit in respect of the Saturdays named at the head of this decision, which were the Saturdays for which he had claimed benefit.

. . . .

5. In order to determine whether or not in the normal course the claimant would work on a Saturday, it is necessary to examine

his employment history for a period preceding the day in respect of which unemployment benefit is claimed.

6. In Decision C.U. 518/49 (reported), in which the Commissioner was discussing the meaning of the expressions "a person who does not ordinarily work on every day in a week" and "to the full extent normal in his case", which occur in the National Insurance (Unemployment and Sickness Benefit Regulations, 1948 [S.I. 1948 No. 1277] regulation 6(1)(e)(ii), the Commissioner said "A claimant who has in fact worked only on some days of the week for a period of a year or more is 'a person who does not ordinarily work on every day in a week', unless there are some exceptional industrial circumstances relevant to his case." The Commissioner then explained that the inference that the claimant did not ordinarily work on every day in a week might be drawn from his employment history of less than a year in certain circumstances.

7. A similar approach was approved in Decision R(U) 22/58 for the purpose of determining under section 4(1) referred to above whether a day was a day on which in the normal course a person would not work, and it was further held in Decision R(U) 14/59 that, if in the year ending with the day for which benefit was claimed, or such other period as might provide a more suitable test in the particular case, the claimant had worked on less than 50% of the days of the week in question (excluding any day of incapacity for work or holiday and days on which he was unemployed because his unemployment had been terminated) that day should be held to be one on which in the normal course the claimant would not work.

8. It is noted that it has not been said in any decision of which we are aware that the period to be examined must not exceed a year and that it was contemplated that exceptional industrial circumstances relevant to the claimant's case would be taken into account.

9. On examining the claimant's employment record for the year preceding the 30th May, 1959 it is found that he worked only 11 Saturdays out of 46 "possible" Saturdays, that is to say, the Saturdays in the year excluding those which were holidays. On the other hand, of the year preceding the 30th May, 1958 is examined, that is to say, the year before the reduction in the hours of work due to the industrial events referred to above, the claimant worked on 42 our of 45 "possible" Saturdays.

10. On behalf of the insurance officer now concerned with this case, it was submitted that it must be said of the claimant that Saturday was a day on which in the normal course he would not work, having regard to his employment history for the year pre-

ceding the 30th May, 1959, but on the claimant's behalf it was submitted that it was inappropriate to look at that year alone because this was a case falling within the exception contemplated by the Commissioner in Decision C(U) 518/49 (reported), namely that the lack of work on Saturdays was due to exceptional industrial circumstances relevant to the claimant's case.

11. To that submission the insurance officer now concerned with this case replied that the expression "exceptional industrial circumstances" had been amplified in subsequent Commissioner's decisions. In Decision R(U) 13/55 the Commissioner had disagreed with the local tribunal who had held that there were exceptional industrial circumstances relevant to the claimant's case. The Commissioner said "There is no evidence to indicate that there were any circumstances relating to his [the claimant's] work which were purely temporary and sporadic and brought about by some conditions unlikely to continue. In the result the claimant can at present derive no assistance from the industrial circumstances which prevailed at his place of employment". This indication as to the meaning of "exceptional industrial circumstances" was, it was submitted, repeated, apparently with approval, in Decision R(U) 33/57. In that case the Commissioner was not prepared to accept the contention that the circumstances were exceptional industrial circumstances. It had been urged that the claimant had been employed in the production of castings, an industry closely linked with the building of new houses, and that the introduction of four-day-a-week working had resulted from a reduction in demand, probably associated with the reduced house building, which in turn was probably due to Government restrictions on local authority expenditure. It was also thought that the introduction of an Australian tariff had reduced the overseas demand. The Commissioner remarked that any estimate of the probable duration of a policy of restricted credit, or of the maintenance of a particular tariff, would seem to be highly conjectural. If, in consequence of factors such as these, short-time working had been introduced in a particular trade and had continued for at least a year, it seemed to him that such short-time working should be generally regarded for the purposes of regulation 6(1)(e)(ii) as having become normal in a particular case if there was no evidence that full-time working was likely to be restored in the near future. He considered whether he would be justified in treating the fact that five-day-a-week working had been resumed by the time that he gave his decision as sufficient evidence that four days a week working was all along "likely to be temporary". He came to the conclusion with some hesitation that it could not be so treated.

12. The insurance officer now concerned with this case submitted that it followed from those decisions that the position as it was on the 30th May, 1959, and on the other dates to which this decision relates, must be considered and that the fact that by the time that appeal was before us there had been a partial resumption of longer hours of work could not assist us in determining whether on the 30th May 1959 the conditions were temporary and unlikely to continue.

13. It seems to us, however, that there is a marked distinction between this case and the other cases with which the Commissioner was concerned in the decision cited by the insurance officer. In those cases, there was only general evidence of recession of trade with possible explanations of the cause. In the present case, however, there was evidence of a definite event causing the recession. Further, the character of the event and the steps which the claimant's employers were taking to overcome their loss of trade made it clear that the recession was on the balance of probabilities temporary and unlikely to continue. The very drastic change of demand from the employers' principle customer, who had made a decision fundamentally affecting the character of the goods which he would require in the future, had made it necessary for the claimant's employers to undertake the exceptional measure of re-tooling, and the claimant's employers were taking the necessary steps. In order to prove that the industrial circumstances were purely temporary and unlikely to continue, the claimant did not have to rely merely on hypotheses as to the cause of the recession of trade or the recent improvement, but was able to point to a specific event, the character of which, in our opinion, enables him to discharge the onus of proving that there were exceptional industrial circumstances relevant to his case, justifying his contention that, in order to determine on what days of the week he would not work in the normal course, a period should be taken into account before these exceptional industrial circumstances supervened.

14. We do not think that the use of the word "sporadic" in the passage quoted in paragraph 11 above justifies the inference that it was intended in that passage to imply that industrial circumstances could not be exceptional within the meaning of Decision C.U. 518/49 (reported), unless they could properly be described as "sporadic" in the sense in which that adjective is defined in standard dictionaries. On the other hand, we wish to make it plain that we adhere to the well established principle that the claimant's employment history for the past year should be taken as the prima facie measure of the extent of employment which is normal in his

case. Looking at the facts of this case, however, we are satisfied that during the year before the 30th May, 1959 there were exceptional industrial circumstances relevant to the claimant's case which would make it inappropriate to rely on the claimant's experience in that year for the purpose of determining the days of the week on which in the normal course he would not work.

15. As, therefore, for the reasons explained above, we are prepared to look further back than one year, we find that in the year from the 30th May 1957 to the 29th May 1958 the claimant worked on 42 out of the "possible" 45 Saturdays, and similar results would be reached by an examination of the claimant's record of work during corresponding periods preceding the 13th and 27th June, 1959. In our opinion, therefore, the insurance officer has failed to prove that for the purposes of section 4(1) of the National Insurance Act, 1957 Saturday is a day on which in the normal course the claimant would not work. Accordingly, the Saturdays named at the head of this decision are to be treated as days of unemployment in the claimant's case.

. . . .

Compensated Days

Social Security (Unemployment, Sickness and Invalidity Benefit) Regulations 1975 (S.I. 1975 No. 564), reg. 7(1)(d)
. . . a day shall not be treated as a day of unemployment if it is a day in respect of which a person receives a payment (whether or not a payment made in pursuance of a legally enforceable obligation) in lieu either of notice or of the remuneration which he would have received for that day had his employment not been terminated, so however that this subparagraph shall not apply to any day which does not fall within the period of one year from the date on which the employment of that person terminated; . . . .

R(U) 7/73 (T)
REASONS OF SIR ROBERT MICKLETHWAIT, Q.C.
. . . .

4. The claimant was employed by a company as a production engineer from 1st June, 1970 to 24th May, 1972. His salary eventually was at the rate of about £2,850 per annum. On 24th May 1972 as a result of a reorganisation and due to no fault on the part of the claimant his employment was terminated by his employers without notice. It is common ground that a month's notice would have been reasonable in his case. On 24th May, 1972 the employers

paid him £725·25 which was intended to be equivalent to the amount of three months' salary.

. . . .

26. I cannot agree with the suggestion first put forward in Decision R(U) 5/73 that a payment in lieu of notice or of remuneration is in its nature a payment made in consideration of the employee's agreeing to forego a legal right (see paragraph 9 to 12 and 21 of that decision). The word "lieu" is of course merely the French word for place. "In lieu of" means simply in place of or instead of. As a matter of ordinary language I am not satisfied that the phrase necessarily has the meaning attributed to it in Decision R(U) 5/73. In many other contexts it clearly does not. I have not heard any suggestion in the words "in lieu of" have become a term of art having a special meaning different from what in my judgment is the ordinary one. Such an interpretation is not an improbable one. If a man entitled to one month's notice is dismissed without notice and is paid a sum equivalent to three months' wages, and both the employers and he agree that it was a payment in lieu of the notice which the employers would in fact have given him though under no legal obligation to do so, I cannot see the slightest reason why he should not be disentitled to the end of the three months. Otherwise he would be receiving unemployment benefit and the equivalent of wages for the same period. Moreover even if in general the words had the meaning suggested, described in Decision R(U) 5/73, in my judgment they could not have them in the context of the regulation, since the insertion of the words in brackets would then make the regulation self-contradictory and the answer to the question posed by the Commissioner in that decision whether the draftsman had not been "beating the air" would be that he had.

27. Nor can I agree with the view expressed in that decision that the words in brackets in the regulation had no significance or effect in cases of that type. In my judgment one change which they made, or helped to make was to abolish the rule in Decision R(U) 37/53. Nor can I agree with the suggestion in paragraph 21 of that decision that in construing the words in brackets one can leave aside Crown employees. If on their true construction they have a certain meaning, it must be the same in the case of Crown employees and others. I cannot see how one can limit or qualify the completely unqualified words in brackets. I think that they abolish the rule in Decision R(U) 37/53 in all cases. One of the main objects of the 1971 amendment was to get rid of the need to investigate the claimant's legal rights especially as to notice.

28. In Decision C.U. 17/72, the Commissioner was dealing with cases of employment terminable by notice; there was no question of a term certain. In paragraph 26 of the decision, however, he expressed the view that the 1971 regulation follows its predecessor in dividing contracts of employment into two categories.

(a) those requiring notice for their termination, and

(b) those expiring by effluxion of time.

He continued that in his view a payment attracting the operation of the regulation must be characterised either as a payment in lieu of notice or as a payment in lieu of the remuneration which the insured person would have received had his employment not been terminated; it cannot be both. I do not feel able to accept this view. Another of the reasons for making the 1971 regulation was to get rid of the difficulty of discriminating between contracts which were for a term certain and those which were not. I cannot think that on its true construction it is under the 1971 regulation still necessary to decide into which class the employment falls.

29. A difficulty about the insurance officer's interpretation of the regulation arises in this way, and it must be faced. Under the provisions in force down to 1966, the amount of the payment was highly material. From 1966 to 1971 it was less important. During that period the way that the regulations worked was as follows:

(a) If a person entitled to four weeks' notice was dismissed without notice, and paid only one week's salary, he was normally held to be disentitled, not merely for the one week but for the four weeks. One possible explanation is that this was based on an inference of *fact*. It was in practice regarded as incredible that the employers would have paid the employee the equivalent of one week's salary whilst at the same time leaving themselves wide open to an action for wrongful dismissal in respect of the other three weeks. The payment was presumed to be in satisfaction of the whole of the employee's rights.

(b) If on the other hand an employee entitled to one week's notice was dismissed without notice, but received four weeks' salary, he was disentitled merely for one week on the principle that the remaining three weeks' salary was not paid pursuant to a legal obligation (Decision R(U) 37/53).

The question arises whether either or both of these results still follow under the 1971 regulation.

30. In my judgment the doctrine referred to in paragraph 29(a) is unaffected by the 1971 change in the regulation. The inference of fact is just as valid as it ever was, subject to the last sentence of the next paragraph.

31. The second doctrine (paragraph 29(b)) in my judgment now no longer applies, having been based on the doctrine in Decision R(U) 37/53, which has now gone. Under the 1971 regulation there is no reason for limiting the period of disentitlement to what I may describe as the period of legal obligation. It is here that the difficulty is created. The regulation speaks of "the remuneration which he would have received for that day had his employment not been terminated". Literally, if it had not been terminated, presumably it would have continued for the rest of his life or until retirement age. In my judgment, however, this difficulty is more apparent than real. If a person entitled to one month's notice is dismissed without notice but paid three months' money, he could not be held to be disentitled for more than three months unless the statutory authorities decided that days after the end of the three months were *in fact* days in respect of which he had received a payment in lieu of notice or remuneration. I cannot conceive of a case where this would be decided. Moreover even in respect of the second and third months it must be remembered that there would be no basis for the presumption referred to in paragraphs 29(a) and 30 above.

32. Neither the words "*ex gratia* payment" nor any such words appear or have ever appeared in the statutory provision, and in my judgment the use of them should be avoided, as far as possible, since they are ambiguous and can be misleading. They may be used to describe a gift, or a payment which a person feels under a moral or ethical but not a legal duty to make. In legal circles they are commonly used to describe the situation where a plaintiff sues a defendant, each of them hopes that he will win but fears that he may lose, and the defendant makes an *ex gratia* payment, with the result that the plaintiff gets some money, though usually less than the full amount of his claim, and the defendant saves his face by not admitting liability or risking a judgment against him. They may also be used to describe a payment made by the Crown to one of its employees which constitutionally it is not legally liable to make. Now that the 1971 regulation has, in my judgment, completely abolished the distinction between payments made under legal obligation and others, there is no longer a true contrast between an *ex gratia* payment and a payment in lieu of notice or remuneration. The use of the phrase is therefore in my opinion better avoided.

33. The remaining question is whether as a matter of fact any of the days in the second and third months were days in respect of which the claimant received a payment in lieu of notice or remuneration. In my judgment, to this question of fact what the employers or the claimant or anyone else have said about it is evidence but is not conclusive. The difficulties facing the statutory authorities are well illustrated in this case where the employers at first said one thing somewhat ambiguously and later said something different. The fact that the total payment exactly corresponded with three months' salary is suggestive that it did come within the regulation, and the claimant's own statement that it was to help to tide him over the period until he found another job supports that suggestion. On the other hand, he had been in the employment just not long enough to entitle him to a payment under the Redundancy Payments Act 1965, so a payment in appreciation of past services as opposed to in lieu of proper notice or more remuneration was not improbable. The claimant has throughout been perfectly consistent in his description of the two elements in the payment and the local tribunal's finding as to his last pay slip is in his favour. On the whole I am prepared to accept the view, now supported by the insurance officer, that the claimant is not disentitled under the regulation in respect of either the second or the third month, on the ground that in fact none of the days in those months is a day in respect of which he received a payment covered by the 1971 regulation. The claimant is therefore entitled to all the benefit which he either received or claimed, and it is unnecessary to go into any questions of review or repayment since these no longer arise.

. . . .

REASONS OF MR. DESMOND NELIGAN AND MR. R. J. A. TEMPLE, Q.C.

. . . .

37. The justification for finding, as the local tribunal found, that the claimant was disentitled to unemployment benefit for a further period of two months proceeded from the isolation of the severance pay (which appears to have been a bounty payment) treating it as a separate payment, allocating it in lieu of remuneration and concluding that it was paid in lieu thereof for a period of two months ending 24th August, 1972 and in respect of that period. Adopting, as we do, the approach of the Commissioner in Decision R(U) 5/73 *supra* paragraph 15 *et seq.* to a similar situation we see no justification for concluding that regulation 7(1)(e) operates in such circumstances to disentitle the claimant in respect of the period from 25th May to 24th August. Consequently he was not

disentitled to unemployment benefit from 6th July to 24th August and was entitled to the benefit that was paid to him for the days included in the period from 6th to 11th July. Accordingly no question of repayment arises.

38. We think it right to refer further to the words in regulation 7(1)(e) "in lieu . . . of the remuneration which he would have received for that day had his employment not been terminated". In the case of a fixed term contract a sum paid in lieu of remuneration presents no difficulty because the days in the period of employment remaining under the contract after its termination are ascertainable. Thus, the period of disentitlement to unemployment benefit (which under the present regulation is not in any case to exceed one year) becomes clear. (We may add that we do not accept the submission that regulation 7(1)(e) "abandons the concept of 'term certain' contracts".) But in contracts other than for a fixed term the regulation, which must be construed strictly since it is a disentitling regulation is not, in our judgment, intended to extend the period of disentitlement beyond the period for which the notice provided, by reason of the fact that the sum paid in lieu of notice was greater than the equivalent remuneration the claimant would have received had he worked out the period of notice. Thus, if the entitlement to notice is one month and a sum equivalent to three months' wages is received, disentitlement to unemployment benefit for the days in the second and third months can only be arrived at by allocating on a daily basis the whole of the excess sum equivalent to two months' wages as being received in lieu of the remuneration for the period had the employment continued.

39. We do not accept that this is the correct approach. It would in many cases involve the insurance officer in prolonged and detailed investigation into daily rates of pay to ascertain the number of days of remuneration represented by the excess and time would be consumed in taking out of account elements representing holiday or bounty payments which are often involved in a terminal sum. We agree with, and adopt, the approach in paragraph 18 of Decision R(U) 5/73 *supra* to which we have already referred. Further, we consider that the regulation, in speaking of "the remuneration which he would have received for that day had his employment not been terminated" creates a substantial difficulty in the selection of days for disentitlement. Bearing in mind that the regulation does not refer to equivalence in any way, but is directed to payments in lieu of notice or remuneration, it seems to us that there is no reason why an amount precisely that of a day's pay should necessarily be allotted, at normal equivalent daily rates, to days sufficient to exhaust the excess. Read literally a

payment in lieu of remuneration which the claimant would have received had his employment not been terminated refers to, and involves, an imprecise and unascertainable period of remunerative employment.

40. In our view, a payment in lieu of remuneration, as now defined by the regulation, should be referred to the days during which the claimant would otherwise have worked; *i.e.* the appropriate period of notice. The only exception where a post-termination period is for consideration is where the employment was for a fixed term, and this is because the days in respect of which remuneration would have been earned are precise and ascertainable.

41. It is, of course, true that the language of the present regulation is different from its predecessors and is now apt to cover the case of the public servant who strictly has no legal right to notice or payment in lieu thereof. The payment under the present regulation, if in fact made, does not require examination as to whether it was made in pursuance of a legal obligation or not and neither the presence nor the absence of a legally enforceable obligation to make it can affect the character of the payment or the object with which it was made.

42. "Notice" in the regulation refers to notice required for the termination of the employment and the period (whether enforceable or not) as ascertainable from the contract of employment, from statute, from the common law or from regulations incorporated in the agreement for employment.

43. In Decision R(U) 37/53 the remaining two months of a payment equivalent to three months' salary was held not to rank as compensation in the payment made in lieu of one month's notice (which was not given) because there was no legal obligation to make the further two months' payment. Under the present regulation the same result (though not for the same reason) would obtain because, as we have already said, if in fact a payment is made in lieu of notice its character and amount are not affected by any obligation to make it.

44. For the reasons we have given we are not able to agree that the regulation now in force enables an employed person entitled to a month's notice, who is paid a sum equivalent to three months' wages "in lieu of notice" when dismissed without notice to be held disentitled to the end of three months because of the "remuneration" provision.

45. It is relevant to add that, although the description given to a terminal payment by the parties may be some evidence of its character, it is by no means conclusive. A payment which is made

truly *ex gratia* (*i.e.* out of kindness) by an employer, and not having the characteristic of either a payment in lieu of notice or in lieu of remuneration, would be outside the ambit of regulation 7(1)(e) but we do not, of course, exclude the possibility of some composite terminal payment being made which includes an element of bounty. If it does that ingredient would not prevent such a composite payment from being within the regulation because of its overriding characteristics.

46. We agree with the Chief Commissioner that, as was said in Decision R(U) 5/73 *supra*, a terminal payment to an employed person when his contract of employment is terminated without notice, or without the full period of notice to which he is entitled, may well have both the characteristics specified in regulation 7(1)(e). In that connection it is relevant to observe that Mr. Nuttall pointed out that at the end of paragraph 16 of Decision C.U. 17/72 *supra*, it was said that a payment cannot have both characteristics but it is, we think, clear from the context in which that was said that the Commissioner was addressing his mind solely to the distinction between contracts requiring notice for their termination and those expiring by effluxion of time. And that that was so, we think, is made even clearer by the Commissioner's reference to a previous decision of his own viz.: Decision C.U. 2/70 (not reported) in which he dealt at some length with the distinction between those two types of contracts of employment.

47. For the above reasons on the application of the regulation in this case we conclude that none of the days in the second and third months were days in respect of which the claimant received a payment in lieu of notice or of remuneration.

Holidays

Social Security (Unemployment, Sickness and Ivalidity Benefit) Regulations 1975 (S.I. 1975 No. 564), reg. 7(1)(i)

. . . where . . . employment has not been terminated, a day shall not be treated as a day of unemployment if it is a day of recognised or customary holiday in connection with that person's employment, unless that person's employment therein has been indefinitely suspended and the day in question is the seventh or a later day . . . in a continuous period of days on which that suspension has lasted. . . .

102/51 (UB)

. . . .

4. Claimant, a third-preference casual docker, is employed at the — Docks. There are about 150 such dockers working at the docks and they represent about 30 per cent of the total dock labour employed.

5. By a holiday pay agreement of 18th November, 1946, made between the — Association and claimant's Trade Union, it is provided *inter alia:* that Easter Monday and Easter Tuesday in each year shall be recognised as public holidays and that in certain circumstances payment shall be made for holidays, including public holidays when a sufficent number of days have been worked during the year. This agreement does not apply to third preference dockers.

6. The question for determination, therefore, is whether Easter Monday and Easter Tuesday are to be regarded as days of customary or recognised holiday for third preference dockers.

7. What then are "customary or recognised holidays"? In (E.)U.D. 18284/32, the Umpire in Great Britain defined such holidays as follows:—

> "Customary or recognised holidays are those days which the employers and workers have agreed (whether expressly or by implication based on acquiescence) shall be non-working days. When those holidays have been defined and determined they become a normal incident of employment and an implied term of contract of service which cannot be varied except by an express or implied agreement between the parties."

> "Unless there is definite evidence to the contrary a claimant who has taken employment in a particular establishment is subject to the holiday conditions prevailing there."

> "The existence or duration of a recognised holiday in any particular establishment must be determined by the agreement or practice observed within the establishment."

> "The onus of proving that there is no holiday, or only a limited holiday, for a particular grade or class of workers, rests upon those who affirm it and the fact must be proved by clear and definite evidence."

8. Also in (E.)U.D. 4796/37, it was decided that once the main body of the employees has agreed to a period being treated as a holiday, it becomes a recognised holiday for all the employees (apart from the excluded grades or classes) including the dissentients.

9. And in (E.)U.D. 4616/37, it was held if it has been the practice for a number of years to close an establishment for the same period of time each year, there arises the presumption that that period has become recognised as a holiday for all employees, whether they receive or do not receive payment for it.

10. In Decision No. 53/48 (revised) (unreported) dated 4th October, 1948. I had occasion to consider the claim of third preference dockers to unemployment benefit for Christmas Day and Boxing Day, 1947 (which days were recognised as public holidays under the agreement). Having decided that although the agreement did not apply to third preference men, I went on to say that I was of the opinion, nevertheless, that they were in fact dockers, as there was no doubt that they attended at the docks most days for work and very frequently obtained it. I then continued as follows:—

> "It is, therefore, necessary to consider what were the recognised holidays for dockers before the agreement came into operation. There cannot be a recognised holiday for only a part of a grade or class of workers but where under a holiday payment scheme, some employees receive wages for a period of holiday and some do not, it may be necessary to regard them as in two distinct classes, even though they may be in the same grade and working side by side. Under such a scheme those who received holiday wages would usually be regarded as on holiday and not entitled to benefit for the days of holiday. But the period of holiday would not necessarily be a recognised holiday for those who did not qualify for holiday wages under the scheme. In their case it would be necessary to consider whether the period in question or any part of it had been a customary holiday in the past, or whether it had become a recognised holiday for reasons other than the decision to make holiday payments to those qualified".

11. When I gave that decision the agreement had only been in operation for a period of less than two years, and I was not prepared to hold at that time that the holidays referred to in the agreement had become the recognised or customary holidays for third preference dockers. The agreement has now been in operation for the past five years and I am of opinion the time has come when it is equitable to say that Easter Monday and Easter Tuesday have now become days of recognised holiday for all dockers, including third preference dockers who would not receive a holiday payment for those two days.

. . . .

R(U) 31/56

. . . .

2. The claimant is a married man aged 52 years, registered for employment as a light labourer. For the past three or four years he has been employed by the Post Office (in Scotland) as a temporary postman at the Christmas-New Year season. He was so employed from the 16th December, 1955 to the 3rd January, 1956. Monday the 2nd January, 1956—being the first week-day of the New Year—was observed as a customary holiday by the postal branch of the Post Office in Scotland, there being no deliveries that day. The claimant did no work on that day. Unfortunately he was not entitled to holiday pay, and so he got no wages for that day. He claimed unemployment benefit for that day.

. . . .

4. The short question in the present case is whether, on the 2nd January, 1956, the claimant was on holiday. The local insurance officer, and on appeal the local tribunal, answered that question in the affirmative, and accordingly disallowed the claim for benefit.

5. If the claimant had been on the permanent staff of the Post Office, with a contract of employment extending over the date in question it would have been clear beyond dispute that he was not entitled to benefit. The point taken by the claimant in the present case is that he was employed as a Christmas casual worker, and his contract of employment as such was on a day-to-day basis. His service were not required on the 2nd January, 1956 and his further day's employment on the 3rd January was again as a casual worker. He submits:—"If my employment is on a day-to-day basis and the Post Office says I am not required on the 2nd January, 1956 it seems reasonable to consider me unemployed on that day notwithstanding the fact that the day may have been a holiday."

6. The question whether a workman employed on a day-to-day basis can be said to be on holiday fell to be considered by the Umpire in various cases under the Unemployment Insurance Acts, and it has also been considered by the Commissioner under the National Insurance Acts. Although a claimant employed on a day-to-day basis may have no certainty that his employment will continue beyond the day on which he is working, it does not follow that his employment is to be regarded, for all purposes, as having finally terminated at the end of each day's work. So to regard it would indeed be to ignore the practical realities of the situation. If a day-to-day worker normally seeks work in a particular market, the presumption is that he becomes bound by such agreements, express or implied, as govern employment in that market, including the agreement which constitutes or recognises a particular day as

a holiday—compare Decision R(U) 18/54, paragraph 5. In a particular case, a claimant might be able to show that although a particular day was a holiday in the market in which he had been working, it was nevertheless not a holiday for him, because when that market was closed or on holiday he normally sought work elsewhere. In the present case I do not think it possible for the claimant so to escape. The day in question was a day in a season during which it had become customary for the claimant to work for the Post Office. There is no evidence that on the 2nd January, 1956 he sought employment elsewhere: and indeed if he had, it is unlikely that he would have obtained it. The fact that he got another day's work from the Post Office on the 3rd January, 1956 suggests that his "idleness" on the previous day was more in the nature of a temporary suspension of employment than an absolute discharge of employment. I must agree with the tribunal that in the circumstances the claimant was on holiday on the day in question. The fact that the holiday was enforced in this case and unpaid, does not, unfortunately, help him (Decision R(U) 2/51). That being so, in terms of the regulation quoted, the day cannot be treated as a day of unemployment, and unemployment benefit is therefore not payable.

. . . .

(On termination of employment, see, now R(U)7/68, *ante*, p. 20.)

Suspensions

(See the Social Security Act 1975, s. 17(3), p. 3, *ante*.)

R(U) 2/75

. . . .

. . . if, within the meaning of the quoted provision, the claimant's employment was suspended by his employers during any of the relevant periods, then he is not entitled to earnings-related supplement for any part of that period. On the other hand, if his employment was not suspended at all or, if suspended, not by his employers then the quoted provision does not apply and the result will be that he is entitled to the supplement for such period.

. . . .

10. It will be appreciated that the issue whether . . . a suspension has to be authorised by a power to suspend conferred on the employer by contract was not raised in R(U) 11/72. There are, however, passages in the decision which have a bearing on it. In paragraph 8 of the decision it is stated that the insurance officer's representative accepted that "there could not be a suspension by

the employer unless the latter had a legal right to suspend". In paragraph 17, which is the concluding paragraph of the joint decision of the Chief Commissioner and Mr. H. A. Shewan, Q. C., the following passage occurs:—

> "Although the insurance officer's representative was prepared to accept that the employer must have a legal right to suspend, which in this case, in view of the arrangement made, the employer clearly had, we wish to reserve this question for consideration in some future case where it arises. We think it well arguable that there can be suspension by the employer where he lays off the employee in fact even though he has no legal right to do so. (In such a case the employee could treat the suspension as a repudiation of the contract and refuse to be employed further in which event there would be a termination of the employment.)"

11. I should like to pay tribute to the care taken by the local tribunal and to the clarity with which their decision is recorded. However, I have come to the conclusion that the chairman's view is to be preferred to that of the majority. My reasons are as follows:—

(*a*) As already mentioned, the deprivation of a supply of electric current prevented the claimant's employers from providing work for their employees during any day on which the supply was cut off. Accordingly, they had to "lay off" their employees on those days. In my view, that is a "suspension" by the employers of the employment of the employees. That the employers had no choice in the matter seems to me to be irrelevant. I think that suspension "by the employer" is expressly mentioned in order to exclude suspension by the employee.

(*b*) In my view, the phrase "suspended by the employer" in section 3(1)(a) refers to a fact, that is to say the fact of suspension by the employer. I do not consider that the statutory provision is concerned with the question whether or not the employer has the legal right to suspend his employee under the terms of a contract of employment. It is concerned only with facts.

Any other view would have the consequence that whenever a question arose concerning the application of this statutory provision, the insurance officer would have to make close enquiry into the terms of the contract of employment of each employee affected and make up his mind on what might well be a difficult question of law. It cannot have been the intention of Parliament that an insured person's title to earnings-related supplement should depend on such a process. It has always been the consistent policy of Parliament to provide an adjudication process which allows of prompt decision and disposal of claims to unemployment benefit. Moreover, in the field of industrial relations a great deal of action is taken without regard to the terms of any contract of employment but with regard to customary forms of behaviour, whether or not sanctioned by a legal provision in a contract. I think that if the view of the majority of the local tribunal were to prevail, the task of an insurance officer in dealing with claims to earnings-related supplement would become so difficult as to verge on the impossible. No doubt the concession recorded as having been made by the insurance officer's representative in R(U) 11/72 misled the majority of the local tribunal in this case. I do not understand why it was made, but it may have been only for the purpose of shortening the argument.

(c) Mr. Nathoo also submitted to me that, even if I failed to come to the view which I have expressed above, then it could be said that the claimant and, no doubt also, his fellow employees did by their conduct consent to the suspensions. It is unnecessary for me to rest my decision on this point, but on the whole I think the point sound.

. . . .

Availability

(See the Social Security Act, 1975, s. 17(1)(*a*), *ante,* p. 2.)

Social Security (Unemployment, Sickness and Invalidity Benefit) Regulations 1975 (S. I. 1975 No. 564), reg. 7(1)(a)

. . . where in respect of any day a person places restrictions on the nature, hours, rate of remuneration or locality or other conditions of employment which he is prepared to accept and as a consequence of those restrictions has no reasonable prospects of securing employment, that day shall not be treated as a day of unemployment unless—

(i) he is prevented from having reasonable prospects of securing employment consistent with those restrictions only as a result of adverse industrial conditions in the locality or localities concerned which may reasonably be regarded

as temporary, and, having regard to all the circumstances, personal and other, the restrictions which he imposes are reasonable, or
(ii) the restrictions are nevertheless reasonable in view of his physical condition, or
(iii) the restrictions are nevertheless reasonable having regard both to the nature of his usual occupation and also to the time which has elapsed since he became unemployed;
(For "adverse industrial circumstances, see *ante*, pp. 40–44.)

R(U) 1/55

. . . .

2. The claimant is a rigger who normally obtains his employment at the S. Docks. The manner in which he obtains employment there is to take his place twice daily at a stand which is situated outside the dock gates and if any employer should require any labour he would go to the stand and thereupon engage the number of workers he required—the claimant possibly being one of those workers.

. . . .

10. It will be convenient here to summarise the conditions A, B, and C to which the chairman and the insurance officer have referred. Those conditions are set out in Decision U.D. 7550/35 and are as follows:—

Condition A. The claimant who leaves home for the purpose of taking a holiday must prove that he was ready and willing to curtail his intended period of absence from his locality on holiday in order to accept at once any suitable employment which might be notified to him.

Condition B. He must prove that he had taken reasonable and satifactory steps to ensure that any opportunity of suitable employment would be brought to his notice without delay. That his place of temporary residence was on the telephone service or had a postal and telegraph delivery which afforded a means of communicating with him which was adequate for the purpose of satisfying this condition.

Condition C. He must prove that there was nothing connected with his absence from his locality or with the position of his place of temporary residence which would have prevented him from accepting at once any suitable employment which might be notified to him.

11. In my view condition B of the requirements of proof set out in Decision U.D. 7550/35 is, in itself, sufficient to show that the claimant was not available for employment as a rigger, for it is

farcical to suggest that prospective employers in the docks, especially at a time when work was slack, would go to the trouble of sending a message to a man who was on holiday and that they would have been prepared to wait for him while all the time there were other men standing by idle, ready and willing to accept employment immediately. The question is not whether there was employment available for the claimant, it is whether he was available for employment, and I think that it strains credulity to the breaking point to assume that the claimant could *reasonably* expect that an opportunity for employment would, in the circumstances, be brought to his notice. Men such as the claimant who want employment in the docks go there and take their place at the stand. Employers of dock labour expect to find labour there; they do not normally expect to have to send messages for men who are not ready to accept employment immediately. The claimant was not in a position to accept *at once* any suitable employment which may have been notified to him and it is manifest that his chances of securing employment while residing in R. for his holiday were substantially reduced. I will go further and say that his chances were remote and that the procedure adopted by him in leaving his address at the employment exchange was a mere formality and had not reality about it. Even if he had left his address with the people who usually employed him, I would want cogent evidence that such people would be prepared to write or telegraph him to come all the way from R. to S. to do a day's work when they knew that there was labour available immediately to call. To say that the claimant was available for employment in this case seems to me to reduce the question to a farce.

12. This case is clearly distinguishable from the cases of those persons who are not casual workers but who expect to be employed for an appreciable time and can usually expect some notice before they accept a situation. Such persons can reasonably expect to have an opportunity to return home and take up the proffered situation. Workers at the docks expect to be taken on immediately or within a few hours. The claimant was in no position to begin work at such short notice.

13. In the result I am satisfied, as was the local insurance officer and the chairman, that no such opportunity could reasonably have presented itself to the claimant while he was taking his holiday at R. and, therefore, I hold that he was not available for employment during the period in question. It follows that he cannot be treated as having been unemployed during that period and, therefore, he was not entitled to unemployment benefit from the 18th to the 25th September, 1954.

. . . .

R(U) 6/72

. . . .

2. The claimant, who is now 62 years of age, was employed for many years, indeed, for the whole of his working life, in the building and construction industry. He has plainly had enormous experience in that trade. He became the technical manager of a large construction company whose head office is in London. He lives some miles out of London at Epsom. Unhappily he suffers from a heart condition and from hypertension. He found that the daily travel from Epsom to London became too much for him. Accordingly, he took the advice of his doctor and retired from his employment as technical manager of the construction company. His employment with the company came to an end on 31st July, 1971.

3. On 6th August, 1971 the claimant went to his local employment exchange to make enquiries about further employment. I am not sure whether he in fact registered for employment but, however that may be, he was required to complete a form UI 672 which is headed "Report on question of availability for employed contributor's employment". It is a familiar form. It has in the past given rise to many decisions and will no doubt continue to do so in the future. The form is designed to enable officials at an employment exchange to be informed of the limits within which a claimant for unemployment benefit is willing to accept employment. It is, in a sense, complementary to regulation 7(1)(b) of the National Insurance (Unemployment and Sickness Benefit) Regulation 1967 [S.I. 1967 No. 330] to the terms of which I refer below. Part 1 of the form is a type of questionnaire to be completed by the claimant. He is, however, clearly informed by a note at the head of Part 1 that his entitlement to unemployment benefit and contribution credits may be affected if he places restrictions on the work or conditions of the employment he is prepared to accept. He is also referred to a leaflet.

4. In the instant case the claimant's answers to the questions in Part 1 of form UI 672 were as follows:—

1. What type or types of employment are you prepared to accept?

—*Answer:* Technical manager.

2. What minimum salary or wages do you require?

—*Answer:* £5,500.

3. Are you available for and prepared to accept full-time suitable employment from Monday to Saturday each week?—*Answer:* Yes.

4. Are you prepared to go anywhere to work?—*Answer:* No. If your answer is "No", what restrictions are you placing on the locality in which you are prepared to work?—*Answer:* Home town or close environs away from London.

. . . .

7. There can, of course, be no doubt whatsoever that the claimant placed restrictions on the nature, rate of remuneration and the locality of the employment he was prepared to accept. There can be no possible argument about that. What was the consequence of his imposing those restrictions? On the available evidence I think that that question admits of only one answer. I think the unavoidable conclusion must be that in consequence of the restrictions he imposed the claimant had no reasonable prospects of securing employment. I understand that the branch of the Department of Employment known as "the Professional and Executive register" expressed the view that there were no prospects of the type of employment specified by the claimant at the salary he stipulated within the locality to which he confined himself. There is no evidence to the contrary. There is nothing to contradict what was said by officials at the Professional and Executive register of the Department.

8. I do not find that surprising. I should have thought it unlikely in the extreme that a man of the claimant's age would secure employment outside London, or outside any large city, as a technical manager at so high a salary as £5,500 a year. In so saying, I do not for a moment overlook the fact that the claimant has had years of experience in his particular trade and is, I doubt not, highly skilled in it. Nevertheless, I feel obliged to hold that it must be said of the claimant that in consequence of the nature, rate of remuneration and locality of the employment he was prepared to accept, that he had no reasonable prospects of securing employment. I therefore hold that 6th August, 1971 cannot be treated as a day of unemployment in relation to the claimant unless he can be assisted by one of the subparagraphs. . . .

9. Sub-paragraph (i) plainly has no application in this case. There is nothing to suggest that the claimant was prevented from having reasonable prospects of securing employment consistent with the restrictions he imposed only as a result of adverse industrial conditions in the locality. There is no evidence that in that particular locality there were any adverse industrial conditions, temporary

or otherwise, Under sub-paragraph (ii) the restrictions must be shown to be reasonable in view of the claimant's physical condition. It is to be noted that the word "restriction" in that sub-paragraph is in the plural. As I have said earlier, the claimant suffers from a heart condition. He also suffers from hypertension. It was for reasons of his health that he prematurely retired at the end of July 1971. I think, therefore, that it might well be said that the locality restriction the claimant imposed when completing form UI 672 was a reasonable restriction. The same cannot, however, be said of the restriction relating to the type of employment he was prepared to accept or to the rate of remuneration for which he stipulated. Sub-paragraph (ii) does not, I find, assist the claimant. The restrictions (in the plural) cannot be said to have been reasonable in view of the claimant's physical condition.

10. I turn finally to sub-paragraph (iii) of regulation 7(1)(b). It is said that, having retired from his employment as technical manager with the construction company in London, the claimant had no usual occupation at the material time; i.e. when he answered the questionnaire in Part 1 of form UI 672 on 6th August, 1971. That may, no doubt, be a possible view. I express no opinion as to that. I do not find it necessary to do so. I assume (though I do not decide) that the claimant's regular occupation on 6th August 1971 may properly be said to have been that of a technical manager. It is, however, to be observed that the word "restrictions" in sub-paragraph (iii) is also in the plural. It may be, again I will assume though not decide, that having regard to the nature of what I have assumed the claimant's usual occupation to be it was reasonable for him to restrict the type of employment he was prepared to accept to that of a technical manager. But it cannot, I think, be said to have been reasonable for him to have restricted the locality in which he was prepared to accept such employment to his "home town or close environs away from London". I find that the restrictions he imposed were not reasonable having regard to the nature of his usual occupation as I have assumed it to be.

11. The period that had elapsed since the claimant became unemployed was, admittedly, an extremely brief one. I do not think, however, that the fact that it was such a brief period is in any way relevant. In my judgment the evidence shows that no matter how long he might wait he would be extremely unlikely to secure employment within the limits of the restrictions he imposed.

12. In the result I hold that in consequence of the restrictions the claimant placed on the nature etc. of the employment he was prepared to accept he had not reasonable prospects of securing employment. I find that he is not assisted by any of the sub-

paragraphs . . . referred to above. I therefore hold that 6th August, 1971, which I repeat is the only day to which the present appeal relates, cannot be treated as a day of unemployment in relation to the claimant.

. . . .

Inclusionary Rules

Regulations provide for a day to be treated as a day of unemployment notwithstanding that prima facie it cannot be ranked as such by reason of the claimant being employed, *i.e.* doing work. There are two instances, nightworkers and persons engaged in subsidiary occupations.

Nightworkers

(See, also, R(U) 15/60, *ante*, p. 27.

R(U) 37/56

11. . . . work beginning on Saturday at 11.30 a.m. and ending on Sunday must be treated as occurring in the week ending on midnight Saturday/Sunday.[16] I do not think that the fact that the work lasted continuously for 29½ hours affects the question.

. . . .

R(U) 18/56

. . . .

5. . . . a question arises whether the claimant may be assisted by invoking . . . the Night Workers Regulation. . . . The general effect of this regulation, where it applies, is to enable a workman whose night employment extends into two calendar days to qualify for unemployment benefit in respect of one or other of these two days. The meaning and application of the Night Workers Regulation were considered very recently by the Commissioner in the case to which Decision R(U) 10/56 relates. In that case the Commissioner held that the Night Workers Regulation did not apply to share fishermen in so far as it was inconsistent with the provisions of the Mariners Regulations. The present claimant is not, however, a share fisherman. But in the course of his decision the Commissioner also expressed approval of the view that "the Night Workers Regulation can have no application in relation to a period of

---

[16] Under the current regulation the work would be appropriated to the day on which the greater part of it fell (Social Security (Unemployment, Sickness and Invalidity Benefit) Regulations 1975 (S.I. 1975 No. 564), reg. 5).

employment which lasts for more than 24 hours on either side of midnight."

6. I respectfully agree. The regulation in question deals specifically with a period of employment (*a*) begun on a Saturday and extending over midnight into Sunday; or (*b*) begun on a Sunday and extending over midnight into Monday; or (*c*) begun on any day other than Saturday or Sunday and extending over midnight into the following day. In each case, that is to say, the period of employment within the purview of the regulation is one which begins at some time within the 24 hours comprising one calendar day, and ends at some time within the 24 hours comprising the following calendar day. The regulation is in all material respects identical with an earlier regulation under the Unemployment Insurance Acts, about which, in Decision 6860/33 the Umpire said: "The Regulation is framed and worded to meet the case of persons on night work whose actual employment is begun before midnight on one day and terminates some time after midnight on the day following. It does not apply and was not intended to apply to the case of persons who, while their periods of duty are usually divided into 'watches' or other periods, are under orders and discipline and liable to perform services at any time of the day or night throughout a continuous period of many days, weeks or months."

. . . .

Subsidiary Occupations

(See **R(U) 6/77,** *ante,* pp. 9–10.)

R(U) 4/77

. . . .

4. On 21 August, 1975 the claimant and his wife opened a gift shop and coffee house (sometimes referred to as a restaurant). The claimant has never denied, and therefore I find, that this was a partnership venture between them and each was in law entitled to half the profits if any. During the periods material to this decision they both worked in the business full time, the claimant himself taking a full part in the day to day running of the business save, perhaps, on occasional days. The shop was open from 9.30 a.m. to 5.30 p.m. each day except on Wednesdays and Sundays. During the first seven weeks of the business it remained open on Wednesday mornings but thereafter it was not opened on Wednesdays at all.

5. The main statutory provision to be applied to the facts which I have related is found in regulation 7(1)(h) of the Social Security (Unemployment, Sickness and Invalidity Benefit) Regulations 1975 [SI 1975 No. 564] which so far as material reads as follows, the paragraphing and capital letters being insterted by me for ease of reference:—

> "7.—(1) For the purposes of unemployment . . . . benefit—
>
> (h) . . . . a day shall not be treated as a day of unemployment if on that day a person is engaged in any employment unless
>
> (A) the earnings derived from that employment, in respect of that day, do not exceed 75 pence, or, where the earnings are earned in respect of a longer period than a day, the earnings do not on the daily average exceed that amount and
>
> (B) unless he is available on that day to be employed full-time in some employed earner's employment and
>
> (C) the employment in which he is engaged is consistent with that full-time employment and,
>
> (D) if the employment in which he is engaged is employed earner's employment, it is not in his usual main occupation; . . . . "

That regulation replaced regulation 7(1)(i) of SI 1967 No. 330 (as amended) and is in substantially the same terms. The word "employment" has been substituted for "occupation" in the opening paragraph. But in my view this alteration makes no material difference.

6. The effect of regulation 7(1)(h) is that if an insured person engages in any employment whatever, including self-employment, no day on which he is so engaged may be treated as a day of his unemployment unless he satifies all the four conditions (A) to (D) in the above quotation. It has been accepted throughout by the insurance officers that in undertaking employment in the shop and coffee house business the claimant did not fail to satisfy condition (B) (*i.e.* he remained available for full-time employment), and did not offend condition (D) (because his employment was not employed earner's employment). They maintain, however, that he failed to satisfy condition (A) (the earnings condition) or condition (C) (the consistency condition). Accordingly, although the local tribunal rested their decision only on a finding that the claimant had not satisfied the consistency condition, the first question for my determination is whether, during the inclusive period 21 August to 13 November 1975, he satisfied the earnings condition either

wholly or in part. Plainly the case is one in which earnings were gained over a period and the daily rate of earning has to be determined by an averaging calculation.

7. When the claimant's title to unemployment benefit was called in question prior to the local insurance officer's decision dated 18 December 1975, the claimant instructed his accountants to prepare an account showing the weekly profit or loss made by the shop and coffee house business since it opened. The accountants carried out his instruction so far as was possible and their account covered the period down to 22 November 1975, a period of 14 weeks. . . . The accountants had to estimate some of the expenditure because its amount was not known at the time; for example no electricity account had been received then.

8. The Social Security Benefit (Computation of Earnings) Regulations 1974 [SI 1974 No. 2008][17] provide guidance on methods of computing earnings, but in the circumstances of this case the relevant regulation, which is 2(3), gives a free hand to the determining authority to select whatever method seems fair having regard to the available evidence. This eminently sensible rule is necessary because evidence of earnings is often very sketchy and the statutory authorities simply have to do the best they can. In the present case both insurance officers have suggested that the reasonable method of calculating the claimant's daily rate of earning is to divide the profit of £159 . . . by the number of working days in the 14 weeks period. This method ascribes to each of the claimant and his wife a daily rate of earnings of just under 95p. The alternative to that choice of method is to work out the claimant's daily earning rate for each week . . . .

9. Of the two possible methods the latter appeals more to my sense of justice than the former. The business under consideration was newly started, and the first fourteen weeks of its existence have no accounting significance. This period is wholly arbitrary from an accounting point of view, simply depending on the accident that the insurance officer happened to take the claimant's benefit position into cognisance at about the end of the 14 weeks. If I could have seen an annual account I would probably have adopted the method suggested by the insurance officer. But neither the local insurance officer nor the local tribunal could wait for the production of an annual account. I think that the right course is to calculate the claimant's daily earning rate separately for each week covered by the account. This is likely to minimise the effects of unavoidable inaccuracies in the accounts, particularly underestimates of expenditure. The result of adopting this approach is

[17] See, now, S.I. 1978 No. 1698.

to ascribe to the claimant a daily rate exceeding 75p only during the weeks ending 11 and 25 October, and 1, 8, 15 and 22 November, 1975. Accordingly, he only failed to satisfy the earnings condition during these 6 weeks out of the 14 weeks dealt with in the account.

. . . .

11. The question whether the claimant satisfied the consistency condition of regulation 7(1)(h) is vexed. The regulation presents a problem of interpretation which, and a solution to which, were explained in the following extract from paragraph 10 of the reported Commissioner's Decision R(U) 4/64:—

> "The next question is whether the occupation which he is following is consistent with full-time employment. If a person following an occupation is available for full-time employment, it might appear at first sight that his occupation must of necessity also be consistent with full-time employment. The idea of "consistency" must however be something different from the idea of "availability", otherwise conditions (2) and (3) would be tautologous. It appears to me that, if an occupation is to be consistent will full-time employment, it must be one which a person can carry on concurrently with the full-time employment for which he is available without interfering with the latter, *and also it must be capable of being so carried on without any substantial reduction in volume or extent.*"

Conditions (2) and (3) referred to in that extract correspond with my conditions (B) (availability) and (C) (consistency), and the underlining at the end of the quotation is mine.

12. Unfortunately I have never felt able to accept the underlined sentence of that quotation. I gave reasons in unreported Decisions CU 9/69 and CU 1/73, and another Commissioner agreed with my view in unreported Decision CU 21/72. I am very conscious of the undesirability of a Commissioner dissenting from a reported Decision, but nevertheless feel compelled to do so in this case. My reasons are as follows:—

   (a) The language of the regulation does not justify the underlined sentence. There are no words in it referring to the insured person's activities in the occupation in question, or to a variation in those activities following engagement in full-time employment. The regulation deals with the nature of the occupation itself, not with the insured person's activities in it while unemployed, and all that is necessary to give it full effect is to hold that the occupation must be *capable* of being followed by the insured person concurrently with full-time employment.

(b) (i) In my view, a historical approach confirms the lack of justification for the underlined sentence. A regulation corresponding to regulation (7)(1)(h) but not identical with it has been in existence since 1948. For a period prior to 1955 there was a provision in it that a day was not to be treated as a day of unemployment if on that day a person was following an occupation "unless that occupation should ordinarily have been followed by him in addition to his usual employment and outside the ordinary working hours of that employment." This formula contemplated that while unemployed a person might work different or longer hours in a subsidiary occupation than he could if employed in his usual employment: but of course, there was then, as now, an earnings condition and if the person earned in excess of the limit thereby provided his title to unemployment benefit was defeated. The accepted view of the effect of the quoted part of the then regulation was expressed in Decision R(U) 11/54, which was in turn explained in R(U) 12/59, paragraph 8 in the following passage:—

"The fact that a claimant for unemployment benefit, *when unemployed,* may follow a subsidiary occupation during hours in which he would have been working, if he had been in full-time employment does not of itself disqualify him for unemployment benefit; see Decision R(U) 11/54, paragraphs 5 and 6."

(ii) The word "consistent" was introduced into the regulation by an amendment made in 1955 and comes from the Report of the National Insurance Advisory Committee on "The Availability Question" published in 1953 (Cmd 8894) which recommended the amendment. The Committee were told that a person whose regular main occupation was a part-time one might be entitled to unemployment benefit at the full rate if he lost employment in that occupation but was able to carry on with his subsidiary, also part-time, occupation; and that he might be better off unemployed than employed. They therefore recommended that any subsidiary occupation which such a man followed during the period of unemployment should be consistent with full-time employment: see paragraphs 49 and 52 of their Report. The emphasis of their recommendation was on the phrase "full-time".

(iii) The Decision R(U) 12/59 from which I have quoted in (b)(i) above was, of course, written some years after the consistency condition was introduced into the law and was written by the same learned author as wrote Decision R(U) 4/64. Evidently he changed his view in the intervening period, but he has not explained why. I do not consider that any change was needed.

(c) The interpretation adopted in R(U) 4/64 could lead to the undesirable result that an unemployed man would be compelled to be unnecessarily idle. So long as he remains available for full-time employment, and does not earn enough to breach the earnings condition, the unemployment insurance funds are sufficiently protected.

(d) Cases allowing a person to work longer hours in a "consistent" occupation while unemployed than he is able to do while in full-time employment are, perhaps not exclusively but mostly, confined to situations in which the unemployed person is self-employed. If he is an employee then he is less likely to be able to adjust his hours of work when he obtains full-time employment elsewhere. These cases are therefore relatively rare. Decision CU 21/72 provides a good example of such a case. On the other hand the case dealt with in R(U) 4/64 is a different kind of case; one in which the occupation in question necessarily failed to be consistent will full-time employment because the work was done in usual working hours and could not be altered to fit in with full-time employment.

13. The occupation or, as it is now called by the 1975 regulation, the employment in which the present claimant was engaged from 21 August, 1975 was self-employment as a part proprietor of a shop and coffee house business. He may have appeared at first sight to have been engaged in the employment of a shop assistant but that was not his employment. He was one of the two owners of the business, self-employed and able to do as much or as little work in the shop as he thought fit. It does not appear that he ceased to be the part proprietor of the business on obtaining full-time employment in 1976, and I must assume that he continued to be such although reducing his activities in the shop. In my judgment his self-employment in business was consistent with full-time employment, and I hold that he satisfied condition (C).

. . . .

Period of Interruption of Employment

17/59 (UB)

(Note: this decision relates to the "continuity" rule, now repealed, whereby benefit for the first three days of a period of interruption of employment (the "waiting days") became payable once a futher nine days of interruption of employment had occurred in the same period. The reasoning, however, applies equally to arranging lay-offs so as to ensure that short periods of interruption of employment can be linked so as to form one long period of interruption of employment thus avoiding loss of benefit for a second and subsequent sets of three "waiting days.")

. . . .

2. . . . it is a question of fact, and of history, on any claimant's actual record whether or not continuity of employment in the sense of that proviso has, or has not, been affected; subject only to the quite general principle of equity, in interpreting the section, that if in any case the facts are such as to lead one to conclude either that a claimant himself has improperly and artificially "arranged" his employment of his own volition (as *e.g.*, in U.D. 5825/36) or, as a corollary, if the employers have so arranged it for the purpose of benefiting their workers under the said proviso, then it is justifiable and right to look beyond the record itself in order to ascertain whether, indeed, there has been a genuine "interruption of employment" within the meaning of the said proviso (as *e.g.*, in U.D. 399/28, or U.D. 120/52). But it is right to say that these cases were decided on clear evidence that this objective was either the sole, or at least the predominant, purpose of the employers.

. . . .

4. Whilst I have paid due attention to the form of the notices displayed by the firm at their factory, these are expressed to be based on "the uncertainty of trade" and, both from those notices and the evidence before the Local Tribunal I think it is only fair to conclude—as the Insurance Officer very properly concedes at paragraph 21—that ". . . there is no evidence that the employers suspended the employment of their workers for the sole purpose of putting them on to unemployment benefit as far as the 28th and 31st August are concerned . . .". It is, however, when the Insurance Officer goes on to submit that ". . . it is not unreasonable to conclude that in arranging the stopping periods as they did the employers had in mind to benefit their workers by saving them the necessity of having to wait three days without benefit (N.I.U.D. 399/28 is of interest in this connection)", that I find myself unable to agree with him on this occasion. The Decision in N.I.U.D. 399/28 to which he refers was based on strong evidence of such an

arrangement, in the form of a letter of the 4th October, 1927, sent to the Local Exchange Manager in connection with another mill of the same employers; and the employers' evidence before the Court of Referees in that case manifestly constituted additional evidence of such an "arrangement". I consider the present case quite different in that there is clear evidence by the employer that "the factory did not close down to assist the workers in their relations with the Ministry of Labour" and that the interruption was occasioned by a seasonal slackness in the trade, the firm preferring to "spread the slackness" rather than closing down completely for successive periods.

5. I do not consider that the evidence is such as to establish clearly—or indeed to any satisfactory degree at all—that the employers' sole, or predominant, motive in so terminating the employment was to preserve continuity of unemployment for their workers. Indeed, if Mr. B—'s evidence is accepted—and though the Local Tribunal came to an adverse conclusion they do not express themselves as rejecting that evidence—the evidence is to the contrary. And, as I have said, I think consideration of employers' motives only becomes relevant if there is tolerably clear evidence of such an arrangement with such a purpose by the employers as that to which I have referred; the Statutory Authorities being otherwise bound, as I see it, to take the record and history of a claimant as they find it, since neither the section nor any other statutory provision of which I am aware, entitles one to do otherwise.

Seasonal Workers

Social Security (Unemployment, Sickness and Invalidity Benefit) Regulations 1975 (S.I. 1975 No. 564, reg. 19

. . . .

(2) in this regulation—

. . . .

"off-season" means, . . . that period of the year (or, if more than one period, the aggregate of those periods) during which he is normally not employed, and for this purpose the expression "period" shall not include any period of less than 7 consecutive days;

"seasonal worker" means a person whose normal employment is for a part or parts only of a year in an occupation or occupations of which the availability or extent varies at approximately the same time or times in successive years; or any other person who normally restricts his employment to the same, or substantially the same, part or parts only of the year; and for the purpose of this definition the following provisions shall apply:—

(i) the expression "part or parts only of a year" shall include any period of time . . . whatever the duration of that period; but where any period or periods of a year during which a person is normally employed is not, or if more than one period . . . do not amount in the aggregrate to, more than seven weeks, that person shall not be treated as a seasonal worker;

(ii) in construing the expression "normal employment", regard shall be paid to factors inherent in the nature or conditions of the occupation or occupations in which that person is engaged, and not to factors abnormal that occupation or occupations notwithstanding that those factors persist for a prolonged period;

"a substantial amount of employment" means employment which is equal in duration to not less than one-fourth (or such other fractional part as may, in the circumstances of any particular case, be reasonable) of the current off-season; "year" . . . means the period of 12 months commencing with the first day in the calendar year on which the person concerned begins a period of normal employment.

(3) The following shall be additional conditions with respect to the receipt of unemployment benefit by a seasonal worker in respect of any day during his off-season—

(*a*) that he has registered for employment . . . throughout the period of 2 years immediately preceding that day . . . other than . . .:—

(i) any period during which he was employed or was incapable of work;

(ii) any inconsiderable period;

(iii) any temporary period throughout which he was not available to be employed by reason only of domestic necessity or compulsion of law, or by reason of any other circumstances of an exceptional character; and

(*b*) that either—

(i) in his current off-season he has had a substantial amount of employment before that day; or

(ii) . . . he can or could reasonably expect to obtain, after that day in his current off-season, employment which, together with his employment (if any) before that day in that off-season, constitutes a substantial amount of employment.

R(U) 5/64 (T)

. . . .

7. Having fully considered all the arguments put forward by and on behalf of the claimant, we are unable to accept his representative's approach to this matter as being correct. As appears from numerous decisions of the Commissioner, the answer to the question whether a person is a seasonal worker is provided, not by considering the conditions in an industry generally, but by an examination of the individual claimant's own record of employment. The definition of a seasonal worker . . . contains the word "normal", and to the great advantage of claimants the Commissioner has accepted the view that, where employment is for a part or parts only of a year, that should generally not be regarded as normal until three years have elapsed. Since individual records of employment over such a long period vary considerably, and the line has to be drawn somewhere, it must necessarily follow that one claimant may be held to be a seasonal worker when another, whose present occupation is very similar, is held not to be. Our duty is to decide on the claimant's record of employment and all the circumstances whether he is a seasonal worker. If he is, then we must say so, irrespective of what has been held or admitted in other cases, though of course we recognise how unfortunate it is that there should be apparent inequalities, one of which has resulted from Decision C.U. 15/63, in which, as we shall later indicate, in our opinion the decision that the claimant was not a seasonal worker was erroneous. The fact that the gaps between the claimant's summer and winter periods of employment happened against his wish and through no fault of his cannot prevent him from being held a seasonal worker. Under the definition . . . even though a person does not (voluntarily) *restrict* his employment, he may still become a seasonal worker against his will if in fact the "availability or extent" of his occupation "varies at approximately the same time or times in successive years". (See for example Decision R(U) 28/56). The words on which the claimant's representative relied so strongly . . . are part of a provision which gives a claimant an excuse for not having registered for employment. It has throughout been admitted that the claimant did register for employment, and he therefore has no need of excuses for not

doing so, and the words relied on accordingly have no relevance to the present case. With regard to hardship and detriment to the fishing industry, our duty is to decide the case by applying the regulation to the facts, and we have no discretion to take into consideration such other matters. With reference to the claimant's objection to the application of the phrase seasonal worker to himself, a large number of cases come before the statutory authorities of persons who unquestionably are seasonal workers but at the same time are deserving, anxious to work, unfortunate and certainly not lazy. No doubt there are some seasonal workers, as there are others, who are lazy, but in our opinion there is no justification for using the phrase seasonal worker as a term of reproach.

8. In our judgment the approach to this matter of the insurance officer now concerned with the case is correct in all respects.

9. The accepted method of deciding whether a person is a seasonal worker as defined has been described in a number of decisions, notably Decisions R(U) 3/51, R(U) 29/51, R(U) 14/53 and R(U) 7/59; and it has been applied in countless other cases. In this case the insurance officer now concerned with it has produced a most helpful chart (on C.I.O. form No. 29A) which displays vividly the pattern of the claimant's employment during recent years. After a continuous summer period of employment from April to September 1961, there was a gap during part of September and part of October, followed by an intermittent but fairly substantial period of employment down to the middle of March 1962, followed by a gap during part of March and part of April, followed in turn by a continuous period of employment down to the 3rd October, 1962. The pattern of the two preceding years is very similar. Prima facie therefore the availability or extent of the claimant's occupation varied at approximately the same times in successive years. The definition of off-season . . . makes it clear that in a case like this, where there are normally two gaps between two periods of employment each year, the off-season is the aggregate of the two gaps. By averaging the periods of employment in the preceding 3 years (Decision R(U) 29/51) the claimant is found to have had an (aggregate) off-season of 45 days excluding Sundays (consisting of the two periods in paragraph 1 above), which is just more than 7 weeks. . . . And the evidence shows that in none of the preceding 3 years did he during his aggregate off-season have as much as 12 days employment, which, being not less than one fourth of 45 days, would have been accepted as a substantial amount of employment and would have negatived any presumption that he was a seasonal worker (Decision R(U) 7/59). We can see no grounds for

saying that the gaps in the employment or the reasons for them were factors abnormal to the employment . . . nor that the 3 years is an inappropriate period or one fourth an inappropriate fraction to take. Accordingly, if the matter be approached in the accepted way, in our judgment the claimant had become a seasonal worker by the 28th September, 1962, if not before.

10. In Decision C.U. 15/63 however the Commissioner on similar materials held that nevertheless the claimant was not a seasonal worker because there was not one month in the whole period of [in that case five years, and not merely] three in which the claimant had been totally without work (paragraph 9 of the decision). It appears from the context that this meant that there had not been one calendar month. In our judgment this approach to the matter is completely novel and is inconsistent with that adopted in many Commissioner's decisions and with the terms of the regulations themselves. The normal employment for "part or parts only of a year" in the definition of a seasonal worker . . . can be of any duration, long or short, . . . subject only to the limitation that, if the remaining parts (that is to say the periods of normal non-employment) do not amount to more than seven weeks, the person is not treated as a seasonal worker. The periods of normal employment may be spread over the year in any manner, but provided that they recur at approximately the same time or times in successive years the person is a seasonal worker. This could happen without there being a single calendar month or a period of a month throughout which the claimant was unemployed. The test applied was therefore inconsistent with the terms of the regulation itself. Further, in paragraph 10 of Decision C.U. 15/63 the Commissioner in effect rejected the averaging process, which has been consistently used since Decision R(U) 29/51. In our judgment, whether or not month meant calendar month, Decision C.U. 15/63 proceeded on grounds completely different from those adopted in countless similar cases, and the decision was erroneous and cannot be supported.

11. It remains to consider whether the claimant satisfied the additional conditions. . . . Admittedly he satisfied that in [reg. 19(3)(*a*) above]. In respect of regulation [19(3)(*b*)] however, the question [of aggregating a number of off-seasons in a year] arises.

12. [References to "the current off-season" occur in a number of places in regulation 19]. In Decision C.U. 15/63 the opinion was expressed that, where an off-season contains more than one part, "current off-season" means that part of the off-season which contains the day for which unemployment benefit is claimed. This view is in accordance with Decision C.U. 8/54 (not reported). And incidental references to the current off-season can be found in

decisions suggesting the same view (see *e.g.* paragraph 11 of Decision R(U) 36/56). If this view is correct, it would mean that in the present case, in respect of a claim for unemployment benefit for any day in the period from the 28th September to the 23rd October, 1962, the question would be whether the claimant satisfied the conditions . . . in respect of this period; "a substantial amount" of employment would mean employment of not less than one fourth . . . of the days from the 28th September to the 23rd October. Similarly, on a claim for any day in the period between the 12 March and the 7th April, 1963, that second period would have to be considered separately from the first.

13. The insurance officer points out, however, that there are very many decisions which imply that, in cases where the off-season is made up of more periods than one, the current off-season is the whole of the aggregate off-season (as defined) which contains the day for which benefit is claimed, and there are many more decisions which show that in practice the calculation is always made on this basis (see e.g. Decisions R(U) 10/55, R(U) 26/55, R(U) 19/60) and R(U) 19/62). She submits that this view is correct.

14. In our judgment the insurance officer's contention on this point also is correct. . . . The claimant's "year", as defined, was the period of 12 months starting in April 1962, the first date in the calendar year when he began a period of normal employment. Accordingly his relevant current off-season was as stated in paragraph 1 above.

15. It remains to consider whether the claimant satisfied [the] regulation . . . during that current aggregate off-season looked at as a whole. The insurance officer now concerned with the case submits that he did so, and she draws attention to the following facts established by the evidence. He needed to obtain only 12 days of employment. Owing to slight irregularities in the dates, he started with, so to speak, a credit of 5 days employment consisting of normal employment which happened to fall in his off-season. He had had odd days of employment during the previous off-seasons. By the 1st April 1963 he had had 12 days of employment and so had complied with [the] regulation. . . . The insurance officer submits that he could throughout reasonably expect the amount required by [the] Regulation. . . . In our judgment this submission in favour of the claimant can be accepted. Accordingly the . . . Regulations put no obstacle in the way of the claimant receiving unemployment benefit during any part of the relevant current off-season.

16. The result is that the claimant's appeal fails in so far as he seeks a finding that he has not become a seasonal worker, but it

succeeds in that the insurance officer has established that the regulations do not prevent him from receiving the benefit during the periods concerned.

. . . .

(As to "averaging", see, now, the following case).

R(U) 4/75 (T)

. . . .

. . . each of the three years considered when the rule is applied should conform with the definition of a year contained in [the] regulation.

. . . .

15. The definition of a year . . . is, in our view, intended to assist in ascertaining a person's off-season whether or not it has any other purpose. But the practice has long been to fix the current off-season of a person held to be a seasonal worker by the averaging process first expounded in the Commissioner's Decision R(U) 29/51. As the Commissioner who decided C.U. 22/73 pointed out in another unreported Decision, C.U. 3/75, the averaging process may lead to a result contrary to regulation 2 because the definition is ignored. It seems to us, as at present advised, that no averaging process will be needed for fixing the opening date of a current off-season. this will be known from what has happened; it will be the first day after the insured person concerned ended his most recent on-season. As to the closing date of a current off-season, the latest possible date will be known. It will be the end of the year as fixed by regulation. . . . However, in some cases it may still be necessary to adopt an artificial method of pre-fixing the closing date in order to apply regulation [19]. If so, it may be that the averaging method is the best that can be done, but we leave the point open.

16. We ought not to conclude this decision without giving expression to the warning that the three year rule is a yardstick and not a magic wand. It does not solve all cases. Particular circumstances will in many cases make the application of the rule inappropriate or unneccessary: see paragraph 17 of the Decision R(U) 14/53.

. . . .

R(U) 19/60

. . . .

6. In the two years from the 16th September, 1957 to the 15th September, 1959, apart from periods of employment and periods of incapacity, the claimant failed to sign (a) from the 15th to the 18th September 1958, and (b) from the 16th March to the 27th April, 1959. Period (a) may be disregarded as "inconsiderable", but period (b) can not. It runs to 37 consecutive days, Sundays not

being counted. it has been ascertained that during this period the claimant was attending classes in the evening and studying during the day for his mate's certificate. It appears that by reason of these studies the claimant was not available for employment. This withdrawal from the field of employment was temporary, and it was for the specific purpose of attaining the mate's certificate, which purpose was in fact achieved at the end of the course. I am therefore able to accept the submission of the insurance officer now concerned with the case, that this period was a temporary period throughout which the claimant was not available for employment by reason only of circumstances which were of an exceptional character. This means that branch (a) of the additional condition is satisfied.

. . . .

Share Fisherman

In order to qualify for unemployment benefit, a share fisherman must prove, inter alia,
"that there was no work on or in connection with the fishing vessel available for him on that day for the reason—
  (a) that on account of the state of the weather the fishing vessel could not reasonably have put to sea with a view to fishing; or
  (b) that the fishing vessel was undergoing repairs or maintenance, . . .;
  (c) that there was an absence of fish from any waters in which the fishing vessel could reasonably be expected to operate;
  (d) that any other good cause necessitated abstention from fishing.
(Social Security (Mariners' Benefits) Regulations 1975 (S.I. 1975 No. 529), reg. 8(6)).

R(U) 19/64
. . . .
4. The first question which arises is whether the claimant is a person to whom [the] regulation applies. he is admittedly a sharefisherman as defined. . . . The fact that he himself is not a part-owner does not take him out of the operation of [the regulation because it] applies where "either the master of *any member* of the crew is the owner or part owner" (the italics are mine), and that was the position of the m.v. B. The contention of the association

is that, having been "paid off" by the owners, the claimant ceased to be a member of the crew; and reference is made to Decision R(U) 29/58. In the case to which that decision relates, the vessel changed over from one mode of fishing to another, necessitating a reduction of the number of crew from 10 to 8. The claimant in that case was one of the superfluous two who were "stood down". The vessel went about its fishing without them. In these circumstances the deputy Commissioner accepted that the claimant had ceased, for the time being, to be a member of the crew. But of course in that case, the vessel had its full crew, for the mode of fishing which it was in fact prosecuting, without the claimant: and that, to my mind, marks a significant distinction from the present case. *A fortiori*, in Decision R(U) 6/63, when the owners of a vessel, being resolved (permanently) to cease fishing with that vessel, laid it up for sale, it was held that its complement had ceased to be members of the crew of that vessel. In the present case I am not satisfied that while the m.v. B. was temporarily idle in the circumstances explained above, the claimant ceased to be a member of her crew . . . although no doubt he was at liberty to take other employment if he could have found it. I hold, therefore, that the claimant in the present case is a person to whom [the] regulation . . . applies, so that, in order to qualify for the receipt of unemployment benefit, he must satisfy the additional conditions contained therein.

5. The claimant must show that there was no work for him on or in connection with the m.v. B. for one or other of the four reasons specified in the regulation. The only one which is, or can be invoked, in the circumstances of this case is that under head (d) of the regulation: namely, "that . . . good cause necessitated abstention from fishing." What is alleged to have constituted the good cause necessitating absention from fishing?

6. The reason as stated by the association is "that there was no economic market for the fish caught": and the association's submission is that "where, as in this case, the claimant knows full well and, if necessary, proves that there was no market for the fish he had caught or would catch for some considerable time ahead (save at fishmeal prices which do not suffice to meet the cost of catching) he has other good cause necessitating abstention from fishing and that, accordingly, this claim should be allowed."

7. It would not be accurate to say that there was *no* market for any fish which the vessel might catch. If there had been no market, so that fish could not have been sold at any price [the] regulation . . . might be held to be satisfied—*see* Decision R(U) 16/53. But that was not the position. The port from which the vessel

operated was open, and there was a market for catches, although a poor one. The evidence is that for some weeks very low prices had been obtained, varying from 76s. to 42s. a cran; and some of the catches had to be sold for fish meal. Selling for fish meal attracts a government subsidy, amounting to 35s. a cran for 20 per cent of the total catch, and 10s. a cran thereafter. At the port in question some 1,600 crans of herring were landed on the 28th November, 1963, and of this some 600 crans were sold for fish meal: and about half of this quantity, it is said, fetched 10s. a cran only.

8. Regulation 14B(2)[18] was made on the 25th February, 1949, and came into operation on the 3rd March, 1949. It was not long before its meaning and implications fell to be considered by the Commissioner. A point similar to that raised in the present appeal was dealt with in an unreported decision of the Commissioner (C.S.U. 1/50) dated the 5th January, 1950. There the Commissioner said—

"For reasons about to be explained I find it unnecessary to consider whether *on proof* that the market for the probable catch was so inadequate as to have that result" [*sc.* that the fisherman would only incur debt on running expenses] "the fishermen concerned could all qualify for unemployment benefit by an agreement that all should abstain from fishing. The ground of my decision in the present case is that I can find no foundation in the evidence before the Local Tribunal and now before me for such a conclusion. The evidence shows that the situation from the standpoint of the share fishermen was regarded as most unsatisfactory, for beyond a market estimated at 200-250 crans provided by liners purchasing for bait, kippering firms and purchasers for curing purposes at prices stated at 89s. 10d., 85s. 10d.-89s. 10d., and 60s. per cran respectively, there was no market for the surplus herring catch except at the figure of 35s. per cran offered by the Herring Industry Board for conversion into fish meal and oil.

The share fishermen maintained that 'the figure of 35s. per cran for surplus herring is regarded by fishermen fish-salesmen drifter owners and others connected with the industry as entirely inadequate and uneconomical in view of the heavy working expenses of herring drifters' and the members of the Local Tribunal appear to have accepted and given effect to that contention as a sufficient justification for the allowance of unemployment benefit, but I am unable to affirm that

[18] Now reg. 8(6), above.

decision. No figures are given indicating even approximately the normal running expenses of the vessels or the remuneration of masters and crews from their shares of profits at what might be called normal times. Nor on the information before me is it possible for me to form any view as to the remuneration that would have been available for them under the conditions that are described as 'unremunerative and uneconomical'—or even how much more or less it would have been than the unemployment benefit that they have claimed, and have been receiving under the decision of the Local Tribunal. It seems obvious that apart from other considerations it would have depended on the amount of the surplus catch.

Accordingly I must allow the appeal of the Insurance Officer."

9. It may be said that the crux of Decision C.S.U. 1/50 was that *it had not been proved* that fishing operations, if carried out, would have resulted in a loss. Later decisions of the Commissioner, however, go rather further than this: they indicate that an allegation that fishing could only have resulted in a loss cannot be entertained by the Commissioner, and is in effect irrelevant to head (d) of the regulation. This appears from the reported Decision R(U) 10/51.

10. In the case to which Decision R(U) 10/51 relates, certain vessels abstained from fishing because of "uneconomic conditions". Financial statements were submitted in that case, showing that members of the crew were receiving (and presumably would have continued to earn) "rather less in all than £3 a week". The Commissioner said—". . . on consideration of regulation 14B as a whole and the terms of sub-paragraph (d) I think that it is clear that it was not intended or contemplated that the statutory authorities should entertain and dispose of claims based on such a ground" [*sc.* namely that fishing would not have yielded a weekly wage exceeding (say) £2 a week for each member of the crew (after allowing for expenses)]"—even if it could be regarded as practicable for them to do so. . . . The opposite view of the scope of sub-paragraph (d) would contemplate the somewhat embarrassing situation of the statutory authorities under the National Insurance Act, 1946 disapproving in effect of the price conditions fixed for share fishermen—by a body with special qualifications and holding special authority to do so—as conditions calculated to ensure for them a fair return for their labour. Apart, however, from such considerations such an interpretation of sub-paragraph (d) would give it a meaning and effect in violent contrast to the meaning and effect of the other sub-paragraphs (a), (b) and (c). . . . For those

provisions plainly contemplate and provide that there will be days and that there may be periods when unemployment benefit *will not be payable* although, after a vessel has put to sea (and whether it be engaged in fishing or not) or during a period in which the vessel has not put to sea because of repairs, the master and crew earn nothing—or their earnings are small or negligible."

11. In Decision R(U) 17/55 (at paragraph 16) the Commissioner said— "Reasonable cause for abstaining from fishing (whether that cause be of an economic nature or otherwise) does not in my view necessarily amount to 'good cause *necessitating* abstention'. It is important to remember that a share fisherman who in fact fishes, and whose catch can only be sold at a loss, does not qualify for unemployment benefit. There is much to be said for the view that in an enterprise such as share fishing the participants must expect days of loss as well as days of profit. And just as a day of fishing at a loss is not compensated by payment of unemployment benefits, it must not be readily assumed that a day of abstention from fishing because of apprehended loss will be compensated by payment of unemployment benefit."

12. in Decision R(U) 22/59, after re-examination of the principles established in earlier cases it was reiterated that 'unprofitability as a commercial venture has been rejected by the Commissioner as the test of 'any other good cause necessitating abstention from fishing'.".

13. It seems to me that in the present case I am being invited to depart from an interpretation of [the] regulation . . . which has been accepted by the Commissioner consistently, in the series of decisions cited above, and doubtless in many others. I see no justification for doing so: particularly as the accepted interpretation seems to me, with respect, to be logical and in accordance with principles. I agree therefore that the claimant has not established that he satisfies the additional condition.

. . . .

On employment benefit in general see Calvert, *Social Security Law,* (2nd ed.) pp. 57–144; Ogus and Barendt, *The Law of Social Security,* pp. 77–107, 131–136.

CHAPTER 2

DISQUALIFICATION FOR UNEMPLOYMENT BENEFIT

THE TRADE DISPUTE DISQUALIFICATION

SOCIAL SECURITY ACT 1975, s. 19(1)

A person who has lost employment . . . by reason of a stoppage of work which was due to a trade dispute at his place of employment shall be disqualified for receiving unemployment benefit so long as the stoppage continues, except in a case where, during the stoppage, he has become bona fide employed elsewhere in the occupation which he usually follows or has become regularly engaged in some other occupation; but this subsection does not apply in the case of a person who proves—

(a) that he is not participating in or directly interested in the trade dispute which caused the stoppage of work. . . .[1]

R(U)1/56

. . . .

5. In a very full note appended to their findings, the tribunal explain the reasons for their decision. Throughout this note there runs the theme that although the men were originally on strike, they were prepared unconditionally to return to work on the 24th September: accordingly it could not be said to be their fault that they were unemployed after that date; and therefore it would be unfair that they should be penalised by being disqualified for receiving unemployment benefit after that date. Thus it is said—"If they had a good reason" (*i.e.* for not getting back to work "not attributed to any fault or neglect on their part it could not be held that the strike continues in such a way as to debar them from unemployment benefit. . . . Surely again if the offer to resume work was unconditional and honestly made that is all that is required. . . . The tribunal is unable to hold that it was the men's

[1] As amended by Employment Protection Act 1975, s. 111. Parallel provisions in previous legislation are: National Insurance Act 1946, s. 13; National Insurance Act 1965, s. 22; Social Security Act 1973, s. 14.

fault that there was not what might amount to a reasonably full resumption of work until about 3rd October, 1955."

6. With respect, these observations seem to me to betray a wrong approach to the question which the tribunal had to decide. The provisions of Section 13(1) of the Act are not directed to disqualification on the ground of *fault*. Where employment has been lost because of a stoppage of work, disqualification is imposed for the duration of the stoppage, provided that the stoppage is (and continues to be) due to a trade dispute. "The manifest object of the subsection is to prevent the insurance fund from being used to finance employees during strikes *or lock-outs* . . . . The merits of the dispute are irrelevant" (Decision R(U) 17/52). Equally, where a stoppage of work originally starting as a strike is continued as a lock-out, it is irrelevant to inquire whose "fault" that is, provided that the continuance of the stoppage is due to a trade dispute. It is of course necessary in the present case to inquire why the stoppage continued after the men had intimated their readiness to resume work. But inquiries on that point should be in no way directed towards attributing blame to the one side or the other. They should be directed simply towards deciding whether the continued stoppage was due to a trade dispute or not.

. . . .

Loss of Employment "By Reason of" Stoppage

R(U)6/71

. . . 2. The claimant is one of a number of temporary dockers at Dundee docks who were without employment for the period stated above. During that period there was a stoppage of work which was due to a trade dispute at his place of employment. The first—and, in effect, the only—question in issue in this appeal is whether his loss of employment was "by reason of" that stoppage of work; so as to involve disqualification for receiving unemployment benefit for the duration of the stoppage, in terms of section 22(1) of the Act.

3. The stoppage of work was a national one, arising from a dispute between dockers and employers as to wage rates. The dispute was reported upon by a Court of Inquiry under the Rt. Hon. The Lord Pearson dated 24th July, 1970. A copy of the Report, published by Her Majesty's Stationery Office as Cmnd. 4429, was included in the case papers furnished to me. As Commissioner, concerned solely with the determination of the insurance officer's appeal from the unanimous decision of the local tribunal

at Dundee, I am not concerned with the merits of the dispute: but the time table of events, and the causal connection of the events, are important. Fortunately there is little or no controversy as to the essential facts.

4. It appears that incoming cargoes at Dundee are substantially represented by (a) jute and (b) timber. In earlier times, jute usually arrived in winter and timber in summer. In more recent years this seasonal pattern has not been so closely followed. From time to time simultaneous arrivals of jute and timber occur. For this and other reasons it is necessary from time to time to supplement the established force of dockers by temporary dockers. The engagement of these temporary dockers is no longer so casual as it used formerly to be. In order that temporary dockers be engaged, authority has to be obtained from the National Dock Labour Board, and in practice authority will be given for the engagement of only that number of temporary dockers estimated to be required over and above the permanent dockers available. An attempt is made to indicate how long the engagement is likely to be for; but it is not always possible to do this with accuracy. It is customary to re-engage men who have been temporarily engaged on previous occasions, and these men may in due course become established as permanent dockers. A week's notice is required to terminate the engagement of a temporary docker. It is thus apparent that under the system, as practised, the employer cannot engage, dismiss or re-engage temporary dockers without a certain time lag: a period must elapse between the decision to engage, dismiss or re-engage, and the implementation of the decision.

5. The employers in the present case obtained authority to engage the claimant and others (numbering in all 26) with effect from 22nd June 1970. It was anticipated that work would be available for the increased task-force for some considerable time: but it was known to all concerned that a national dock strike was pending. On 1st June 1970 the Workpeople's Side of the National Joint Council for the Port Transport Industry had given one month's notice of their intention to terminate the current Docks Agreement. The temporary dockers so engaged did not wish to be involved in the threatened strike: and so it was clearly understood on both sides that their engagement was to terminate before any strike began. Meanwhile the threat of strike became more imminent, with a probably starting date of 14th July, 1970. On 24th June, 1970 formal notice of termination of the current Agreement was given, and on 9th July 1970 notice was given calling for an official national dock strike, to start on 14th July, 1970. The claimant's employers had in fact given him his due notice of

discharge, as they were obliged to do, in anticipation that the strike would start on that date. The claimant worked up to and including 13th July, 1970. On 14th July, 1970 the strike started.

6. The short and simple—but not entirely easy—question which emerges is whether the claimant's loss of employment, in these circumstances, was by reason of the stoppage of work. To this question, a simple, but—as I think rather superficial—answer was given by the local tribunal. They said "No. He received notice of termination of employment". It is no doubt true that the claimant's employment terminated, in a sense, because the stipulated period of notice had expired. But in a deeper sense it terminated because the anticipated strike had occurred.

7. At the oral hearing of the appeal the claimant was represented by an officer of his association who put forward his case with, if I may say so, great ability and reasonableness. His contention, as I understood it, was that the claimant's employment had come to an end, not simply for the rather technical reason that the period of notice had expired, but also because it had been contemplated from the beginning that it should terminate (in the events which happened) on 13th July, 1970. But it must be observed that when the engagement was entered into, no terminal *date* could be, or was, specified. Essentially, the duration of the engagement was to depend, not on a specified *date*, but on a specified *event*: namely the strike, or, perhaps more accurately, the non-withdrawal of the notice of strike. The fact that the employer had to give 7 days' notice of discharge was irrelevant to the *cause* of discharge. It merely had to be given, as matter of machinery, 7 days prior to whatever date was anticipated, or known, to be the date when the strike would begin. Having considered the matter carefully I am satisfied that the endurance of the claimant's employment was not in any true sense based on a period of time, but was dependent on the occurrence, or anticipated occurrence, of an event: namely the stoppage. On the evidence before me I am satisfied that he lost his employment by reason of the stoppage, not merely in respect that the particular engagement came to an end, but also in the sense that from 14th July, 1970 there continued to be work available for him, which he would or could have continued to have, but for the strike.

8. In his written submission the insurance officer also relied upon what is called the "12 days' rule", formulated by the Umpire under the old Unemployment Insurance Acts, and adopted, in some cases at least, by the Commissioner under the National Insurance Acts. Manifestly if a person whose employment is casual or irregular falls out of work at or shortly before a stoppage of work at

a place where he normally seeks work, it may be very difficult to determine, as matter of fact, whether his loss of employment was due to the stoppage or due to causes unconnected with the stoppage. If the loss of employment occurred within 12 days of a stoppage, the Umpire presumed that the loss of employment was by reason of the stoppage. There is an obvious element of arbitrariness in this so-called rule: and it may well be that, having regard to the general decasualisation of dock labour, the inference or presumption which it embodies is less readily justifiable nowadays in relation to dockers. But in the present case I do not find it necessary to invoke the "12 days' rule" in order to arrive at any conclusions: and accordingly I simply reserve my opinion as to the validity and applicability of the rule in present-day circumstances.

9. Once the conclusion is reached that the claimant's loss of employment was by reason of the stoppage of work in question, it is not suggested that he can escape the net of section 22(1). He did not obtain other employment, and he obviously had a direct interest in the dispute. It is common ground, also, that the stoppage continued up to and including 1st August, 1970: the reference to 31st August (on form L.T.3 (T.D.)) is a transcription error. There must therefore be disqualification for the period stated in paragraph 1 above.

. . . .

"Stoppage"

R(U) 7/58

. . . .

2. The claimant, a cabinet maker, and certain fellow-workers withdrew their labour at 4.30 p.m. on Friday the 7th December 1956 by reason of a trade dispute, either two or three (the exact number is irrelevant) of their fellow-workers having had their employment terminated on the ground of redundancy.

3. It is conceded by the claimant's association that he is disqualified for receiving unemployment benefit so long as a stoppage of work at his place of employment continued by reason of this action. They contend, however, that no such appreciable stoppage of work occurred as constitutes a "stoppage of work . . . at his place of employment" within the meaning of section 13(1) of the National Insurance Act, 1946, or alternatively, that, if it did, it had ended on the 17th December 1956, or at the latest, on the 1st January, 1957.

. . . .

4. It appears that the labour force at the claimant's place of employment was about 90 and a representative of the employers stated before the local tribunal at the hearing of the claimant's appeal that after Monday the 10th December 1956 the factory carried on with about 50 per cent. staff of operators and he considered that between 25 per cent. and 50 per cent. of the labour operatives were replaced from time to time. He stated that output of work was considerably reduced as a result of the shortage of labour.

5. The claimant's association have stated that 38 persons, including the claimant, withdrew their labour, 5 adult males, 17 adult females, 6 juvenile males and 10 juvenile females. Three workers were dismissed on the grounds of redundancy during the week before the stoppage of work by the claimant and his colleagues and it had been stated that further dismissals would be necessary.

6. It appears that in a local newspaper published on the 21st December 1956 the managing director of the claimant's employers was reported to have claimed "we are managing to replace the dismissed staff", and in another local newspaper published on the 11th January, 1957 he was reported to have said that "he had taken on new employees and was now about six short of the original number. The firm was operating as usual". (The exact position as to replacements is set out later in this decision.)

7. On the 12th December, 1956 letters had been addressed by the managing director of the employers to the persons who had withdrawn their labour, inviting them to see him and discuss any grievances they had and saying that he could only assume from the events which had taken place during the last few days that it was not their wish either to see him or to return to work. That might or might not be the case. Nevertheless, he was extending the opportunity for them to do so, and the offer would remain open until Monday next, the 17th December. There were no conditions attached to the offer. He added that, if it was not the desire to resume their duties, he must assume conclusively that they no longer wished to work there. That, with regret, would naturally leave him with no other alternative but to give them a week's notice of his intention to terminate their agreement with the company. He looked forward to hearing from them between the date of his latter and Monday next.

8. No response being received, on the 17th December, 1956 the works manager of the claimant's employers sent to the claimant and the others concerned their insurance cards and stated that the holiday pay due to them would be available for collection at certain named dates in that week.

. . . .

12. . . . . certain further inquiries were made of the claimant's employers. In reply, they allege that the number of persons who withdrew their labour was 41, not 38 as alleged by the claimant's association. (This slight discrepancy is insufficient to affect the result of this appeal.) The employers point out that they were all production workers. They agree that the majority of those workers had resumed their employment on the 21st January, 1957, and add the information that they finished on the 18th February, 1957. They state that the company's production was reduced during the period of the dispute by 50 per cent.

13. As to the replacement of labour, they state that up to the 3rd January, 1957 19 workers had been taken on, by the 9th January, 1957 a further 5, and by the 16th January, 1957 a further 2.

14. It is also stated by the insurance officer now concerned with this case to have been confirmed that 17 workers, including the claimant, who had withheld their labour, resumed work on the 21st January, 1957 and that payment of unemployment benefit had been resumed on that date to those still unemployed. The claimant's association say that 14, not 17, workers resumed work on that day, but that discrepancy is not material.

15. In Umpire's Decision 2191/37, a decision of the Umpire under the former Unemployment Insurance Acts, it was stated that, where a considerable number of men with one accord ceased to carry on with their work, it seemed to him that there must inevitably be a stoppage of work, provided that an appreciable interval of time elapsed before the men returned to work or their places were filled by other men. That seems to me to be a reasonable conclusion and I can see no sufficient reason for not taking a similar view in interpreting the National Insurance Act, 1946, section 13(1).

16. As in this case some 38 production workers, including the claimant, out of a working force of 90 or thereabouts withdrew their labour at 4.30 p.m. on the 7th December, 1956. I think it an unavoidable conclusion that a stoppage of work then occurred at the claimant's place of employment, even though some of them were juveniles.

17. It is inapt to speak of the claimant as disqualified for receiving unemployment benefit on that day because he was not entitled to unemployment benefit on that date, but from and including the next day, Saturday, the 8th December, 1956, he was, in my view, disqualified for receiving unemployment benefit.

18. It now remains to consider until what date the stoppage of work can properly be said to have continued.

19. In Decision R(U) 25/57 it was held that the principle applied in Umpire's Decision 4665/26 should be applied to claims under the National Insurance Act, 1946. So far as is material to this case, that principle was stated thus:—

> "Where the dispute is settled, whether by a general settlement of a settlement affecting only the particular factory, workshop or premises at which the applicant was employed, the stoppage of work which was due to the trade dispute comes to an end when there is a general resumption of work following such settlement, though, as decided in No. 801 (1920 Act), not necessarily immediately after the settlement.

> "But a stoppage of work may come to an end without any settlement of the dispute, by the workers returning to work in a body, or by driblets, or by their places being taken by other men. In such cases the stoppage of work comes to an end when the employers have got all the workers they require, that is, when work is no longer being stopped or hindered by the refusal of workers to work on the employers' terms or hindered by the refusal of workers to work on the employers' terms or the refusal of employers to employ the workers on the workers' terms.

> "It may be that the employers cannot at once re-employ all the workers who are willing to work because the work has to be reorganised, or because repairs necessitated by the stoppage of work have not been completed. But when work is again proceeding normally and is not being held up either by the men holding back or by circumstances directly resulting from the stoppage of work, the stoppage of work is at an end."

20. Applying that principle, it seems to me that the employers in the present case could not be said to have all the workers they required at any rate until the 21st January, 1957, by which date the insurance officer now concerned with this case has conceded that the stoppage of work may be regarded as having come to an end. Up to the 16th January, 1957 the employers had been engaging replacements for the workers who had withdrawn their labour and on the 17th January, 1957 the employers, as part of the terms of settlement of the dispute, agreed to restart at least 14 workers on the 21st January, 1957. I see no sufficient reason for not thinking that they still needed these additional workers at that time. The

replacements which they had obtained were obviously not sufficient to enable the factory to resume normal working.

21. I have not overlooked the fact that in the later part of February 1957 the claimant's employers no longer needed so large a labour force. That may have been due to general trading conditions at the time or it may have been a condition of affairs partly brought about by the sudden withdrawal of their labour by the claimant and his fellow-workers and the consequent sudden reduction in production. In either event, I do not think it enables me to say that the reasonable inference to be drawn from the evidence looked at as a whole is that "work was no longer being stopped or hindered by the refusal of workers to work on the employers' terms or the refusal of employers to employ the workers on the workers' terms" at any time from the 8th December, 1956 to the 20th January, 1957, both dates included.

22. That being so, I must hold that the stoppage of work continued for that period and the claimant was disqualified for receiving unemployment benefit. It will be noted that at the head of this decision I have omitted any reference to the 20th January, 1957. That was a Sunday and unemployment benefit was not in any event payable for that day.

. . . .

Stoppage "Due to" Dispute

R(U) 17/52 (T)

8. . . . . The question is what is meant by "stoppage of work *due* to a trade dispute" in Section 13(1)? Section 13(1) reproduces the language of the corresponding provisions of the Unemployment Insurance Acts which had been the subject of decisions of the Umpire extending over many years. It is reasonable therefore to assume that the view taken by the Umpire of the principal questions arising on the interpretation of the section was not contrary to the intention of the Legislature when passing the Act.

9. It is we think clear that the view taken in the Umpire's decision was that to be due to a trade dispute within the meaning of Section 13(1) a stoppage of work must be in the nature of a strike or lockout, that is to say it must be a move in a contest between an employer and his employees, the object of which is that employment shall be resumed on certain conditions. If a stoppage was not designed for this purpose but was the result of a decision to cease to be employed or to give employment (as the case may be) it would not in our opinion be due to a trade dispute within the

meaning of the subsection, notwithstanding that his decision was taken because of the existence of a trade dispute.

10. We refer to the following decisions of the Umpire to illustrate his view of the subsection. In Umpire's Decision 2461/28 (reported in selected decisions given by the Umpire from the 19th April, 1928, to the 12th March, 1930, at p. 117) the Umpire said ". . . The simple issue of notices by an employer unaccompanied by an invitation to negotiate fresh terms affords presumptive evidence that no dispute exists. Decision 458/20. It is however necessary to take into account all the circumstances surrounding the issue of the notices and the subsequent conduct of the parties, and evidence on these points may demonstrate (as it does in this case) that the notices were issued as part of the trade dispute. Decision 7791/20 (*sic*—this reference should be 7991/20)." In Umpire's Decision 4850/26 the Umpire said: "In my opinion a stoppage of work which was due to a trade dispute means not merely a cessation of work but a cessation of work due to the unwillingness of men to work or the employer to give employment *so long as some matter in dispute is unsettled*, and a stoppage of work in this sense comes to an end when for any reason the employers no longer have employment to offer on any terms and will not again employ men at the colliery in question on any terms." In Umpire's Decision 415/27 the claim for benefit was allowed because although there had been a stoppage of work which was due to a trade dispute the continuance of the stoppage during the period for which benefit was claimed was held not to be due to the trade dispute because the dispute had been settled and the delay in reopening the colliery was not due to any want of repair resulting from the stoppage of work but to an independent cause as the result of which the employers were not during that period prepared to offer employment on any terms. Again in Umpire's Decision 9959/29 (reported), explained in Umpire's Decision 3127/35 (reported), it was held (in accordance with earlier decisions) that even though a stoppage of work began as the result of a trade dispute, if after the men were willing to resume work on terms acceptable to the employer the stoppage was prolonged by the employer for a certain period as a retaliatory or disciplinary measure the stoppage of work during that period could not be regarded as due to a trade dispute. On the other hand, the mere fact that the employer takes steps to replace men who are on strike or have been locked out does not prove that a stoppage of work pending their replacement is not due to a trade dispute. Umpire's Decision 1480/27. We may add that even if the question were free from authority we should reach the same conclusion as that indicated in the Umpire's decisions.

11. The question into which category a stoppage must depend upon the facts of the particular case. The mere fact that notice to terminate employment is given is not usually significant. Such notice is commonly required by the contract of employment and the fact that it is given is not inconsistent with an intention to resume employment on fresh terms. It may be clear from the course of the previous negotiations and the number of employees and employers involved that neither side intends or can afford a permanent severance of relations and that the withdrawal of labour by the employees or of employment by the employer is a trial of strength intended to result in a resumption of relations when the trial is over. On the other hand, if the position at the time the stoppage of work occurs is that although there had been a trade dispute the employer or the whole body of the employees concerned (as the case may be) are no longer willing to employ or be employed by the other part on any terms, the stoppage of work will not be due to the trade dispute but to the determination of one or both parties to have no further relations with each other.

12. It remains to apply these considerations to the present case. It is to be observed that the business in question was on a comparatively small scale, employing only about 50 persons. Further, the dispute did not involve any other firm nor was any trade union or employers' association concerned in it. It is also to be observed that the business was suffering from a shortage of raw material, the purchase of which had been prohibited before the stoppage began. In these circumstances it would be less unlikely that the employer should determine to sever relations permanently with the employees in question than it would be in the case of a dispute involving a large firm or a number of firms who could not expect to continue business except with the assistance of the greater part of the employees who had ceased to be employed. As we have said, the mere facts that Mr. P. gave the claimant and his fellow employees notice which was apparently unconditional and that he took immediate steps to replace them might not be of much significance in the case of a stoppage involving a large number of employees. These facts would however confirm the view that a final severance of relations was intended by Mr. P. if there were other evidence to justify it. There is such evidence, for Mr. P. says that the reason why he gave notices was that he expected trouble on the following Monday and did not want the trouble to spread to other workers. The only meaning we can place on this statement is that Mr. P. knew that owing to the shortage of materials he would have to dismiss other employees or put them on short time and thought that as the men to whom his statement applied had

made trouble over the dismissal of Mr. K. they would probably make further trouble over other dismissals and alterations of working conditions. In order to avoid such trouble he decided to get rid of them. It is true that the claimant and the other men involved had given a week's notice themselves on Friday the 20th April, but that notice would not have been effective till the following Friday and we cannot doubt that when they presented themselves for work on the Monday they were prepared to work their notice out. The stoppage of work therefore was not due to their notice but to the employer's action in dismissing them. If the reasonable interpretation of the employer's action were that it was not intended as a final severance of relations but as a means to coerce the men concerned into acquiescing in the dismissal of Mr. K., the inference would have been that the stoppage was due to a trade dispute. In our view, however, the true inference from the evidence taken as a whole is that the stoppages was due to Mr. P.'s determination to get rid of men whom he regarded as trouble makers and not to a strike or lock-out designed to enforce the acceptance of particular terms of employment. In our opinion, therefore, the stoppage was not due to a trade dispute within the meaning of Section 13(1) and the disqualification under Section 13(1) cannot stand. We think it well to add that we regard this as a somewhat exceptional case and that in our opinion this decision is not likely to apply to stoppages on a larger scale in which trade unions are involved on the one side and employers' association on the other.

. . . .

R(U) 1/65

. . . .

7. The substantial point in this appeal is whether the local tribunal have correctly interpreted and applied Decision R(U) 17/52.

8. The local tribunal no doubt had in mind paragraph 9 of Decision R(U) 17/52 which says—

> "It is we think clear that the view taken in the Umpire's decisions was that to be due to a trade dispute within the meaning of section 13(1) a stoppage of work must be in the nature of a strike or lock-out, that is to say it must be a move in a contest between an employer and his employees, the object of which is that employment shall be resumed on certain conditions. If a stoppage was not designed for this purpose but was the result of a decision to cease to be employed or to give employment (as the case may be) it would not in our opinion be due to a trade dispute within the meaning of the

sub-section, notwithstanding that this decision was taken because of the existence of a trade dispute."

The last sentence in that paragraph—"If a stoppage . . . was the result of a decision to cease to be employed or to give employment (as the case may be) it would not . . . be due to a trade dispute . . . notwithstanding that this decision was taken because of the existence of a trade dispute"—has I think given rise to some difficulty and misunderstanding. In the present case the local tribunal evidently read it as meaning that if in the course of a stoppage which is due to a trade dispute an employer determines that he will never again engage a particular employee or group of employees then, so far as that employee or group is concerned, the stoppage of work which is due to the trade dispute is at an end and becomes replaced by a stoppage of work which is due to a different cause, viz. the employer's determination to sever relations for ever with that employee or group, with the result that the employee or group is not disqualified by section 13(1). It appears to me (with respect) that so to read Decision R(U) 17/52 is to misinterpret it.

9. That decision concerned a small factory with about 50 employees manufacturing straps and fittings for the watch trade. There was a trade dispute smouldering in the background between the employer and the riveters, three in number, over homework. There was also a shortage of materials and the employer decided to make a reduction in staff. He gave notice to a riveter. Six workmen then gave a week's notice to the employer. The next day the employer dismissed these six men at an hour's notice and one of them (the claimant in that case) later obtained judgment for a week's wages as damages for wrongful dismissal. The crucial question was whether the stoppage of work suffered by the dismissed men was due to a trade dispute. In this complicated situation, in which there was some conflict of evidence on the facts, the tribunal of Commissioners who sat in that case decided that, on the whole, the stoppage was not due to a trade dispute but was due to the employer's action in dismissing men whom he regarded as troublemakers. The Commissioners said (at the end of paragraph 12) "We think it well to add that we regard this as a somewhat exceptional case and that in our opinion this decision is not likely to apply to stoppages on a larger scale in which trade unions are involved on the one side and employers' associations on the other." Essentially Decision R(U) 17/52 is a decision on fact. It decides that although there be a trade dispute in existence, a stoppage of work may be due to a quite different cause; in that case the

stoppage was held to be due to the employer's determination, at an opportune time when materials were short, to get rid of men whom he regarded as troublemakers. It by no means follows from this decision that, if an employer determines to dismiss for ever certain employees, the stoppage of work for them cannot be due to a trade dispute. It still remains to ascertain whether the employer's determination is itself a move in a trade dispute or is an original and separate cause of the stoppage as it was held to be in Decision R(U) 17/52.

10. In cases arising under section 13(1) of the Act it is always essential to distinguish between the stoppage of work and the trade dispute. In the present case there was undoubtedly a trade dispute within the meaning of section 13(6)(b) in that there was a dispute between employer and employees connected with the terms of employment, that is to say whether the agreement alleged by the employer was valid. The employer was seeking to enforce the agreement on pain of dismissal. The welders resisted by walking out of work in a body. The employer treated the walk-out as a breach of contract justifying instant dismissal. The stoppage of work for the claimant began when he walked out. Clearly at that point it was due to the trade dispute.

11. The local tribunal found as a fact that the employer had no intention of re-employing the claimant, a member of the Boilermakers Society. I accept that finding. I agree that the evidence shows that after the walk-out the employer intended not to engage or re-engage any member of the Boilermakers Society. It is then said for the claimant that this fixed determination of the employer to sever all relations with members of the Boilermakers Society ended the original stoppage and introduced a new cause for a further stoppage and that as soon as the claimant received his notice of dismissal the stoppage which was due to the trade dispute was at an end. That proposition seems to me to be contrary to reason. When a stoppage of work is due to a trade dispute (as here) a decision by an employer never to re-engage a particular man or group of men, or a decision by that man or group of men never to accept employment again with that employer on any terms, seems to me quite clearly to be not a termination of the stoppage of work but a perpetuation of it. I can see no ground whatsoever for holding that a stoppage of work which is due to a trade dispute ceases to be due to that trade dispute simply because the employer decides in regard to certain workmen involved in the stoppage that the stoppage as between him and them is to be permanent.

12. I am thinking of course of the kind of stoppage in which an employer hopes ultimately to restart his business, or the part of it affected by the stoppage, as soon as terms have been agreed with employees. If in the course of a stoppage an employer decides never to re-open his business, because of economic or other reasons, or if a trade dispute has been settled but work is not restarted by reason of causes independent of the trade dispute, no doubt in these and such-like cases a fresh cause of stoppage would be held to have replaced the trade dispute. Umpire's Decisions U.D. 4850/26 and U.D. 415/27 referred to in paragraph 10 of Decision R(U) 17/52 deal with cases of this kind.

13. The capital distinction between Decision R(U) 17/52 (on which the local tribunal relied) and the present case is that in R(U) 17/52 the tribunal of Commissioners held that the stoppage of work was *not* due to a trade dispute at all; although there was in existence a trade dispute, the stoppage was held to be due to the employer's determination permanently to dismiss certain employees. On the facts it was held that their stoppage of work was due to dismissal and not to a trade dispute. In the present case, however, the claimant's stoppage of work was quite plainly due to the trade dispute. He walked out in furtherance of the trade dispute and stopped working. The company, by refusing to re-engage him on any terms, made the stoppage as between themselves and him permanent, but in my judgment the stoppage was still clearly due to the trade dispute.

14. Of course this does not mean that the claimant is permanently disqualified for receiving unemployment benefit. If, in terms of section 13(1), "during the stoppage of work, he has become bona fide employed elsewhere in the occupation which he usually follows or has become regularly engaged in some other occupation" the disqualification is lifted. Furthermore, disqualification applies only "so long as the stoppage of work continues". It is well settled that this refers to the general stoppage and not to the stoppage of an individual claimant. A general stoppage of work comes to an end when the employers have all the workers they require so that work is no longer being stopped or hindered by the refusal of workers to work on the employers' terms or by the refusal of employers to employ workers on the workers' terms; see Decision R(U) 25/57. In the present case, the general stoppage came to an end when work was resumed on Monday the 10th August, 1964. In any event disqualification for the claimant would have continued only until and including Saturday the 8th August, 1964 even though his own individual stoppage of work had continued thereafter.

15. In conclusion, it appears to me that Decision R(U) 17/52 cannot properly bear the interpretation put upon it by the local tribunal in the present case and which has I think been sometimes put upon it in the past. In essence it decides only that a stoppage of work which is due to a dismissal is not, for the dismissed employee, due to a trade dispute. In my judgment it affords no authority for holding that, if a stoppage of work *is* due to a trade dispute, a determination by either party to sever relations permanently with the other brings the stoppage to an end. I hold that the claimant lost employment by reason of a stoppage of work; that the stoppage was due, and continued to be due, to a trade dispute; and that he is thus disqualified for receiving unemployment benefit for the duration of the stoppage, *i.e.* from the 1st May, 1964 to the 8th August, 1964.

. . . .

R(U) 3/71

. . . .

2. This is one of six appeals arising out of disqualification for receiving unemployment benefit resulting from a stoppage of work which was due to a trade dispute at a plant of Vauxhall Motors Ltd. at Ellesmere Port. The brief history of the matter, as it affects the appeals, is that there was a pay dispute at the plant which affected all hourly paid workers in every department of the plant. On the morning of 24th September, 1969, an unofficial meeting of workers was called by the shop stewards' committee. A resolution calling for complete withdrawal of labour on 9th October, 1969 was rejected but a further resolution that there should be an immediate "work to rule" was adopted. This was put into effect on the same day. The result was that a number of employees declined to work to instructions and a number of incidents arose as to complaints about machines and the like and, as a result, a number of employees were "laid off" by the employers. In the result some 5,000–6,000 employees either refused to work or were "laid off".

3. Although each appeal is a separate matter, it would be unrealistic to regard each in isolation and each must be considered in relation to the general background of the conditions at the place of employment at the time. The insurance officer has submitted, and it was not disputed at any of the oral hearings before me, that a substantial number of employees had resumed work by 10th November, 1969 and that disqualification for receiving unemployment benefit should end on 8th November, 1969. In view of the evidence and in the absence of any disagreement, I accept that as

the terminal date for any disqualification. There were in fact two trade disputes at the plant at the same time. An earlier dispute affected press operators and it is not necessary to deal with that in this decision.

4. This is an appeal by the insurance officer from the decision of the local tribunal who found that the question of the safety of a machine is not a trade dispute within the meaning of Decision R(U) 4/65. It was decided in that decision that a trade dispute could be about a non-financial matter and that it followed that a direct interest in such a dispute would be non-financial. In that appeal the dispute was about the heating in a shed. The expression "trade dispute" is defined in section 22(6)(b) of the National Insurance Act 1965 and attention has often been drawn to it. The definition is wide and in deciding whether or not there is a "trade dispute" the merits of the dispute do not enter into the matter. It is difficult to see how the local tribunal could have reached the decision they did in the present appeal.

5. Mr. N. Blackshaw represented the insurance officer at the hearing of all the appeals before me and the claimant appeared in person and gave evidence in this appeal. Apparently on the morning of 24th September, 1969 a machine operator received an injury to his right hand when operating a machine which he said performed a cutting stroke whilst it was in a switched off position. According to the evidence before me he lacerated a finger. The operator considered the machine was dangerous, the foreman examined the machine and considered it was safe. The operator referred the matter to the claimant, who is a production machinist and was the shop steward for the section. The claimant advised the machine operator to carry on until he could get the safety engineer to examine the machine. The machine was evidently not examined by the safety engineer and was used, apparently with safety, by the night shift 24th/25th September, 1969. On the morning of 25th September, 1969 the claimant contended that the machine did not comply with the Factories Act 1961, section 14(1) as regards safe fencing. The foreman either contended that it did or that it was not dangerous. The foreman did not call the safety engineer and the claimant said that the operators were not prepared to accept the foreman's decision as he was not a "competent person" within the meaning of the Factories Act 1961. There is no reference to examination by a "competent person" in section 14 of the Act. This applies to periodical inspection of chains, ropes and lifting tackle as in section 26(1)(d) of the Act. The claimant also referred to section 143 of the Factories Act as to the duties

of persons employed and to a pamphlet issued by the employers on the safe operation of machines.

6. The result of this dispute was that when an operator was asked to operate the machine in the usual manner he refused and was "laid off" on behalf of the employers. As a result a group of employees followed in sympathy and on 25th September, 1969, 53 employees, including the claimant either withdrew their labour or were "laid off". The claimant said in cross-examination that he and members of his group had attended the meeting on 24th September, 1969 when the resolution to "work to rule" was adopted. He also said that the guards were not on the machine which had been operated in that way for possibly 18 months before the disagreement and was still operated in the same way after 8th November, 1969, when the trade dispute ended, until the factory inspector inspected the machine on 9th December, 1969.

7. The claimant referred to another incident on 23rd August, 1969 as to a fault in another machine which the foreman, not the same foreman concerned with the machine on 24th/25th September, 1969, refused to admit and refused to call in the safety engineer. The claimant put in documents to show that the production supervisor decided that the report on the safety incident was completely true and that the foreman concerned had been reinstructed in his responsibility. I observe that in the report signed on behalf of the work's committee reference is made to the result being "Dispute situation". As far as I am aware there was neither a withdrawal of labour nor a "lay off" of employees following that situation. The claimant said that he raised the matter at the earliest meeting of the management trade union joint consultative committee, which was on 8th December, 1969 because the committee had not met during the currency of the trade dispute. The minutes of the meeting contain the following—

> "91. SAFETY ENGINEER
>
> It was re-iterated that should there be a need for the services of a Safety Engineer on a section, contact will be made by area supervision.
>
> Instances where there is not a resolution of a safety problem at shop floor level should be processed through the grievance procedure.

8. It is to be noted that that dispute as to the safety of a machine did not lead to a stoppage of work or to a "lay off" of employees. Evidently there was a grievance or dispute procedure available for such cases. Mr. Blackshaw referred to the evidence of similar disputes occurring on or about 24th/25th September, 1969. One

concerned a Gildmeister machine which the operator considered unsafe to run. The foreman and manager considered that it was safe but the operator still refused to operate it and was asked to "clock-out". There is evidence in the other appeals of objection being taken to performing tasks all of which, in my judgment, fit into a pattern of industrial action. No doubt the employers also took counter industrial action, which may have taken the form of asking men to perform tasks which it was probable they would refuse to do. There follows an instruction given to the particular employee or group of employees to "clock-out" and their refusing to do so, so that the incident is not classed as a withdrawal of labour but a "laying off" by the employers. All these events and incidents were, in my judgment, moves in the trade dispute which had as its basis a dispute as to the rate of remuneration of all hourly paid workers at the plant. In my judgment, the claimant was participating in the dispute. He was himself an hourly paid worker and was thus directly interested in the trade dispute.

9. Having listened to and considered the evidence in this and the other appeals I have no doubt that in this case, as in the others, the claimant lost his employment by reason of a stoppage of work which was due to a trade dispute at his place of employment. . . .
. . . .

"Trade Dispute"

Social Security Act 1975, s. 19(2)(b)
'trade dispute' means any dispute between employers and employees, or between employees and employees, which is connected with the employment or non-employment or the terms of employment or the conditions of employment of any persons, whether employees in the employment of the employer with whom the dispute arises, or not.

R(U) 1/74

11. . . . Prior to the visit of the pickets from Doncaster, there was no dispute at the claimant's place of employment and it is the claimant's case that at no time was there any such dispute between his employer on the one hand and himself or any of his fellow employees on the other hand, or between any employees of his employers. These assertions are correct, and at first sight it might seem strange that a trade dispute could be, so to speak, imported from outside to the site on which the claimant was working. It is natural to think that if there was to be found a trade dispute at the

claimant's place of employment there had to be either a dispute between his employer and the employer's employees, or one in which the employees of that same employer were in dispute with each other. This is not, however, correct.

14. . . . a trade dispute can exist when employees from elsewhere picket a place of employment which, until their arrival, was free from dispute. The fact of picketing does not of itself indicate that there is a trade dispute in progress, because trade unionists may undertake picketing or other industrial activity from some personal motive. . . .

17. My analysis of the present case is that there was no trade dispute at the claimant's place of employment prior to the arrival of the pickets from Doncaster. There was then a trade dispute, imported by the pickets, between those men and the claimant's employer. It is arguable that there also developed a dispute between the pickets and the claimant himself and possibly others of his fellow employees who did not want to stop work. . . .

R(U) 5/77

. . . .

21. In so far as the subject matter of the dispute is concerned, that is to say who should for protective clothing which the employers were willing to provide on payment, I do not find anything which would take the dispute out of the definition in section 19(2)(b) of the Act. In Decision R(U) 4/65 the Commissioner, pointing out the wide terms of the definition in section 13(6) of the National Insurance Act 1946, illustrated it by saying (paragraph 8), "One can visualise a trade dispute about conditions of employment . . . . *e.g.* a dispute about the provision of safety clothing or equipment . . . .". In Decision R(U) 3/71 the Commissioner expressed the view that a dispute on the safety of a machine, involving consideration of duties under section 14(1) and section 143 of the Factories Act 1961, could be a trade dispute (paragraph 4).

22. The claimants contended that the dispute was not a trade dispute because it was not "connected with . . . . the terms of employment or the conditions of employment", and thus did not fall within the terms of section 19(2)(b). They contended, as the local tribunal had found, that it was connected with the statutory provisions of the 1974 Act. I do not find myself in agreement with the approach that the dispute is therefore to be regarded as unconnected with the terms or conditions of employment. The scheme of the 1974 Act in laying down the general duties of employers and employees was to produce a framework for detailed regulations

and approved codes of practice to replace existing enactments and regulations hitherto in force; see section 1(2) of the Act and the relevant statutory provisions in Schedule 1.

23. I do not think it necessary to consider whether the 1974 Act inserts by implication additional terms into the contracts of employment between employers and employees. In my opinion the 1974 Act, providing for health and safety at work, imposes obligations and confers rights on both parties, which are connected with the employment, or the conditions of employment of the employees. Any dispute concerning such obligations or rights must in my view necessarily be "connected with the employment" or "connected with . . . . the conditions of employment", and therefore by definition be a trade dispute.

24. A further point relied upon by the claimants was based on the Decision of the Umpire 306/29. In that case the terms upon which the employers were prepared to settle a dispute were in breach of the provisions of the Coal Mines Regulations Act 1908. The Umpire held, following Decisions 2358/20, 3015/20 and 6926/20, that because the terms offered entailed a breach of the act of 1908 and were illegal, it could not be held that the stoppage of work in that case was due to a trade dispute. The then definition of "trade dispute" in section 47(1) of the Unemployment Insurance Act 1920 corresponds with the present statutory definition, and there is no significant difference between section 8(1) of the Unemployment Insurance Act 1920 as then applicable and the applicable statutory provisions of section 19(1) and (2)(a).

25. At the resumed hearing by the local tribunal on 10th November, 1976, and before me, it was conceded by Counsel that there had been no breach of the provisions of the 1974 Act. The submission made was that there would have been a breach by the employers of section 2 (to ensure, so far as is reasonably practicable, the health, safety and welfare at work of all their employees) and a breach by the employees of section 7 (to take reasonable care for the health and safety of themselves) had the men worked in certain areas without protective clothing. It was conceded that section 9, forbidding any employer to levy any charge in respect of anything done or provided in pursuance of any specific requirement of the relevant statutory provisions, did not apply.

26. I do not think that I should adopt the approach of the Umpire in Decision 306/29 and follow him by inquiring into the question of the legality or otherwise of the employers' proposals in the dispute. It is true that there was a short period when former statutory provisions would have involved the statutory authorities in a consideration of the merits of an alleged trade dispute. Section

E

4 of the Unemployment Insurance (No. 2) Act 1924 amending section 8(1) of the Unemployment Insurance Act 1920 would have involved enquiry into whether agreements were being contravened, but by section 6 of the Unemployment Insurance Act 1927 the provision in question, inserted ʹby the No. 2 Act of 1924, was removed.

. . . .

28. In Decision R(U) 17/52, paragraph 8, a Tribunal of Commissioners considering the situation (and provisions) to which I have referred in paragraph 26 above pointed out that such provisions had been repealed before the Unemployment Insurance Act 1935 and that both in section 13(1) of the National Insurance Act 1946 and in the Unemployment Insurance Act 1935, which it replaced. "The disqualification is made absolute and consequently the merits of the dispute are irrelevant". In Decision R(U) 12/60 the Commissioner said, paragraph 8, "In determining questions under section 13(1) of the Act, the statutory authorities are not concerned with the merits of the parties' actions. The statutory authorities are concerned with whether the situation which is shown to exist is in fact the situation described in section 13(1). If it is, then the consequences prescribed by section 13(1) must follow, and there is no provision for mitigating these consequences on the ground that a claimant had merit on his side, or that he had a legal right to do what he did".

29. For the above reasons I do not consider that I should follow an apply the approach of the Umpire, and enquire into the question what would be the effect of the employers' offer had been accepted, and involved myself in consideration of the legal merits of the dispute.

30. If, however, I ought to follow the Umpire and consider the submission to which I have referred at paragraph 25, based on the Umpire's approach, I am not satisfied that the terms upon which the employers were prepared to settle the dispute were in breach of any provision of the 1974 Act. They were prepared to provide protective overalls for work in affected areas. In return they require employees to agree to pay for them on a weekly basis.

31. If, on the Umpire's approach, the terms offered had been accepted by the employees they would have returned to work with protective clothing for which they had agreed to pay. That would not have been in breach of the 1974 Act and illegal, and the parties were free to negotiate on the question of payment for the protective clothing. What they could not agree or negotiate about was that employees should resume work in areas affected by dust which was injurious to health without protective clothing, but this was

not what acceptance of the employers' terms would in my opinion have entailed.

32. My conclusion is that there was a stoppage of work on 15 June, 1976 due to a trade dispute at the place of employment, and that the stoppage ended on 3rd January, 1977.

. . . .

Place of Employment

Social Security Act 1975, s. 19(2)(a)

'place of employment' in relation to any person, means the factory, workshop, farm or others premises or place at which he was employed, so however, that, where separate braches of work which are commonly carried on as separate businesses in separate premises or at separate places are in any case carried on in separate departments on the same premises or at the same place, each of those departments shall for the purposes of this paragraph be deemed to be a separate factory or workshop or farm or separate premises or a separate place, as the case may be.

R(U) 1/70

. . . .

13. . . . the first question for decision is whether the Trim Shop where the strikers worked, in the River Plant, was part of the claimant's place of employment as defined by section 22(6)(a). This question must be considered in two stages, since clearly that paragraph falls into two parts, namely the first part preceding the words, "so, however," and the second part from and including those words to the end of the paragraph.

14. It is common ground that, since it is for the insurance officer to show that the case comes within section 22(1), it is for him to prove the matters under the first part of paragraph (a). Mr. Cherrill accepted at the hearing however that once the insurance officer has done so it is then for the claimant to allege and prove matters under the exception created by the second part.

15. On the first question the insurance officer's contention is that the whole Estate or alternatively the three plants referred to as "Dagenham Operations" constitute one "factory, workshop, farm or other premises or place" within the meaning of paragraph (a).

16. The definition of "place of employment" is a very wide one. The inclusion in it of a farm, which may well be intersected by a road or a railway, supported this view. The presence of, and

necessity for, the exception in the second part does not suggest that the first part should be narrowly construed. It has always been widely construed by the Commissioner. The relevant defintion of "factory" in the Oxford English Dictionary is "A building, or buildings, with plant for the manufacture of goods; a manufactory; works." The evidence establishes that some of the components used in the assembly plant were brought in from outside and some of those manufactured at Dagenham were used in Ford factories elsewhere. The main purpose, however, of the operations on this Estate was to build motor vehicles. The operations known as Dagenham Operations, carried on in the three plants with which we are concerned in these appeals, had as their purpose the manufacturer of particular types of motor vehicle. In the circumstances I am satisfied that the insurance officer's contention is correct. In my judgment the Estate was for national insurance purposes a factory for the production of motor vehicles and not merely a number of factories for the manufacture of component parts of them. Even if I had taken a different view on this, I should have accepted that the three plants called Dagenham Operations constituted one such factory and not merely three or more. I therefore hold that the Estate as a whole comes within the definition of place of employment in the first part of section 22(6)(a). The remedy in the case of such large premises as these lies in the second part, where it applies.

17. As to the second question, I assume in favour of the claimant that each of the relevant Plants or the Trim Shop could be regarded as a department for the purposes of paragraph (a). Nevertheless that is not sufficient. The exception would only apply if they were separate places or premises, where separate branches of work were carried on, which are commonly carried on as separate businesses in separate premises or at separate places. The only evidence relied on in relation to the words "commonly carried on" was that of a witness from the company that, when difficulties were encountered as a result of the action of the strikers, the Company was able to obtain trim from one alternative source. Against this was the evidence of Mr. Haynes, a very experienced and responsible insurance officer. Shortly before the hearing before me he had instituted enquires in various directions on the question. His evidence was objected to by Mr. Monier-Williams and Mr. Johnson, though not by Mr. Cherrill, but it will be convenient to deal with the objections here. They were based on two grounds: firstly surprise, in that the evidence had not been made available before the first day of the hearing; and secondly that the evidence was hearsay. In my judgment neither of these objections can prevail. None of the three

representatives wished to avail himself of an adjournment to enable him to seek further evidence. The fact that the evidence was hearsay goes to its weight but not its admissibility (*Regina* v. *Deputy Industrial injuries Commissioner, Ex parte Moore* [1965] 1 Q.B. 456, printed as an Appendix to Decision R(I) 4/65). The evidence obtained by Mr. Haynes is in my judgment persuasive and convincing and, being practically uncontradicted, I accept it. It shows that in a few factories seat assemblies, complete with the frame as well as the trim, are manufactured, but in my judgment it establishes that trim manufacture is certainly not commonly carried on as a separate business and indeed is probably not carried on at all except by the one supplier whom the company prevailed on to do the work when they were in difficulties. It was not argued that separate branches of work were carried on in either the Assembly Plant or the Body Plant or some subdivision of them, which were commonly carried on elsewhere, and in view of the nature of the work being done I am satisfied that they were not.

. . . .

Bona Fide Employment Elsewhere

R(U) 6/74

. . . .

5. In Decision R(U) 39/56 a Commissioner dealt with the case of a boilermaker who, having lost employment as the result of a stoppage of work due to a trade dispute, and being consequently under disqualification, obtained spells of employment in his usual occupation elsewhere. In the circumstances of the case the Commissioner held that the claimant had not proved that he had become "bona fide employed" so as to terminate the disqualification. This conclusion appears to have been based mainly on the consideration—see paragraph 9 of the decision—that the interim employment was "a temporary expedient to tide him over the period of the stoppage" and "no permanent severance of relations [with the original employer] was intended". The tribunal appear to have inferred—not without justification—from what was said in Decision R(U) 39/56, that if an *interim* employment turned out to be not permanent, it could not be regarded as bona fide. The tribunal were not, I think, informed that the author of Decision R(U) 39/56 subsequently modified the views expressed in that decision, and that other Commissioners had subsequently questioned, or indeed disagreed with, those views. Unfortunately these subsequent observations do not appear in any reported decision.

. . . .

7. At first sight, the necessity for providing the exception is not entirely evident, since when a person under disqualification obtains employment he ceases, by that fact, to satisfy the primary condition of entitlement to unemployment benefit: so that even if disqualification were not thereby terminated, it would cease to have practical effect. But it is important to note that the provision is for *termination*, and not merely *suspension*, of the disqualification: and it has never, so far as I know, been contended that a disqualification terminated by the obtaining of employment revives if that employment should end while the relevant stoppage is still in being. (A quite separate disqualification might of course fall to be imposed, in certain circumstances, arising out of the termination of the *interim* employment.) The obtaining of employment by a person under disqualification . . . may thus constitute a means of getting rid of a disqualification, which might otherwise be of indefinite duration. In certatin circumstances this might be regarded as a mischief, or abuse. The insertion of the words "bona fide" or "regularly"" (as the case may be) appears to have been designed to defeat such an apprehended mischief or abuse by providing that it is only if the employment obtained is "bona fide" or "regular" (as the case may be) that its obtaining is to have the effect of terminating the disqualification.

8. What then is the meaning of "bona fide" in the present context? Reference to Stroud's Judicial Dictionary (2nd ed.) shows that the use of the phrase, in legislation, has been extensive and peculiar; and in some contexts almost unintelligible. But the basic connotation is simply that of "honesty"— *i.e.* honesty of motive or intention. To my mind the term "bona fide" in the present context implies (a) that the employment is taken up for an honest motive and (b) that it is genuine employment.

9. Having regard to the basic meaning of the term, I can see no justification for equiparating it (in this context) to "permanently" or "with the intention of permanently severing relations with the original employer".

10. There is nothing *prima facie* dishonest or mischievous in a person, who finds himself out of work and under disqualification, seeking and obtaining employment, even if it turns out to be temporary, or even if he knows from the start it is likely to be temporary, so long as he takes it up for a proper motive—*e.g.* to have a job and earn a livelihood. It would no doubt be dishonest or at least mischievous, if he took up the employment, knowing it was likely to be of short duration, merely thereby to rid himself of the disqualification and requalify immediately for benefit; or if

for a similar motive he purported to take up employment which was merely a sham. The probable duration of the employment (viewed propsectively) or its actual duration (viewed in hindsight) is simply an element which, taken along with other circumstances, may go towards showing whether the employment was or was not "bona fide". But the fact that an employment has turned out to be of short duration cannot *by itself* justify the inference that it was not "bona fide".

11. In the present case: if, as appears, the local tribunal judged that the claimant's employment with B was not bona fide merely because it was only temporary, they were not justified in doing so. As the insurance officer's representative at the hearing submitted (in favour of the claimant) the tribunal applied the wrong test.

12. It appeared to me highly relevant to ascertain the nature of the claimant's employment with B and how he came to take it up. In answer to questions the claimant explained that he was a man of 54, with a wife and family. He was not a member of a union and he got no strike pay. He was thus very short of money. Although he could not know for certain, he thought that the stoppage was likely to be lengthy. He heard of a vacancy at B, a firm for which he had worked on a previous occasion. The firm of B was not associated in any way with A. The vacancy at B was for a maintenance fitter, his customary occupation. The "job" to be done at B was to participate in the routine dismantling, servicing and rehabilitation of mechanical equipment in a particular department. His employment was thus expected, in the first instance at least, to be temporary, till this particular job was completed. It was, however, possible that this would be only the first of a succession of similar operations in other departments, and that he might be kept on. He took this employment with B in order to earn a wage and support his family. He repudiated the suggestion (which I thought it right to put to him) that this was merely a "dodge" to get rid of his disqualification. He would have liked permanent employment with B, even in preference to A. He was, however, discharged when the first "job" was completed, and did not obtain other employment until the stoppage at A. ended and he returned there.

13. I thought the claimant's evidence candid. I saw no reason to doubt that his employment with B was "bona fide" employment. The member of the solicitor's office of the Department of Health and Social Security, Mr. R. A. Sanders, who represented the insurance officer at the oral hearing, also expressed himself as unable to challenge the claimant's evidence, and on that basis was prepared to concede that by taking up the employment with B the

claimant had "become bona fide employed" in terms of the section, so as to bring his disqualification then to an end. I do not doubt that the concession was rightly made.

. . . .

Participating, Direct Interest

R(U) 3/69

. . . .

2. The claimant was employed as a joiner's labourer by Tarmac Civil Engineering Limited, (Tarmac), on work at the Shellstar Site, Ince Marsh near Chester. Amongst other contractors working on the site was Chemical Construction (G.B.) Limited, (Chemico). The mechanical trades employed by Chemico became involved in August 1968 in a dispute, the nature of which was a trade dispute and which involved Chemico employees, union officials and Chemico; but the matters in dispute did not involve Tarmac and their own employees.

3. Apart from the evidence afforded by the documents on the file, two witnesses were called before me to give evidence. They were Mr. John Lamb, the project manager for Tarmac, and Mr. Michael O'hare, a district officer of the claimant's union. I accept their evidence. Mr. lamb told me that Tarmac were engaged on the construction of stores, laboratories and offices on the site. Chemico worked in different areas of the site, and if occasion arose for the employees of the one concern to go on to the area of the other permission was necessary. Tarmac and Chemico operated under separate and distinct agreements in so far as remuneration of their employees was concerned. The sole access to the site was by a public road, and Chemico strike pickets, active on and after 7th September, 1968, were stationed strategically at a roundabout some 1¼ miles from the perimeter of the site where they had effective control of all access to and from the site. The picketing was effective, involving some 200–300 men and some 50 police. The pickets, noisy, militant and successful, stopped every car approaching the site entrance, and remained effective for weeks. The management were not prepared to risk damage to the site installations by bringing men in to work in the early hours of the morning, and in the result the office staffs were compelled to operate away from the site.

Mr. O'Hare, who agreed with Mr. Lamb's evidence, stated that his members derived no advantage from the strike. In his opinion, and he had had experience of many strikes, the pickets made it impossible for men to get to work, and he described the situation as ugly and dangerous. The claimant tried to report for work daily from 9th September to 20 September. I accept that he (with others) was physically prevented over this period from getting to his work by militant pickets who effected their object that no work at all should be done at the site. The claimant was laid off by his employer on 20th September 1968 having been paid to that date.

. . . .

6. . . . The case was argued before me on the basis that, of the requirements, the claimant had failed to prove that under proviso (a) he was not participating in or directly interested in the trade dispute which caused the stoppage of work, and these were the only issues raised for determination on the appeal. . . .

9. . . . decisions of the Umpire under the 1924 Act and there-after, under similarly worded sections, are of assistance. (Unemployment Insurance Act 1935 section 26(1); National Insurance Act 1946 section 13(1).)

10. Decisions of the Umpire 1677/1925, 1764/1925 and 1765/1925 support the view that, notwithstanding an extension of the area of dispute, participation, financing and a direct interest in the dispute do not necessarily follow. In Decision 1677/1925 a stoppage of work occurred at the pits where the applicants, "safety men", were employed on 24th June, 1925, which was due to a trade dispute between members of the Miners' Federation and their employers, relating to matters in which the applicants were in no way interested. Shortly after 3rd July they were prevented from continuing to work, owing to the violence of strikers. The Umpire said "In my opinion the stoppage of work of the applicants was not due to a second trade dispute but was only a step taken by the strikers against their employers in their efforts to make the general stoppage of work more effective." The applicants succeeded in showing that they were not participating in or financing or directly interested in the trade dispute which caused the stoppage of work, and that they did not belong to a grade or class so doing or directly interested. In Decision 1764/1925 a blacksmith, employed at a colliery, was attacked by strikers on his way to work and forced to return. The Umpire held that "The applicant did not become a participant or directly interested in the dispute by his having been prevented from going to work by force or intimidation on the part of the men on strike".

11. Decisions 1677/1925 and 1764/1925 were referred to by the Umpire in Decision 1022/1938; and two extracts were quoted, as I think appears, with approval. He drew attention to the use of the word "prevented" in both decisions, and said "The material word in the two quotations in the preceding paragraph is 'pre-

vented'. A different situation arises when persons refrain from working or presenting themselves for work, not because they are prevented by violence or intimidation from so doing, but because they acquiesce in a request not to do so." Such acquiescence he held to amount to participation. There is no question of acquiescence in the claimant's case.

12. Apart from relying on decisions before 1925, Mr. Haynes submitted that Decision R(U) 2/53 governed the matter. It is plain however from the decision itself that the claimant in that case belonged to a grade or class of workers of which, immediately before the commencement of the stoppage, there were members employed at his place of employment some of whom were participating in and directly interested in the dispute. Thus the claimant was disqualified under proviso (b)[2] to section 13(1) of the National Insurance Act 1946, and it was accordingly unnecessary to deal with the question posed by the activities of the pickets. He also relied on an unnumbered decision (not reported) on Commissioner's File C.W.U. 20/68.

13. In the decision on Commissioner's File C.W.U. 20/68 the Commissioner had occasion to consider Decision R(U) 2/53 in connection with the case of a claimant prevented from getting to work by the violence of pickets. He declined to find participation in a dispute which was not of the claimant's seeking, which he was anxious to avoid, and in which he only became involved by reason of well-founded fears of violence. In *Punton* v. *Ministry of Pensions and National Insurance (No. 2)* [1963] 1. W.L.R. 1176 Phillimore J. (as he then was) expressed the view, of section 13(1) of the National Insurance Act 1946, that participating in or financing involve active support by the claimants.

14. The claimant lost employment by reason of a stoppage of work due to a trade dispute at his place of employment. The trade dispute which caused the stoppage was either the original dispute, regarded as extended to the claimant by the perimeter confrontations with the pickets, or a second dispute arising out of the confrontations, ancillary to the original dispute. Whichever dispute caused the stoppage, I am not prepared to hold that the claimant, who was prevented by violence and obstruction from getting to his place of work, participated in either.

15. It remains to consider whether the claimant proved, as the local tribunal found he had, that he had no direct interest in the trade dispute which caused the stoppage. The local tribunal found that this dispute was that between the claimant and the pickets, and was a trade dispute as far as he was concerned. Whichever

[2] Since repealed, see *ante*, p. 83.

dispute caused the stoppage it is common ground that the claimant's only "interest" in either case was to be allowed to resume his employment. Whatever changes the settlement of either dispute might have brought about, the claimant himself did not stand to gain or to lose anything in his conditions of work, in his terms of employment or in amenity.

16. A non-participating person may be held to be directly interested in a dispute which has produced a stoppage causing him to lose employment, because, for example, the amount of work available would be affected if the dispute were to be settled in a particular way (see Tribunal Decision R(U) 1/60). But here no change in the conditions of employment of the Chemico mechanical trades on strike would have had any effect on the claimant, and the incidents of his employment, as distinct from his employment itself, would not have been affected.

17. The object of any settlement of a trade dispute is to bring about the resumption of work on the part of those who have lost employment. The purpose of the provisos to section 22(1) is to enable benefit to be paid where the claimant proves, among other requirements, that he is not directly interested in the trade dispute. If the prospect of continuing in employment and resuming work on the settlement of a trade dispute which has produced a stoppage leading to a loss of employment on the part of the claimant be held sufficient of itself to make him directly interested within the meaning of proviso (a), no claimant who has lost employment owing to a stoppage of work due to a trade dispute would ever succeed in obtaining benefit. The proviso (a), whilst in form indicating requirements, which, if proved, would enable a claimant . . . to escape disqualification, would be otiose and impossible of application.

18. It can, I think, be gathered from the Umpire's decisions of 1925 that, where intimidation and violence on the part of pickets, designed to make a strike effective, had resulted in loss of employment, the Umpire was not prepared to hold that a direct interest in the dispute was thereby imposed on a person thus prevented from working. These decisions, following upon the then recently enacted Unemployment Insurance (No. 2) Act 1924 (which by section 4(1) introduced the escape provisos), survived the passing of the Unemployment Insurance Act 1927 and the Unemployment Insurance Act 1935, where section 26(1) reproduced the provisions under which the decisions had been given; nor was any legislative step taken to reverse or modify the Umpire's approach to this question (referred to in Decision 1022/1938) when the National Insurance Act 1946 was passed, and the National Insurance Act

1965, section 22(1) is in terms identical with section 13(1) of the 1946 Act.

19. For the above reasons I prefer the approach of the Umpire, and hold that the claimant did not become directly interested in the dispute (however regarded) merely by his having been prevented from going to work by force or intimidation on the part of the pickets.

20. The stoppage ended on 26th October, 1968. Before it ended a new factor arose. Work should have been resumed by Tarmac employees on 21st October, 1968. The Amalgamated Society of Woodworkers lodged a claim for loss of wages for the period of the dispute on behalf of their joiner members against Tarmac, and instructed their members not to report for work. The joiners, with the other employees at Tarmac were employed under a common contract of employment as regards payment for periods of lay off, and there was a possibility, if the claim was not successful, that the terms of employment would be altered. All employees of Tarmac were thus directly interested in the outcome of the claim for loss of wages and in the dispute about it. The claimant, in common with his fellow employees continued to lose employment by reason of a stoppage due to what I consider to be a trade dispute at his place of employment, although that dispute had not caused the original stoppage (see Decision R(U) 12/60).

21. Finally, (the question arising out of the appeal on Commissioner's File C.U. 888/68, heard with this appeal) consideration must be given to the effect which this trade dispute between Tarmac and its employees may have had on the position of those in non-mechanical trades employed by Chemico. It was a trade dispute at their place of employment producing a stoppage directly affecting Tarmac employees. A phased resumption of work by Chemico employees started on 15th October, 1968. It is not, however, clear that, had the Tarmac employees restarted work on 21st October, 1968, the non-mechanical trades employed by Chemico would have done so. I am not satisfied that the continued loss of employment by the Chemico non-mechanical trades on and after 21st October was because of the stoppage caused by the action of the Tarmac employees. The initial loss of employment by the Chemico non-mechanical trades was due to the stoppage connected with the original dispute. In these circumstances, in my view, their continued loss of employment for the period 21st October 1968 to 26th October 1968 is to be ascribed to the stoppage of work due to the original dispute, and it is in respect of that dispute, for the whole period during which the Chemico non-mechanical trades lost employment, that the questions of participation and direct interest

are relevant. On these questions, as regards that dispute, I have already expressed my opinion and conclusions.

. . . .

R(U) 14/71

. . . .

10. Counsel for the claimant maintained that the claimant did not have any direct interest in the trade dispute which had arisen as a result of the strike of the toolroom workers. He maintained that the claimant's interest in the dispute involving the toolroom workers was too remote to warrant a decision that the claimant had a direct interest in the said dispute. He founded in particular on a recent decision by a Commissioner dated 23rd July, 1971 (Decision R(U) 13/71) in which the Commissioner stated, "Without attempting to define precisely what is meant by "direct interest", I think that a claimant should not be regarded as having a direct interest in another person's dispute for purposes of section [19(1)] unless there is a close association between the two occupations concerned, and the outcome of the dispute is likely to affect the claimant, not at a number of removes, but virtually automatically, without further intervening contingencies." He maintained that applying that dictum to the present case the claimant should not be regarded as having a direct interest in the trade dispute under consideration. The legal representative for the insurance officer now concerned with the case contended that the question of what amounted to "direct interest" could not be precisely defined, and that such an issue must always depend on the particular facts and circumstances of each case.

11. When the workers in an industry or even in a particular factory strike because they wish an increase in their wages it is clear that other workers in the same industry or in the particular factory in question will be interested in the outcome of such a dispute. My understanding of the Commissioner's Decision R(U) 13/71 is that the Commissioner in question considered that it was of importance in such cases to remember that the expression used in [19(1)] . . . was not "interested" but "directly interested" in the trade dispute under consideration. The Commissioner in that decision made clear that he was not attempting to define precisely what was meant by "direct interest" in a trade dispute, but I have no doubt that his observations in that connection may well be helpful in cases involving the question of "direct interest". I do, however, agree with the legal representative of the insurance officer now concerned with the case that the question of whether

a person is directly interested in a trade dispute must always depend very much on the particular facts and circumstances of each case.

12. In my opinion it is clear that all the hourly-paid workers at the said three Rolls Royce factories were very much involved at the time under consideration with the question of the general increase of wages which was being negotiated between the management of Rolls Royce and the joint negotiating committee. The main reason for the strike of the toolroom workers on 8th January 1971 was that they considered that the management of Rolls Royce had been lethargic in arranging a realistic wage level. As stated in paragraph 5 above the 1968 agreement expressly provided that the relationships or differentials in basic pay between the hourly-paid workers had to be maintained. I have reached the conclusion that all the hourly-paid workers who were laid off by the management as a result of the strike of the toolroom workers were clearly directly interested in the trade dispute which had arisen as a result of the demand for a realistic wage level. In those circumstances I have decided that the claimant, because of the provisions of section 22(1) of the 1965 Act, falls to be disqualified for receiving unemployment benefit in respect of the period set forth in paragraph 1 above.

. . . .

R(U) 8/72
. . . whatever formulation is used the concept which must be expressed is that of a break in a chain of causation. Supposing that the outcome of a trade dispute might lead to a change in the terms of employment of a person, then that person will have a direct interest in the dispute if the change would occur without any act or event breaking the chain of causation between such outcome and the change. On the other hand, his interest will not be direct if some act or event must be interposed between the outcome of the dispute and the occurrence of the change. I believe that this is what the learned Commissioner who decided R(U) 13/71 meant by "further intervening contingencies".

. . . .

SELF-INDUCED UNEMPLOYMENT

Social Security Act 1975, s. 20(1)
A person shall be disqualified for receiving unemployment benefit for such period not exceeding 6 weeks as may be determined . . . if—

(a) he has lost his employment . . . through his misconduct, or
has voluntarily left such employment without just cause;
(b) after a situation in any suitable employment has been properly notified to him as vacant or about to become vacant,
he has without good cause refused or failed to apply for
that situation or refused to accept that situation when
offered to him;
(c) he has neglected to avail himself of a reasonable opportunity
of suitable employment;
(d) he has without good cause refused or failed to carry out any
official recommendations given to him with a view to
assisting him to find suitable employment, being recommendations which were reasonable having regard to his
circumstances and to the means of obtaining that employment usually adopted in the district in which he resides;
or
(e) he has without good cause refused or failed to avail himself
of a reasonable opportunity of receiving training approved
by the Secretary of State in his case for the purpose of
becoming or keeping fit for entry into, or return to, regular
employment.[3]

Misconduct, Voluntary Leaving and Failure to Avail

R(U) 2/77

. . . .

2. The facts of this case and the course of events leading to the
situation with which I have to deal arising out of this claim to
unemployment benefit, are as follows. On 22 July, 1974 the claimant became employed by the British Railways Board as a railman,
his precise duty being as a plate-layer. Under the Contracts of
Employment Act 1972 he received the statutory notice of the terms
and conditions of his employment, by which it is apparent he set
great store. It provided, among other matters, that his contract
could be terminated without notice in the event that he was guilty
of misconduct. Paragraph 9 reads as follows:—

"9. Trade Union Membership:—
Your attention is drawn to the fact that under Section 5 of the
Industrial Relations Act, 1971, every employee shall, as
between himself and his employer, have the right:—

---

[3] Parallel provisions in previous Acts are: the National Insurance Act 1946. s. 13;
the National Insurance Act 1965, s. 22(2); the Social Security Act 1973, s. 14(2).

(a) If he so desires to be a member of a Trade Union of his choice;

(b) The right to be a member of no Trade Union or to refuse to be a member of any particular Trade Union; and

(c) . . . .

The Industrial Relations Act, 1971, provides it to be an unfair industrial practice for any employer to prevent or deter a worker from exercising any of the rights above mentioned or to dismiss, penalise or otherwise discriminate against him by reason of his exercising any such right."

3. The claimant was not then nor did he thereafter become a member of any trade union. He continued with his employment, and no complaint has ever been raised against him in relation to the work he was employed to do.

4. By the Trade Union and Labour Relations Act 1974 (31 July, 1974), the Industrial Relations Act 1971 was repealed, and with amendments, the dismissal provisions of section 24 of the Industrial Relations Act 1971 were thereafter contained in Schedule 1 paragraphs 6(5) of the 1974 Act. This provided:—

"(5) Dismissal of an employee by an employer shall be regarded as fair for the purpose of this Schedule if:—

(a) it is the practice, in accordance with a union membership agreement, for all the employees of that employer or all employees of the same class as the dismissed employee to belong to a specified independent trade union, or to one of a number of specified independent trade unions; and

(b) the reason for the dismissal was that the employee was not a member of the specified union or one of the specified unions or had refused or proposed to refuse to become or remain a member of that union or one of those unions:

unless the employee genuinely objects on grounds of religious belief to being a member of any trade union whatsoever or on any reasonable grounds to being a member of a particular trade union, in which case the dismissal shall be regarded as unfair."

5. In July 1975 the British Railways Board entered into a union membership agreement in respect of employees of a class of which the claimant was a member with the National Union of Railwaymen, the Associated Society of Locomotive Engineers and Fire-

man, and the Transport and Salaried Staffs Association. The agreement required that any member of the staff of the Board who was not a member of a recognised trade union at 1 August, 1975 should apply to join one of the recognised trade unions by 31 October, 1975. The claimant's situation was clearly affected by the new injected condition of employment.

6. The agreement was brought to the claimant's notice. He declined to join any union. According to the evidence of Mr. Hyland, a representative of British Railways who attended the local tribunal hearing, and which evidence I accept, the claimant gave as his reason for declining to join that the compulsion to do so was a denial of his freedom. From his written observations it appears that the claimant also took his stand on the terms of his original contract of employment, and also had a grievance, in that having applied in March, 1975 to work overtime he was not offered such work until July 1975, notwithstanding that such work had been offered to others.

7. The claimant's refusal to join a union was treated by his employers as a claim for exemption, and on 25 February 1976 his case was considered at York. The claimant attended. It was decided that his claim for exemption failed. At that stage the Trade Union and Labour Relations (Amendment) Bill was about to become law, and the claimant appreciated that if it did the only valid ground for not joining a union which would thereafter make his dismissal unfair would be on religious grounds. The Bill in fact became law on 25 March, 1976, and the words "or on any reasonable grounds to being a member of a particular trade union" in paragraph 6(5) of Schedule 1 to the 1974 Act were repealed. The claimant maintained his position, declining to join.

8. By letter of 15 March, 1976 the claimant was informed by his employers as follows. "I have to advise you that by reason of your non-compliance with the terms of the agreement on trade union membership dated July 1975 your service will no longer be required as from Saturday, the 17 April, 1976." So he was dismissed; his discharge for non-compliance took effect, and on 19 April, 1976 he claimed unemployment benefit. Benefit was not paid; enquiries were made in the usual course as to the circumstances in which he had become unemployed.

9. The claimant thought he had been unfairly dismissed. On 4 June, 1976 an Industrial Tribunal decided he had not been unfairly dismissed, since in evidence on that day the claimant frankly said he had no genuine religious objection to joining a trade union.

10. A decision on his claim to unemployment benefit was given on 12 July, 1976. He was held disqualified for the inclusive period

19 April, 1976 to 29 May 1976 because he had lost his employment through misconduct, and on his appeal to the local tribunal, on 24 September, 1976 they upheld the disqualification but only for three weeks from 19 April, 1976, and on the ground that he had voluntarily left his employment without just cause.

. . . .

12. It is to be noted that the proceedings before the Industrial Tribunal and the issues I have to decide involve consideration of similar facts. Such facts as are common, however, involve different issues and different considerations, and the issues arise under different statutory provisions. Findings of fact by the Industrial Tribunal are cogent evidence. I may act on them, but they do not bind me (Commissioner's Decision R(U) 2/74).

. . . .

14. *Whether the claimant lost his employment through misconduct.* Misconduct is not defined in the 1975 Act nor in its predecessors, but its characteristics in a social security context have been defined by the Umpire, and in many decisions of the Commissioners since. As early as 1928 the Umpire held in Decision UD 98/28 that disqualification was not punitive under the provisions of section 8(2) of the Unemployment Insurance Act 1920, but was designed to protect the Unemployment Insurance Fund "against claims by those who have brought about their unemployment through their own wrongful or unreasonable action." It has been variously defined by the Umpire as "misconduct . . . of a kind which renders the claimant unsuitable for his employment" (UD 18984/31) and "some failure of duty which the claimant owed to her employer . . . or . . . conduct . . . as to render her not suitable for the continuance of her employment" (UD 5546/35).

15. In Decision R(U) 24/55, paragraph 8, the Commissioner held that it meant "simply such misconduct as would lead a reasonable employer to terminate a claimant's employment", and in Decision R(U) 7/57, paragraph 6, it was equated with conduct showing that the claimant was not a fit person to hold the particular employment. Cases abound illustrating the many facets of industrial shortcomings, disobedience, faulty workmanship, idleness, unauthorised absence, some types of carelessness and conduct in greater or lesser degree connected with the employment adversely affecting the claimant's proper discharge of duties. It has been held to import some wrongful act or omission by the claimant, and to conform to what can fairly be described as blameworthy conduct. Mr. Brockman accepted that there must be blameworthiness; (Decision R(U) 8/57). It is not necessary for the purpose of the Act that there should be dishonesty in the conduct alleged to be

misconduct, or indeed, conduct which would amount to misconduct in a moral sense, although unfortunately such cases do occur, and findings of misconduct in the sense of the term as it is used for social security purposes may properly be made. In my view "misconduct" in the sense it is used in a social security context, is conduct which is causally but not necessarily directly connected with the employment, and having regard to the relationship of employer and employee and the rights and duties of both, can fairly be described as blameworthy, reprehensible and wrong.

16. The submission of the insurance officer now concerned, supported by Mr. Brockman, is that the claimant's non-compliance with the injected condition that he should join a union in order to remain employed was misconduct on his part. It is said that he provoked his employer to dismiss him; that he had made himself unsuitable for his job; that he was blameworthy, because he caused himself to become a potential charge on the National Insurance Fund, although it is not submitted that every dismissal, regarded as fair within the meaning of the Trade Union and Labour Relations Act 1974–1976, automatically attracts the description of misconduct to the conduct which provokes it.

17. The local tribunal (and I think it important to appreciate that included in its composition one member was from a panel of persons representing employed persons and one member from a panel of persons representing employers and insured persons other than employed persons) unanimously rejected any question of misconduct. They held that by its ordinary meaning misconduct "is an indictment of a person's character as an employee" and that "it implies an element of blameworthiness, a charge against the employee that he has wronged his employer by his behaviour". I see nothing erroneous in this approach. They held that the evidence showed that the claimant was a satisfactory platelayer, and that there was no complaint about his work, his attendance record, or his obedience to reasonable orders.

18. It has been submitted, however, that I should not restrict the meaning of "misconduct" to its ordinary meaning and as hitherto applied, but that I should consider it in a wider ambit, such as is shown from the case of *Owen* v *Nicholl* [1948] 1 All E.R. 707 where under the County Courts Act 1934 section 89 an arbitrator's "excusable slip" in admitting evidence not adduced by the parties was described by the Court as "technically called misconduct". I do not find the case of assistance in what I have to decide in a social security context.

19. It cannot be doubted that the onus on proof of establishing misconduct is on those who allege it. For the employed person it

is an emotive word, and a finding of misconduct produces an entry in a man's record of employment which may have a continuing and adverse effect on his prospects of future employment. Notwithstanding the change in industrial relations brought about by the legislation affecting the claimant's position as an employed non-union man who would not agree to become a member of a union, my view is that "misconduct" for social security purposes has retained its essential characteristic of wrongfulness in the sense I have previously described.

20. I enquire therefore what it was, having regard to his then obligations, that the claimant did, or refrained from doing, which was wrong. The employers were asked whether he had been discharged "because of unsatisfactory conduct of any kind?". In relation to his work and the performance of his contractural duties they alleged nothing. Their reply was that it was now a condition of employment with British Railways that staff must be members of a trade union, and that despite several approaches the claimant refused to join a union, and it was therefore necessary for his services to be terminated. Mr Brockman submitted that this was misconduct on the claimant's part through which he lost his employment because the claimant would not change his mind, abandon his objections and conform to the new conditions for continued employment.

21. The position of claimants to benefit who were discharged from or who left employment because of their views in relation to trade unions has been considered in decisions both of the Umpire and of the Commissioners. In Decision UD 5546/35 a claimant lost her employment because as the employers said, "she joined a trade union in defiance of our wishes". A majority of the Court of Referees found she had lost her employment because of misconduct. The Umpire disagreed. In the course of his decision, quoting from Decision UD 1528/26 he said "A man has as much right to refuse to leave a union as he has to refuse to join a union and it has been held in a number of cases that when a man is discharged rather than comply with such a demand he does not leave voluntarily without just cause and is not discharged for misconduct". Continuing, he said "I fail to find any difference in principle between a case in which a claimant refused to leave or join a union and one in which he refuses to give an undertaking that the will not join a union as a condition of his continued employment. The general principle applicable in all such cases is that a worker is entitled to resist any attempt to restrain the exercise of his legitimate rights as a citizen, so long as that exercise is not a breach of the terms of his existing contract of employment,

and so long as that exercise does not render him incapable of or unfitted for the due performance of the duties of his actual or prospective employment, and that he is entitled to regard as unsuitable any employment the terms of which offend against this principle".

22. The views above enunciated in Decision UD 1528/26 were quoted and endorsed by the Commissioner in Decision R(U) 38/53, where a voluntary leaving by the claimant, in what was described as the exercise of an undisputed right to decide whether he would be become a member of a trade union, was held to be with just cause.

23. I do not consider that in declining to join a union and thus not complying with the injected condition for further employment, the claimant was guilty of misconduct within the meaning of section 20(1)(a). No doubt he was fairly dismissed, but he lost his employment primarily because his employers wished to carry out their obligation to others. I agree with the decision of the local tribunal in this respect. In my view it would be wholly inappropriate to describe the claimant's non-compliance, for which the employers dismissed him, as misconduct through which he lost his employment.

24. *Whether the claimant left his employment volunatarily without just cause.* The employers who were asked "If the claimant left voluntarily what reason did he give?", did not answer the question. Plainly the question could not in terms be answered, because he had given no reason for leaving; he was dismissed. What I am asked to do is to apply what Decision R(U) 16/52 and others have enunciated, namely that it is an established principle of unemployment insurance law that if a person acts deliberately and knowingly in a way which makes it necessary for the employers to dismiss him he may be regarded as leaving his employment voluntarily. But in Decision R(U) 4/51 the Commissioner discussed certain decisions given under the unemployment insurance legislation prior to 1948, and held that a claimant cannot be regarded as voluntarily leaving his employment without just cause if he is discharged for refusing to pay union dues because he has a genuine grievance with his union.

25. Decisions R(U) 9/59 and R(U) 5/71 accept that in appropriate circumstances it may be proper to hold that an employee who brings about his own dismissal by failing or refusing to implement the conditions of his employment has left voluntarily within the meaning of the provision.

26. The concepts of "treating as", "regarding as" and "deeming to be" if not statutorily provided for, are in my opinion to be

applied both with caution and restraint. They are conclusions which at best may not wholly accord with the facts, and at worst may contradict them. I have no doubt that in this case the leaving of the employment was because of dismissal, because, in turn, the employers for good industrial reasons were anxious to implement their arrangement with the unions. I see no reason to impute to the claimant the last thing he had in mind, namely a volition to leave his employment, which he would have been content to pursue as a non-union man.

27. It seems to me, additionally, that as a result of Commissioner's Decision R(U) 7/74, where the claimant refused to accept alternative employment or to work non-contractual overtime, it is plain that those who are dismissed for refusing to accept summary changes in the terms of their employment—as was the claimant in this case—are not to be treated as having left voluntarily. Further in Commissioner's Decision R(U) 5/71 (to which I later refer) where registration would have made it lawful for the claimant's employment to have continued, dismissal consequent on his refusal to register was held not to produce a situation in which he could be held to have voluntarily left. As was held in that case, so I hold in this, that it would be a misuse of language to describe the claimant as having voluntarily left. Having regard to that finding the question of just cause does not arise for consideration.

28. *Whether the claimant neglected to avail himself of a reasonable opportunity of suitable employment.* It was submitted that because the employment offered was the claimant's regular employment it was suitable for him; that as the only change was the introduction with legislative approval of a requirement to join a union, that change could not make the employment unsuitable for the claimant; and that since his non-compliance with the condition to join a union was unreasonable *vis à vis* the National Insurance Fund, he could not show that the employment had become unsuitable for him. If I hold the employment was not suitable, it will be unnecessary to consider the question of "neglected to avail himself" or "reasonable opportunity", the further requirements of section 20(1)(c).

29. Section 20(1)(c) does not provide a definition of suitability. Subsection (4) describes three sets of circumstances in which the statutory authorities are compelled to find that an employment is unsuitable, and one in which they are compelled to find it suitable. (See Decision R(U) 5/68, decided with reference to section 22 of the National Insurance Act 1965). No question, however, arises in this case of the application of the subsection.

30. On an analysis of the situation, I am invited to hold that in the circumstances of his case the exercise of his right to object and not to accept the new condition, and which resulted in fair dismissal, attracted a collateral disqualification for receiving unemployment benefit under section 20(1)(c). Mr Brockman conceded the possibility that such disqualification would arise repeatedly and continuously if, on each occasion that similar offers of employment in the industry were made, the claimant was to maintain his objection to a union membership. So he would not only lose his livelihood but would also be deprived of the support of the unemployment insurance scheme.

31. I am wholly in agreement with the proposition stated in Decision R(U) 5/71 that in an appropriate case a person's attitude towards some feature of a proposed employment may properly be regarded as making that employment not "suitable" in his case; or as making the opportunity of such employment not a "reasonable" opportunity; or possibly as making it inappropriate to describe his attitude as "neglect" of anything. In that case the Commissioner was concerned whether the claimant's objections to registration (he was a "certificated" teacher) were reasonable, having regard to the fact that a system of registration was a *fait accompli*. It had been established by law as the basic qualification for teachers employed by an education authority in Scotland. On the facts it was held that the claimant's refusal to register (which would have ensured his continued employment) was not reasonable, and that the condition of registration did not make the employment unsuitable, or make the opportunity of such employment unreasonable. So the claimant in that case incurred disqualification under section 22(2)(c) of the National Insurance Act 1965.

32. There are, I think, substanital differences between the facts and circumstance of that case and this. As regards Decision R(U) 5/71 Parliament by amending regulations had provided for Scotland that the basic requirement for the employment as a local authority teacher was registration. In the present case it cannot be said that Parliament has in terms enacted that membership of a trade union is a basic requirement for the employment, although it has become so for the claimant through the lawful agreement negotiated by the employer with the unions. The requirements to register had no effect on the employment as a teacher, which would continue as before. The same cannot be said of the claimant's offered employment with British Railways. No doubt his plate-laying activities would continue unchanged, but membership of a union would entail financial obligations and the expectation that he would

conform to union practices an industrial relations, a very different situation from that considered in Decision R(U) 5/71.

33. The Commissioner in Decision R(U) 5/71, in considering the reasonableness of the claimant's objection, referred to conscientious objections in the strict sense, operating in the sphere of morals or religion such as may be admitted as exempting the holder from complying with some term of employment. He did not think that the objection to registration in that case, at the most intellectual and held as a matter of strong conviction, was an exempting condition. It is not, of course, necessary that a reasonable objection should be grounded only on religious or moral reasons. The circumstances of each case must be considered, and domestic, personal and financial reasons are examples of circumstance which have been held to make employment unsuitable for the claimant concerned.

34. The decisive factor on the question of the suitability of the continued employment must lie in the validity and weight to be attached to the claimant's objection to the injected condition, and whether I think the objection reasonable. He has described it as a moral objection, offering the view that being compelled to join a union was a denial of his freedom. I have found that his noncompliance was not misconduct; the local tribunal found, *vis-à-vis* his employers, that his objection was reasonable.

35. I appreciate the trivial and idiosyncratic objections to an employment may be disregarded as of no weight. Equally, I bear in mind, as it was submitted that I should, the changed situation in the industry affecting the claimant consequent upon recent legislation. In so doing it is hardly possible that I should be expected to insulate myself from the knowledge that the claimant's expressed views are shared by many others, and thus do not derive from the insubstantial perversities of an individual eccentricity.

36. It would I think, be implicit in a finding that for the purpose of section 20(1)(c) the employment offered was suitable, that I should have accepted that the claimant's objection to the injected condition was not reasonable and the disqualification would in effect operated primarily because he declined to join a union for the reasons he advanced. I consider the claimant's views, sincerely held, are of no less weight and are no less valid than as if the case had been, for example, that he had a religious objection to Sunday working, or an objection based on teetotal principles to an occupation involving the supply of intoxicants on licensed premises, or if, being a vegetarian, he objected to work in a butcher's shop. I see no reason why, in considering his objections as he expresses them to be, I should now be any the less liberal in my approach

to "suitability" than was the Umpire or the Commissioner, to whose decisions I have previously referred in paragraphs 21 and 22 above.

37. My conclusion on the submission is that for the purpose of disqualification . . . the claimant's objection to the particular feature of the continued employment he was offered was reasonable, and that in terms of the provision the employment was not suitable for him. As stated in paragraph 28 it is not necessary to consider the further issues raised . . . but on my finding of unsuitability it is clear that the opportunity itself could not be reasonable.

. . . .

R(U) 2/71

. . . .

7. . . . . I think that where at an oral hearing the insurance officer for the first time seeks to support disqualification on a different ground, very special precautions are necessary. Here the insurance officer disqualified the claimant for the period stated at the head of this decision [*from 14th August to 20th September, 1969*] on the ground of misconduct and nothing else. In his written submission to the local tribunal he cited the part of the statute dealing with misconduct but not the words dealing with voluntarily leaving the employment. He supported the decision on the ground of misconduct only. No doubt in may cases the evidence relevant to misconduct is to a large extent the same as that relevant to justification for leaving. And when adjourning the case the chairman of the tribunal recorded that the question was "the real reason why the applicant left his job". But even if this was served on the claimant I do not think that it would necessarily have conveyed to his mind that disqualification on any ground other than misconduct was being considered. A claimant, particularly an inexperienced young man, may not know that leaving voluntarily without just cause is a ground for disqualification. Unless a claimant is specifically told he may not know that it is the ground relied on against him. Where, therefore, the written submission does not make matters clear, I think that it would be desirable for the chairman of the tribunal to record in terms that the insurance officer's new contention has been explained to the claimant. In this case I am by no means convinced that the claimant fully understood the issue which eventually was being tried.

. . . .

R(U) 1/71

. . . .

2. From May 1967 to June 1969 the claimant, a single man in his thirties, was employed as a gardener by the Parks Department of a Corporation. On 29th May, 1969 he pleaded guilty on the advice of his solicitor to having committed an act of gross indecency with another man on 13th April 1969 (a Sunday) for which, having consented to be dealt with summarily, he was fined £10. This was an offence under section 13 of the Sexual Offences Act 1956. Section 1 of the Sexual Offences Act 1967 lays down circumstances in which gross indecency with another male person is not a criminal offence, it being for the prosecution to prove the absence of such circumstances. In the present case it is not alleged that the claimant committed the offence during his employment or on his employers' premises, but there is no evidence of the circumstances which made a defence under the 1967 Act not available.

. . .

5. This was one of two appeals by claimants whose cases were otherwise completely unconnected but contained the common element that each of the claimants had been disqualified under section 22 for misconduct consisting of a sexual offence or offences outside the employment. (The other is on Commissioner's File C.U. 735/69 (Decision C.U. 8/70 (not reported)).)As I could not remember any precedent for such a disqualification, I invited the insurance officer to deliver a further submission dealing with three points. I am greatly indebted to him for the trouble to which he has gone in looking into the matter. His answers to my questions are as follows.

6. Firstly, on the question whether there is any precedent in decisions of the Umpire or the Commissioner for disqualification as a result of a sexual offence committed outside the employment the insurance officer has been unable to find any precedent at all except a decision on Commissioner's File C.S.U. 3/69 given last year. In that case the offence consisted of indecent behaviour towards a girl aged 12, the claimant was a temporary civil servant at an army camp, the military personnel had requested that his employment be terminated and there was a possibility that he would come in contact with the families in the camp married quarters.

7. On the second question whether such an offence is accepted by the Courts as misconduct justifying summary dismissal the insurance officer refers to only two cases, neither of them very modern ones. These however seem to me to be clearly distinguishable. In *Atkin* v. *Acton* (1830) 4 C. & P. 208, 172 E.R. 673 there had been a series of incidents when the employee, being alone on

the employers' premises with a maidservant, made attempts to take indecent liberties with her, on one occasion putting a handkerchief into her mouth to prevent her crying out. This happened in and not outside the employment. In *Pearce* v. *Foster* (1886) 17 Q.B.D. 539 Lord Esher M.R. said that if a servant's conduct was so grossly immoral that all reasonable men would say that he could not be trusted the master might dismiss him. The immoral conduct in that case, however, was very heavy gambling on the stock exchange by a confidential clerk. I am certainly not satisfied that Lord Esher was using "immoral" in the sense of sexual immorality.

8. On the third question whether the fact that the offence was committed outside the employment had been accepted by the Commissioner as a ground for reducing the period of disqualification, the insurance officer was unable to refer to any case where he had done so.

9. My researches reveal that in Decision C.U. 381/51 (not reported) the Commissioner did reduce the disqualification from six weeks to one week in a case of misconduct outside the employment. He wrote: ". . . I take into consideration that the matter giving rise to the claimant's loss of employment occurred outside his working hours and had nothing whatever to do with his employment, and that there is no reason for supposing that it will ever occur again." An examination of the file for that case shows that the misconduct consisted of an indecent assault by a commercial traveller, a single man aged 33, on his fiancée. Before the case began the assize judge advised all women present to leave the Court. The case seems to have arisen out of a quarrel between the claimant and his fiancée who were living together. The assize judge put the claimant on probation for 12 months. The employers terminated the claimant's employment as a traveller selling ribbons. Apart from that case, there is an *obiter dictum* in paragraph 8 of Decision R(U) 24/55.

10. The misconduct referred to in section 22 is often described as industrial misconduct. The reason no doubt is to show that the word is not there used in the same sense as in some other jurisdictions: in divorce adultery is often spoken of as misconduct. Misconduct under section 22 has a much wider meaning, but the word "industrial" does not appear and never has appeared in the statute. The commonest cases of misconduct are in the employment, but it has long been accepted that that is not essential. If a person loses his employment by reason of misconduct which has a sufficient connection with the employment, it may not matter that it was committed outside the employment. Common examples are those of the man employed as a motor vehicle driver who loses

his licence as a result of his driving outside his employment and is disqualified for driving; there is an obvious link between the disqualification and his work. Similarly a person who commits offences of dishonesty outside his work may be disqualified under section 22, since most employers regard a thief as unsuitable to have about their premises. The principle acted on by the Umpire is stated in Halsbury's Laws of England, 2nd Edition, volume 34, page 526, paragraph 610 as follows:—

> "A claimant discharged for offences committed outside work-ing hours is not guilty of misconduct unless the offence is directly connected with his employment or is such as adversely to affect his suitability for it."

A restatement of the matter by the Commissioner in similar terms is to be found in paragraph 12 of Decision R(U) 20/59.

11. I think that the case of sexual offences outside the employ-ment present considerable difficulty. Disqualification for miscon-duct has been part of our law since 1911. The fact that it has been so difficult to find precedents suggests that such offences have in the past not generally been treated as misconduct. In my judgment however as a matter of law they can be so treated, and it is a question of fact whether in the particular case they should be. In many cases a sexual offence may have nothing whatsoever to do with the employment. I think however that there may be special circumstances where they may do so. The commercial traveller's case (paragraph 9 above) is a good instance. The employers may well have thought that there was a real danger that when visiting houses trying to sell ribbons, probably to women who might often be alone in the house, the claimant might attempt some sort of liberties. Further, there are some employments where the employer has a legitimate interest in the conduct of employees even outside the employment. One example may be that of a person who holds a special position, *e.g.* a school teacher. Another may be that of an employee of a government department or a local authority, who rightly feel that their employees should maintain a high stand-ard of conduct at all times.

12. In the present case the claimant was convicted before the local justices, and no doubt the case would have been reported in the local papers. The employers' view that as a result he was unsuitable to continue his employment is some evidence of the fact that he was, though of course it is not conclusive. The local tribunal, with their local knowledge and experience, unanimously took the same view. The claimant's evidence is uncontradicted that he was not required to work in public parks, but a gardener employed by

a corporation may have opportunities of embarrassing the public by some form of indecency. The claimant has not given oral evidence at any stage in this case. On the whole, though I think the case is somewhat near the line, I am not prepared to dissent from the view of the local tribunal that the claimant's conduct constituted misconduct within the meaning of section 22.

13. The insurance officer submits that the full six weeks' disqualification was rightly imposed[4] and relies on Decision R(U) 24/64 as showing that the nature of the misconduct is the only ground for a reduction. That decision however related to a bus driver who had lost his driving licence through driving his private car uninsured. There was therefore an obvious direct connection between the offence outside the employment and the claimant's suitability for the employment. The Commissioner was not considering a case where the situation was otherwise.

14. It seems to me that as the misconduct becomes less and less closely related to the employment there is more and more justification for reducing the period of disqualification. If this was the approach to the matter of the Commissioner in Decision C.U. 381/51 I agree with it. In the present case it seems to me that the claimant's offence was not at all closely related to the employment, and that in the circumstances a very substantial reduction in the period is justified. (This is the course which the local tribunal would have wished to take if they had felt justified in doing so.) I have reduced the period to one week—so far as section 22 is concerned. Whether this will help the claimant at all in view of the fact that he still may face disqualification owing to the lateness of his claim and the further fact that he obtained employment for himself as from 30th June I do not know.

. . . .

R(U) 20/64

. . . .

2. The claimant, who was serving as a sergeant in a county police force, was at liberty to retire at the end of either 25 or 30 years' service but was bound to retire at the age of 55. He was due to complete 25 years' service on the 26th February, 1963 when he would be 47 years of age. In January 1963 the Chief Constable wrote to him inquiring his intentions. The claimant replied, but there is no evidence of the contents of his reply. On the 28th January 1963 the assistant Chief Constable wrote to the claimant saying that he quite understood the claimant's problem and as the claimant was intending to leave sometime within the next two

[4] See R(U)8/74, *post*, p. 142.

months the assistant Chief Constable advised him to take on the other employment which he had in mind, at any rate for the time being, as an increase in the civilian establishment of the force had not yet been approved and it was too early for them to guarantee that they could employ the claimant at headquarters immediately on his retirement. On Saturday the 13th April, 1963 the claimant retired from the police force being then aged 47. On Monday the 15th April he claimed unemployment benefit and the insurance officer decided that he must be disqualified for receiving unemployment benefit for six weeks on the ground that he had voluntarily left his employment without just cause.

3. If a police officer in the claimant's county signifies his intention of retiring after either 25 or 30 years of service he may be allowed to occupy his own house for the last three years of service. At the beginning of 1962, when the claimant was serving at B, he made arrangements through a Building Society to buy his own house at H, 2 miles away from B. Unfortunately he was then moved to A, which is about 11 miles from his house at H. It was not possible for him to live in his own house and serve at A owing to the hours at which some of his turns of duty ended and began—in the small hours of the morning when no transport was available—and indeed the Chief Constable would not allow it. It was also not possible for him to lodge at A and maintain a home of his own at H owing to the expense of the latter. He applied to be allowed to serve nearer his own house but his application was not granted. He moved into occupation of his own house on the 11th February, 1963 having hitherto lived in police houses.

4. Before retiring the claimant visited about six prospective employers and 'he also applied to the Chief Constable for employment in a civilian capacity. On the 15th April, 1963—the first day of unemployment—he had already had one interview with the firm which subsequently engaged him and he was then awaiting another interview with them in the following week. He took up employment with this firm on the 1st May, 1963.

5. He contends that he had just cause for leaving the police force on the 13th April, 1963 because it was not practicable for him to continue to serve in the force and at the same time live in his own house; further that he had taken active measures before retiring to obtain other employment and had excellent prospects of obtaining it; and finally that he had never before claimed unemployment benefit.

. . . .

7. . . . those who assert that the claimant left voluntarily must prove it, and . . ., when they have done so, it is then for the

claimant to prove that he did not leave without just cause. This is the strictly accurate way of putting the matter; a slight change of emphasis may be involved in the phrase, frequently used in practice, that the claimant must prove that he had just cause for leaving. Each of these matters must be proved on balance of probabilities.

8. The basic purpose of unemployment benefit is to provide against the misfortune of unemployment happening against a person's will. Section 13(2) however clearly recognises that it may be payable in certain cases where the claimant leaves voluntarily, if he does not do so without just cause. It is not sufficient for him to prove that he acted reasonably, in the sense of acting reasonably in his own interests. The interests of the National Insurance Fund and other contributors have to be taken into account as well. "The notion of 'just cause' involves a compromise between the rights of the individual and the interests of the rest of the community. So long as he does not break his contract with his employer, the individual is free to leave his employment when he likes. But if he wishes to claim unemployment benefit he must not leave his employment without due regard to the interests of the rest of the community. . . ." (Decision C.U. 164/50 (not reported)). This has been expressed in different ways in many decisions; see Decisions R(U) 14/55, paragraph 5 and R(U) 23/59, paragraph 12. The difficulty however lies in making a comparison between such very different elements.

9. In deciding the question of just cause it is essential to remember throughout that the question is the one arising on the very words of the statute, and it is not permissible to substitute any other test. Further, "It is not practicable to lay down any hard and fast rule to guide the Statutory Authorities as to the precise circumstances in which just cause or no just cause for leaving is shown. Each case must depend upon its own particular circumstances" (Decision R(U) 14/52, paragraph 5). Nor should the various elements in the case be considered in water-tight compartments. It is necessary to look at the whole circumstances at the relevant time in order to determine whether in a fair sense it can be said that he did not leave without just cause. It may however be helpful to draw attention to certain types of case which occur frequently, in order to give guidance as to the way in which the Commissioner has regarded these problems.

10. In Decision R(U) 14/52 already referred to the Commissioner approached the matter by considering the necessity of being assured of suitable alternative employment unless there were circumstances justifying the claimant in leaving without it. We think that it may

be helpful to approach the matter from the opposite direction, considering first some circumstances in which a person may be held to have just cause for leaving his employment although he has no alternative employment to go to, and discussing then the effect of alternative employment or a prospect of it where there are no such circumstances or they are not sufficient to constitute just cause.

11. It is clearly established that some feature of the claimant's existing employment may justify him in leaving it immediately without any regard to the question of other employment. This is illustrated by many decisions including C.U. 248/49 (reported), R(U) 15/53, R(U) 38/53, R(U) 18/57, C.U. 46/59 and C.U. 1/64, the two last not reported. But the circumstances must be pressing. If, for example, the claimant has a grievance in connection with his employment, it may be reasonable to expect him to take such steps as are open to him through the proper channels to get it remedied rather than to leave immediately without doing so.

12. It is equally well established that circumstances in the claimant's personal or domestic life may become so pressing as to justify him in leaving without regard to the question of other employment. Illustrations of this are to be found in decisions such as R(U) 14/52 itself, R(U) 19/52 and R(U) 31/59. The need to take a quick decision about housing accommodation sometimes creates an urgency justifying the claimant in leaving; see, for example, Decision C.U. 49/57 (not reported). Many cases of this type depend on some circumstance affecting the health of the claimant or some person living with him.

13. In both classes of case referred to in the last two paragraphs there must be some urgency in the matter. Otherwise it often has to be held that the claimant could have taken some step other than leaving his employment when he did so. This is merely a particular application of the more general statement that the claimant ought to take such steps as are reasonably open to him to avoid voluntarily becoming unemployed and dependent on the National Insurance Fund.

14. Where the claimant either gives no reason at all for leaving or gives reasons which do not amount to just cause for doing so, the question frequently arises how the situation is affected by his having made arrangements for other employment or having prospects of other employment either immediately following his old employment or shortly afterwards. This commonly arises in cases where either the claimant moves house to some other district, which necessitates his moving his employment, or he leaves his employment simply because he wants a change of employment.

15. In our judgment the fact that a man moves house to a different district does not automatically or in itself provide him with just cause for leaving his employment in his old district when he does so. If a sentence in Decision C.U. 21/59 (not reported) had meant this in our judgment it would have been erroneous. But the fact that a man has moved or is moving house is an element to be taken into account with all the other circumstances in considering whether he has just cause. And the reasons for his moving may make it an important element. Further, there may be developments and difficulties in connection with his move which may make it an extremely important element, for example, if a situation unexpectedly develops whereby it becomes impracticable for him to avoid a short period of unemployment. Manifestly, a mere desire to change one's employment does not of itself constitute just cause.

16. In such cases it has been said that, generally speaking, a man should be assured of having suitable alternative employment to go to before he leaves that which he already has, or at least he ought to have very good reason for supposing that his chances of securing alternative employment in the immediate future are such that he will not be relying on unemployment benefit (Decision R(U) 14/52). In other decisions the matter has been put somewhat differently by saying, for example, that in general a person should not leave settled employment before he is reasonably assured of another situation at no distant date (Decision C.S.U. 13/56 (not reported)) or that he should take all reasonable steps to secure alternative employment before leaving that which he has (Decision C.U. 20/59 (not reported)).

17. Having fully considered the insurance officer's argument in the present case we think that the second approach to the matter described in paragraph 10 above is to be preferred to that suggested by these last decisions. We agree with the insurance officer that it is impossible to lay down any period of time representing a gap between employments, or any degree of probability of fresh employment, which will give an automatic answer to the question whether the claimant has shown just cause for leaving. We think that there is a distinction between on the one hand having suitable employment to go to, as where there is an actual promise of employment, and having only prospects of employment on the other. It may be reasonable to expect a claimant who has only prospects to take some step before leaving, such as communicating with the employment exchange to see whether his prospects cannot be made more certain. We think that there may be cases where an actual promise of immediate suitable new employment may

afford just cause in the absence of any other circumstances, but that such cases will probably be rare. Apart from them, we agree with the insurance officer that arrangements for, or promises or prospects of, other employment may be effective as an *additional* factor which may help the claimant to prove just cause. For example, where a man by reason of such circumstances as are mentioned in paragraphs 11 and 12 above almost establishes just cause, the fact that he has a promise or prospects of other employment may serve to tip the scale in his favour, or alternatively may provide grounds for reducing the period of disqualification. In considering these matters of course the strength of his chances of employment and the gap, if any, likely to occur between the two employments must be taken into account.

18. The claimant relies on the fact that he has never before been unemployed and has never drawn unemployment benefit, and that he has only drawn sickness benefit for 5 weeks when he was injured on duty. The insurance officer has rightly drawn attention to the fact that in some recent unreported decisions suggestions have been made that this might be directly relevant. Having had the advantage of hearing his full argument we are satisfied that this idea is erroneous. The fact that for half a century there has been no reported decision supporting it is strong evidence that the claimant's previous record has not been considered to be directly material. The insurance officer accepts and we agree that a man's record, either good or bad, may be indirectly relevant. It may show that in the past he has been willing or unwilling to work, able or unable to find employment for himself quickly, and responsible or irresponsible in terminating his employment. But the statute makes no provision by which a person can be deemed to have just cause when in fact he has not, and it is not open to the Commissioner, when just cause is not proved, to allow the claim for benefit on the ground that the claimant has a good record. In fact in the present case the claimant's record really throws no light on the matter either way. He had been serving in the police force all his adult life and no question of other employment had ever arisen. His record therefore throws no light on the question whether on this occasion he would have been likely to leave without just cause, and it can have no effect on our decision.

19. There is no doubt in this case that the claimant voluntarily left his employment. It is therefore for him to show that he did not do so without just cause. There is no suggestion that there was any unsatisfactory feature about his employment in the police force which would help him to prove just cause. We are not satisfied that the true inference from the facts is that the purchase of his

house caused him to retire. From the evidence it seems to us much more probable that he had decided to retire after 25 years, hoping perhaps to obtain civilian work with the police force after his retirement and that he bought or took steps to buy the house at H, to live in when he retired after 25 years. We should need strong evidence to show that he bought it in order to retire many years later. We cannot accept his suggestion that the purchase of the house of itself provides just cause for leaving his employment. The question then is whether the prospects of employment which he had, combined with the other circumstances, could justify a finding of just cause for leaving. In our judgment they do not do so. In fact there was a gap of a fortnight between the end of the one employment and the beginning of the other, and there is no evidence justifying the inference that the claimant ever thought that that gap would be either shorter or longer. Although the case is somewhat near the line, we do not feel justified in holding that the claimant has established that there were no steps which he could reasonably have been expected to take to avoid a gap between the two employments. All the events occurred in a comparatively small area, and this is not one of those cases where a claimant's new home is so far from his old one that it was impracticable to make arrangements at a distance. And we do not see how those efforts which he had made to obtain employment which he knew to have been unsuccessful—such as his attempt to obtain civilian employment with the police—can help him to prove just cause.

20. In our judgment however there are circumstances in this case, including his efforts to obtain employment, which justify a modest reduction in the period of disqualification. As the claimant was unemployed for only a fortnight this presumably will not help him, but we make the reduction as this decision may be a precedent in future cases.

. . . .

Suitable Employment

Social Security Act 1975, s. 20(4)

. . . employment shall not be deemed to be employment suitable in the case of any person if it is either—

    (a) employment in a situation vacant in consequence of a stoppage of work due to a trade dispute; or

    (b) employment in his usual occupation in the district where he was last ordinarily employed at a rate of remuneration lower, or on conditions less favourable, than those which he might reasonably have expected to obtain having regard to those which he habitually obtained in his usual employment in that district, or would have obtained had he continued to be so employed; or

(c) employment in his usual occupation in any other district at a rate of remuneration lower, or on conditions less favourable, than those generally observed in that district by agreement between associations of employers and employees or, failing any such agreement, than those generally recognised in that district by good employers;

but, after the lapse of such an interval from the date on which he becomes unemployed as in the circumstances of the case is reasonable, employment shall not be deemed to be unsuitable by reason only that it is employment of a kind other than employment in his usual occupation if it is employment at a rate of remuneration not lower, and on conditions not less favourable, than those generally observed by agreement between associations of employers and of employees or, failing any such agreement, than those generally recognised by good employers.

R(U) 5/68

. . . .

11. Paragraphs (a), (b) and (c) differ from the concluding words both in the subject matter with which they deal and in the way in which they operate.

12. Paragraphs (b) and (c) relate only to employment in the claimant's usual occupation. Like paragraph (a) they operate as a shield behind which a claimant can shelter from disqualification based on an allegation that a proposed employment is suitable. If the conditions in any one of the three paragraphs are satisfied, the statutory authorities are forbidden, whatever they may think of the merits of the case themselves, to decide that the employment is suitable. The converse however is not true. Nobody would dream of suggesting that simply because the employment is not in a situation vacant in consequence of a stoppage of work due to a trade dispute therefore automatically it is suitable. And the same applied in the case of paragraphs (b) and (c).

13. The concluding words do not deal at all with employment in the claimant's usual occupation, but only with "employment of a kind other than employment in his usual occupation". They operate in precisely the opposite way to paragraphs (a), (b) and

(c). Their effect is that if the *only* reason for saying that the employment is unsuitable is that it is employment of a kind other than employment in the claimant's usual occupation, the statutory authorities, if the conditions in the concluding words are satisfied, are forbidden to say that it is unsuitable. (I think that the operation of these concluding words must be extremely limited in view of the presence of the all important word "only"). Here again however the converse is not true. If the concluding words do not compel the statutory authorities to decide that the employment is suitable, that does not mean that they must necessarily decide that it is unsuitable.

14. The effect of subsection (5) therefore is to describe four sets of circumstances in which a decision is compulsory; the statutory authorities have no discretion in the matter. In three cases the compulsory decision is favourable to the claimant, in one it is adverse to him.

15. In the present case paragraph (a) does not apply. Paragraph (c) does not apply since the employment proposed was in the claimant's district. The concluding words do not apply because it was in his usual occupation. Three grounds for compelling me to decide the question of suitability one way or the other are therefore eliminated. The only one left for consideration is paragraph (b).

16. As to paragraph (b), I am prepared to assume against the claimant that he cannot shelter behind it and that I am therefore not compelled to hold the employment unsuitable. This makes it necessary for me to decide as a matter of fact, taking into account all the relevant circumstances, whether the employment was suitable, I have no doubt that in deciding this I am entitled to take into consideration all relevant matters, even though some of them are mentioned in subsection (5).

17. Having carefully considered all the evidence I am satisfied that the suggested employment was unsuitable for the claimant. It is true that he had been unemployed for some months. On the other hand he visited the proposed employers and they had an ample opportunity of correcting their description of the terms of employment if they had made a mistake. I must take it that the offer was of £11 plus (whatever that may mean) for the first four weeks. This was far below what these employers had promised the union that they would pay to a skilled man. Such an offer was in my judgment wholly inappropriate to a skilled man, who incidentally had been doing even more skilled work than the proposed work.

18. It is unnecessary to consider whether there may be cases where suitability and good cause depend on different considera-

tions. In my judgment this is not such a case, and the claimant had good cause for refusing or not applying for the situation.

. . . .

Refusal of Training

2/57 (UB)

. . . .

2. It is, in the first place, clear that the approval by the Ministry is an *ad hoc* decision, *i.e.,* that it is not merely a general approval of the training course as a valuable course and carried out under proper and suitable conditions, but is approval to the course as suitable for the particular claimant "in his case". The use of these words "in his case" in my opinion means that the Ministry has, and must be taken by the Statutory Authorities to have, considered adequately the suitability of the training facilities for the particular claimant concerned, and in fact found them generally suitable for him or her. How far, then, is it open or proper for the Statutory Authorities to examine the suitability of the training, the "reasonableness" of the opportunity given to make use of it, or the objections of a claimant to the training or its conditions? A closer scrutiny of Section 12(2)(*e*) does, in my opinion, afford guidance on these points. In my opinion, once the approval of the Ministry has been given to the training in the particular claimant's case, it is no longer open to the Statutory Authorities, or to anyone else exercising their duties under the Act, to consider or decide whether or not, *e.g.,* the claimant is physically, occupationally, or temperamentally suited to that class of training, but they must in fact accept that the facilities so approved are suitable "in his case for the purpose of becoming or keeping fit for entry into or return to regular employment"; since the Ministry has been entrusted by Parliament with the duty of so deciding. But this leaves a wide field of consideration and decision remaining under the sub-section as within the province, and duty, of the Statutory Authorities.

3. It will be noted that it is merely the training itself which is to be approved by the Ministry and the Ministry is not fixed with the statutory responsibility of deciding whether the opportunity given to the claimant of receiving such approved training is "reasonable" or not. The Ministry with the knowledge and facilities available to it, is responsible for examining the course of training, *as such,* not merely *in vacuo,* but as a course for the particular claimant. But all other matters are entrusted to the care of the Statutory

Authorities. In my opinion, this quite wide area of jurisdiction includes consideration of:—

(i) "Whether the claimant has without good cause refused or failed to avail himself" of an opportunity of such training. In this respect every avenue of investigation would be open, save only the question whether the training was generally suitable as such for the claimant. I say "generally" and "as such", because obviously there might have been a change since the Ministry's decision, *e.g.*, the claimant might have suffered some incapacity for the course, since the decision was given, which would constitute "good cause", To select from a variety of circumstances which could properly constitute "good cause", domestic circumstances, a promise of regular employment, disability, or travelling difficulties occur to one. I do not attempt to exhaust the list, and in my opinion any *individual* circumstances, of which the Ministry could not normally be aware, are within the proper consideration of the Statutory Authorities.

(ii) Whether the claimant has, in fact, "refused or failed to avail himself" of the opportunity. This would involve consideration of the terms of the offer, how it was communicated to the claimant, if so communicated at all, and his response or reaction to any such offer.

(iii) Whether any opportunity given was "reasonable" in all the circumstances. To some extent, I think, consideration of this issue may overlap (i) and (ii) above, but in my opinion it clearly involves consideration also whether, first of all, there was intelligible communication to the claimant of an offer of the training, given in time for him to avail himself of it and in a proper manner; and, secondly, whether it was otherwise "reasonable". Even, for example if it had been approved by the Ministry in relation to the claimant an offer of training might not be considered "reasonable" if it were made on a day when the claimant was unwell or was being interviewed for work by an employer. And it may be noted that though such approval by the Ministry would presumably extend often over a period of time several opportunities of taking up such training might be offered within such period of time, any one of which might be reasonable and others unreasonable. And I am very clear that the vesting in the Ministry of such a right to approve in no way extends to consideration of all the day-to-day reasons and circumstances of an individual claimant, nor would the Ministry be likely to consider it desirable or administratively expedient that it should do so.

. . . .

Period of Disqualification

R(U) 8/74 (T)

. . . .

16. . . . the section entrusts to the statutory authorities a discretion, which must be exercised judicially taking into account all the circumstances relevant to the question whether the claimant should be disqualified at all and excluding extraneous matters. We also agree that disqualification for six weeks is not necessarily appropriate only in the most serious cases. We do not agree that there are only two possible approaches, one starting at the top and working down and the other starting at the bottom and working up. We think that the references to disqualification not being a penalty may have been misunderstood. In the cases the subjects of U.D. 6279/33 and U.D. 98/28 referred to in it, which were both misconduct cases, the claimant had been convicted of a criminal offence and fined, and it was the circumstances of those offences that constituted the misconduct in each case. It was argued on behalf of the claimants that as they had been fined they ought not to be penalised further by being disqualified for the full period. It was in the course of explaining why this contention could not prevail that the word penalty was mentioned.

17. The history of the sections shows a gradually increasing emphasis on discretion in the adjudicating authorities. The 1911 Act contained no discretion: the disqualification was for six weeks, no more and no less. Under the 1920 Act it was six weeks or a shorter period not less than a week. Under the 1934 and 1935 Acts it was six weeks or a shorter period. Since 1946 it has been a period not exceeding six weeks. The emphasis on the six weeks has completely disappeared. Parliament could in 1946 have enacted that the disqualification—on all or any of the various grounds drawn together in section 13(2)—was to be for six weeks or such lesser period as the determining authorities might for special reasons decide. Parliament did not do so. It left the statutory authorities a completely unfettered discretion subject only to the requirement that it must be exercised judicially. In our judgment this is the clear meaning of the opening words of section 22(2), which

must be the same, no matter which paragraph of the subsection is under consideration, though of course the application of them may vary according to the individual circumstances.

18. We are not satisfied that the "heavy burden" approach as set forth in Decision R(U) 17/54 has in fact been generally accepted by the Commissioners. An examination of many cases in Dr. Jenkins's Index under the various headings (voluntarily leaving, misconduct etc.) shows that in a substantial number of cases the Commissioner has reduced the period from the one which the local tribunal has imposed. The same is true of many other cases which are neither reported nor numbered. It may be that the use in such cases of the word "reduced" has given the erroneous impression that the Commissioner was treating six weeks as being the normal starting point and was "reducing" the period below that when in fact he was merely reducing the period ordered by the local tribunal. Decision R(U) 12/72 is clearly distinguishable. The subsection under consideration there specifically stated the period of disqualification, and the Tribunal of Commissioners felt unable to depart from or dissent from the long line of authority holding that the subsection meant precisely what it said. In the present case however we are clearly convinced that the interpretation in paragraph 3 of Decision R(U) 17/54 which, with its reference to a burden of proof on the claimant which will seldom be a light one, substantially limits the discretion of the statutory authorities, is erroneous.

19. We fully appreciate the difficulty of administering this provision in such a manner as not to lead to large discrepancies between the treatment of different claimants. Once however it is accepted, as the insurance officer does accept, that in every case the individual circumstances must be considered, differences in treatment to a certain extent are inevitable. Section 22(2) is one of the comparatively rare instances in national insurance law where Parliament has entrusted to the determining authorities a discretion which in percentage terms is very substantial. The period of disqualification in one case may be more than thirty times as long as in another. The amounts may not be very large (except perhaps where there are numerous dependants) but they are very important to many claimants. We were assured on behalf of the insurance officer that, apart from occasional lapses, insurance officers do apply their minds to the question of the length of the disqualification, and we hope that they will continue to do so. In doing so, no doubt, they will have regard to the more recent decisions of the Commissioners, remembering that in matters of this kind times and attitudes change.

20. In our opinion the matter is fairly summarised by the Commissioner Mr. Lazarus in paragraph 7 of his decision on Commissioner's file C.U. 273/73 where he wrote:

> "7. I do not find helpful the proposition that the maximum period should be imposed unless the insured person concerned proves that there are mitigating circumstances. The Act says nothing about the insured person having to prove mitigating circumstances, and in my view the exercise of the statutory discretion should not be fettered by what I would call a "burden of proof" approach. Naturally, in exercising the discretion the determining authority should take into account all the relevant circumstances. The statement that, if there are mitigating circumstances, they should impose a disqualification period less than the maximum is not materially different from the statement that they should choose the period in accordance with the merits of the case. It seems to me that the correct approach is to adhere firmly to the statutory language, regarding each case as one in which a sensible discretion has to be exercised in such manner as the justice of the case requires."

We agree.

. . . .

CHAPTER 3

BENEFITS RELATING TO SICKNESS

A number of different social security benefits relate to sickness and
disablement. A range of important and generally higher-level benefits is
available for cases of industrial injuries (see *post*, Chapter 6). Under the
social security Acts, sickness benefit has always figured as one of the most
important contributory benefits and to it has now been added a long-term
cousin, invalidity benefit. In recent years, important new non-contributory
benefits have been introduced—attendance allowance is well known; non-
contributory invalidity pension, invalid care allowance and mobility allowance have now been added.

SICKNESS BENEFIT

(See Social Security Act 1975, ss. 14–18, *ante*, pp. 1–3.)

"Day"

C.S. 363/49(KL)

. . . .

2. The claimant visited his doctor between 9 a.m. and 10 a.m.
on 24th March, 1949, which was a Thursday, and obtained a
medical certificate on form Med.2B to the effect that he had
remained incapable of work by reason of influenza up to and
including that day and that he would be fit to resume work on that
day. He in fact intended to resume work, if he could, that evening
on night shift, which began at 10 p.m. He did so resume work.
The night shift lasts until 5.30 a.m. the next morning.[1] It is clear,
therefore, that the claimant was not incapable of work throughout
the period of 24 hours from midnight on 23rd/24th March, 1949,
to midnight on 24th/25th March, 1949.

3. . . . . an insured person is entitled to sickness benefit "in respect
of any day of incapacity for work" which forms part of a period
of interruption of employment and . . . a day is not to be treated
as a day of incapacity for work unless on that day the claimant is,
or is deemed in accordance with regulations to be, incapable of
work by reason of some specific disease or bodily or mental dis-

[1] See, now, the "nightworkers' regulation," *ante*, pp. 63–64.

145

ability. If 24th March is a day of incapacity for work, it clearly forms part of a period of interruption of employment, because the claimant was admittedly incapable of work on 23rd March and . . . "the expression day or interruption of employment means a day which is a day . . . of incapacity for work", and . . . "any two days of interruption of employment . . . within a period of six consecutive days shall be treated as a period of interruption of employment". Further, the claimant, if he was incapable of work on 24th March, was clearly so incapable by reason of a specific disease, namely, influenza.

4. The point at issue in this case, therefore, is whether in respect of the claimant 24th March, 1949, was "a day of incapacity for work". . . .

5. "Day" is not expressly defined . . . but its *prima facie* meaning is the period of 24 hours from midnight to midnight. That such is the sense in which the word is used . . . is confirmed by noting, for example, that . . . it is provided that "Sunday or such other day in each week as may be prescribed shall not be treated as a day of unemployment or of incapacity for work and shall be disregarded in computing any period of consecutive days". "Consecutive days" clearly refers to the days of the week, and Sunday lasts from midnight to midnight, as do Monday, Tuesday, Wednesday and the other days.

6. It has already been decided in Decision No. C.W.I 10/49 (reported) that a claimant cannot be held to be entitled to injury benefit in respect of a day, unless he is incapable of work throughout that day, subject to two exceptions. One of these exceptions arises from an express provision of the . . . Act, . . . under which that decision was given. The second exception is a case where the period during which the claimant is incapable of work can be ignored under what is known in law as the *de minimis* rule. That rule may be expressed shortly by saying that the law does not concern itself with trifles, and, consequently, a period of capacity for work of negligible duration will be ignored.

7. In this case the period during which the claimant was capable of work on 24th March, 1949, even if it be assumed to have lasted only from 10 p.m. to midnight, was clearly not of so negligible a duration as to be capable of being ignored under the *de minimis* rule.

Social Security (Unemployment, Sickness and Invalidity Benefit) Regulations 1975 (S.I. 1975 No. 564), regs. 3(2), 7(1)(g)

3(2). A person who at the commencement of any day is, or thereafter on that day becomes, incapable of work by reason of some specific disease or bodily or mental disablement and does no work as an employed earner or self-employed earner on that day shall be deemed to be so incapable of work throughout that day.

. . . .

7(1)(*g*). A day shall not be treated as a day of incapacity for work if a person does any work on that day, other than—

    (i) work which is undertaken under medical supervision as part of his treatment while he is a patient in or of a hospital or similar institution, or

    (ii) work which is not so undertaken and which he has good cause for doing,

and from which, in the case of work of either description, his earnings, if any, are ordinarily not more than £9·00 a week.

"Specific disease or bodily or mental disablement"

R(S) 6/59

. . . .

2. At the times to which this decision relates the claimant was employed as a long-distance lorry driver, working either for himself or his brother. Between the 2nd April, 1955 and the 12th May, 1958 the claimant was in hospital as an in-patient for 68 periods in hospitals all over the country and on no less than 18 occasions he entered one hospital, after having left another hospital in a different town earlier on the same day. At the time to which this appeal relates he travelled from hospital by driving his motor lorry.

3. Records from a number of hospitals show that he attended the hospital complaining of symptoms which suggested the presence of a disease in the kidney or the ureter and investigations and, on occasions, even operations were carried out without any disease being diagnosed. On a number of these occasions he told inconsistent stories about previous operations carried out upon him and never told a frank story of his medical history. On a number of occasions he left hospital before the investigations were complete.

4. The deputy chief medical officer of the Ministry of Pensions and National Insurance explained at the hearing of the claimant's appeal to the Commissioner that the claimant's case was a typical case of Munchausen's syndrome.

This is a strange condition in the nature of malingering and the motive has never been clearly ascertained, but a doctor who had made a special study of this disease was of the opinion that one of the following mechanisms may be involved:—

(*a*) a desire to be the centre of interest and attention;
(*b*) a grudge against doctors and hospitals, which is satisfied by frustrating or deceiving them;
(*c*) a desire for drugs;
(*d*) a desire to escape from the police;
(*e*) a desire to get free board and lodging for the night, despite the risk of investigations and treatment.

5. Supplementing these scanty motives there probably exists some strange twist of personality.

6. The medical officer stated that he could not find any evidence of a cause having been ascertained for the symptoms of which the claimant complained at the hospitals which he attended from the 2nd April, 1955 to the 12th May, 1958. He agreed in reply to questions by the claimant that, if a calculus was present in the ureter, it would be painless while stationary, but painful if it moved, and that long distance lorry driving might make it move, but the medical officer pointed out that he could find no evidence in the very extensive information supplied by the hospitals of a stone having been found in the ureter.

7. In the medical officer's opinion, the condition known as Munchausen's syndrome was a defect of character, rather than a mental disorder. Persons with Munchausen's syndrome knew that there was nothing wrong with them; in that respect they were different from the true psychotic, who was not really aware of his condition.

8. I was assisted in this case by a medical assessor who agreed with the view of the medical officer that the claimant's was a typical case of Munchausen's syndrome and that that syndrome should be regarded as a defect of character, a refusal to accept the evidence of frequent complete examinations showing that no physical disorder existed and a persistence in representing to hospitals the presence of symptoms suggesting that disorder, when he already knew that on investigation they had been shown not to be symptoms of any such disorder. My medical assessor was not prepared to regard the condition as either a disease or a mental disablement. Although by the false and incomplete stories that the claimant had told he had caused investigations to be made which in some cases would have rendered him incapable of work, those investigations failed to disclose any disorders from which the claimant was suffering.

. . . .

11. . . . the Munchausen's syndrome of itself did not render the claimant incapable of work. He drove his lorry for long distances in the short intervals between his hospital admissions. Further,

although in some cases he was rendered incapable of work by investigations which he caused to be carried out at the hospitals, there is no evidence that they discovered the claimant to be suffering from any disease or bodily or mental disablement. As was pointed out in Decision R(S) 1/58, "normally, evidence that a claimant is an inpatient in hospital is regarded as evidence that he is incapable of work and entitled to sickness benefit, even though he has been admitted only for investigation and whether or not a specific disease has been or is identified during his stay there because a man cannot be expected to work, if there are reasonable grounds for belief that he is suffering from a disease, while the matter is under investigation at hospital. But there may be cases where the evidence looked at as a whole justifies the inference that this prima facie evidence of incapacity is rebutted because the claimant in going to hospital has an ulterior object in view unconnected with his health, and no evidence of his incapacity for work is found on investigation."

12. If I felt satisfied, therefore, that the claimant's condition was a psychosis, so that, despite the absence of organic disease, it was reasonable to infer that the symptoms of which he complained were real to him with the result that he attended hospital in the genuine belief that benefit might be derived from doing so and for the genuine purpose of having their cause ascertained, I should hold that there was no evidence to rebut the prima facie evidence of incapacity provided by his presence in hospital as an inpatient for the purpose of investigating those symptoms. But on the facts of this case I am not so satisfied. The balance of probabilities appears to me to support the view that the claimant's condition was due to a defect of character and not to disease or mental disablement.

No other disease or bodily or mental disablement was found on investigation at the various hospitals, and, accordingly, the claimant has been unable to establish that during any of the periods named at the head of this decision he was incapable of work by reason of some specific disease or bodily or mental disablement. . . .
. . . .

Incapacity for work

R(S) 8/53
. . . .

2. The claimant is 30 years of age. He has had his right leg amputated just below the thigh and wears an artificial leg. He is

a rubber worker but owing to a heavy fall of snow and the ensuing icy and dangerous condition of the roads in the district where he lives, he was unable to get to his place of work during the period mentioned above. His doctor certified on the 28th November, 1952 that the claimant was incapable of work by reason of "Prosthesis—impossible for him to attend work because of snow": the doctor added that the claimant had not attended work since the 25th November, 1952. "Prosthesis" is the medical term for the replacing of an absent part by an artificial one, in this case the right leg. The claimant has claimed sickness benefit for the period when he was prevented from attending work by the snow and ice.

3. . . . In order to succeed the claimant must prove that he was, or was deemed in accordance with regulations to be,

> "incapable of work by reason of some specific disease or bodily or mental disablement"

within the meaning of . . . the . . . Act. . . . He was, however, not incapable of work by reason of his bodily disablement; he was perfectly capable of work but was incapable of getting to work. If his work could have been brought to his home, or if he could have been transported to his place of work, he could have done it. The claimant was not incapable of work, but was prevented by circumstances beyond his control from reaching his place of employment. A disabled man, who was capable of work but was obliged to use a conveyance to reach his place of work, could not be said to be incapable of work if his conveyance were to break down and so prevent him from reaching his place of employment.

4. The only regulation which could have any relevance is Regulation 3(a)[1a] . . . but this does not help the claimant because he was not at the material time under medical care in respect of his disablement and furthermore his doctor has not certified that by reason of his disablement he should abstain from work. The doctor merely says that it was impossible for him to attend work.

5. The claimant was not incapable of work by reason of his bodily disablement, and there is no regulation in accordance with which he can be deemed to have been so incapable.

. . . .

[1a] See, now, the Social Security (Unemployment, Sickness and Invalidity Benefit) Regulations 1975 (S.I. 1975 No. 564), reg. 3(1)(a), *post*, p. 153.

R(S) 2/78

. . . .

2. The claimant, a former furniture salesman now aged 48, was in receipt of sickness benefit or invalidity benefit continuously from 23rd August, 1976. On 13th January, 1977 he was examined by an officer of the regional medical service of the Scottish Home and Health Department who pronounced him incapable of work at his normal occupation, but capable of work within certain limits (which he indicated). He diagnosed the claimant as suffering from osteo-arthritis of spine (main condition) with hypertension as a secondary condition. His report was "This man has fairly good spinal movements, but is unsuited to work involving lifting or bending. He also has moderate hypertension. I think he might manage limited work". The claimant's doctor continued to advise him to refrain from work, and the claimant did so, and continued to claim and receive invalidity benefit. On 8th February, 1977 another medical officer of the same service examined him and reported rather more fully on his condition. He too pronounced the claimant capable of work within certain limits, and agreed that "he is fit for light employment as described. A course of rehabilitation would not only be of value but would be also welcomed". The claimant's doctor continued to advise him to refrain from work, and she is said to have expressed the opinion that he was unfit even for rehabilitation: but there is no direct evidence of this.

. . . .

5. The main contention on behalf of the claimant was that it was too early to apply the test of capacity for work other than his normal work: (it being assumed, rather than established, that his normal work was that of furniture salesman). Here the "alternative work" test had been applied after only 6 months of incapacity. Reference was made to Decision R(S) 7/60, in which it was only after 7 years of certification that the claimant was disallowed benefit on application of the "alternative work" test: and to Decision R(S) 10/61, in which the claimant's appeal was allowed. But the circumstances of these cases were so entirely different from those of the present case that their citation is not helpful.

6. In terms of section 17(1)(a)(ii) of the Social Security Act 1975 the relevant question for determination is whether on each or any of the days in question the claimant was incapable of work by reason of some specific disease or bodily or mental disablement. (In this case no question of "deeming" incapacity arises.) And "work" in this paragraph means "work which the person can reasonably be expected to do". There is no specific direction that at any stage the claimant's capacity for work should be considered

only in relation to his normal work. The earlier National Insurance Acts did not include the parenthetical words "work in this paragraph, meaning work which the person can reasonably be expected to do". The addition of these parenthetical words appears to recognise, in brief expression, the validity of the definition of "incapable of work" enunciated by a Tribunal of Commissioners in Decision R(S) 11/51, as follows "A person is incapable of work within the meaning of [the statute] . . . if, having regard to his age, education, experience, state of health and other personal factors, there is no work or type of work which he can reasonably be expected to do. . . ." In Decision R(S) 7/60, after quoting the foregoing, the Commissioner said, "I would be quite prepared to agree that, in a case of temporary illness of short duration, a claimant's capacity for work should be judged by reference to his normal field of employment because he could not in such circumstances reasonably be expected to embark on a new career, but, when a claimant's disabilities last for a long period the field of employment to be taken into account must be enlarged. . . ."

7. The Commissioners have never, so far as I am aware, purported to lay down any specific period which must elapse before the "alternative work" test falls to be applied: and it is apparent to me that any attempt to do so would be quite inappropriate. In practice, I understand, insurance officers rarely apply the "alternative work" test until at least 6 months or thereby. This is mainly for administrative reasons: and as a result the Commissioners have rarely been called upon to adjudicate on cases where the test has been applied after less than 6 months.

8. The statute, however, does now explicitly refer to "work which the person can reasonably be expected to do": just as the Commissioners' definition did. Reasonableness, rather than any specific measure of time, is the crucial matter. It is not normally reasonable, in the case of a short-term incapacity, to expect a claimant to change his occupation. If incapacity is continued, it may become reasonable to do so. Just at what stage must depend on the circumstances of the particular case: not merely age, education, experience and state of health, but other possible factors such as the nature of the claimant's normal occupation, how long he has been engaged in it, whether his incapacity for it is likely to be permanent or long-continued, whether he is likely to be adaptable to a new form of employment, and possibly whether he is due to retire at no distant date. There can be no specific time limit for all cases.

9. Having considered all the available information as to the circumstances of the instant case, I am satisfied that by 25th

February, 1977 the time had come when the claimant could reasonably have been expected to attempt other work than that of furniture salesman, within the restrictions indicated by the regional medical officer. By that date it was not in the least unreasonable to apply the "alternative work" test. The weight of the evidence is to the effect that by that date he was not incapable of such alternative work. He therefore failed to prove incapacity for work within the meaning of section 17(1)(a)(ii) of the Act. His claim was rightly disallowed.

R3/60(SB)

1. The question for consideration in this case is:—

Whether sickness benefit is payable to the claimant from and including the 31st March, 1960, to the 12th May, 1960, and in particular whether the claimant has proved that she is, or is deemed in accordance with regulations to be, incapable of work by reason of some specific disease or bodily or mental disablement.

. . . .

4. It is pointed out by the Insurance Officer that the claimant, during the period under consideration, performed a number of household duties, and in this connection reference is made to reported Decision No. 1/53 (S.B.). In that case the learned Umpire may well have thought that the claimant was capable of performing a greater number of household duties than she was prepared to admit. Be that as it may, the decision in each case depends upon its own particular facts as ascertained from the evidence. If the claimant's capacity for domestic work appears to be so limited that no employer would normally be expected to engage and remunerate her she should be treated as being incapable of remunerative work—see, for example, paragraph 6 of Decision R(S)11/51, a decision of a Tribunal of Commissioners in Great Britain.

5. The evidence in the present case suggests to me that at the material time the claimant was capable of very light housework only, and I would not have expected any employer to be willing to engage and remunerate her.

. . . .

Deemed incapacity

Social Security (Unemployment, Sickness and Invalidity Benefit) Regulations 1975 (S.I. 1975 No. 564), reg. 3(1)

3.—(1) A person who is not incapable of work may be deemed to be incapable of work by reason of some specific disease or bodily or mental disablement for any day on which either—

(*a*) (i) he is under medical care in respect of a disease or disablement as aforesaid.

(ii) It is certified by a registered medical practitioner that for precautionary or convalescent reasons consequential on such disease or disablement he should abstain from work, and

(iii) he does not work; or

(*b*) he is excluded from work on the certificate of a Medical Officer for Environmental Health and is under medical observation by reason of his being a carrier, or having been in contact with a case, of infectious disease.[2]

Proof

(See Social Security (Medical Evidence) Regulations 1976, (S.I. 1976 No. 615).)

R(S) 1/67

. . . .

6. I think it is right to make certain observations about the relevance and materiality of the claimant's record of previous claims. The Commissioner has more than once affirmed that a claimant's record of previous claims may legitimately be taken into consideration in determining whether incapacity has been proved. But caution must be exercised in drawing inferences from it. The fact that a man has a long record of claimed incapacities, is *by itself* quite ambiguous. It may mean that he is a person who is prone to claim incapacity on unsubstantial grounds. But is may equally well mean that he is a person in poor health who is genuinely incapacitated from time to time. To jump to a conclusion, from a claimant's previous record *alone*, would therefore generally be to beg the very question at issue. If, of course, the record contains unambiguously suspicious features, or if it is allied to other suspicious circumstances, that may be quite a different matter. Even so, there may be a danger of over-estimating the significance of a long record of claims. If a man has a long enough

---

[2] As amended following unreported Commissioner's Decision C.S. 1/78, by the Social Security (Unemployment, Sickness and Invalidity Benefit) Amendment Regulations 1978 (S.I. 1978 No. 394). *Cf.* R6/62(SB).

record of short term claimed incapacities, it is very probable that some of the periods involved will be periods of holiday: if the incapacity is genuine, the fact that it occurs at a holiday time makes it no less so. Similarly, a long enough record of short term claimed incapacities will almost certainly mean that some at least of the references to the regional medical officer will be abortive because a "final" certificate will have been issued: but, if the short-term incapacity was genuine, the fact that it ended before the regional medical officer's examination could take place, does not make it any less so.

7. In the present case there is ample evidence that the claimant is a person whose health is not robust. The hospital report already referred to shows that in childhood he had scarlet fever and nephritis, and that later he had mitral stenosis (for which operative treatment was carried out) and a posterior infarction. He remains subject to bronchitis, with breathlessness of Grade I severity. "He thus has atrial fibrillation, residual mild mitral stenosis and an old posterior infarction." The case papers do not contain any specific medical assessment of the effects of these conditions on the claimant's probable capacity for work from time to time: but it seems to me that, where a man is known to have some definite physical weakness or disability, his record of claimed incapacities falls to be regarded in a rather different light from that of a man whose general health is believed to be robust.

8. The other feature of the present case which has caused me particular concern is that I suspect that the local tribunal were considerably influenced by the fact that in the evidence before them there was no confirmation of the truth of the claimant's explanation of his absence from home on 9th August, 1966: indeed the implication was that his explanation was false. It has now been shown, in my judgment, to have been true. I should add that, as a result of the oral hearing before me, the claimant was not convicted of falsehood in any particular. Indeed, when his evidence was capable of confirmation from other sources, it was in fact confirmed.

9. In the whole circumstances, I find no sufficient justification for rejecting the evidence of incapacity constituted by the medical certificates on which the claim is founded. Incapacity is sufficiently proved, and accordingly sickness benefit is payable for the period in question.

. . . .

Disqualification

Social Security (Unemployment, Sickness and Invalidity Benefit) Regulations 1975 (S.I. 1975 No. 564), reg. 12(1)

A person shall be disqualified for receiving sickness or invalidity benefit for such period not exceeding 6 weeks . . . if—

(*a*) he has become incapable of work through his own misconduct, except that this disqualification shall not apply where the incapacity is due to venereal disease or, in the case of a woman who is not a wife, or being a wife, is separated from her husband, to pregnancy or

(*b*) he fails without good cause to comply with a notice in writing given by or on behalf of the Secretary of State requiring him to attend for and to submit himself to medical or other examination on a date not earlier than the third day after the day on which the notice was sent and at a time and place specified in that notice; or

(*c*) he fails without good cause to attend for, or to submit himself to medical or other treatment; provided that this disqualification shall not apply to any failure to attend for or to submit to vaccination or inoculation of any kind or to a surgical operation unless the failure is a failure to attend for or to submit to a surgical operation of a minor character and is unreasonable; or

(*d*) he fails without good cause to observe any of the following rules of behaviour, namely:—

(i) to refrain from behaviour calculated to retard his recovery, and to answer any reasonable enquiries (not being enquiries relating to medical examination, treatment or advice) by the Secretary of State or his officers directed to ascertaining whether he is doing so;

(ii) not to be absent from his place of residence without leaving word where he may be found;

(iii) to do no work for which remuneration is, or would ordinarily be payable. . . .

4/53(SB)

. . . .

The claimant is a hairdresser and taxi owner and the medical evidence is that he is incapable of work by reason of bronchial asthma. . . .

The claimant admits that on occasions he drives his taxi for short runs and obtains payments of small amounts. His doctor had advised him to keep out-of-doors as much as possible and that since walking induces breathlessness he sees no harm in getting the necessary fresh air by driving his taxi occasionally. . . .

In a somewhat similar case the Commissioner in Great Britain disqualified a claimant for helping at a stall in a market without payment (C.W.S. 25/50(KL)).

In that case the claimant's doctor had advised the claimant to be out in the open air as much as possible. The Commissioner added that the doctor's advice would not justify the claimant working to an appreciable extent; that the onus is on claimant to show good cause and that it is inadvisable to depart from the plain simplicity of the regulation that a person shall not do work which is, or would ordinarily be, paid, and at the same time draw sickness benefit, unless he can clearly show good cause for doing so. In the case in question the Commissioner did not find good cause to be shown.

I agree with the views expressed by the Commissioner. This claimant has not even as good a case as the one the Commissioner was dealing with as the claimant in Great Britain was not being paid a wage whereas this claimant admits that he does receive payments on occasions. . . .

. . . .

R(S) 9/51

. . . .

2. The claimant, who is a member of the Mother Church and of the Seventh Church of Christ Scientist and has been a Christian Scientist for 38 years, appeals from a decision of a Local Tribunal upholding the decision of a local Insurance Officer that from and including the 26th July, 1950 to the 4th September, 1950 the claimant was disqualified for receiving sickness benefit on the ground that she had failed without good cause to attend for or submit herself to medical examination.

3. The district manager of the Christian Science Committees on publication for Great Britain and Ireland acting on behalf of the First Church of Christ Scientist in Boston, Massachusetts, also appeals in support of the claim.

4. The sole question in dispute is whether the claimant had good cause for refusing to attend for or submit herself to medical examination. The claimant contends that it would be inconsistent with her religious beliefs to submit to a medical examination. The burden of proving good cause rests upon the claimant. In his observations on the appeal the Insurance Officer now concerned drew attention to the definition of good cause given in Decision

C.S. 371/49 (reported) namely, "some fact which having regard to all the circumstances (including the claimant's state of health and the information which he had received and that which he might have obtained) would probably have caused a reasonable person of his age and experience to act (or fail to act) as the claimant did." A definition or other general statement in a decision of a judicial authority must always be interpreted with due regard to the fact that it was made with reference to a particular subject matter or state of facts and is not necessarily intended to apply to other states of facts, even though such an application would be warranted by the literal meaning of the statement. If they could not rely on this principle of interpretation judicial authorities would be compelled either to refrain from any general statements or to guard such statements with so elaborate an incrustation of exceptions and qualifications as to render them useless as guides in other cases.

. . . .

6. . . . . a claimant's conviction that to comply with this regulation would be contrary to the principles of his religion would be good cause for his refusing to do so, whether or not the determining authority was satisfied that the conviction was reasonable. It is relevant in such a case to inquire whether the claimant's religion requires that he should refuse to comply with the regulation and (if it appears not to do so) whether the claimant has any reasonable ground for supposing that it did, but in my opinion these two questions are only relevant as tests of the sincerity of the claimant's alleged conviction that he is bound in conscience to refuse to comply with the regulation; the value of such tests will vary in accordance with the temperament, mental power and education of the claimant. . . .

. . . .

ATTENDANCE ALLOWANCE

SOCIAL SECURITY ACT 1975, s. 35

(1) A person shall be entitled to an attendance allowance if he satisfies prescribed conditions as to residence or presence in Great Britain and either—

(*a*) he is so severely disabled physically or mentally that, by day, he requires from another person either—

> (i) frequent attention throughout the day in connec-
> tion with his bodily functions, or
> (ii) continual supervision throughout the day in order
> to avoid substantial danger to himself or others;
> or
> (b) he is so severely disabled physically or mentally that, at
> night, he requires from another person either—
>> (i) prolonged or repeated attention during the night in con-
>> nection with his bodily functions, or
>> (ii) continual supervision throughout the night in order to
>> avoid substantial danger to himself or others.

R(A) 1/73

. . . .

9. . . . . any question whether a person satisfies either of the two conditions, to which I will refer as "the medical conditions" . . . is for decision not by the insurance officer or the local tribunal with an appeal on fact as well as law to a National Insurance Commissioner . . . but by the Board, who have power to delegate any of their functions. . . . The Board or a delegate have power to review their decisions, the claimant and the Secretary of State must be notified in writing of a review decision and the reasons for it. . . . The only right of appeal to a Commissioner is, with leave, against a review decision and only on any question of law arising on such a decision. . . .

. . . .

13. In considering this it is important to remember that the Commissioner's functions are limited. An attendance allowance being a benefit under the . . . Act . . . the actual award or refusal to award the allowance is made by the statutory authorities; there is a right of appeal against such a decision on any ground to a Commissioner. But the question whether either of the medical conditions is satisfied is for decision by the Board or their delegate, whose decision is binding on the statutory authorities. And an appeal against a decision of the Board or its delegate on the medical conditions lies only against a determination on review on any question of law; there is no appeal on the facts. Parliament has entrusted the decision of the medical questions to a single central medical authority, whose delegates for the purposes of determination under section 5(6) must be medical practitioners and must act in accordance with any directions of the Board (*ibid*). Obviously one of the purposes is to secure so far as possible uniformity and fairness of treatment as between the extremely numerous claimants

throughout Great Britain. Against this background it would be most unfortunate if the Commissioner, in the guise of deciding questions of law, were in trust substituting his own layman's opinion on the facts or the medical inferences to be drawn from them. This makes it particularly important to recognize both the limits beyond which the Commissioner has no power to act and the tests to be applied in deciding whether a decision of a question is erroneous in point of law.

14. The test was stated by a Commissioner, Mr. Temple, in Decision C.A. 1/72 (to be reported as R(A) 1/72). His statement is based on the judgment of Lord Widgery C.J. in *Global Plant Ltd.* v. *Secretary of State for Social Services* [1972] 1 Q.B. 139. In that judgment reference was made to an earlier judgment of Diplock J. (as he then was) in an unreported case which in turn referred to Lord Radcliffe's statement of the matter in a tax case *Edwards (Inspector of Taxes)* v. *Bairstow* [1956] A.C. 14. Briefly stated, the five grounds listed by the Commissioner are:—

(*a*) error of law on the face of the decision;
(*b*) no evidence to support the decision;
(*c*) that the decision was one which no person acting judicially and properly instructed as to the relevant law could have given;
(*d*) that it was contrary to natural justice; and
(*e*) insufficient statement of the reasons.

15. The first question arising on the supervision condition is what is meant by "continual" and "supervision". In Decision C.A. 5/72 (not reported) another Commissioner, Mr. Neligan, drew attention to the fact that the word is "continual" and not "continuous" and that the former is wider than the latter. In Decision C.A. 8/72 (not reported) I ventured some further comments on the meaning of supervision. I thought then and still think that there is a close link between attention and supervision. If a person is liable to require attention at unpredictable intervals it may be necessary for someone to be continuously available to provide attention when it is needed. In such a case the requirement of continual supervision could properly be found. I think too that there is a danger of not starting the enquiry at an early enough point. If one starts with the fact that the disabled person is living with relatives who are looking after him, and then asks oneself to what extent he requires supervision, that is beginning at the wrong point. It might indeed be helpful to ask also whether without substantial danger the disabled person could be by himself in a house at any rate for periods long enough to make any supervision

that there was not continual. In the end there was little dispute on this point. Mr. Parke, a member of the solicitors office of the Department of Health and Social Security, accepted on behalf of the Secretary of State that James' parents were supervising him within the meaning of the condition whilst he and they were in the house, even though in different rooms, provided that they were up and about and not asleep in bed. In my judgment this last qualification is too narrow. If the situation was that one or other of the parents would have woken up if he had called to them and would have given him any attention necessary, in my judgment the Board would certainly be justified in holding that supervision was in fact being provided. Moreover the claimant was clearly supervising James when she escorted him to school, whether or not what she was doing amounted also to attention. Attention and supervision in my judgment can clearly overlap and be provided simultaneously. The question of course is whether supervision was required, not whether it was in fact provided. But the Board would probably agree that evidence that supervision (or attention) was in fact provided is strong evidence that it was required; mothers would be unlikely to exhaust themselves by providing it unnecessarily *for years.*

16. This still leaves the question whether the supervision was required "to avoid substantial danger to himself". (There is no question in this case of danger to others.) On this point paragraph 12 of Mr. Neligan's Decision C.A. 5/72 was referred to. That paragraph, however, referred to the particular mongol child concerned in that case and was not intended to apply to every case. In some cases supervision may be required for reasons other than danger but not to avoid danger. The question whether continual supervision from another person in order to avoid substantial danger is required is one to be determined in the light of the circumstances of each individual case.

17. My attention was not drawn to any Commissioner's decisions in which the meaning of the phrase "substantial danger" has been discussed. The phrase should not be too narrowly construed. Substantial danger can result not only from a fall but from exposure, neglect, and a good many other things. Mr. Parke for the Secretary of State submitted that it meant a real risk of serious harm. Mr. Janner quoted dictionary definitions and relied on one contrasting substantial with imaginary, unreal or apparent only. It is clear, however, from dictionaries, including Stroud's Judicial Dictionary, that the word has many meanings in different contexts, and it probably would not be helpful for me to suggest a paraphrase. I may, perhaps, however, quote what was said by Viscount Simon

L.C. in *Palser* v. *Grinling* [1948] A.C. 291 when considering in a Rent Act case the phrase "a substantial portion of the whole rent". His Lordship said at page 317: " 'Substantial' in this connexion is not the same as 'not unsubstantial', *i.e.*, just enough to avoid the 'de minimis' principle. One of the primary meanings of the word is equivalent to considerable, solid, or big. It is in this sense that we speak of a substantial fortune, a substantial meal, a substantial man, a substantial argument or ground of defence. Applying the word in this sense, it must be left to the discretion of the judge of fact to decide as best he can according to the circumstances in each case . . . " . . . .

R(A) 1/75

. . . .

12. The claimant relies on the view expressed by the Chief Commissioner in Decision C.A. 8/72 (unreported) paragraph 14: "If a person is liable to require attention at unpredictable intervals, it may be necessary for someone to be continually at hand that is to say in attendance so as to provide the attention when it is needed. In such a case a requirement of continual supervision could in my judgment properly be found." This view was repeated in Decision R(A) 1/73 paragraph 15. She relies on the evidence of doctors, and the factual situation since her stroke, and contends that her case falls within the following sentences from paragraph 3 of Decision C.A. 7/73 (unreported): "It may well be that a person sleeping either in the next room or the same room as the disabled person should be held, in some circumstances, to be exercising supervision over the disabled person. The question depends upon the facts of the particular case."

13. It should I think be emphasised that the above decisions do not in any way lay down that in the circumstances referring to a finding of a requirement for continual supervision must be made, or indeed that supervision is necessarily being exercised. Whether the circumstances in question constitute supervision, whether it is continual, and the separate question whether continual supervision is required and for what purpose are findings which may, not must, be made, and as paragraph 15 of Decision R(A) 1/73 makes clear the question is whether supervision is required, not whether it is provided. So even if the Board had concluded that what the claimant's husband did and was prepared to do for her at night was supervision and was continual (as she contends), the question for their decision was whether she required it for the purpose of avoiding substantial danger to herself or others. That question was for the Board alone to decide.

14. In my view the characteristic nature of "continual supervision" is an overseeing or watching over, considered with reference to its frequency or regularity of recurrence (see Decision C.A. 5/72 (not reported), paragraph 8), and if the Board, having regard to the claimant's disabilities, consider that such is required for the purposes laid down by the Act, the question whether what has been or is being done fulfills that requirement is itself not relevant. I do not see the question for the Board as being whether this or that arrangement in any particular case is supervision within the meaning of the statutory language; the question is whether the claimant in the particular case *requires* continual supervision within the meaning of the statutory language.

15. I do not find any indication in the decision of the Board that they misdirected themselves on the characteristics of "supervision" or "continual supervision". Whilst they refer to "watching over", it is plain that they did not reject consideration of supervision of a passive nature (based on the continual availability of the claimant's husband to give assistance and thereby supervision on call) being required by the claimant; appreciating, as I find they did, the characteristics of supervision, they were not bound to find that it was being exercised, or if exercised was required on occasions or at times other than when the claimant was assisted to get out of bed and visit the toilet. In this connection it may be noted that their reference to the Decision of the Chief Commissioner for Northern Ireland, appeal No. 12/72 (AA) paragraph 5, to the effect that while supervision may be of a passive nature it is not necessarily exercised by someone who is asleep within earshot, and is merely available to come to the assistance of a severely disabled person when summoned by a voice or by the ringing of a bell, was taking a view favourable to the claimant. This is because reference to the decision, as reported, shows that the Board interpolated the word "necessarily" which does not appear in the decision. Inasmuch as the finding that the claimant does not require continual supervision throughout the night to avoid substantial danger to herself or others was based on what I consider to be an accurate appreciation of the statutory language, and is supported by the evidence and primary facts as found, I am of the opinion that the Board made no error in law in reaching their conclusion. Since an appeal does not lie on any other ground, my decision must be that the appeal is disallowed.

. . . .

R. v. National Insurance Commissioner, Ex parte Secretary of State for Social Services [1974] 1 W.L.R. 1290

LORD WIDGERY C. J. . . . . in considering here what is on the face of it an ordinary English word "night" prima facie the giving of a meaning to that word is not a matter of law at all. However, though "night" is one of the commonest English words in its ordinary usage, it does have different shades of meaning and the decision of the correct shade of meaning to give to the word in a particular context requires consideration of the context, and thus becomes a matter of construction and therefore a matter of law.

We are told that dictionaries describe night as being the period between sunset and sunrise, and no doubt for many purposes that is its only true meaning. It would not be a misuse of the language however to say a particular public house closed at 10 o'clock "last night" even though by reason of the latitude and the time of the year the sun was shining at that time. The word "night" is used loosely to describe the latter part of the day. It would be entirely wrong, in my judgment, when considering section 4 of the Act to give "night" the sort of "sunset to sunrise" meaning to which I have referred. The purpose of the Act and the provision it seeks to make is not related to whether the sun is shining or not; it is related to the domestic routine of the house and the distinction between day and night in section 4 is no doubt made because the giving of attention to a sick or disabled person may be far more onerous at night, when the attendant has to get out of bed in the middle of his sleep, than it would be in the middle of the day when the house is alive and people are about and ready to respond to the call of the sufferer. That is why I think this section distinguishes service by night from service by day. Therefore one must give a meaning to the words "night" and "day" which is consistent with that background.

Like the commissioner I am not going to attempt to give any single definition of "night" for present purposes for the very good reason I do not think it can be done. The argument before us has been at one in a number of respects; both Mr. Slynn and Mr. Brown invite us to regard the night for the purpose of the section as being that period of inactivity, or that principal period of inactivity through which each household goes in the dark hours, and to measure the beginning of the night from the time at which the household, as it were, closed down for the night. I would commend to boards dealing with this difficult question in future that they should look at the matter in that way. It was fairly suggested in argument that the night begins at the time when in a hospital or an army barracks "lights out" is ordered; the night begins when everything closes down, people put the lights out and go to sleep. It has been suggested also that night for this purpose begins when a child who having run about during the day is eventually put to bed, kissed by his mother, told to go to sleep, the light is put out and the door is shut. For that child it is perfectly sensible to describe "night", as beginning when the child was settled down for the night in that way.

In future when these matters come before attendance allowance boards, I would recommend them first to instruct themselves as a matter of law in the meaning of "night" which I have given to it, namely, the coming of night according to the domestic routine of the household. When they have done that there is no more law to bother about; from then onwards it is for them to decide, using their good sense and medical knowledge what services are fairly to be described as rendered at night and what are fairly to be described as rendered by day, and if they conscientiously apply themselves to the problem and reach a conclusion which a sensible board might have reached in the circumstances, then their decision is final because it is their function and their function alone to weigh the considerations which may be urged upon them. . . . .

Melford Stevenson and Talbot J.J. concurred.
(See, now, R(A)1/78. On "bodily functions," see R(A)3/78).

Non-contributory Invalidity Pension

R(S)5/78
. . . .
2. It is convenient to deal with the appeal and matters arising under separate headings.

Statutory provisions relevant to the appeal
3. Section 36 of the Social Security Act 1975 provides:—

"(1) Subject to the provisions of this section, a person shall be entitled to a non-contributory invalidity pension for any day on which he is incapable of work, if he has been so incapable for a period of not less than 196 consecutive days ending immediately before that day.

(2) A person shall not be entitled to such a pension if he is under the age of 16 or receiving full-time education; and a woman shall not be so entitled if—
　(a) she is married and either—
　　(i) she is residing with her husband, or

(ii) . . . or
(b) . . . .
except where she is incapable of performing normal household duties".

. . . .

4. Regulation 13A of the Social Security (Non-Contributory Invalidity Pension) Regulation 1975 [S.I. 1975 No. 1058] inserted by amendment (regulation 2 of the Social Security (Non-Contributory Invalidity Pension) Amendment Regulations 1977 [S.I. 1977 No. 1312]) is as follows:—

"Circumstances in which a woman is or is not to be treated as incapable of performing normal household duties
13A.—(1) A woman shall not be treated as incapable of performing normal household duties unless she is so incapable by reason of some specific disease or bodily or mental disablement.
(2) Where as a result of such a disease or disablement a woman—

(a) is unable to perform to any substantial extent, or cannot reasonably be expected to perform to any substantial extent, normal household duties; or
(b) in the absence of substantial assistance from or supervision by another person, is unable to perform to any substantial extent, or cannot reasonably be expected to perform to any substantial extent, such duties,

she may be treated as incapable of performing such duties.
(3) Where a woman is living as a member of a household in circumstances in which, were she capable of performing normal household duties, she might ordinarily be expected to be responsible for performing such duties in that household—

(a) if in the circumstances existing in that household as they relate to the performance of normal household duties therein she would fall to be regarded as incapable of performing such duties, she may be so regarded notwithstanding that she would not be so regarded in substantially different household circumstances; and
(b) if in the circumstances existing in that household as they relate to the performance of normal household duties therein she would not fall to be regarded as incapable of performing normal household duties, she may be treated as not so incapable notwithstanding that she would be or fall to be treated as incapable of per-

forming such duties in substantially different household circumstances."

Scope of the appeal

5. There is no dispute that the claimant is incapable of work within the meaning of section 36(1) of the Social Security Act 1975. The only question for decision on the appeal is whether she establishes that she is also incapable of performing normal household duties as prescribed by the regulations.

. . . .

Normal household duties

9. "Normal household duties" is not defined either in the Act or in the regulations, but various household activities are listed in the claim form and supplemented by the medical report in connection with the grading of functions. Since households vary in their composition, facilities and environment the normal household duties of one household may well include duties which do not arise for another, although basic household duties are in large measure common to both.

10. The submission on behalf of the insurance officer was that light household duties were now the claimant's normal household duties, and because she was able to perform them to a substantial extent she failed to qualify for this benefit.

11. This approach to normal household duties, that is to say, the sphere of household duties limited by the degree of the claimant's incapacity would lead to what I think is an unacceptable conclusion. The greater the incapacity the less can be done; a claimant, whose incapacity was almost total and whose only household duty, for which she had a slight impairment of function, was for instance, dusting from a wheelchair, would fail, on the ground that she performed her normal household duty to a substantial extent. Such a result seems to me to be incongruous and wrong.

12. In my opinion the "normal household duties" for consideration for a claimant living in a private household are not those in the limited sphere of activity circumscribed by the claimant's inability to do more, but are the normal household duties appropriate to her own circumstances, all of which, if she were capable, she would be expected to do. I express no view on the position of claimants living in hotels, hostels, nursing homes and similar establishments.

13. I am fortified in this view by the terms of regulation 13A(3) providing for cases where, as here, a woman is living as a member of a household in circumstances in which, were she capable of

performing normal household duties, she might ordinarily be expected to be responsible for performing such duties in that household. The emphasis is that the incapacity test is attached to the claimant's own household, in relation to the duties therein which a capable housewife would perform.

14. In summary, in my view, regulation 13A requires a subjective test, in that it is the claimant's own incapacity for normal household duties which is to be considered, judged, however, by reference to the objective standard of the duties which a capable housewife would perform were she in the claimant's situation, in that particular household and in that environment.

Substantial extent

15. Both representatives referred me to dictionary definitions of the word "substantial". The statutory provisions do not define it. It is in my opinion an ordinary English word not used in the regulations in an unusual sense. It should therefore be given its ordinary meaning, weighty, ample, or considerable. The word has many meanings in different contexts. Guidance on the approach may perhaps be found in the speech of Viscount Simon L.C. in *Palser* v. *Grinling* [1948] A.C. 291. The phrase for consideration in that Rent Act case was "a substantial portion of the whole rent". At page 317 of the report His Lordship said "'Substantial' in this connexion is not the same as "not substantial", *i.e.*, just enough to avoid the "de minimis" principle. One of the primary meanings of the word is equivalent to considerable, solid, or bit. . . . Applying the word in this sense, it must be left to the discretion of the judge of fact to decide as best he can according to the circumstances in each case . . . " In *Cozens* v. *Brutus* H.L. [1973] A.C. 854 Lord Reid at p. 861 spoke to like effect. "It is for the tribunal which decides the case to consider, not as law but as fact, whether in the whole circumstances the words of the statute do or do not as a matter of ordinary usage of The English language cover or apply to the facts which have been proved."

. . . .

(See, now, S.I. 1978 No. 1340)

On Mobility Allowance, see Social Security Act 1975, S. 37A, Mobility Allowance Regulations 1975 (S.I. 1975 No. 1573) and R(M)1/78, R(M)2/78.

CHAPTER 4

MINOR BENEFITS

WIDOWS' BENEFITS

SECTIONS 24–26 of the Social Security Act 1975 provide for payment of widows' benefits of three types:

Widow's allowance payable at a high rate for the first 26 weeks following upon the death of the husband, regardless of age or dependants;

Widowed mother's allowance, payable from the end of the above allowance period to a widow with dependent children so long as the dependency continues.

Widow's pension, now payable where the widow is over 40, either at time of death of the husband or upon cessation of the dependency conferring title to the mother's allowance. Pension is payable on a sliding scale from age 40, being payable at the full rate at age 50 or over.

All benefits are suspended during cohabitation; remarriage disqualifies. For title to be established at all, there must originally have been a marriage and the husband must have died.

Marriage

R(G) 18/52

. . . .

19.   Having regard to the terms and objects of the . . . Act . . . it seems to us reasonably plain that "widow" . . . means a woman who was married to her husband by a marriage in the sense in which that term is used in the law of Great Britain, that is to say—"the voluntary union for life of one man and one woman to the exclusion of all others" per Lord Penzance in *Hyde* v. *Hyde and Woodmansee* L.R.1 P.D. 130 at p. 133.

. . . .

R(G) 10/53

. . . .

2. On the 31st March, 1934 the claimant went through a ceremony of marriage with D.D. D.D. was her father's brother, that is to say, her uncle.

3. By the Marriage Act, 1835 Section 2 "all marriages which shall hereafter be celebrated between persons within the prohibited degrees of consanguinity or affinity shall be absolutely null and void to all intents and purposes whatsoever."

4. The prohibited degrees may be found conveniently set out in Part I of the First Schedule to the Marriage Act, 1949.

5. A marriage of a woman with her father's brother is within those degrees.

6. The claimant's marriage was accordingly, null and void to all intents and purposes whatsoever. She is not, therefore, the widow of D.D.

7. The facts that she can produce a marriage certificate and that the police have taken no action are wholly irrelevant.

R(G) 2/73 (T)
(Note: this decision deals only with the law applicable in England and Wales.)

4. From what the claimant has written it appears that very soon after the marriage she found that it had been a disastrous mistake from her point of view. It is unnecessary to go into the distressing details. On the claimant's petition a decree nisi of nullity was pronounced on 27th September 1972 on the ground of wilful refusal to consummate the marriage, and on 9th November, 1972 that decree was made absolute. The claimant then asked for payment of her widow's pension (which as a result of the National Insurance Act 1970 would now have been at a higher rate) to be restarted. This however was refused, and the insurance officer then reviewed the original award and decided that from and including 6th April, 1971 widow's benefit was not payable because on 31st March, 1971 the claimant had remarried.

. . . .

6. The tribunal . . . referred to Commissioner's Decision R(G) 3/72 and section 5 of the Nullity of Marriage Act 1971 which provides as follows: "A decree of nullity-granted after the commencement of this Act on the ground that a marriage is voidable shall operate to annul the marriage only as respects any time after the decree has been made absolute, and the marriage shall, notwithstanding the decree, be treated as if it had existed up to that time."

They referred to the Report of the Law Commission and went on to express the following views. Section 5 had not altered the application of Decision R(G) 3/72. The Law Commission had retained nullity as a remedy for wilful refusal to consummate the marriage and rejected the alternative of dissolution. Annulment had different consequences from dissolution and the differences were preserved by the 1971 Act. The only effect of section 5 was to resolve the conflict between the civil cases decided before that Act many of which were referred to in Decision R(G) 3/72. In the present case from 31st March, 1971 to 9th November, 1972 the claimant was "a widow who had remarried" (section 28(4) proviso), but upon the decree of annulment being made absolute she reverted to the status of widow and ceased to be a remarried widow. Section 5 had not affected this. The concluding paragraph of their reasons was as follows: "In our view the effect of Section 5, and in particular the words "shall operate to annul the marriage only as respects any time after the decree has been made absolute" is that the Appellant is to be treated, with effect from 9.11.72, as if she had never contracted the marriage to [Mr. S.] that is, for the purpose of Section 28(4) National Insurance Act 1965 as a widow who has never remarried. Between 31.3.71 and 9.11.72 however she is to be treated as a "remarried widow" exactly as the Commissioner treated the widow in paragraphs 18 and 19 of Decision R(G) 3/72."

7. In our judgment this argument is not correct. The matter is dealt with in paragraph 19 of Tribunal Decision R(G) 1/73 as follows:—"If section 5 had stopped at the words "after the decree has been made absolute" it might have been argued that after the decree had been made absolute it is to be treated as having made the marriage void as from the date of the marriage. We do not say that this argument would have prevailed, since it could be said that this would not have altered the position before section 5 came into force. No one had doubted that before the 1971 Act the decree made the marriage void from the date of the marriage. The problem was how that fact affected the various situations which were the subject of the decisions of the Courts. Section 5 however does not stop at the words "after the decree has been made absolute". It continues with words which if that interpretation of the first part of the section were adopted would flatly contradict it. The words "notwithstanding the decree" show that the concluding words are dealing with the treatment of the decree after it has been made absolute. The effect is that even after the decree the marriage has to be treated as if it had existed from the date of the marriage to the date of the decree absolute." In face of this it seems to us impossible for these reasons and those given in Tribunal Decision R(G) 1/73, which should be read together with this decision, to hold that any part of the period after the remarriage was not "any period after the widow's remarriage" within the meaning of section 28(4). On this ground the insurance officer's appeal must (subject

to what follows) succeed, and we need not refer to any other matters (see paragraph 4 of Tribunal Decision R(G) 1/73).

8. The additional question arising in this appeal results from the fact that the formal documents recording the decree nisi and the decree absolute were expressed in the old forms and not the new ones. In paragraph 6 and the following paragraphs of Tribunal Decision R(G) 1/73 reference is made to the history of the enactment of section 5 on 1st July, 1971 to come into force on 1st August, 1971, to the practice direction of 19th July, 1971 altering the forms as from 1st August 1971 and the amendment of the Matrimonial Causes Rules as from 1st January, 1972. It is unnecessary to repeat those paragraphs in this decision. The decree nisi as actually recorded in this case was in the old form (see paragraph 9 of Tribunal Decision R(G) 1/73); it stated that the judge decreed that the marriage be pronounced and declared to have been and to be absolutely null and void. The decree absolute was similarly in the old form (see paragraph 11 of that decision).

9. The local tribunal did not rely on this point in their reasons, and it has not been put forward on behalf of the claimant. Nevertheless we thought it right to consider it. In our judgment it cannot avail the claimant. It is true that the direction and the amended Rules lay down the new forms in which decrees are to be recorded. Section 5 however does something different. It enacts what are to be the legal consequences of a decree of nullity on the ground of voidability after a certain date. In this case there can be no doubt that such a decree was pronounced and made absolute. It follows in our judgment that, in whatever form it may have been recorded, the legal consequences for National Insurance purposes are those stated in section 5.

10. The claimant has mentioned that on 28th February, 1973 Mr. S. died, and she naturally wishes to know whether she has any rights to widow's benefit as his widow. On this point we accept the insurance officer's submission. The decree absolute of the 9th November, 1972, some three months before Mr. S.'s death, terminated her marriage to Mr. S. and he thereupon ceased to be her husband for the purposes of section 28, and she did not upon his death become his widow. Moreover there are no regulations entitling her to be treated as such. She therefore can have no rights to widow's benefit by virtue of Mr. S.'s contributions.

. . . .

(S. 5 of the Nullity of Marriage Act 1973 was replaced by s. 16 of the Matrimonial Causes Act 1973.)

Proof of death

R(G) 1/62

. . . .

2. The claimant who was born in 1907, was married to J. T. H. (who was born in 1905) in 1925. She and her husband had four children. In 1935 J. T. H. deserted the claimant and the children. It is thought that he went off with another woman to London, and that he changed his name. J. T. H. was a railwayman. According to the records of his approved society his Health and Pensions insurance ceased on the 31st December, 1936. He has not been heard of, by the claimant or the children or (so far as is known) by any of his own relatives, since 1935. In consequence of his desertion, the claimant and her children had to receive public assistance, and accordingly inquiries to find J. T. H. were carried out by the police as well as by the claimant privately. These investigations failed to establish either J. T. H.'s whereabouts or his death.

3. The claimant now claims a widow's pension, in respect of her husband J. T. H.'s insurance. The first thing she must do, in order to succeed, is to show that she is a widow. The claimant was advised to obtain a decree of Court under the Presumption of Life Limitation (Scotland) Act, 1891; and she did so. On the 10th May, 1960 the Sheriff found that J. T. H. "has disappeared, that he has not been known to be alive after 30th September, 1935, and that he is to be presumed to have died on 30th September, 1942", The claimant asks me to accept this decree as establishing the presumed death of J. T. H., and consequently as establishing that she is a widow.

4. I regret that I cannot do this. The Act of 1891 is an Act of limited scope. Its main purpose is to enable the property of a missing person to be dealt with—*see* section 3—subject to restoration if the missing person turns up within 13 years—*see* sections 6 and 7. Section 11 specifically provides that the Act "shall not apply to any claim against the insurers under a policy of assurance upon the life of any person who has disappeared, and the person or persons claiming under such policy shall be required in any question with the insurers to prove the death of the person whose life is insured in the same manner as if this Act had not been passed". Moreover, the Act cannot be used as a means of establishing *status*. A person who has been married and whose spouse had disappeared cannot use a decree under this Act in order to establish that she is free to re-marry. In the case of *Brady* v. *Murray*, 1933 *S.L.T.* 535, Lord Moncrieff said—"The statutory

presumption of limitation of life [under the 1891 Act] avails only for the statutory purpose of regulation of property, and is without effect upon questions of status."

5. The fact that I must reject the Sheriff's decree for present purposes is not so regrettable as might at first appear: for the reason that in all probability acceptance of it would not benefit the claimant. If I were to proceed upon the Sheriff's decree, I should have to accept that the date of the presumed death of J. T. H. was the 30th September, 1942. A question as to satisfaction of the contribution conditions would then arise: and while contribution questions under the National Insurance Acts are for determination by the Minister, and not by the Commissioner, it seems apparent, *prima facie* at least, that if J. T. H. be presumed to have died on the 30th September, 1942 (his Health and Pensions insurance having ceased on the 31st December, 1936) there would be no satisfaction of the relevant contribution conditions either under the old Contributory Pensions Acts or under the present National Insurance Acts.

6. It would of course be open to the claimant to establish her status as a widow by satisfying a Court of Law at common law that J. T. H. is, or should be presumed to be dead. For the purposes of her claim to widow's pension it would be sufficient for her to satisfy the Commissioner that J. T. H. is, or should be presumed to be, dead. (This was done successfully, for example, in the case to which Decision R(G) 4/57 relates). But in considering whether death has been established, or should be presumed, the Commissioner would have to have regard to the principles of the common law: and one principle of the common law of Scotland is that a man is presumed to survive to the normal limit of human life. J. T. H. cannot possibly be said to have reached that limit, for, if alive, he would now be only 56 years of age. The presumption of survival is capable of being rebutted by evidence tending to establish death, such as, for example, evidence that the claimant was last seen setting out on a dangerous mission, or known to have been at the site of some calamity at the time the calamity occurred. There is no such evidence in the present case. On the contrary: J. T. H. was a man who had a motive for disappearing, and such evidence as there is points towards deliberate disappearance rather than death. In these circumstances I find it impossible to be satisfied that J. T. H. is dead, and that the claimant is a widow: and on that basis her claim to widow's pension must fail at the outset.

. . . .

Cohabitation

R(G) 5/68

. . . .

2. The claimant became a widow on 25th September 1967 when her husband whom she married in 1958 died. She left him some 12 months after the marriage due, she alleges, to his cruelty and obtained employment as a fashion buyer. When she left that employment she was recovering from a major operation and had nowhere to live. She was offered and accepted accommodation in his flat by Mr. D. whom she had known for about 35 years. She stayed at the flat until she was able to work again and obtained employment at Swindon. She became ill and, on leaving her employment about March 1963, returned to live in Mr. D's flat where she continued to live until 6th May, 1968.

3. The claimant said that she and Mr. D. were old friends and that they neither slept together nor were there any sexual relations between them. He was a true colleague and their relationship was more that of brother and sister than of husband and wife. Mr. D. was rarely at the flat himself as his work involved travelling and when he returned to the flat at week-ends he slept on a settee in the living room as there was only one bedroom in use. Since March 1963 she had adopted the surname and was known as Mrs. D. This was in order to allay gossip by neighbours and also to deceive the landlord of the flat so that, in the event of Mr. D's death, the claimant would be able to obtain the tenancy of the flat. She had not sought employment since taking up residence in Mr. D's flat in March 1963 and he had provided for her needs. Mr. D. paid her a weekly sum, latterly £5 a week, to cover all household expenses including her keep which she spent at her discretion. If they went household shopping together Mr. D. paid for the provisions. During this period she had no other income.

4. . . . widow's allowance and widow's pension shall not be payable, amongst other circumstances, for any period during which a widow is cohabiting with a man as his wife.[1] The local tribunal on substantially the same evidence as was before me decided by a majority that cohabitation had not been established and that benefit was payable. The chairman dissented and would have found cohabitation proved on the basis of previous decisions of the

---

[1] The Social Security Act 1975, ss. 24(2), 25(3), 26(3) now (as a result of amendments effected by Social Security (Miscellaneous Provisions) Act 1977, s. 22(2)) speak of "any period during which she and a man to whom she is not married are living together as husband and wife."

Commissioner. The insurance officer has appealed from the majority decision.

5. The local tribunal recorded a unanimous finding that there was not sufficient proof of sexual relations which would until September 1967 have constituted adultery. They found the claimant frank and accepted her account of the household arrangements and matters incidental. I find no reason to differ from those unanimous findings. The question whether or not proof of sexual relations was vital to their decision appears to have been the root of the disagreement. It was decided as long ago as Decision C.G. 214/50 (K.L.) paragraph 3, that it is the general relationship of the widow and the man that has to be looked at. Proof of sexual relations is not an essential element of cohabitation between a man and a woman. Indeed in the Courts ". . . cogent evidence is required for proof of adultery" (per Lord Pearce in *Blyth* v. *Blyth* [1966] A.C. 643 at page 673) as one result of such a finding might be to bastardize issue. An insurance officer is not in a position to decide such questions when disputed and, apart from other considerations, neither the local tribunal nor the Commissioner, who have no authority to compel the attendance of witnesses, have the necessary facilities for deciding such questions. Moreover, such a finding is not necessary but, if sexual relations are admitted, that is strong evidence of cohabitation.

6. In the variety of ways in which human beings arrange their affairs it must always be a question of fact whether or not a man and a woman are cohabiting as man and wife. There is the relationship of a man and his housekeeper in which sometimes the relationship is strictly that of employer and employee and sometimes is a euphemistic description of a man and his mistress; or the relationship may be one of companionship. A man and woman might be living together in the same household each under their own names, each earning their own living and each contributing to the general expenses. There are a variety of circumstances which must be examined in order to decide whether or not a widow is cohabiting with a man as his wife.

7. In my judgment, there is cogent evidence that a man and a woman are cohabiting together as man and wife when they are not only using the same accommodation but the woman has assumed the surname of the man, as in the present case. Whatever may be the reason, whether to avoid gossip or to acquire the benefit of accommodation in the event of death, in such circumstances the inference is unavoidable, in the absence of compelling evidence to the contrary, that the woman wishes to pass herself off as the wife of the man with whom she is living. Household and

financial arrangements are personal matters not easy to ascertain but the use of names which implies that a man and a woman are husband and wife is compelling evidence that they are cohabiting as such.

8. In the present case it is not disputed that during the relevant period Mr. D. was providing the claimant with her keep and accommodation and that she had no other resources. Whatever the reasons may have been for such an arrangement, in my judgment it is clear beyond argument that during the period relevant to this appeal the relationship between the claimant and Mr. D. constituted cohabitation by the claimant with a man as his wife within the meaning of the statutory provisions.

. . . .

MATERNITY BENEFITS

Maternity benefits (Social Security Act 1975, ss. 21, 22) are of two types:
   1. Maternity grant, a lump sum payment payable on either wife's or husband's contributions;
   2. Maternity allowance, payable weekly on the wife's own contributions (if any).

R(G) 1/67

. . . .

2. On 15th December, 1965 the claimant was pregnant, and a doctor signed a certificate on form Mat. B.1 that she might expect to be confined in the contribution week which would include 28th February, 1966. The claimant was at that time married to her first husband.

Monday 27th December, 1965 was the first day on which she had reached a stage in her pregnancy which was not more than nine weeks before that contribution week.

On 20th January, 1966 a decree of divorce dissolving her marriage was made absolute. She thereby ceased to have a husband.

On 21st January, 1966 she first claimed a maternity grant by submitting by post a claim on form B.M.4, with which she enclosed the certificate on form Mat. B.1 (I am satisfied that this is correct, though the claimant's evidence at first suggested otherwise.)

On 19th February, 1966 the claimant was confined.

Monday 28th February to Sunday 6th March, 1966 was the week expected at the date of the certificate to be the week of confinement. On 24th March, 1966, the claimant remarried.

3. The claimant admits that she is not entitled to the grant by virtue of any contributions of her own. The insurance officer admits that each husband, by any date which I might hold to be the material date, satisfied the contribution conditions . . . But the insurance officer submits that, since the claimant had no husband from 20th January to 23rd March, 1966, which period included the dates of the claim, the confinement and the expected week of confinement, the claimant is not entitled to the grant by virtue of the contributions of either of her husbands.

. . . .

10. In Decision R(G) 1/52 . . . the Commissioner held, on a claim by virtue of the fact of confinement, that "husband" . . . did not include a man who at the date of the confinement was not yet married to the claimant. In that case the order of events was confinement—marriage—claim. . . . As the date of the claim was not and indeed could not have been earlier than the date of the confinement the question did not arise whether the man must also have been the claimant's husband at the date of the claim.

11. In Decision R(G) 1/65 the Commissioner was dealing with a claim based on expectation of confinement. There the order of events was: claim (made within 9 weeks of the expected week of confinement)—decree absolute—expected week of confinement. In that case therefore there was a period between the dates of the claim and the decree absolute when three circumstances coexisted: the claimant had a husband who satisfied the contribution conditions, her confinement was expected to occur within 9 weeks and she had made a claim. The Commissioner allowed her appeal and awarded the grant, observing that once her title to maternity grant had accrued she could not lose it by her decree nisi subsequently being made absolute, in the absence of any express enactment to that effect. The Commissioner commented (in relation to the type of case before him) that there was no requirement that at "the relevant time" the "relevant person" should still be the claimant's husband.

12. The insurance officer admits that if the present claimant had made her claim one day earlier it would have succeeded. She submits that having been made one day after the date of the decree absolute it fails on the grounds that, to succeed, the claimant must have had a husband at the date of the claim, that the claimant had not, and that therefore Decision R(G) 1/65 is distinguishable. . . .

13. In her claim made on 21st January, 1966 the claimant made it clear that she wished the substituted condition to apply, and it may help to clarify matters if I write out section 23(1) (so far as material) substituting that condition. The sub-section would read:

"Subject to the provisions of this Act, a woman shall be entitled to a maternity grant . . . if she is pregnant and has reached a stage in her pregnancy which is not more than nine weeks before that in which it is to be expected that she will be confined and either—

(a) she or her husband satisfies the contribution conditions set out in paragraph 2(1) of Schedule 2 to this Act; . . . "[2]

14. This provision is referring to that particular stage in the claimant's pregnancy which she reached on 27th December, 1965. At that stage she fulfilled all the conditions: she was pregnant; it was to be expected that she would be confined within 9 weeks; she had a husband who fulfilled the contribution conditions. Fulfilment of these conditions in no way depends on her having a husband at "the relevant time" (cf. paragraph 6 of Decision R(G) 1/65).

15. In my judgment the insurance officer's contention that the claim must fail because at the date of the claim the claimant had no husband is erroneous. I do not think that any inference can be drawn from the insertion in regulation 3(b) of the words "on the date of the making of the claim", which modify the contribution conditions in relation to certain special cases of death and attainment of pensionable age. What does seem to me important is this. Section 48[3] makes it a condition in this case of the right to benefit that the claimant claims it in the prescribed manner. She did so. A condition that she claims it during her marriage is (in this case) more onerous. I should hesitate long before interpreting any regulation as attaching such a condition to the title to benefit. . . .

16. Taking all these considerations into account I hold that the claimant did satisfy the further condition in section 48 even though she had no husband when she claimed. I do not think that this in any way conflicts with Decision R(G) 1/65; I am merely carrying the reasoning of that decision one step further in favour of the claimant. There the claim preceded the decree absolute, so no question arose under section 48, and the Commissioner did not mention that section in the decision and did not think it necessary, when quoting regulation 3(b), to include the final phrase. The decision turned on the considerations discussed in paragraph 14 above. It follows that in my opinion the headnote to Decision R(G) 1/55 (for which of course the Commissioner is in no way responsible) is erroneous.

[2] See, now, the Social Security Act 1975, s. 21 and the substituted condition set out in the Social Security (Maternity Benefit) Regulations 1975 (S.I. 1975 No. 553), reg. 3.
[3] See, now, the Social Security Act 1975, s. 79.

17. For these reasons my decision is as stated in paragraph 1 above, and it is not necessary for me to consider whether the claimant could have succeeded by virtue of the fact of confinement in reliance on the contributions of either of her husbands. In saying this I must not be taken as even suggesting any doubt of the correctness of the conclusion reached in Decision R(G) 1/52.

. . . .

R(G) 2/68

. . . .

2. The claimant was first married on 8th September, 1961 but that marriage was terminated by divorce on 22nd January, 1966. The claimant was confined on 9th January, 1967 and gave birth to twins. On 7th February, 1967 she married R. On 8th February, 1967 the claimant claimed maternity grants in respect of her said confinement. The local insurance officer decided that maternity grants were not payable to the claimant, and, after an appeal by the claimant, a local tribunal reached a similar decision. The claimant thereafter brought the present appeal to the Commissioner.

. . . .

5. . . . . In R(G) 1/52 the claimant had been confined on 27th April, 1951 at which date she had no husband. On 5th June, 1951 she married a man with whom she had been living and then claimed maternity grant and attendance allowance. She, herself, was unable to satisfy the relevant contribution conditions, but she contended that her husband did. The Commissioner held that she was not entitled to maternity grant and attendance allowance and in paragraph 5 of his decision he stated:—

> "Having regard to the context in which the word 'husband' appears in Section 14 referred to above, I am satisfied that it does not include a man who was not the claimant's husband when she was confined, even though he became her husband at a later date. If the word 'husband' in the Section was not otherwise limited to the man who was the claimant's husband at the date of her confinement, it would have been unnecessary to have provided in Subsection (7) for the case of a husband who had died before that date."

6. The claimant in the present case cannot herself satisfy the necessary contribution conditions, and she therefore can only be entitled to maternity grants in respect of her twins if she can show that she is entitled to rely on the contributions of either her first or her second husband.

7. The legal representative of the insurance officer now concerned with the case submitted at the oral hearing before me that although the Commissioner had reached the right conclusion in R(G) 1/52, the reasoning which led the Commissioner to reach that conclusion could not be regarded as being sound. The said legal representative submitted that the presence of section 14(7) in the 1946 Act had not in itself warranted the conclusion that maternity grant was not payable unless the claimant had a husband at the date of her confinement. He further submitted in regard to the present case that he could not maintain that the presence of subsection (6) in section 23 of the 1965 Act[4] in itself meant that the claimant could not be found entitled to maternity grants because she had not a husband at the date of her confinement. I would say at this stage that I agree with these submissions. The said legal representative, however, contended that the terms of section 23, when read as a whole, made clear that the claimant in the present case could not be found entitled to maternity grants since she had not had a husband at the date of her confinement.

8. The terms of section 23 are very wide and I have found difficulty in reaching my decision regarding the question at issue in this appeal. I have, however, finally decided that the claimant is not entitled to maternity grants since she did not have a husband at the date of her confinement who satisfied the contribution conditions. I feel that in the absence of provisions to the contrary when a statutory benefit is payable on the occurrence of a certain event subject to certain conditions being satisfied, there can be said to be a presumption to the effect that the benefit is only payable if the conditions are satisfied on the date on which the event happens. There is nothing in my view in section 23 to rebut that presumption. Indeed the section in my opinion contains provisions indicating that the presumption applies in the present case. Subsection (2), for instance, provides that except where regulations otherwise provide a woman shall not be entitled to a maternity grant in respect of a confinement if *on the date of the confinement* she is outside Great Britain. This to my mind is an indication that the date of confinement should be taken to be the vital point of time for deciding entitlement to maternity grant in claims based on actual confinement. I have already stated that I agree that subsection (6) does not in itself warrant the conclusion that a woman (who does not satisfy the contribution conditions) can only get maternity grant if she has a husband at the date of confinement who satisfies the contribution conditions. Nevertheless I consider

---

[4] See, now, the Social Security Act 1975, s. 21.

that it can be said that the presence of subsection (6) is at least a pointer to the conclusion that the above-mentioned presumption should be applied in the present case. In all the circumstances I have decided, as already stated above, that the claimant is not entitled to maternity grants in respect of her twins who were born on 9th January, 1967 since she did not have a husband on that date who satisfied the contribution conditions.

. . . .

DEATH GRANT

Death grant is payable "in respect of the death of any person . . ." (Social Security Act 1975, s. 32)

R 1/68 (D.G.)

. . . .

2. The facts of this case are not in dispute; and it is common case that the claimant's wife was delivered of a still-born, premature, infant on 24th August, 1967; the expected date of confinement up to that moment having been 18th September, 1967, according to the medical practitioner's letter of 20th September, 1967. . . . in order to create an entitlement under the statute, there must first have been a person alive whose subsequent death then becomes the circumstance attracting a death grant. And, as the Great Britain Commissioner observed at paragraph 4 of Decision R(G) 3/51: "Breathing is the criterion of life and birth, and a child or foetus is said to be still-born if it never breathed". Where a child is "still-born" (which is the actual description contained in the medical certificate of 20th September, 1967), there has never been a living person in existence, and, therefore, no "death of any person", in the words of the sub-section already cited. Or, as the Great Britain Commissioner observes, in paragraph 3 of Decision R(G) 3/51:

"It is impossible to speak of the death of a person, unless that person, in this case the child, lived."

5. It follows that I am unable to allow the present appeal. But having read the letters between the claimant and the Ministry of Health and Social Services dated respectively 13th September, 1967 and 15th September, 1967, I think it is right that I should endeavour to give some help and guidance on the disputed paragraph contained in the Ministry's letter of 13th September, 1967,

that ". . . as it has been held that a still-born child has never been a person, no grant is payable in such a case."

6. It is clear that this statement is based upon the headnote to Great Britain Commissioner's Decision R(G) 3/51 (though it goes a little further than the headnote itself), and in the light of this fact I have no wish to criticise the letter of 13th September, 1967, and that is not my purpose in adding a further paragraph to the present decision. Undoubtedly, however, this whole question of the nature, significance, and correct description of a child *en ventre sa mère* is a sensitive one, the degree of sensitivity varying sometimes with the religious persuasion of the parents. I think I should say quite firmly, therefore, that in my opinion the headnote prefacing the Great Britain Commissioner's Decision R(G) 3/51 is misleading, commencing as it does "HELD that a still-born child is not a person . . .". Nowhere in his actual judgment does the learned Great Britain Commissioner say that; and, indeed, by the clearest implication he says the direct opposite when he observes "It is impossible to speak of the death of a person, unless that person, in this case the child, lived". (The underlining is mine.) What the Commissioner said was that the child never became a living person—a significantly different statement, in my view, and one beyond which there is no need to go. And diffident though I am about criticising the headnote to a Great Britain Commissioner's decision, I consider that I ought not to shrink from doing so when a point involving it is directly raised, as it is in the present case, and since that headnote is, in my view, clearly misleading on the face of the decision itself. One need perhaps only add that the Commissioner's view that the child was not a living person receives support from the general law outside national insurance matters and from the decided cases, *e.g. R.* v. *Handley,* 13 Cox 79, in which it was held that "A child is born alive when it exists as a live child, breathing and living by reason of breathing through its own lungs alone, without deriving any of its living or power of living by or through any connection with its mother." And, consequently, if the child has not attained to life in this way, its death cannot be said to have occurred.

7. Unfortunately, this statement of the law applicable under the statute cannot avail to create in the claimant an entitlement to a death grant, for reasons which will, I hope, be clear; and, accordingly, I must dismiss his appeal."

. . . .

GUARDIAN'S ALLOWANCE

Guardian's allowance is payable to a person in respect of a child of his family where child benefit is payable in respect of that child and either:

1. both of the child's parents are dead; or
2. one of the child's parents is dead and the person claiming the allowance shows that he was at the date of the death unaware of, and has failed after all reasonable efforts to discover, the whereabouts of the other parent; or
3. one of the child's parents is dead and the other is in prison.

(Social Security Act 1975, s. 38(2).)

R 2/61 (P)

. . . .

3. In February, 1960, the claimant applied for a guardian's allowance in respect of her niece, M.G., who was born on 26th November, 1947. The child's mother, Mrs. M.G., died on 18th November, 1959, and the claimant stated that the whereabouts of the child's father have not been known since 1953.

. . . .

5. On the 3rd May, 1960, the claimant was interviewed by an Officer of the Ministry to whom she stated that she met the child's father once about six years ago and since then she has been completely ignorant of his whereabouts. She also stated that some time within the last six years the child's mother received a letter from her husband in which he said he was thinking of going to Canada. Claimant did not know the address from which this letter was written except that it "was somewhere in England". The mother replied to the letter but the reply was returned marked undelivered.

6. The claimant was interviewed again on 19th May, 1960, to ascertain if she had made any enquiries about the father's whereabouts after the mother's death. She was able to add very little to what she had already stated. She was unable to give any information about any relatives the father might have had. She understood that his parents were dead and that he had been brought up in —, by a grandmother or an aunt. She knew of no relatives of the father who could assist her in tracing him. In effect she had never tried to trace him and she said she would not know how or where to start making enquiries.

. . . .

14. The intermediate question before me is, therefore, whether in the circumstances of the present case the claimant can be said to have made all reasonable efforts to discover the whereabouts

of the other parent, in this case the father. Her own answer on this aspect of the case was that she would not know how or where to start making inquiries, and had never tried to trace the father. And in appealing to the Local Tribunal against the Insurance Officer's decision she commented that "There did not appear to be any reasonable inquiries I could make". Even on the most liberal view, can the position so described be said in any true sense to meet the requirements of the regulations to which I have referred? I do not think it can. In giving judicial interpretation to a regulation of this nature I am very conscious that it is important so to construe it that practical, and not an artificial, effect may be given to it. Clearly, for example, it would be undesirable—and I have no doubt it would also be contrary to the intention of Parliament—that a claimant who had made purely formal gestures towards ascertaining the other parent's whereabouts—perhaps knowing that they had no chance at all of succeeding—coupled with a declaration that all possible efforts had been made, should qualify: whilst another claimant, perhaps doing his or her best to find the vanished parent but less skilled at instituting inquiries or describing any efforts made, should fail to qualify.

15. In my opinion there are three separate considerations . . . which it becomes the duty of the Statutory Authorities to examine in each case, viz.:

(i) The person claiming the allowance must show that he was at the date of the death of the deceased parent unaware of the whereabouts of the surviving parent.

(ii) There must be "efforts to discover" those whereabouts which are, or would have been, "reasonable" in the opinion of the Statutory Authorities: *i.e.*, there must, in the circumstances of the particular case, be avenues of inquiry open to the particular claimant and which it would have been reasonable to expect him or her to have pursued with the knowledge and facilities available to him, the rest under the amended regulation clearly being a subjective one. Anything more than this it would, in my view, be unreasonable to expect a claimant to do. Anything less would not satisfy the requirements of the regulation—*i.e.*, to put the paragraph negatively, no reasonable effort to discover the surviving parent's whereabouts must be neglected by a claimant.

(iii) The onus lies upon the person claiming the allowance to show that he has made such efforts to the best of his particular ability.

16. The Insurance Officer in his written submission requests guidance on two further points, viz., (a) "whether a person has made all reasonable efforts. If she had made no effort, but pleads with some justification that there did not appear to be any efforts she could reasonably take;" and (b) whether efforts made within the lifetime of the parent now deceased could be regarded as sufficient, provided they were shown to have been made. As to the first query, I think it is best answered by stating that there could, in my view, and exceptionally, be a case in which the Statutory Authorities might consider that by reason of quite unusual circumstances such as the length of time involved or the search previously made for a missing person, to require further "efforts" would be a mere artificiality, and to expect them would be unreasonable. Such a case would be very exceptional and one would normally anticipate that such circumstances would in practice lead to very slight efforts being acceptable rather than to acceptance of the fact that nothing whatever had been done to seek to trace the missing person.

17. As to the second query, though indeed in practice such efforts would be made more usually after the death of the deceased parent, there is, in my opinion, no necessity that this should be so in order that they be taken into account. With efflux of time the value of past efforts made may in some cases—and by no means in all—diminish, since there may be some up-to-date further steps to seek to trace the missing person which could be regarded as reasonable. But, subject only to this comment, the efforts required by the regulation might have been made just as readily before as after the death of the deceased parent.

18. I agree, furthermore, with the Insurance Officer's suggestion that the efforts can and should properly be taken into account as soon as made. The regulations are concerned not with the possible ultimate results of those effects but with the subjective test of whether the claimant has made them and they have been unsuccessful.

19. I also agree with the Insurance Officer's further suggestion that, though the reappearance of a missing parent in such circumstances may not always be in the best interests of a child, that is not a factor which the Statutory Authorities can take into account in administering the regulations any more than the factors adverted to in the Great Britain Commissioner's Decision R(G) 4/59. It is, indeed, only one of a number of relevant factors and is clearly a matter of policy for Parliament and somewhat outside the scope of the statutory judical authorities.

20. Having set out my general views on this regulation in some detail at the request of the Insurance Officer. I turn now to the circumstances of the instant case. I have given careful consideration to the facts but I am quite unable to hold that "all reasonable efforts" have been made by the claimant to trace the whereabouts of the father. The latter disappeared in 1953, and the present claimant—his sister-in-law—met him once, about six years ago, in N. And apart from a reference to one letter, received by the child's mother some time within the last six years and stating that he was thinking of going to Canada, there has been no further contact and, apparently, no further inquiries. I have endeavoured to approach the claimant's position most sympathetically, but even assuming that there are no local relations of the child's father—as to which there have been no real inquiries at all—there are obviously many and various lines of inquiry reasonably open to the claimant, through the Police, the Passport Office and Canada House, to mention only the first that occur to one. Nor am I able to draw the inference suggested by the Local Tribunal that to ascertain such facts as are known the claimant must have made considerable efforts at various times. I agree with the Insurance Officer's submissions on this aspect of the case at paragraph 16 I am unable to avoid the conclusion that—as indeed she frankly concedes—the claimant made no such efforts. In my view a number of sources of inquiry were readily open to her, and without pursuing at least some of these she cannot be said to have made "all reasonable efforts" to discover the father's whereabouts. Sympathetic as I am to the claimant, to hold otherwise would in my view, merely render the regulations ineffectual, and be clearly contrary to their provisions.

. . . .

CHILD'S SPECIAL ALLOWANCE

A woman whose marriage has been terminated by divorce is entitled to child's special allowance where, *inter alia*, the husband is dead and was, before his death, contributing at the statutory rate to the cost of providing for the child in respect of which the allowance is claimed (Social Security Act 1975, s. 31).

R(G) 3/60

. . . .

3. The claimant was married on the 20th December, 1939, but was subsequently divorced and the decree was made absolute on

the 29th May, 1945. A maintenance order was made in favour of her and her child. With effect from the 27th May, 1950, the order was reduced to one of £2 a week free of tax in respect of her maintenance and £1 a week free of tax in respect of her child. The evidence at that time was that her former husband was unemployed and living on his capital.

4. In 1952 she obtained employment and by mutual agreement the £2 a week which her former husband had been paying to her ceased to be paid by him, but he continued to pay regularly the £1 a week in respect of her child. He had been incapable of work from the 20th December, 1956 to the 21st June, 1957, when he retired, and thereafter was in receipt of a retirement pension until his death on the 28th September, 1958. He also received 33s. 6d. a week from the 15th February, 1957 until his death from the National Assistance Board on the ground of his personal need. No allowance was made to him to assist him to continue payment of maintenance for the child under the Court Order.

5. The claimant has stated, after communicating with the Inland Revenue office, that during the income tax year 1956/1957, £30 was paid to her in respect of her child, but that during the following income tax year no payment was made owing to her former husband's total incapacity for work through illness. The claimant has agreed that thereafter no payments were made to her by her former husband in respect of her child.

6. In the result, therefore, it is clear that from some date before April 1957 until his death on the 28th September 1958 the claimant's former husband had paid nothing to her in respect of the maintenance of her child.

7. In order to qualify for a child's special allowance, the claimant has to prove (among other things) that her husband "had before his death been contributing" at not less than the prescribed weekly rate to the cost of providing for her child.

8. It was decided in Decision R(G) 5/59 that the expression "had before his death been contributing" meant in the context "had immediately before his death been contributing", subject to this qualification, that if at that particular time there had been a temporary and involuntary cessation of contributions, that break in the contributions could properly be ignored. It was explained that the design and intention of the section was clearly to compensate a divorced woman who had been deprived of financial assistance for the maintenance of a child by the death of a former husband. In such circumstances, the fact that at some time in the past before he died he had contributed to the cost of the child's maintenance, but had ceased to do so (for other than a temporary

and involuntary reason) before his death would have resulted in no loss to the claimant by reason of his death.

9. The Commissioner has also decided that, in determining the question whether a cessation of contributions has been temporary and involuntary, the period of a terminal illness may be disregarded. In speaking of a terminal illness, the Commissioner was referring to a short period in hospital immediately before death, where within a short time after admission it was clear that the husband in question was a dying man. (*See* Decision R(G) 15/59.)

10. On the facts of the present case set out above, though I would agree that the cessation of contributions by the claimant's former husband was involuntary, I do not think it possible to hold that it was temporary. Her husband had been certified to be incapable of work for six months before his retirement in June 1957 and thereafter until his death he had to receive assistance from the National Assistance Board for his own needs. There was no prospect of his being able to resume the payment of any contribution towards the maintenance of his child. Further, the period of incapacity which had started in December 1956 cannot be regarded as a terminal illness in the sense in which that phrase is used in Decision R(G) 15/59 referred to above. That expression related to a period when a person was dying, not to a long period of incapacity which ultimately terminated in death.

11. In the result, I cannot hold that the claimant has been able to prove that her late husband had before his death been contributing to the maintenance of his child, as that expression has been interpreted.

. . . .

CHAPTER 5

RETIREMENT PENSIONS

SECTIONS 27–30 of the Social Security Act 1975 set out conditions of entitlement to different categories of retirement pension. Although conditions of entitlement to each category differ, attainment of pensionable age, retirement (or deemed retirement), and notice are common to all. Notwithstanding the attainment of pensionable age, pension is not payable if retirement is deferred, in which event a higher pension will become payable later. For important incidents of entitlement, see Social Security Pensions Act 1975.

Proof of Age

R(P) 1/75
1. This is an appeal by the claimant from the decision of a local tribunal who decided that he had not attained pensionable age. He contends and his solicitors submit that the evidence establishes that he was born on 6th August, 1906. This case is a further example of the difficulties confronting the statutory authorities where the claimant, a Pakistan subject of poor instruction who signs by mark, is called upon to prove his age, when the fact is that his origins lie in a rural village in the District of Mirpur, Azaz, Kashmir, where at the time of his birth (if it be as late as 1926 as various documents no doubt based on his passports suggest) registration of birth was not compulsory until the reforms initiated by the Basic Democracies Order 1959 were put into effect in 1960.
2. The documentary evidence is contradictory and in general far from satisfactory. The claimant's case is that he arrived in England in 1959 and was absent in Pakistan from 20th January, 1968 to 10th January, 1970, since when he has lived in England. This absence is shown by a Passport No. 317104 issued on 29th September, 1961, but the records of the Department of Health and Social Security have no earlier reference to the claimant than a recorded arrival in England from Pakistan on 14th March, 1961, his then passport being AB 010316 giving his date of birth as 25th April, 1926. Since that date he has held the passport 317104 (renewed) and Passport No. AC 964545 issued on 24th February, 1972 at Bradford which records his date of birth as 5th August,

1926 as did passport 317104. When he applied in 1970 for a national insurance card, and on the occasion of a claim for sickness benefit in February 1973, his date of birth was given as 5th August, 1926, and that date again appears on an application for a Certificate of Exemption on the ground of small income made on 23rd October, 1970.

3. In support of his contention that he was in England prior to 14th March, 1961 the claimant relies upon a Form A16 said to have been issued to him for an interview on "Monday, 6th Apr 1960", and sent by the Department's local office at Bolton Road, Bradford to the claimant at Bradford. The 6th April, 1960 was a Wednesday: the form is unsigned, although it bears the appropriate stamped address of the local office. It was printed on "12/68". I have no further evidence about it, but having regard to the above it is clear that, if the claimant's assertion that he received it in April 1960 was a material factor in the consideration of the date of his birth, considerable further investigation would be necessary.

4. There is no satisfactory explanation of how the claimant's original "passport age" was given as 25th April, 1926 making him 20 years younger than he now asserts. The passport was obtained through a travelling agent to whom a village friend gave the details. The claimant has stated that he did not see the details, neither did his friend ask his age, but I think the transaction conforms to a well known practice, it being appreciated that work is more likely to be obtained by the young immigrant from Pakistan rather than by the old.

5. The claimant has produced a printed form of certificate completed on 1st November, 1971 by the District Medical Officer, Mirpur. He obtained it on the expiry of his current passport, having been told by a friend that his age was "wrong". It certifies "as per record of the office Affidavit the date of birth" that the claimant, son of Ali Haider of the village Marchola was born on 5th August, 1906. When the record of the office is, by whom and when it was made and any other relevant particulars are not vouchsafed. The certificate was sent to the claimant by his father.

6. Further to support the appeal a second certificate of 20th August 1974 on a similar form was obtained, completed by the District Medical Officer, Mirpur. It certifies (with some attention to the deletion of printed words not material) "as per affidavit the date of birth" that the claimant was born on 5th August, 1906. Not unnaturally the insurance officer now concerned commented that the source of the Affidavit was not given, that it was not produced and was sworn on a date unknown. The claimant's solicitors contend that the certificate is of the highest value being

based on an affidavit by the claimant's father, but the fact is that the certificate is based on hearsay, on the content of an unknown document, and evidence not produced is not evidence. In this connection it may be pertinent to observe that on 18th December, 1973 the claimant's solicitors asked for a speedy hearing of the claimant's appeal to the local tribunal on the ground that the claimant's father was seriously ill. The local tribunal sat on 15th January, 1974 and the claimant (through an interpreter) gave evidence. He said that his father was then dead. On 23rd October, 1974 the claimant's solicitors, who had enquired as to the source of the affidavit, the deponent then being unknown, wrote "We wrote to our client, through his interpreter, and are informed that Mr. Ali Haider lives in the same village, he being [the claimant's] father. He naturally can give first class details of his own son, . . ."

7. The above circumstances do not enable me to rely to any degree on the documentary evidence produced by the claimant to establish that he was born in 1906.

8. Nevertheless, documentary evidence of the registration of a birth is not the only method of proof available to establish how old a claimant is, and medical evidence may be resorted to. Plainly the weight to be attached by any medical opinion will vary according to the nature of any physical examination, the degree to which the accepted signs of age are explored, and the certainty or lack of certainty expressed by the medical opinion.

9. I therefore turn to a consideration of the medical evidence in this case. On 13th March, 1974 the claimant, in connection with sickness benefit was examined by a medical officer of the Department. He doubted whether the claimant was then only 47 years of age (born in 1926) and said "He seems a very old man to me". At the local tribunal hearing the claimant relied upon the evidence of Dr. Ellis. It is evident from what he is recorded as saying that at his examination of the claimant he had given the most careful consideration to all the indices of age. He stated that the claimant had the appearance of early senility, with bowing of the spine due to ageing and osteoarthritis in nearly every joint. He found atrophy of the genital organs, muscles and skin, showing senile changes. He found arteriosclerosis, blood pressure and a comprehensive picture of great age. The ribs he found to be almost completely fixed, the eyes and nervous system to be poor. There was loss of all teeth. His conclusion was that the evidence pointed to an excess of 70 years, and he believed the claimant to be over 65 years of age.

10. It must I think be borne in mind that cases which are true are sometimes accompanied by items of evidence, unsatisfactory

and unworthy of credence, introduced from a desire to improve a case, or in the case of an illiterate immigrant claimant (who may have something to hide) from fear or anxiety or merely from a desire to please authority. It may be accepted, as the local tribunal found, that there were omissions and inconsistencies in the claimant's statements, but whatever he may have said or done and whatever agents abroad in his behalf did on the matter of his passport, it cannot be said that any of these matters impinge in any degree on what the doctors found on their examination of the claimant. Their examinations were impersonal and factual, and the physical signs of old age present on examination can hardly be thought to be influenced or affected by the character of the person examined or by passport photographs, which are notoriously unreliable as true likenesses of the sitter.

11. I reject the documentary evidence from Pakistan. I accept the conclusions of the medical evidence, and my decision is that the claimant has established he is of pensionable age and was born in 1906.

. . . .

Retirement in General

141/49(P)

. . . .

4. The provisions . . . of the Act have been the subject of a number of decisions by me and by the Umpire in Great Britain. I agree with the views expressed by the Umpire in Great Britain and I therefore enunciate the following definitions and principles, with necessary comments thereon, for future guidance.

5. *"Retirement"*.—"Retirement" is used in relation to a person who has reached an age (65 for men and 60 for women) when he or she may be contemplating retiring from work, so that Section 19[1] has reference to a retirement which is induced or affected by the attainment of that age [UP. 10/47]. Retirement before pensionable age, though it is not retirement within the meaning of Section 19 may have a bearing on subsequent events and may have to be taken into account. [UP. 10/47, UP. 74/47].

6. "Retirement" does not mean retirement from the gainful occupation in which the claimant is at present engaged because the purpose of Section 19(2)(*b*) of the Act is to determine whether the claimant can be treated as having retired from regular employ-

[1] See, now, the Social Security Act 1975, s. 27.

ment whilst continuing in that occupation. In my view the word
"retirement" has reference to some occupation in which the claimant was previously engaged, either as his or her main means of
livelihood or in such circumstances that it can be regarded as
having been his or her usual or normal occupation. [UP. 10/47].

7. *"Retired"*.—The ordinary meaning of the word "retired" in
the sense that it is used in Section 19 implies the giving up of a
business, profession, calling or means of livelihood. It therefore
means much more than temporary suspension from employment
and implies a retirement which is final and permanent. So that if
the correct decision is that the claimant may be treated as having
retired from regular employment, his status as a retired person is
thereby established and it cannot be affected by anything that he
may do subsequently. [UP. 84/47]. The only events which can
affect a decision that a claimant has retired are that the decision
is reversed on appeal or is revised on account of disclosure of fresh
evidence *which was in existence at the date of the original decision*
and which shows that the original decision was wrong.

8. The onus of proving that he has retired within the meaning
of Section 19 of the Act rests on the claimant.

9. *"Treated as retired from regular employment"*.—The foundation of every claim to retirement pension is the claimant's allegation that he has retired from regular employment or, as it is
sometimes expressed, that he has retired from work. If he gives
satisfactory evidence that he has actually retired and has no gainful
occupation and does not intend to engage in such, no further
question arises. If, on the other hand, the claimant is engaged or
intends to engage in a gainful occupation that *prima facie* negatives
the alleged retirement. [UP. 68/47].

10. *"Intends to engage"*.—In deciding whether a claimant can
be treated as retired, it is necessary to take into account not only
what he is actually doing but also his intentions for the future. If
he states that he intends to engage in any gainful occupation, his
title to retirement pensions would have to be determined in the
same way as if he were actually engaged in that occupation. If, on
this basis, he cannot be treated as having retired, the position is
not affected by the fact that he has not recently had any work and
has no immediate prospects of any.

11. *"Gainful occupation"*.—The expression "gainful occupation" is not defined in the National Insurance Act or in the regulations, but in its ordinary meaning it is an occupation in which
a person is engaged with the desire, hope and intention of obtaining
for himself, directly and personally, remuneration or profit in
return for his services and efforts [UP. 56/47].

12. *"Only occasionally or to an inconsiderable extent".*—The occupation of working a croft, like the occupation of working a farm or carrying on any other business from day to day is a continuous occupation and, therefore, it cannot be said that the claimant is engaged in it "only occasionally" or only "to an inconsiderable extent" (as to which see UP. 4/47). It has then to be considered whether the claimant is engaged in the occupation "in circumstances not inconsistent with retirement" [UP. 131/47]. Any such occupation is not limited to the amount of active work which the claimant performs nor can its extent be measured by the amount of profit which it yields [UP. 161/47].

13. It follows from the principles set out in the preceding paragraph that a claimant who is engaged in a gainful occupation as a self employed person cannot under any circumstances be treated as being engaged therein "only occasionally" or only "to an inconsiderable extent". It also follows from the terms of Section 19(2)(*b*) of the Act and the definition of the expression "gainful occupation", that the amount of profit derived from the occupation is not material.

14. *"Otherwise in circumstances not inconsistent with treatment".*—In view of the foregoing definitions it will be clear that a farmer or other self-employed person cannot be regarded as being engaged in a gainful occupation "only occasionally" or only "to an inconsiderable extent". He is in fact, engaged in a continuous occupation, notwithstanding that he may do little manual work, or that his actual duties are confined to supervision, management, etc. It will, therefore, be necessary to ascertain whether there has been any alteration in the conditions of the occupation occasioned by his having attained pensionable age, and to determine whether, in the light of any such alterations, he is engaged in the occupation "in circumstances not inconsistent with retirement".

15. When a claimant bases his alleged retirement on the fact that he has changed his occupation, or on the fact that he has altered the conditions of the occupation in which he is engaged, he can rarely, if ever, prove retirement unless he can show the existence of specific circumstances which have caused him to make that change or alteration, and the Statutory Authority is satisfied that the specific circumstances justify a finding of retirement. A desire on the part of the claimant to earn something in addition to a retirement pension is not a specific circumstance. [UP. 68/47]. This decision was given in the case of a weaver who reduced her working hours in order to qualify for a pension.

16. The following decisions have been given on the question whether farmers, poultry keepers, etc., could be treated as retired

from regular employment on the ground that they were engaged in a gainful occupation "in circumstances not inconsistent with retirement".

> "If he has not actually retired in the full meaning of the term, I cannot say that he could properly be held to be engaged in farming 'only occasionally' or 'to an inconsiderable extent', because what work he may do on the farm must be said to be done throughout the year, and there is no evidence to show that if it is done by him at all it is done 'to an inconsiderable extent'.

> I have to ask myself, does the evidence support the view that the claimant is engaged in his gainful occupation 'in circumstances not inconsistent with retirement'?

> On a farm of this size which the claimant owns, however, there are many activities in which he can be engaged which are not beyond his powers, and there is no evidence that the extent of the holding has been materially reduced since he reached pensionable age.

> The burden of proving that he has retired within the meaning of Section 19(2) is upon the claimant and, in the circumstances, I cannot say that he may be treated as having retired from regular employment". [UP. 39/48].

> "I am of the opinion that the claimant is unfit for heavy farm work, but I am of the opinion that he is still capable of performing the lighter work on the farm and there is no reason for supposing that he is unable to, and does not, manage the farm". [U.D. No. 25/49(P) (unreported)].

> "The claimant admits that there is no change (except that he is not now as fit as he was) in the running of the farm since he became the owner in 1937. The stock and crop are substantially the same now as heretofore, and there appears to be no alteration in the conditions of his employment occasioned by his having attained the age of 65 years". [U.D. No. 77/49(P) (unreported)].

17. Giving due weight to the above-mentioned decisions I now set out the circumstances any of which may militate against the granting of a retirement pension to a person alleged to be engaged in the occupation of farming:—

(1) That although, due to physical or mental infirmity, he is unable to perform the same amount of work as formerly he still retains the ownership of his farm, stock and farming implements and continues to reside on the farm.

(2) That he supervises, manages, or takes anything to do with the farm, or gives any advice as to the running of it.

(2) That the banking account in connection with the farm is in his name.

(4) That he attends markets or fairs to buy or sell stock.

(5) That the milk licence, and subsidies payable by the Ministry of Agriculture are in his name.

(6) That he recruits labour or takes anything to do with the running of the farm.

. . . .

Deemed Retirement

Social Security Act 1975, s. 27(3)

. . . a person may . . . be treated as having retired from regular employment at any time after he has attained pensionable age—

. . . .

    (*b*) notwithstanding that he is, or intends to be, an earner, if—

        (i) he is or intends to be only occasionally or to an inconsiderable extent, or otherwise in circumstances not inconsistent with retirement, or

        (ii) his earnings can be expected not to exceed, or only occasionally to exceed [the earnings rule limit][2] . . .

(See 141/49(P) above).

R(P) 8/51

. . . .

2. The claimant attained the age of 65 years on the 2nd February, 1950. He was gainfully occupied as a tailor for 30 or 40 hours a week, doing odd jobs, but for a single employer. About the end of June, 1951, the employer went into hospital and the claimant's work for him ceased.

3. The claimant, therefore, on the 9th July, 1951, posted what purported to be a notice of retirement on the appropriate form B.R.55 (Rev.). On this form he stated that he had retired from regular employment on the 30th June, 1951, and that he had not at present any gainful occupation. In answer to question (iv) "Do you intend to have any gainful occupation in future?" he stated "Hope to". He did not answer the specific questions as to what

[2] See the Social Security Act 1975, s. 30.

the future occupation would be or how many hours or what earnings he expected it would involve.

4. The form was returned to him for the proper completion of question (iv), which has to be answered Yes or No, and of the subsidiary questions. He then replied "Yes" to question (iv), and stated that his intended occupation was that of a tailor and that he expected to work 15 hours a week and to earn £1 15s. a week.

. . . .

11. It is the intention of the claimant at the moment when he proposes to retire which counts. Assuming that that intention does not satisfy Section[27], then (provided the intention was a reasonably possible one) the mere fact that he is unfortunate enough not to achieve his intention cannot alter the nature of his intention retrospectively. He cannot be treated as having retired until his intention complies. . . .

. . . .

13. The work which the present claimant intended to do could not be described as occasional; for it was his intention to keep on doing it if he could. Nor could it be said that he intended to engage in it only to an inconsiderable extent; to establish this he must show that he intended to engage in it for not more than 12 hours a week or for not more than one quarter of the normal hours of his previous full working week in that occupation whichever is the greater. Further, I do not think it can be said that he intended to engage in the occupation "in circumstances otherwise not inconsistent with retirement", in view of the number of hours which he proposed to work.

14. The question which has caused me some difficulty is whether it can properly be said that the claimant's figures of hours and earnings really represented his intention, or whether they were merely a vague hope which had little prospect of being achieved; see Commissioner's Decision C.P. 120/49 (not reported). I have come to the conclusion that it is not possible to regard these figures merely as a vague hope . . .

. . . .

R(P) 8/54 (T)

. . . .

2. The claimant attained the age of 60 on the 15th September, 1953 and subsequently gave notice of retirement stating that she intended to retire from regular employment on the 12th October, 1953, but to continue in her occupation in the school meals service, working 12½ hours a week. That was the occupation at which she had been working since January, 1943. In her early years she had

worked in domestic service but on her marriage in 1916 she had given up work and had not taken up work again until January, 1943.

. . . .

7. The claimant cannot show that she is engaged in her occupation of school meals attendant "only occasionally" for she works regularly 12½ hours a week, apart from periods of holiday, nor can she show that she is engaged in that occupation "to an inconsiderable extent" because, as was held in Decision C.P. 33/49 (reported), 12½ hours a week is too long a period.

8. It remains to consider, therefore, whether the claimant is engaged in her occupation "otherwise in circumstances not inconsistent with retirement".

. . . .

13. It is clear from the use of the word "otherwise" . . . that the Legislature contemplated that the circumstances in which a person was engaged in an occupation might justify his being treated as having retired from regular employment, even though he was not engaged, or did not intend to engage in his occupation only occasionally or only to an inconsiderable extent.

14. In order to decide whether a claim falls within [(i)] it is therefore necessary to have regard to the circumstances of the occupation looked at as a whole. The number of hours worked though material is not conclusive (unless the hours are short enough to justify a finding that the occupation is engaged in only to an inconsiderable extent). Similarly the fact that the claimant's earnings have been reduced to a sum such that, if she were entitled to a retirement pension, her earnings would not cause the amount of that pension to be reduced would not in itself satisfy [(i)]. (See Decision R(P) 1/52.)[3] It is necessary to look at all the circumstances of the occupation, including the sort of work involved, and, if the work is of a kind which a retired person might reasonably be expected to do and there is no other feature in the occupation which would render it unreasonable to speak of a person engaged in it as having retired from regular employment, the occupation will satisfy [i].

15. In the present case we hold that work in the school meals service for 12½ hours a week is not inconsistent with retirement. It is the type of work which a person, who had retired from regular employment but wanted to add to some extent to her means, might well undertake and in our view there is no feature in the occupation which would render it unreasonable to speak of a person engaged

---

[3] This is no longer true: see the Social Security Act 1975, s. 27(3)(*b*)(ii).

in it as having retired from regular employment. (Compare Decision R(P) 15/52.)

16. Though this interpretation of Section [27] has not been expressly formulated in previous decisions of the Commissioner we think that it is consistent with their general trend. There are however two decisions which call for comment.

17. In the course of Decision C.P. 33/49 (reported) (referred to above), in which the questions were whether a school meals attendant working more than 12 hours a week could be said to be engaged in her occupation only to an inconsiderable extent and how the number of hours a week should be calculated, it was said "it is clear on the facts of this case that it could not be said that she was engaged in it 'in circumstances not inconsistent with retirement '". The facts in that case are indistinguishable from those in the present case but in our view the statement quoted above in inconsistent with subsequent decisions of the Commissioner and should not be followed nor should a case be approached on the basis that it is necessary for the claimant to show some specific circumstances causing a change of occupation or an alteration in the terms of an occupation. Attention should be directed to the nature of the occupation itself. Accordingly the passage quoted above from Decision C.P. 126/49 (reported) should no longer be treated as correct.

18. In the present case therefore it is unnecessary to decide whether or not the claimant could properly be said to have retired from regular employment . . . in 1916 (when she married) because it can be said of the only occupation in which she has been engaged since she attained pensionable age, or in which she intends to engage, that she has been engaged and intends to engage in it in circumstances not inconsistent with retirement.

. . . .

R(P) 1/69

. . . .

2. The question whether the amount payable to the claimant by way of a retirement pension falls to be reduced or extinguished has formerly been the subject of an appeal to the Commissioner. That question was then decided in the claimant's favour in respect of the inclusive period from 12th July 1965 to 10th April, 1966. See Decision R(P) 4/67.

3. The facts, so far as material for present purposes, as then found by the learned Commissioner were that, following his retirement from regular employment as a partner in a firm of accountants, the claimant was awarded a retirement pension under the

National Insurance Act from 9th July, 1965; that after his retirement the continuing partners were jointly and severally liable to pay him an annuity; and that on 30th June, 1966 he received a cheque for £1,000 from the firm with a covering letter which said: "We have pleasure in enclosing our cheque for £1,000 in payment for the advisory services you rendered to this firm in the year ended 31st March 1966."

4. The learned Commissioner, for the reasons given in his decision, upheld the local tribunal's decision that the sum of £1,000 paid to the claimant at the end of June 1966 did not constitute earnings derived from a gainful occupation and was therefore irrelevant to the computation of the amount payable to the claimant by way of a retirement pension under the National Insurance Act. It was, however, emphasised (see paragraph 10 of Decision R(P) 4/67) that the decision related solely to the claimant's pension rights for the period from 12th July, 1965 to 10th April, 1966 and the Commissioner added: "It is important to note that throughout that period the claimant had no hope or expectation of being paid for consultancy services. In relation to later periods . . . it may well be relevant to consider the effect of the senior partner's intimation that two more payments of £1,000 were likely to be made."

5. A further payment was in fact made to the claimant and in a letter dated 29th July, 1967 he informed the Ministry that on the previous 30th June he had again received a cheque for £1,000 with a covering letter saying that it was a payment for the advisory services he had rendered to the firm in the year ended on 31st March, 1967. The purpose of the payment, the claimant said, was the same as in the previous year, namely to augment the retirement annuity payable to him under his partnership agreement. He added: "As in the previous year, the Inland Revenue will no doubt deduct earned income relief in making an assessment on me in respect of this income." In a later letter dated 11th December, 1967 the claimant wrote that in the income tax return that he had made on 10th May, 1967 he included the sum of £1,000 in the section headed "Other Profits of Yourself or Your Wife" and that he had described it as "Fee for advisory services rendered to [the firm of accountants] in year to 31st March, 1967". He said that in a covering letter to the inspector of taxes he explained that the fee for advisory services which he received in 1966/67 was purely discretionary on the part of [the firm] and that he did not then know whether any similar payment would be made in 1967/68 but that he would notify the inspector of any amount he might receive. I assume that he did so. The claimant was awarded earned income relief in respect of

two payments of £1,000 both of which he himself described as a "Fee for advisory services".

. . . .

8. I agree that the fact that the claimant was awarded earned income relief on a sum accruing over a period after he retired would not, of itself, show that he had derived earnings from a gainful occupation for, as the learned Commissioner pointed out at paragraph 11 of Decision R(P) 4/67, such treatment merely reflects the view of an inspector of taxes on a question of law arising under the Income Tax Acts. However, the claimant himself on two occasions described the sum of £1,000 which was paid to him by his former partner as a "Fee for advisory services" and obtained earned income relief on that basis. In other words, he represented to the inspector of taxes that he had received a sum of money by way of remuneration for services rendered which is plainly inconsistent with the contention that he was not following a gainful occupation from which he derived earnings which . . . includes remuneration from a gainful occupation. The claimant thus seeks to blow hot and cold which, as the learned Commissioner said in the decision referred to above, "is something which the law does not tolerate".

9. In my judgment, on the evidence now before me, the sum of £1,000 which the claimant received on 30th June, 1967 clearly constituted earnings derived from a gainful occupation and, since, if that sum be treated as accruing from week to week, the amount payable to the claimant by way of a retirement pension would, under section 30(7) of the Act of 1965[4] be reduced to nil, no sum on account of a pension under the National Insurance Acts can be payable to him during the period with which this appeal is concerned.

10. That would be enough to dispose of the case but I should, I think, add that the claimant makes the point that under section 525(1) of the Income Tax Act 1952 "earned income" means not only any income arising in respect of any remuneration from any office or employment of profit held by the individual, but also any income arising in respect of any pension, superannuation or other allowance, deferred pay or compansation for loss of office, given in respect of the past services of the individual. "This", the claimant says, "surely illustrates the fallacy of treating the [earned income] relief as a test whether or not I am following a 'gainful occupation' for the purposes of the National Insurance Acts." In my opinion it does no such thing. The sum of £1,000 which the claimant

---

[4] See, now, the Social Security Act 1975, s. 30(1).

received at the end of June, 1967 was not, and in the circumstances of this case could not have been, income arising in respect of any pension, superannuation or other allowance given in respect of the claimant's past services, nor was it deferred pay or compensation for loss of office. All these expressions are inapt in relation to a payment made by continuing partners to a retired partner. Moreover it was expressly described both by the firm and by the claimant as a payment or fee for advisory services rendered by the latter to the former during the year ended 31st March, 1967. In terms of section 525(1) earned income relief could, therefore, only have been awarded on the basis that the sum of £1,000 was income arising from an employment of profit—that is that it was a reward for services rendered. The claimant cannot in my judgment be heard to say for the purpose of obtaining relief from tax due to the Crown that he received £1,000 as a reward for services, and thereafter, for the purpose of avoiding a reduction in the amount of his State pension, that he did not have a gainful occupation from which he derived earnings during the period under review.

. . . .

CHAPTER 6

INDUSTRIAL INJURIES

In order to qualify for industrial injuries benefits, an employed earner must either:

1. have suffered personal injury caused by accident arising out of and in the course of employed earner's employment[1]; or

2. have suffered a disease or personal injury prescribed in regulations as being due to the nature of that employment.[2]

The onus of proving prima facie entitlement normally rests upon the claimant. Sections 50(3) and 52–55 of the Social Security Act 1975, however, may relieve the claimant of this onus to some extent.

Benefit is of three types: (1) injury benefit, a short-term benefit (six months) payable at a higher rate than sickness benefit; (2) disablement benefit, payable in respect of a loss of faculty and carrying supplements in appropriate cases (such as special hardship allowance, payable where the disablement reduces the earning capacity of the claimant) and (3) death benefit, payable for dependents.

The basic conditions of entitlement have changed little since originally formulated in the Workmen's Compensation Act 1897. Decisions under the workmen's compensation legislation may, therefore, retain a contemporary relevance.

"Personal Injury"

R(1) 7/56

. . . .

2. The question raised by this appeal is whether damage caused to an artificial limb constitutes "personal injury by accident" within the meaning of Section 7 of the Act above mentioned. . . .

. . . .

4. The insurance officer decided that the claimant had not suffered personal injury. The local appeal tribunal, however, after remarking that "personal injury" is not defined in the Act above mentioned, took the view that as soon as a person acquires an

---

[1] The Social Security Act 1975, s. 50(1).

[2] *Ibid.* s. 76 and see the Social Security (Industrial Injuries) (Prescribed Diseases) Regulations 1975 (S.I. 1975 No. 1537), as amended by S.I. 1975, No. 2241, S.I. 1976 No. 1628, S.I. 1977 No. 250.

artificial limb it becomes part of his person and that if such a limb is damaged as a result of an industrial accident, which prevents work, the owner suffers personal injury; they felt that injury benefit and not sickness benefit was the appropriate benefit, and decided that the claimant had suffered personal injury by industrial accident. The insurance officer now appeals from that decision.

5. I cannot, with respect, agree with the tribunal. In my judgment, "personal injury" as used in Section 7 means injury to the living body of a human being. Damage to some artificial appendage of the body—such as spectacles, false teeth, or a wig, or an artificial limb—may well cause incapacity for work, but such damage cannot, in my view, constitute "personal injury." I am supported in my opinion by two early unreported decisions of the Commissioner, C.S.I. 13/49 and C.I. 172/49, in both of which it was held that the breaking of an artificial leg is not a personal injury.

. . . .

R(I) 19/60

. . . .

9. The medical evidence submitted for the claimant is, not that his incapacity was due to a strain pure and simple, but that it was due to coronary occlusion. The evidence of the senior medical officer . . . satisfies me that, in the circumstances of the case, the coronary occlusion was not brought about by a strain such as the claimant describes as having happened on the 24th October 1958. It is still, however, proper to consider whether on the 24th October 1958 the claimant suffered anything which may properly be described as a "personal injury caused by accident".

10. There seems no reason to doubt that the incident described by the claimant as having happened on the 24th October 1958 did in fact occur. In a sense, no doubt, it occasioned a severe strain to the claimant. (This is a point stressed by the claimant's association in their observations in support of the appeal.) But the word "strain" is—as it seems to me—a rather ambiguous word. No doubt the trained athlete who runs "all-out" in a race, or who exerts himself to the utmost in lifting a heavy weight, suffers in the process a "strain"—in the sense that his physical faculties are put to almost intolerable stress for the time being. But in such a case the strain is transient and after a short rest the athlete returns to normal. There is no lasting physiological change for the worse. A "strain" does not amount to "injury" unless there be some significant physiological change for the worse which lasts for an appreciable time. In the present case there is no evidence that the strain imposed upon the claimant when the weight of the coal

hutch came upon him brought about any physiological change for the worse for any appreciable time—unless one accepts the theory that it brought about the coronary thrombosis which occurred two days later; and that theory, for the reasons stated, I reject. Accordingly, in my judgment, the claimant fails to prove (as matter of reasonable probability) that on the occasion in question he suffered any "personal injury" in the sense of the Statute. That being so, the question whether his subsequent incapacity was the result of such injury does not arise.

. . . .

Causation

R(I) 54/52

. . . .

5. The question at issue in this appeal is whether the death of the claimant's late husband did or did not "result from" the pneumoconiosis. That question involves both a legal and a medical question and this appeal was brought by the Insurance Officer now concerned in this case primarily for the purpose of obtaining guidance on the manner in which the whole question should be approached.

6. It has to be remembered that a claimant can be said to have proved a fact, if she proves that the probability that it was so is so high that in the ordinary affairs of life we should accept that it was so. It does not matter that there is a possibility that it was not so. On the other hand, an event or a cause and effect, cannot be said to be proved if it remains a matter of mere speculation whether it was so or not. (Compare Decisions C.I. 159/50 (reported) and C.I. 401/50 (reported).)

7. The death need not be a direct or a natural or even a probable consequence of the accident if in fact it is a result of the accident. It is enough that the accident caused or contributed to or accelerated death, and the accident may be said to contribute to the death if it causes such a state of things in the man's body that he is physically more susceptible to the cause which ultimately kills him. (Compare Decision C.I. 147/50 (reported).)

8. On the other hand, it has to be remembered that a chain of causation has to be traced. "If the chain of causation is broken by a *novus actus interveniens* (a new intervening cause) so that the old cause goes and a new one is substituted for it, that is a new act which gives a fresh origin to the after-consequences". (See per Collins M. R. in *Dunham* v. *Clare* [1902] 2 K.B. 292 at p. 296.)

9. It is not enough to say that, but for the accident or prescribed disease, the deceased would not have died at the time at which and in the way in which he did die. This was illustrated in the case of *Dunnings* v. *Cavan* [1911] S.C. 579 when the Lord President said "Suppose a workman has met with an accident and has been put on a stretcher in order to be removed to hospital and then on the way to hospital he is killed by lightning, or shot by a lunatic, or is run over by an omnibus. In all these cases it would be true to say, as the Sheriff has said here, that but for the accident the man would not have died at the time at which and in the way in which he did die, because if the accident had not happened the man would have been at work, not on the stretcher. But nevertheless, in all these cases a new cause was introduced and it would be out of the question to say that death resulted from the accident".

10. It is not apt in the determination of questions of causation under the National Insurance (Industrial Injuries) Acts that too much subtlety should be introduced. If I may adapt the words used by Lord Loreburn L.C. in *Clover, Clayton & Co. Ltd.* v. *Hughes* [1910] A.C. 242 at p. 247 I should say that the Statutory Authorities ought to consider whether in substance, as far as they can judge on such a matter, the death came from the disease (cancer in the present case) alone, so that, whatever the condition of health of the claimant's late husband in other respects, death would probably have come substantially at the same time or whether the prescribed disease (pneumoconiosis in this case) from which the claimant's late husband was suffering contributed to his death. In other words, in the particular circumstances of this case, would his life probably have been prolonged by the performance of an operation if he had not suffered from pneumoconiosis? If the claimant could establish that proposition she would be proving something more than that but for the pneumoconiosis her late husband would not have died when he did, she would be proving that his pneumoconiosis affected a vital decision, namely whether or not the surgeon should operate, upon which the duration of his life depended.

11. I have thought it right to deal with the principles of law upon which this case must be determined since the matter was argued before me in some detail. But even accepting this view of the law which is a view most favourable to claimants that I can adopt and more favourable than the alternative view discussed in the course of this appeal, I do not feel able to decide this appeal in the claimant's favour. I might, relying on the surgeon's evidence, hold that, if the claimant's late husband had not been suffering from pneumoconiosis, an operation probably would have been performed, but as the claimant's representative, who was himself a

doctor, very fairly pointed out in the course of this appeal, apart from cases of death on the operating table, there would have remained two possibilities, first, that secondary deposits would have already developed, in which case the operation would have failed, and, secondly that the operation might have been in time. No one can say which of these alternatives would have resulted, but bearing in mind the nature of the cancer from which her late husband was suffering and the development of secondaries found in the post-mortem examination, when he died some five months after the operation was being considered, I feel that it would be pure speculation on my part if I held that it was more probable that the operation would have been in time to prolong the life of the claimant's late husband, than that it would not have been. I was advised by my Medical Assessor that at a hospital which specialises in diseases of the chest, the experience has been that when the chest is opened with a view to the removal of a lung in cases of cancer, in two-thirds of the cases it is found that the growth is too advanced for a chance of cure, and that of the remaining one-third operated on no more than one-quarter of those cases are alive and well five years afterwards, though he agreed that in more than one-quarter of this third, life would be prolonged for a while. It would not, no doubt, be wise to generalise from the experience of a single hospital, but, having reviewed the evidence in this case, I can find nothing to justify my holding that the life of the claimant's late husband would probably have been prolonged if he had not had pneumoconiosis. (It was not contended that the pneumoconiosis had in any way caused or accelerated the development of the cancer).

. . . .

R(I) 3/56 (T)

. . . .

8. The question whether a period of incapacity which is the immediate consequence of an event occurring at a time when a claimant is not in the course of his employment can nevertheless be held to result from an accident which admittedly arose out of and in the course of the claimant's employment is a difficult one and it was thought desirable to take the opportunity to reconsider in the light of the experience gained in the six years which have elapsed since Decision C.I. 114/49 (reported) was given whether the exposition given therein of the legal principles involved in "second accident" cases could be improved. We have received valuable assistance in this task from the representative of the insurance officer now concerned who made an exhaustive review

of the relevant decisions of the Courts under the Workmen's Compensation Acts. Having considered these decisions in the light of the submission made on behalf of the insurance officer at the oral hearing we are of opinion that the explanation given in Decision C.I. 114/49 (reported) of the principle to be applied in "second accident" cases was substantially correct and that the disallowance of the claim in the case to which that decision related was in accordance with that principle. We think however that some of the language used in the decision might lead to misapprehension of the legal position and as we have reconsidered the problem involved in the light of the decisions of the Courts under the Workmen's Compensation Acts we think it better to state our view of law relating to "second accident" cases in our own words than to suggest emendations of particular sentences in Decision C.I. 114/49. Our decision should therefore be treated as superseding the statement of the law relating to "second accidents" given in Decision C.I. 114/49 (reported).

9. In our opinion the decisions of the courts under the Workmen's Compensation Acts warrant the following propositions:

(1) Where the immediately preceding cause of the incapacity is an industrial injury (i.e., an injury by accident arising out of and in the course of the claimant's employment) the claimant will be entitled to injury benefit notwithstanding that some pre-existing weakness or disabilty resulting from a previous non-industrial accident or any other cause has been an effective cause of the injury by industrial accident. This is so because under Section 7(1) of the National Insurance (Industrial Injuries) Act 1946 the claimant is only required to prove that the injury in respect of which he claims benefit should be "caused" by industrial accident and that he should be incapable of work "as the result" of that injury. He is not required to prove that the industrial accident was the sole cause of the injury or that the incapacity was solely the result of the industrial accident. But he must prove that the industrial accident was *an* effective cause of the injury from which the incapacity for work resulted. (By "effective cause" we mean "causa causans" not a mere condition ("causa sine quâ non").)

(2) It follows from the fact that the claimant is not required to prove that his incapacity was solely caused by industrial injury that if the immediate cause of his incapacity is an injury by non-industrial accident the claimant will be entitled to injury benefit if he can prove that a previous

injury by industrial accident was *an* effective cause of the injury by non-industrial accident, which was the immediate cause of his incapacity. *Hodgson* v. *Robins, Hay, Waters and Hay,* 7 B.W.C.C. 232.

(3) If, while the claimant is still incapacitated for work as the result of a condition produced by injury by industrial accident, that condition is aggravated and the period of incapacity prolonged as the result of injury by a non-industrial accident the claimant will be entitled to injury benefit for the extended period of incapacity so long as the condition produced by the industrial injury continues to be an effective cause of the claimant's incapacity. This will be so even though the industrial accident was not an effective cause of the non-industrial accident, *Brown* v. *Kent* 6 B.W.C.C. 745; *Laverick* v. *William Gray and Co., Ltd.,* 12 B.W.C.C. 176.

10. It must be added that the question whether an injury by an industrial accident was an effective cause of a subsequent non-industrial accident or of an extended incapacity is one of fact which must be decided by the determining authority from a common sense point of view in the light of the evidence available in the particular case. The decisions of the courts under the Workmen's Compensation Acts and those of the Commissioner under the National Insurance (Industrial Injuries) Acts can therefore only be regarded as illustrating the view of the appellate tribunal as to the proper approach to the problem.

11. In the present case we are on the whole of opinion that the claim should succeed. As stated above, the evidence before us (some of which was not available to the local appeal tribunal) shows that when he set off to work on the 13th January the claimant had not really recovered from the effects of the first accident and was not fully capable of work. We think that he grabbed the railings because he was slithering on the snow and that this action caused some strain which lit up the semiquiescent pain in his back and made clear to him that he was not fit to go back to work. In our opinion, therefore, the case falls within the principle upon which such cases as *Brown* v. *Kent* supra and *Laverick* v. *Gray* supra were decided namely that the claimant's incapacity for work was demonstrated and prolonged by the incident in question and was therefore "the result of the [industrial] accident" of the 29th December, 1954.

12. The facts differ widely from those of the case which was dealt with in Decision C.I. 114/49 (reported). There the claimant had been back at work as a miner for three days and there was no

suggestion that he had experienced any difficulty in doing his full work. The second accident consisted of slipping and falling on ice and the only way in which it was suggested that the industrial accident contributed to the second accident was that the claimant was (as he said) "forced to put more pressure on one foot than on the other" which "actually contributed to the fall". Persons who are free from any disability frequently slip and fall on ice and there was no satisfactory evidence that the industrial accident was an effective cause of the fall.

. . . .

"Accident"

Fenton v. Thorley & Co. Ltd. [1903] A.C. 443

EXTRACTS FROM THE JUDGMENT OF LORD MACNAGHTEN:

The Court of Appeal held that the injury which Fenton sustained was not "injury by accident" within the meaning of the Act. In so holding they followed an ealier decision of the Court in the case of *Hensey* v. *White*[3], which in its circumstances is not distinguishable from the present case. In *Hensey* v. *White* . . . a passage was cited from the opinion of Halsbury L.C. in *Hamilton, Fraser & Co.* v. *Pandorf & Co.*[4], in which his Lordship said: "I think the idea of something fortuitous and unexpected is involved in both words 'peril' or 'accident.'" Founding themselves upon that expression, the learned judges of the Court of Appeal held in *Hensey* v. *White* . . . , as they have held here, that there was no accident, because (to quote the leading judgment) there was "an entire lack of the fortuitous element." What the man "was doing," it was said, "he was doing deliberately, and in the ordinary course of his work, and that which happened was in no sense a fortuitous event." To the expression as used by Lord Halsbury in the passage in which it occurs, no possible objection can be taken; but it is, I think, to be regretted that the word "fortuitous" should have been applied to the term "injury by accident" in the Workmen's Compensation Act. If it means exactly the same thing as "accidental," the use of the word is superfluous. If it introduces the element of haphazard (if I may use the expression), an element which is not necessarily involved in the word "accidental," its use, I venture to think, is misleading, and not warranted by anything in the Act . . . Now the expression "injury by accident" seems to me to

[3] [1900] 1 Q. B. 481.
[4] (1887) 12 App. Cas. 51.

be a compound expression. The words "by accident" are, I think, introduced parenthetically as it were to qualify the word "injury," confining it to a certain class of injuries, and excluding other classes, as, for instance, injuries by disease or injuries self-inflicted by design. Then comes the question, Do the words "arising out of and in the course of the employment" qualify the word "accident," or the word "injury," or the compound expression "injury by accident"? I rather think the latter view is the correct one . . . . the expression "accident" is used in the popular and ordinary sense of the word as denoting an unlooked-for mishap or an untoward event which is not expected or designed . . .

There is, . . . a recent decision of the Court of Session in Scotland to which I should like to call your Lordships' attention, and in which I agree entirely. It is the case of *Stewart* v. *Wilsons and Clyde Coal Co., Ltd.*[5] . . . A miner strained his back in replacing a derailed coal hutch. The question arose, Was that an accident? All the learned judges held that it was. True, two of the learned judges expressed an opinion that it was "fortuitous," but they could not have used that expression in the sense in which it was used in *Hensey* v. *White.*[6] . . . What the miner did in replacing the hutch he certainly did deliberately and in the ordinary course of this work. There was nothing haphazard about it. Lord M'Laren observed that it was impossible to limit the scope of the statute. He considered that "if a workman in the reasonable performance of his duties sustains a physiological injury as the result of the work he is engaged in" . . . "this is accidental injury in the sense of the statute." Lord Kinnear observed that the injury was "not intentional" and that "it was unforeseen." "It arose," he said, "from some causes which are not definitely ascertained, except that the appellant was lifting hutches which were too heavy for him. If," he added, "such an occurrence as this cannot be described in ordinary language as an accident, I do not know how otherwise to describe it."

. . . .

R(I) 42/51

. . . .

2. The claimant had been employed since March, 1950, as a pug feeder in a brick works. He and another man worked together. They took it in turns to lift blocks of marl into the pug from ground level. The height to which they had to lift the blocks was about

[5] 5 F. 120.
[6] [1900] 1 Q. B. 481.

six feet and they had some steps to enable them to reach the entrance to the pug. They each lifted approximately 700 of these blocks daily. The blocks weighed about 56–60 lbs. each. In addition there were other operations, which I need not set out in detail but which no doubt were a considerable strain.

3. Towards the end of January or the beginning of February, 1951, the claimant felt an aching pain in the left side of his chest, and when he ultimately consulted a doctor he was found to be suffering from strained chest muscles

4. I do not doubt that this condition was due to his work, but the claimant has no recollection of any particular incident and it seems clear that the condition was the result of a gradual process and not accident. Having regard to the principles laid down in Decision C.I. 257/49 (reported), I feel obliged to agree with the decision of the Local Appeal Tribunal, who dealt with the claimant's case with great care and set out the reasons for their decision very fully.

5. The Insurance Officer drew my attention in the interests of the claimant to Decision C.I. 29/49 (reported) in which an elderly man who had strained his heart by lifting heavy weights was held to have suffered injury by accident. It may be that the medical evidence in that case provided ground for holding that there had occurred a culminating strain which could properly be called accident, but in the light of subsequent decisions, such as Decisions C.I. 257/79 (reported) and C.I. 83/50 (reported), some of the general observations in Decision C.I. 29/49 (reported) appear to me to be too widely expressed. The distinction between "process" and "accident" had not at that time been made clear in Commissioner's decisions, and I must decide the present appeal taking into account the later decisions.

. . . .

R(I) 77/51

. . . .

2. The claimant, who is 63 years of age, has been a locomotive driver since 1919 and has driven all types of engines. In 1945, however, owing to high blood pressure and shingles, he was placed on shunting duties on tank engines under the advice of the railway company's medical officer, who used to examine him every year at Swindon. In July, 1949, this doctor noticed a protrusion in the region of the claimant's navel, but the claimant, when questioned, then said it caused him no discomfort. By the 27th July, 1950, the protrusion had grown more pronounced, and the railway medical officer recommended a surgical belt. The claimant's own doctor,

however advised an operation. The claimant continued at work until he went into hospital on the 10th August, 1950. The operation was successfully performed on the 11th August, 1950. The protrusion was an umbilical hernia, and the issue in this appeal is whether the hernia can properly be held to have been caused "by accident arising out of and in the course of his employment" as a locomotive driver.

. . . .

6. The Tribunal gave their finding in the following terms:—

. . . The Tribunal is satisfied that claimant's incapacity was due to the worsening of his hernia through a strain or strains suffered in March, 1950, while he was operating a stiff reversing lever on engine 5774.

. . . .

8. The Insurance Officer submits that the decision is not in accord with the principles laid down in Decisions C.I. 257/49 (reported), C.I. 83/50 (reported) and R(1) 42/51. In those cases it was held respectively that Raynaud's phenomenon, tuberculosis, and strained chest muscles were not the result of injury by accident but of a gradual process. It appears to me, however, that that principle is not applicable here. The injury appears to me to be the result of a series of ascertainable and specific incidents in that each severe strain would cause a minute widening of the tear in the muscular wall or a further minute protrusion of the bowel. As Lord Porter said in *Roberts* v. *Dorothea Slate Quarries Ltd.* 41 B.W.C.C. 154, "The distinction between accident and disease has been insisted upon throughout the authorities, and is, I think, well founded . . . I do not know . . . that any explicit formula can be adopted with safety. There must nevertheless come a time when the indefinite number of so-called accidents and the length of time over which they occur take away the element of accident and substitute that of process". The present case appears to me to be one of injury not from a long-continued process but from the cumulative effect of a series of separate ascertainable minor accidents met with at work, as in *Burrell* v. *Selvage* 14 B.W.C.C. 158.

. . . .

Reg. (Curry) v. **National Insurance Commissioner [1974] N.I. 89 (N.I.C.A.)**
EXTRACTS FROM THE JUDGMENT OF LOWRY L.C.J.: . . .

The concept of "injury by accident" has been current since 1897 and the authorities are embarrassingly numerous and conflicting. So I shall first consider on my own account the meaning of "accident" in its ordinary sense. At its most colourless the word means, a happening, a fortuitous occurrence or something which happens by chance. It cannot in the Act mean simply "a happening" or else the words "accident" and "by accident" would have no limiting function. More specifically an accident means an unlooked-for mishap or an untoward event which is not expected or designed. An accident which results in personal injury can be external to the victim, as when scaffolding collapses or machinery breaks down, or internal or peculiar to the victim, as when a man trips and falls or strains his back. When mishaps of either kind arise out of and in the course of the victim's employment, they are industrial accidents.

In time the courts grafted onto these simple ideas a new concept: if a workman as a result of a series of incidents consisting of accidental occurrences (each one of which may have been insignificant if viewed in isolation) suffered injury, he was regarded as having suffered personal injury by accident. One would still expect that each incident must qualify to be regarded as an "accident" before the cumulative effect to the series of incidents could be held to have produced injury by *accident*, because, if a workman is injured by a series of incidents none of which was an accident he could not properly be said to have been injured by accident. We shall see whether this limitation on the new concept has invariably been observed.

Clearly enough, personal injury consisting of damage to the hearing could be caused by an accident external to the victim, as by a deafening and accidental explosion in a gas-works, and possibly by a series of such explosions. And, as an example of an accident internal or peculiar to the victim, one could imagine a case where the victim faints and falls into a position where his eardrum is damaged through being brought temporarily and unexpectedly into close proximity to a very noisy machine. Equally, on the other hand, one can envisage a workman in a quarry sustaining damage to his hearing as a result of a controlled explosion or, I would suggest, a series of controlled explosions, occurring in the ordinary course of quarrying operations.

The respondent suggests, not without authority, that the word "accident" ought to receive a liberal interpretation, having regard to the presumed intention, formerly of the Workmen's Compensation Acts and now the National Insurance Acts, that workmen should not lightly be excluded from benefit: Halsbury's Statutes 3rd ed. vol. 23 pp. 478–480 and cases there cited; *R.* v. *Industrial Injuries Commissioner* [1966] 2 Q.B. 31, 45D. One may recognise this principle provided that one does not lose sight of the points that the word "accident" must have a limiting effect and that section 54 involves the proposition that there are diseases and personal injuries arising out of and in the course of employment which cannot be attributed to accident and only some of which are intended by Parliament to be prescribed. In *Fenton* v. *Thorley* [1903] A.C. 443, it was held that the word "accident" in the Workmen's Compensation Act 1897 is used in the popular and ordinary sense and means a mishap or untoward event, not expected or designed. It is a reminder that the popular and ordinary sense of the word is paramount.

. . . .

It is now necessary to see how these views are affected by the authorities, and for this purpose I would first refer to *Roberts* v. *Dorothea Slate Quarries Co. Ltd.* [1948] 2 All E.R. 201 in which the House of Lords held, affirming both the county court judge and the Court of Appeal, that a workman's incapacity caused by silicosis was the result of a continuous process going on substantially from day to day over a period of years and could not be said to be the result of an accident or a series of accidents, each one of which was specific and ascertainable. Much attention has been given to a part of Lord Porter's speech at p. 205 which was quoted by the learned commissioner and O'Donnell J. Both sides have cited the passage to their purpose. The respondent in particular contends that in the present case there were "specific and ascertainable accidents", even if this could not be said in the *Dorothea* case and that the present case ought to be distinguished on the further ground that the incapacity was produced over a period of months and not years. Before commenting on these points, I would refer to the speech of Lord Du Parcq in the *Dorothea* case where he made an observation which is very relevant to most of the authorities that have been or could be cited (p. 208):

> "Your Lordships are engaged in construing an Act of Parliament and that duty is not to be performed by deducing from dicta contained in earlier judgments principles which may seem to follow from them. The pursuit of such a course of reasoning may take one on an interesting and attractive journey, but it is all too likely to lead to a destination far removed from any end contemplated by the legislature. Each step may be thought to justify a further advance, until at last the borderline is crossed which divides the reasonable interpretation of the statute from an unwarranted extension of its provisions."

I might refer to remarks in a similar vein by Lord President Dunedin in *Coe* v. *Fife Coal Co.* [1909] S.C. 393, which were adopted by Lord Shaw in *Clover Clayton & Co. v. Hughes* [1910] A.C. 242, 256.

While the regular screeches of the saw may be identifiable as separate specific and ascertainable incidents, that does not, without more, qualify them to be called accidents or show that the respondent's injuries were sustained by accident, and, while Lord Porter referred to a continuous process "which gradually and over a period of years produces incapacity," that does not mean that everything which fails to come within that description is to be called an accident or a series of accidents. The learned commissioner's citation from the speech of Lord Reid in *Cassell & Co. Ltd. v. Broome* [1972] A.C. 1027 is most apposite and could be applied with good effect to the observations of Lord McLaren in *Stewart v. Wilsons and Clyde Coal Co.* (1902) 5 F. 120, where he said:

> "If a workman, in the reasonable performance of his duties, sustains a physiological injury, as the result of the work he is engaged in, I consider that this is accidental injury in the sense of the statute."

These words were very much in point in the context in which they were used but, as Lord Shaw points out in *Hughes'* case [1910] A.C. at p. 259, they cannot by applied indiscriminately without obliterating the meaning of the word "accident". The fact that Lord Shaw was of the minority in *Hughes'* case is immaterial for the purposes for which I have referred to his speech. In the cases where injury was held to be the result of an accident if has usually been possible to point to a specific occurrence which ought not to have happened. This has been sufficient to justify the decisions, albeit some of them have been majority decisions, in favour of accident in *Fenton v. Thorley* [1903] A.C. 443, *Brintons v. Turvey* [1905] A.C. 230, *Ismay, Imrie & Co. v. Williamson* [1908] A.C. 437 (in which I confess to being much attracted by the dissenting opinion of Lord Macnaghten), *Clover, Clayton & Co. Ltd. v. Hughes* [1910] A.C. 242 and *Grant v. Kynoch* [1919] A.C. 765.

Partridge Jones & John Paton Ltd. v. James [1933] A.C. 501 is a case which I find difficult to follow, since it seems to be an extension of *Clover, Clayton & Co. Ltd. v. Hughes*, which itself must be very close to the line. The decision in *Fife Coal Co. v. William Young* [1940] A.C. 479 can be attributed to the fact that a time on 27 April, 1938, when the claimant was in the same crouching position for half an hour and sustained a "dropped foot", was identified by the Court of Session and the House of Lords (who reversed the findings of the Sheriff-substitute) as the occasion of an accident. In reaching his conclusion Viscount Caldecote L.C. laid stress on Lord Macnaghten's disapproval in *Fenton* v. *Thorley* of the word "fortuitous" and also on Lord McLaren's opinion in *Stewart* v. *Wilsons and Clyde Coal Co.* Neither of these points provides any escape from the necessity to be able to find an "accident", but the latter, it seems, is to be found in the incident of 27 April, 1938.

The respondent relied on *Fitzsimons* v. *Ford Motor Co. Ltd.* [1946] 1 All E.R. 429, where the Court of Appeal decided that a workman who contracted Reynaud's disease through using a fettling machine which was electrically operated and vibrated 2,800 times a minute had been injured by accident, since each vibration of the machine constituted a tiny blow to workman's hand. The Court of Appeal reversed the decision of the learned county court judge that the workman's injuries were not caused by accident and held that there was no evidence to support that finding (which, incidentally, was a negative finding). In my opinion the judgment of the court in the *Fitzsimons* case is wrong and fails to identify any incident or series of incidents which could properly be called an accident or series of accidents. *Brintons* v. *Turvey, Grant* v. *Kynoch* and *Burrel* v. *Selvage*, which the court purported to follow, can all be easily distinguished on that ground: a series of accidents is as fit to be relied on as a single accident, but a series of *incidents* does not without more assume the character of a series of *accidents*.

In *Hughes* v. *Lancaster Steam Coal Collieries* [1947] 2 All E.R. 556 the Court of Appeal applied its own decision in the *Fitzsimons* case, among others, but in my opinion it was unnecessary to do so in order to arrive at the result.

The next case in point of time was *Roberts* v. *Dorothea Slate Quarries Co. Ltd.* [1948] 2 All E.R. 201, to which reference has been made already and in which many of the cases mentioned in argument and in this judgment were reviewed (although not the *Fitzsimons* case). Because the *Roberts* case arose out of the effect of normal, although harmful, working conditions, it repays the careful study which it has received in the course of argument.

One then comes to *Pyrah* v. *Doncaster Corporation* [1949] 1 All E.R. 883, and *Roberts* v. *Penrhyn* which is reported at a footnote to the *Pyrah* case on p. 891. In the *Pyrah* case a nurse was awarded compensation by the county court judge as having contracted tuberculosis "by accident" and the Court of Appeal, by a majority, upheld the decision, distinguishing the *Dorothea* case. In the *Penrhyn* case a workman whose hip became arthritic after prolonged contact with a vibrating pneumatic drill failed to prove accidental injury. I am fully persuaded that the *Penrhyn* decision is in accordance with what I believe to be the principles on which one decides whether an accident or series of accidents has occurred, and the reasons given by the majority for their decision in the *Pyrah* case do not impinge on those principles.

I would just notice a hint in the *Dorothea, Pyrah* and *Penrhyn* cases that something which happens often may lose the character of an accident and assume that of a process. With respect, I do not subscribe to this approach, preferring to consider as the real question whether an incident or series of incidents can qualify to be called an accident or series of accidents.

Finally, I consider that it is a mistake in the respondent's favour to take from its context in the *Dorothea* case Lord Porter's reference to a "continuous process . . . which gradually and over a period of years produces incapacity" and a base thereon an argument that something which happens within a few months, as in this case, is an "accident". I need refer only to the observation of Jones L.J. in *Ex parte William Starr*. I respectfully agree with all he says about that case and with what Thompson J. is reported to have said in his judgment.

"Injury by accident" is a phrase which has been re-enacted in the light of many decisions. If, therefore, a clear line of authority could be found, it would go far to establish the meaning of the words in question. But if the thread is tenuous and some of the reasoning, with respect, implausible, one is thrown back (and this may be for the best) upon interpretation of the words in what one conceives to be their ordinary meaning.

It appears to me unrealistic to say that the respondent met with an accident every time the high-pitched noise assailed his ears. All he did was to experience the routine associated with his work and his argument, if sound, would turn every assault of dust or noise into an accident. If the saw had emitted unwarranted noises through lack of maintenance then I could see that injury "by accident" would be likely to occur.

I do not agree that the special sensitivity of the victim converts a routine incident into an industrial accident. It is, in one sense, an accident (of birth, health or physical make-up) that a person is vulnerable to what might otherwise be harmless influences, but this is not something which arises out of that person's employment. I respectfully adopt the general observation of Lord Loreburn in *Ismay, Imrie & Co.* v. *Williamson* [1908] A.C. 437:

> "To my mind the weakness of the deceased which predisposed him to this form of attack is immaterial. The fact that a man who has died from a heat-stroke was by physical debility more

likely than others so to suffer can have nothing to do with the question whether what befell him is to be regarded as a accident or not".

A predisposition to be injured is not an industrial accident. It is true that, if an industrial accident occurs, the vulnerable man may be more severely injured, or may be injured where a normally healthy man would not, but that is a different matter.

I have referred earlier to the forthright conclusion of law apparently reached by the learned commissioner. The application for an order of certiorari, however, specified his error of law as "holding . . . that the applicant had not sustained an industrial accident." The learned judge who granted the order was, as I understand it, equally forthright in holding that the *right* answer was that the respondent had been injured by an industrial accident. He did not say that the commissioner's error lay in holding that he *could* not attribute the respondent's deafness to accident.

My own view is that on the facts found there is only one correct answer, that given by the learned commissioner, but, should I be wrong in that, I still consider that the court, in the exercise of its discretion, ought not to grant an order of certiorari because, if it was open to the commissioner, as I think it must have been, to hold that the respondent was not injured by accident, then I believe that he is certain to do so even if we inform him that in our opinion it was open to him to hold either way.

. . . .

"Arising out of and in the course of"

Weaver v. Tredegar Iron Co. Ltd. [1940] 3 All E.R. 157 (H.L.)
EXTRACTS FROM THE JUDGMENT OF LORD WRIGHT:

My Lords, this appeal raises the ever-recurring problem of the true construction, or rather the true application to the facts of the case, of the words of the Workmen's Compensation Act. 1925, s. 1, "accident arising out of and in the course of the employment." The particular aspect of the words here in question is not the causal, but the time, element: "the course of the employment." It is when, on the facts of this case, the employment terminated.

It has long been held that the course of the employment is not determined by the time at which a man is actually occupied on his work. There may be intermissions during the working-hours when he is not actually working, as, for instance, times for meals or refreshment, or absences for personal necessities. Moreover, the course of the employment may begin or end some little time before or after he has downed tools or ceased actual work. The simplest case is when a man in a large factory or works has to go a substantial distance before he leaves his employer's premises and goes into the public street. As LORD DUNEDIN said in *Stewart (John) & Son (1912), Ltd. v. Longhurst . . .* , at p. 256:

> No one, for instance, would doubt that if a collier was injured in the cage on his way to the face at which he was to work that the injury arose in the course of his employment, though the face might be a mile away from the pit bottom; nor would anyone doubt that if the same man were starting from his house in the village and was injured while in the street before he approached the precincts of the colliery the opposite result would be arrived at.

Here LORD DUNEDIN is distinguishing between risks which a man incurs as an employee and those which he incurs as an ordinary member of the public. To the same effect, LORD ATKINSON said, at p. 258:

> In argument some distinction was attempted to be drawn between the case where the workman has to traverse the private property of the employer to get to his work, and that where to do so he has to traverse the private property of another with the consent of that other. I do not think that is a sound distinction. When a man walks along the public streets to get to his work he is doing something which he has a perfect right to do irrespective altogether of his employment. The right does not spring from his employment at all. It belongs to him as a member of the public.

There LORD ATKINSON is drawing the same distinction as LORD DUNEDIN. I find in these expressions, of which other instances may be found in the authorities, a general criterion for deciding when the employment begins and ends. In *Stewart's* case, . . . the man was employed on a barge which was in a dock. To reach it, he had to traverse the premises of the dock company, over which his employer had no control, but had secured permission for the man to pass from and to his work. He was injured while doing so, in consequence of a risk attaching to those premises. It was held that the accident arose out of and in the course of his employment. LORD DUNEDIN, at p. 257, quoted with approval the words of PICKFORD, L.J.:

> The workman in this case in order to get to the actual place of work, had to enter and leave premises on which he had no

right to be and no reason for being, except by the conditions of his employment, and in crossing them to encounter dangers which he would not have encountered but for that employment.

I have quoted these passages from *Stewart's* case . . . because they seem to me to be precisely applicable to this case, save in one respect, which does not seem to me to constitute a distinction. In *Stewart's* case . . . the workman could not get to the barge save by crossing the dock premises. In the present case, Weaver could have left the colliery without resorting to the platform. In fact, however, "practically all the workmen used it." It is the employers' duty to provide means of access to and egress from the work. Both access and egress are in this respect on the same footing. In *Parker* v. *Black Rock (Owners)* . . . at p. 730, LORD PARKER, while holding against the man's claim, was willing to concede that the arbitrator might have found that the quay which the deceased seaman was using to regain his vessel was the proper and usual method of regaining the ship, and thus might be considered as the access to the ship, so that an accident happening during the course of using that access might be, within the cases, an accident in the course of the employment. That is not an express decision, but indicates that it may be enough if the access was proper and usual. There are several decisions of this House which recognise that there may be a sort of notional extension of the employer's premises (or, more correctly, of the place where the employer is carrying on the particular work, which may include a place such as the barge in *Stewart's* case . . . , or the spot on the highway in *Sparey* v. *Bath Rural District Council* . . .) so as to include an area which the workmen pass and repass in going to and leaving the actual place of work.

It is, I think, true to say that, in the various authorities, at least in this House, where this notional extension has been recognised, the actual or assumed state of things has been that there was no alternative way of access or departure. In one of the latest of these authorities (which have all been cited at great length, and which I need not discuss in detail), it was said in *Northumbrian Shipping Co., Ltd.* v. *McCullum* . . . by my noble and learned friend LORD MACMILLAN in an opinion concurred in by the other Lords, at p. 670:

> If in going and coming from his work he has to use an access which is part of his employer's premises, or which he is only entitled to traverse because he is going to or coming from his

work, he is held to be on his master's business while he is using that access.

There LORD MACMILLAN uses the word "has," meaning, I presume, that it was the only access. That was so in the facts of that case, but does the fact that there is an alternative access exclude the same result, assuming that the access is proper and usual, and is provided by the employers? The words of the Act are very general, no doubt designedly so. Experience has shown how infinitely various may be the facts to which the words are to be applied. In *Stewart's* case . . . LORD BUCKMASTER uttered a warning against the mistake involved in attempting to define a fixed boundary between the cases which are within the statute and those which are without. He said, at p. 259:

> This it is almost impossible to achieve. No authority can with certainty do more than decide whether a particular case upon particular facts is or is not within the meaning of the phrase.

The realities of each case must be regarded. Is there any difference in substance if the man in leaving the work has a choice of two permitted ways over adjoining premises before he reaches the public highway, instead of only one? I cannot see why there should be. Nor could the Court of Appeal in *Foster* v. *Edwin Penfold & Co. Ltd.* . . . , where the accident befell a man when using a permitted means of egress at a place where he was allowed to go, not as a member of the public, but only in virtue of his employment. It was held to be immaterial that there was an alternative way of egress. The man has parked his car on a private wharf adjoining the employers' premises. He was not bound to go home by car, though to do so was usual. ROMER, L.J., in holding the case to be within the Act, said, at p. 259:

> He was, however, bound as part of his service to leave the employers' premises, and he was entitled to leave them by an permissible way and in any permissible manner. He was leaving them by a permissible way and in a permissible manner, and the accident occurred before he had finally got free from those premises and was in a public place, that is to say, on the public highway.

I agree completely with that statement. I think that it applies to the facts of the present case. In my opinion, when Weaver got into the train, and not before, he was in what may be called a public place—so as to include an area which the workmen pass and repass in going to and leaving the actual place of work.

It is, I think, true to say that, in the various authorities, at least in this House, where this notional extension has been recognised, the actual or assumed state of things has been that there was no alternative way of access or departure. In one of the latest of these authorities (which have all been cited at great length, and which I need not discuss in detail), it was said in *Northumbrian Shipping Co., Ltd.* v. *McCullum* . . . by my noble and learned friend LORD MACMILLAN in an opinion concurred in by the other Lords, at p. 670:

> If in going and coming from his work he has to use an access which is part of his employer's premises, or which he is only entitled to traverse because he is going to or coming from his work, he is held to be on his master's business while he is using that access.

There LORD MACMILLAN uses the word "has," meaning, I presume, that it was the only access. That was so in the facts of that case, but does the fact that there is an alternative access exclude the same result, assuming that the access is proper and usual, and is provided by the employers? The words of the Act are very general, no doubt designedly so. Experience has shown how infinitely various may be the facts to which the words are to be applied. In *Stewart's* case . . . , LORD BUCKMASTER uttered a warning against the mistake involved in attempting to define a fixed boundary between the cases which are within the statute and those which are without. He said, at p. 259:

> This it is almost impossible to achieve. No authority can with certainty do more than decide whether a particular case upon particular facts is or is not within the meaning of the phrase.

The realities of each case must be regarded. Is there any difference in substance if the man in leaving the work has a choice of two permitted ways over adjoining premises before he reaches the public highway, instead of only one? I cannot see why there should be. Nor could the Court of Appeal in *Foster* v. *Edwin Penfold & Co., Ltd* . . . where the accident befell a man when using a permitted means of egress at a place where he was allowed to go, not as a member of the public, but only in virtue of his employment. It was held to be immaterial that there was an alternative way of egress. The man had parked his car on a private wharf adjoining the employers' premises. He was not bound to go home by car, though to do so was usual. ROMER, L.J., in holding the case to be within the Act, said, at p. 259:

He was, however, bound as part of his service to leave the employers' premises, and he was entitled to leave them by any permissible way and in any permissible manner. He was leaving them by a permissible way and in a permissible manner, and the accident occurred before he had finally got free from those premises and was in a public place, that is to say, on the public highway.

I agree completely with that statement. I think that it applies to the facts of the present case. In my opinion, when Weaver got into the train, and not before, he was in what may be called a public place—that is, on a public railway, which he was entitled, by contract with the railway company, to use like other members of the public. The platform was not a public place. It was specially provided by arrangement with the employers for the use of the respondents' men. The public had no right of access to it. There was no public means of access to it. It was provided solely as a means of access to, and egress from, the colliery. There was no contractual obligation on the man to use it, but there was clearly a practical compulsion, because practically all the men used it. It was beyond question a proper and usual means of access and egress, provided by the company for that very purpose. I cannot see why the bare possibility that a man may leave the work by road, walking or bicycling, can made a difference. When Weaver was knocked off the platform, he was still surrounded by his fellow-workmen, and the risk of being knocked off by the jostling crowd was a risk still incidental to his employment. The platform was in that respect a dangerous place, just as much as the dock premises which the man was crossing were in *Stewart's* case . . . . He had not become an ordinary member of the public, and had not disentagled himself from his employment. He was, accordingly, still in the course of his employment.

Reg v. Industrial Injuries Commissioner, ex p. A.E.U. [1966] 2 Q.B. 31

LORD DENNING M.R. Mr. Culverwell was employed as a semi-skilled fitter by British Cellophane Ltd. at a factory in Somerset. He was entitled in the course of the morning to have a break which lasted from half-past ten to twenty minutes to eleven. At the beginning and end of it a buzzer sounded. On July 15, 1963, he left off working shortly before 10.30 a.m., and after going to the refreshment room and having a cup of tea he went to a part of the factory where there was a little smoking booth in which the men were allowed to smoke. They were not permitted to smoke in the workshops. When he got there the smoking booth was full. Only three people could get in at a time. He stayed in a recess outside the smoking booth with two other men for at least five minutes, waiting for his turn, as he said, to go into the smoking booth, and he was rolling a cigarette. This smoking booth was quite close to a passageway. At 10.45 a.m., while he was still there, squatting on the floor, a fork-lift truck was driven past, going from one part of the factory to another. The driver, coming along without looking, ran into Culverwell and he was severely injured. He had a broken leg, a broken pelvis and a dislocated hip. We are told that he has made a claim at common law against his employers which has been settled by a payment to him. He claims that he is also entitled to industrial injuries benefit.

. . . .

As I listened to the argument today which Mr. Bridge has put forward, I felt he was going back to the old narrow interpretations of this section. He took us back to the early cases of *Parker* v. *Black Rock* (*Owners*), and *St. Helen's Colliery Co.* v. *Hewitson.* Those decisions give me a shock even now, that the House should have decided them as they did. But Mr. Bridge relied on them. He said that the rule of law still was, as stated by Lord Parker of Waddington in the *Black Rock* case:

> "In order to make it an accident arising out of the employment the absence from the vessel must be in pursuance of a duty owed to the employer."

This idea that a duty is necessary is all wrong. It does not stand with the decision of the House of Lords itself in *Armstrong, Whitworth & Co.* v. *Redford,* where there was no duty on the young woman to go to and from the canteen, and yet she was held to be in the course of her employment. Nor does it stand with the decision of the Court of Appeal in *Knight* v. *Howard Wall Ltd.,* where a boy, who was having his midday meal in a canteen, was injured by a dart. There was no obligation on him to go there. Yet it was held to be in the course of his employment. In *Harris's* case Lord Atkin made it clear that a duty is not necessary:

> "There are many things done which the workman is not obliged to do, for he is given a complete discretion as to what to do and where (within limits) to do it, as for instance, in the case of gamekeepers, and often gardeners. Accidents happen to workmen when taking their meals or in other respects not pursuing for the moment their employment."

Nevertheless it is in the course of his employment, even though he is doing something which it was not his duty to do. Thus, when Culverwell went down for the break, when he was there waiting to go into the smoking booth, it was in the course of his employment, although he did not go in pursuance of any duty owed to his employer.

. . . .

What is the position when a man overstays his tea-break or his meal-break? I do not think that the mere fact of overstaying his time takes him out of the course of his employment: certainly not when it is done without thinking. Even if it is done negligently or disobediently, it does not automatically take him outside the course of his employment. He is only taken out of the course of his employment when the circumstances show that he is doing something of a kind different from anything he was employed to do.

This brings me to the passage which Mr. Pain criticised in the commissioner's judgment. The commissioner said:

> "The first matter which the claimant must establish if he is to succeed in his claim is that at the time of the accident he was in the course of his employment: in other words, that the course of the employment had not been interrupted. It can, of course, be interrupted even during working hours and in the factory, if a claimant either goes away from work for purposes of his own, or at his place of work does something which has nothing to do with his employment, or if, being away from his place of work, he does not return to it when he should. The burden of proof is on the claimant to establish his case on balance of probabilities."

Mr. Pain says that that was an erroneous direction in point of law. I do not think it was erroneous. The key word in the passage is the word "can." The course of employment *can* be interrupted in some circumstances: but not necessarily so.

Take the first class where "a man goes away from his work for purposes of his own." An illustration is where a man goes from one end of a factory to the other to compare notes on football pools. He is not acting in the course of his employment. It would be different if he went to get a tool or to go to the lavatory.

Now take the next class, where a man "at his place of work does something which has nothing to do with his employment." An illustration was given by Lord Atkin in *Noble's* case. If the guard of a train takes it on himself to drive the train and is injured while driving, he is outside the course of his employment. Another illustration is the case which Mr. Bridge mentioned, which was heard by the Divisional Court a little while ago, where a man was employed to hook goods on to a crane and, instead, took it on himself to drive a fork-lift truck. There he was outside the course of his employment.

Take the third class where "being away from his place of work, he does not return to it when he should." An illustration can be taken from *Knight* v. *Howard Wall Ltd.* Suppose the boy in the canteen, instead of going back to his work at the end of the meal, had stayed on for half an hour or an hour playing darts with the rest of the men in the canteen. By overstaying his visit to the canteen he would be taking himself completely out of the course of his employment, because he would be doing something of a kind different from anything he was employed to do.

All of those classes which the commissioner mentioned are, I think, justified when you remember that his words were: "It *can* be interrupted," not *will* be interrupted.

Eventually this case comes down to this: was what this man did (in overstaying his break in the morning) reasonably incidental to his employment? Was he merely overstaying the break negligently or even disobediently? Or was he doing something entirely different, using this extended break for purposes of his own for an indefinite time quite unconnected with his employment? It must be remembered that five minutes had gone past after the end of the break and he was still waiting to smoke a cigarette. It might have been a long time, for all that appears, before he returned.

This is one of those questions, which, as it seems to me, the legislature has decided should not be brought up to the courts of law for decision, but should be entrusted to the specialised statutory authorities for determination. It may occasionally be of use, if there is a real error of law, for a case to be brought before this court, but not in such a case as this. No error of law is shown here.

I would agree that in the ordinary way if a man while at his place of work, during his hours of work, is injured by a risk incidental to his employment, then the right conclusion usually is that it is an injury which arises out of and in the course of the employment, even though he may not be doing his actual work but chatting to a friend or smoking or doing something of that kind. But he may take himself out of it if he does something of a kind entirely different from anything he was employed to do. That is what the commissioner found here. The man was overstaying his tea-break for so long that he was taking himself out of his employment. I would dismiss the application.

Davies and Salmon L.JJ. delivered concurring judgments.

Reg. v. National Insurance Commissioner, ex. p. Michael [1977] 1 W.L.R. 109

LORD DENNING M.R.: . . . Let me take first the case where a man plays football in a team for the factory or firm where he works. For instance, a bank often has its own team. If one of the players is injured, the accident may properly be said to arise "out of" his employment: but it does not arise "in the course of" it. That seems as clear as can be. But it is said that policemen are a special case. And for these reasons: if a policeman is particularly good at a sport or game, he is expected by his superiors to use his skill for the benefit of the force. Each county force enters teams for the various competitions. Success is a matter of great pride. It improves morale. As well as physical fitness. So policemen are encouraged by the authorities to take part. The costs incurred by the games are provided out of police funds. The players are selected and named in the orders issued to the force. Each player who represents the force is allowed to take eight hours each month out of his duty time in order to play. He is considered to that extent to be "on duty." So he is paid for it. But, in addition, he is expected to play during his off-duty time without extra pay. None of this is, in strictness, compulsory. But a young man looking for promotion ought to play for the force when he can. If he goes off and does other things, it would do him no good.

It may be suggested that if a police constable is playing football for the force in his "on duty" time an accident during that time arises "in the course of" his employment: whereas it would not do so if it happened during his "off duty" time. That distinction was upheld in another case by a commissioner, Mr. Lazarus Q.C. in Decision R(I) 3/67, but it was not pursued before us. All agreed it should make no difference. When two police teams are playing, some men may be doing so in "on duty" time, others in "off duty" time; and some part of each. It would be most unfair to make any distinction on that ground. Nor can it make any difference whether the game is played at home or away, or on a neutral ground. The one thing which seems to distinguish the policeman from the bank clerk is the extent of the support which is given officially by the police authorities. It is, or may be assumed to be, greater than is given by a bank.

The problem must be resolved by reference to the words of the statute. In deciding in one case in favour of an injured policeman (who was playing in his on duty time) Sir Robert Micklethwait Q.C. said that the concept of "in the course of his employment" has gradually been widened over the last 30 years. He held that a man is now to be regarded as entitled to injury benefit if he is injured while doing something "which is reasonably incidental to his employment." This test of "reasonably incidental" is to be gathered from the speeches of Lord Sumner, Lord Parmoor, and Lord Wrenbury in *Armstrong, Whitworth and Co. Ltd.* v. *Redford* [1920] A.C. 757, 777, 779 and 780, respectively. It was applied by the county court judge in *Knight* v. *Howard Wall Ltd.* [1938] 4 All E.R. 667, with the approval of this court. It was followed by this court in *Reg.* v. *Industrial Injuries Commissioners, Ex parte Amalgamated Engineering Union (No. 2)* ("the *Culverwell* case") [1966] 2 Q.B. 31, 48, 50, 51. But in all those cases the workman was at the premises where he or she worked and was injured while on a visit to the canteen or other place, for a break. The words "reasonably incidental" should be read in that context, and limited to cases of that kind. They are not part of the statute and should not be extended to other cases without careful consideration. Take a case where a man is going to or from his place of work on his own bicycle, or in his own car. He might be said to be doing something "reasonably incidental" to his employment. But if he has an accident on the way, it is well settled that it does not "arise out of and in the course of his employment": see *Alderman* v. *Great Western Railway Co.* [1936] 2 K.B. 90 and *Netherton* v. *Coles* [1945] 1 All E.R. 227. Even if his employer provides the transport, so that he is going to work as a passenger in his employer's vehicle (which is surely "reasonably incidental" to his employment), nevertheless, if he is injured in an accident, it does not arise out of and in the course of his employment: see *Vandyke* v. *Fender* [1970] 2 Q.B. 292, 305. It needed a special "deeming" provision in a statute to make it "deemed" to arise out of and in the course of his employment: see section 8 of the Act of 1965.

Applying those cases, it seems to me plain that if this policeman had an accident while driving his own car to the football ground it would not arise out and of in the course of his employment. Even if he was travelling with the rest of the team in a coach provided by the police authority, it would be the same. He would not be able to rely on the "deeming" provision of section 8, because he was not travelling to or from his "place of work." By no stretch of imagination could the football ground be called "his place of work."

. . . .

R(I) 12/75 (T)

. . . .

2. The facts of this case are not in dispute. The claimant at the relevant time was employed by a county council as a home help. As such she was given a weekly programme of work by the county's home help organiser which was sent by post to her home. Ordinarily she would be required to attend each day to help in more than one home (referred to by her employers as a "duty point") but during the week in which the relevant accident occurred she worked throughout her working day at a single duty point, the same place on each day from Monday to Friday.

3. The claimant's working day was from 8.30 a.m. when she was expected to arrive at her first (or only) duty point of the day until 4.30 p.m., when she might leave her last (or only) duty point. The claimant was entitled to be paid for the time at duty points and at the same rate for the time spent in travelling between duty points. She was also paid at the same rate for time in excess of twenty minutes each way spent in travelling between home and her first (or only) duty point and between her last (or only) duty point and home. She was also reimbursed her fares. She made her claim for payment by completing a form prepared by the county council on which she indicated the time of arrival at and departure from duty points, travel time and expenses etc. In practice she hardly ever attended at the council offices, but completed her claim forms at home posting them to the county council, and her wages were sent to her by post at home.

4. The distance between the claimant's home and the duty point which she worked throughout the relevant week was about six miles. The journey, partly in two buses and partly on foot, occupied 55 minutes, so that the claimant was entitled to 35 minutes' paid travelling time each way. At 8.20 a.m. on the day in question the claimant when ten minutes from her duty point slipped while walking on an icy footpath in a public road and fell, injuring her back. She was not immediately incapacitated for work and she continued as usual to her duty point. During the following week on 5th December 1973 she became incapable of work and claimed injury benefit.

. . . .

11. . . . The principle on which the issue to be determined has recently been stated by Lord Widgery C.J. in the High Court in *Regina* v. *National Insurance Commissioner, Ex parte Fieldhouse*, reported as an appendix to Commissioner's Decision R(I) 9/74, who said:—

"The learned Commissioner . . . proceeds to consider the principle upon which the issue should be determined, and in paragraph 6 of his written decision he says this: "The question whether a person who meets with an accident on the public highway while travelling to or from his home has been the subject of numerous decisions of the Commissioner, I do not propose to enter into a lengthy discussion of them. As a general principle the decision in such cases turns on the answer to the question: 'Was the journey in the course of which the claimant was injured a journey on duty or simply a journey to or from duty?' In it a comparatively early decision. [R(I) 18/55], the learned Commissioner put it this way: 'The question at issue is whether on the particular journey he was travelling in the performance of a duty, or whether the journey was incidental to the performance of that duty and not merely preparatory to the performance of it. That question can be determined only by looking at all the circumstances of the case. The fact that a man is paid travelling time or travelling expenses, taken by itself, does not prove that he is travelling in the course of his employment: it may be no more than a means of recompensing him for having the inconvenience of travelling'."

I pause there to observe that the test posed for himself by the Commissioner is accepted by both Counsel as correct, and in my judgment is correct. One can express the legal issue thus: it is whether on the particular journey he was travelling in the performance of a duty or whether he was travelling incidental to the performance of a duty, or whether on the other hand his journey was merely preparatory to the performance of the duty."

This is the test in the case of a journey to work, and an analogous test is relevant in the case of the journey from work. So long as the test applied is correct the question whether a journey is made in the course of employment is one of fact.

12. Applying this test to the present case we ask the question whether the claimant's journey to work on the day of the accident was made in fulfilment of an express or implied obligation to her employment or was it incidental to that employment? Whatever may be the position where a person is employed to work for some of his time at home, we do not think that it is in general helpful to consider whether, because a person for his own convenience performs minor functions connected with his work at home which he could equally perform elsewhere, his home is his base. Indeed in Decision R(I) 18/55 the decision went in favour of the claimant

notwithstanding an express finding (in paragraph 9) that the claimant did not normally use his home as his base. Equally in our
opinion the length of journey, long or short, is not material to the
question whether it is in the course of an employment. We think
that the doubts on this point expressed by the Commissioner in
Decision R(I) 3/71 were well founded.

13. Approaching the matter in this way one would have no
difficulty in finding that a commercial traveller, for instance, is
employed to travel and call on customers and is in the course of
his employment when travelling. Other cases may be less clear but
whenever it is found that the duties of an employed person include
either regularly or from time to time travelling to and interviewing
or calling on customers or others at times or in a sequence, which
it is in his discretion to decide in the area of his operations, there
is some evidence on which a finding can be based that such travelling
is in the course of his employment. In this connection we refer,
as well as to the cases cited by Lord Gifford, to Decision R(I)
4/70.

14. On the other hand, as was pointed out in paragraph 10 of
Decision R(I) 2/67, there is a clear distinction between these cases
and that of a person who has defined hours and a fixed place of
work, even though it may not be the same place each day or indeed
even though it be more than one place in any one day. In the
present case we reject both Lord Gifford's criticism of paragraph
10 above referred to and his submission that because the employers
paid for the claimant's travelling time above twenty minutes she
had a duty to travel by a reasonable route. In our judgment it was
simply a condition for payment of travelling time that she should
so travel.

15. The primary question is what was the scope and ambit of
the claimant's employment, or put more simply, what was she
employed to do? In our judgment the claimant was employed, not
to visit or travel, but to work as a home help at the duty points
at which the council instructed her to work and present herself
there at the proper time. She had fixed hours of work and fixed
places of work where her duties were to be performed. On the
day of her accident she had only one place of work, but we do not
think the position would have been different if the claimant had
been directed to go to a second duty point later in the day. Her
journey to work was not, as we find, undertaken in the course of
her employment but was preparatory to the performance of her
duties. In our judgment Decision R(I) 2/67 was correct and
Decision C.I. 7/66 should not be followed.

16. In the present case the local tribunal preferred an unreported decision to a reported decision, and we heard submissions on behalf of both the insurance officer and the claimant on the question of precedent which makes it appropriate to state the position where previous decisions of Commissioners are referred to and submissions are made as to their persuasive or binding effect.

17. There have been nearly 60,000 Commissioners' decisions since 1948, and they fall into the following categories (a) unnumbered decisions (b) numbered decisions and (c) reported decisions.

> (a) Unnumbered decisions which represent the vast majority of decided cases comprise those in which well established principles of law have been applied to the facts as found or in which the sole issues have been of fact. They were not thought by their authors to reflect any usual circumstances or to contribute to the development of the law, save in some cases to reinforce accepted lines of authority
>
> (b) Numbered decisions are those to which the Commissioner concerned has had a number allocated with a prefix beginning with the letter 'C'. This ensures a limited distribution of the decision as being of interest, either on its facts, or because it develops the application of some legal principle or because it is the first decision applying the provisions of some statute or regulation, or simply because the Commisioner for some reason wishes his decision to receive a wider distribution than that given to unnumbered decisions, which are identified by the number of the Commissioner's file (also prefixed 'C') at the foot of the decision.
>
> (c) Reported decisions are those selected for reporting. They are so selected by the Chief Commissioner from numbered decisions and are primarily so selected if he is satisfied that they deal with questions of legal principle and that they command the assent of at least a majority of the Commissioners. Reported decisions are printed by Her Majesty's Stationery Office having a number with a prefix beginning with the letter 'R' and are available to the public once printed. They are collected together in bound volumes available at intervals of four years. They are distributed to all insurance officers and local tribunals and gain added weight after publication in so far as they are applied and followed without criticism. About 2,000 Commissioners' decisions have been reported since 1948. A digest of these decisions is also published by Her Majesty's Stationery Office.

18. In addition to single Commissioner's decisions, decisions may be given by a Tribunal of three Commissioners nominated in accordance with what is now section 116 of the Social Security Act 1975 to decide a question of law of special difficulty. Such decisions are almost invariably reported.

19. Commisioners speak with equal authority. All their decisions whether unnumbered, numbered or reported may be cited to Commissioners, local tribunals and insurance officers. Where they decide questions of legal principle they must be followed by insurance officers and local tribunals in cases involving the application of that principle, unless they can be distinguished. It should be borne in mind that similarity in underlying facts does not automatically give rise to similarity in the principle to be applied and questions of fact should not be elevated into questions of legal principle.

20. If confronted with decisions which conflict, insurance officers and local tribunals must prefer the decision of a Tribunal of Commissioners (whether a unanimous or majority decision) to that of a single Commissioner. A reported decision, for the reasons given in paragraph 17(c), should *prima facie* be given more weight than an unreported decision. Subject to the foregoing insurance officers and local tribunals must choose between conflicting decisions and there is no obligation on them to prefer the earlier to the later or *vice versa*.

21. In so far as the Commissioners are concerned, on questions of legal principle, a single Commissioner follows a decision of a Tribunal of Commissioners unless there are compelling reasons why he should not, as, for instance, a decision of superior Courts affecting the legal principles involved. A single Commissioner in the interests of comity and to secure certainty and avoid confusion on question of legal principle normally follows the decisions of other single Commissioners (see Decision R(G) 3/62 and R(I) 23/63). It is recognised however that a slavish adherence to this could lead to the perpetuation of error and he is not bound to do so.

22. The insurance officer, local tribunals and Commissioners on questions of legal principle are all bound to follow the decisions of the High Court and Superior Courts.

. . . .

Presumption that an Accident arising in the Course of Employment Arose out of it

(Now the Social Security Act 1975, s. 50(3).)

R. v. National Insurance (Industrial Injuries) Commissioner, Ex p. Richardson [1958] 2 All E.R. 689

The applicant, Clifford Richardson, was employed by Salford Corporation as an omnibus conductor. On 7th August, 1954, he was standing in uniform on the platform of his bus making up his way bills, when the driver of the bus, noticing a number of youths standing in the roadway, slowed down the bus. Two of the youths jumped on to the platform of the bus, and one of them kicked the applicant in the stomach. The applicant fell to the floor and knocked his head on the stairs of the bus, receiving head injuries and injury to his right eye. The applicant was not robbed. Previous to the assault on the applicant the youths had assaulted other persons.

. . . .

LORD GODDARD, C.J., stated the facts and continued: The question arises whether the applicant is or is not entitled to claim disablement benefit because, to claim disablement benefit, the insured person must suffer injury caused by accident arising out of and in the course of his employment. The National Insurance (Industrial Injuries) Commissioner has held that the accident did not arise out of his employment, although it arose in the course of his employment, because, on the evidence before him, it was not shown that the applicant was specially singled out by reason of any particular circumstance connected with his employment, such as that he was wearing a particular uniform or might have money on him. The commissioner held that it was an attack made on the applicant as a person in the street, as these youths had been attacking other people.

This is a motion for certiorari on the ground that the commissioner misdirected himself with regard to the law, because, so it is said, the onus of proof was put on the applicant whereas, according to counsel for the applicant's contention, the onus of proof was on the insurance officer. Counsel has conceded that the question comes, in the end, to the true construction of s. 7(4) of the National Insurance (Industrial Injuries) Act, 1946. Sub-section (4) provides

"For the purposes of this Act, an accident arising in the course of an insured person's employment shall be deemed,

in the absence of evidence to the contrary, also to have arisen
out of that employment."

Therefore, if a person proves merely that he suffered an accident
in the course of his employment, and there is no other evidence,
then it is to be deemed that the accident arose out of the employment. If, however, the facts which are in evidence before the
commissioner can amount to evidence to the contrary, then the
presumption disappears, and it is then for the applicant to prove
that the accident did arise not only in the course of but also out
of his employment. The words of the sub-section are not "in the
absence of proof to the contrary" or "unless the contrary is
proved"; the words of the sub-section are "in the absence of
evidence to the contrary". That has been held by commissioners
quite correctly, in my opinion, to mean no more than that, if there
is evidence before the commissioner that the accident does not
arise out of or in the course of the employment, then there is no
presumption at all and it is left to the parties to prove the case in
the ordinary way. It is always necessary to bear in mind that, where
this court is asked to grant certiorari, this court has no power to
sit as a court of appeal on the facts. The only ground on which we
are asked to grant certiorari in this case is that, on the face of the
decision, there is an error of law. The error of law which is alleged
is that the commissioner misdirected himself with regard to the
onus of proof and held that there was an onus on the applicant
instead of there being an onus on the insurance officer. That does
not seem to me, with all respect to counsel for the applicant's
argument, to be right. It is not here a question of the onus of
proof. The question is: Was there evidence to the contrary? If
there was, it is left to the applicant to make out his case. There
being, in my opinion, evidence before the commissioner which
would prevent the presumption which otherwise would arise from
being applicable, he has come to the conclusion that the accident
did not arise out of and in the course of his employment. It is not
for this court to sit as a court of appeal from him on that. In my
opinion, there is no error of law on the face of this decision and
the commissioner has correctly interpreted s. 7(4) of the Act of
1946. For these reasons this application fails.

Slade and Devlin J.J. delivered concurring judgments.

R(I) 1/64

. . . .

3. The applicant, a married man aged 36, is a post office telephone engineer. On the 16th November, 1962 it was his duty to visit a number of telephone call boxes, travelling by means of a van provided, to investigate and rectify faults. In the course of this duty he visited a street telephone kiosk in S. Street, where a fault had been reported. He examined the apparatus. While he was doing so a young man opened the door, wishing to telephone: but the applicant was still working on the apparatus. The applicant completed his work, checked everything was in order, and entered this in his book. The next thing which he remembers is that he arrived home, bleeding from a wound in the head. He was sent to hospital where he was found to have certain injuries about the head and face. It was suspected that his skull might have been fractured, but x-ray examination was negative of this. The hospital diagnosis was "Head injury with retrograde amnesia". There is no reason to doubt that the loss of memory was genuine and complete. At hospital it was assumed that the claimant had been assaulted. However that may be, he was certainly not robbed.

. . . .

9. As I see it, there was really no evidence to show that the accident did *not* arise out of the applicant's employment. He himself had no recollection covering the relevant time. No eyewitness was traced. The circumstantial evidence was so slight and inconclusive as to be—in my opinion—immaterial. I agree that there were lots of speculative possibilities: but I think that "evidence" in the sense of section 7(4) means something more than speculative inference, although it means something less than "proof". If there was no evidence that the accident did *not* arise out of the applicant's employment, section 7(4) applies, and the accident is deemed to have arisen out of the employment.

10. It may be that the tribunal considered that there was sufficient circumstantial evidence to establish the probability of an assault. The case seems to have been put to them on the assumption that the applicant's injuries had been sustained by way of an assault, and that this could not be considered to arise out of the employment unless it were shown that the employment involved a special liability to assault. This was no doubt at one time a correct approach: but I do not think it is so since the coming into force of section 2 of the Family Allowances and National Insurance Act 1961. In terms of that section, an accident arising in the course of employment, caused "by another person's misconduct" is to be treated as arising out of a person's employment, provided that the

insured person did not himself induce or contribute to the happening of it by his conduct outside the employment or by any act not incidental to the employment. Accordingly, even if it were thought that there was evidence in this case to justify the inference that the applicant came by his injuries by way of assault, such evidence would not constitute evidence that the accident did not arise out of his employment.

. . . .

Acts Contrary to Orders, etc.

(Now the Social Security Act 1975, s. 52.)

R(I) 41/55

. . . .

2. On the 2nd February, 1955, while the claimant was driving a dumper at the quarry where he was employed, the dumper went over the edge of the quarry carrying the claimant with it, and the claimant was seriously injured. He claimed injury benefit. On the 16th May, 1955 the local appeal tribunal (affirming the decision of the local insurance officer) disallowed the claim, holding that the accident was not an industrial accident. This was a majority decision. The findings of the majority were as follows. "The claimant sustained an accident on 2.2.55 at C—— Quarry while he was employed there. Claimant's employment at the time was a holeborer. He was driving the dumper at the time of the accident without the permission of his employers. The accident did not arise out of and in the course of the claimant's insurable employment." One member of the tribunal dissented, his reason for dissent being recorded as follows:—"At the time of the accident the claimant was a spare dumper driver."

3. The claimant's appeal was heard by way of oral hearing before me. The claimant is a young man of 17 years. He was legally represented. He and a fellow-workman (who is his brother-in-law) and the quarry foreman gave evidence. In addition to this evidence and the material which was before the tribunal I also had a statement dated the 1st September, 1955 from the employers, relative to the claimant's duties.

. . . .

10. Reference was . . . made to Section 8 of the Act: the general purport of which is in certain prescribed circumstances to bring back within the scope of employment an act which otherwise would have fallen to be regarded as outwith the scope of employment in

respect that it was prohibited or unauthorised. (It has of course been held by the Commissioner in a number of cases—and I respectively agree—that Section 8 does not operate so as to *extend* the scope of an insured person's employment.) In the present case it is admitted that the claimant's act of driving the dumper was not directly prohibited. The evidence as to whether, on the occasion in question, it was or was not authorised is conflicting. It is not necessary—for the purposes of the present decision—to determine that question: for even if the act of driving the dumper on the occasion in question was without instructions from the employer, the claimant is entitled to succeed by virtue of the provisions of Section 8. I am satisfied that the act of driving the dumper was done for the purposes of and in connection with the employer's trade or business: and—as has been shown above—I am also satisfied that the accident would have been deemed to have arisen out of and in the course of the claimant's employment had the act (of driving the dumper) not been done without the instructions of the employer. I hold therefore that the conditions under which Section 8 comes into operation are satisfied, and that accordingly the accident can be deemed to have arisen out of and in the course of the claimant's employment, which, it is not disputed, is insurable employment.

. . . .

R. v. d'Albuquerque, Ex p. Bresnahan [1966] LL.L. R. 69

LORD PARKER OF WADDINGTON, C.J.: In these proceedings, Mr. Stocker moves on behalf of a widow, Mrs. Mary Jane Bresnahan, for an order of *certiorari* to bring up and quash a decision of the Deputy Commissioner for the National Insurance (Industrial Injuries) Acts, 1946 to 1964. whereby he decided that the death of the applicant's husband was not caused by an accident arising out of and in consequence of his employment, and accordingly that she was not entitled to industrial death benefit. The grounds for claiming relief are that there is an error of law on the face of the Deputy Commissioner's decision.

. . . .

The accident arose in the following circumstances: the deceased was a dock labourer working with others on the loading of a ship in the Liverpool docks. A time came when there were some pallet boards on the quay which were in the way of the loading and had to be removed. There was a man also employed in the gang, if I may use that expression, engaged in this loading whose duty it was to drive a fork lift truck. A time came when he left that fork lift truck with the engine running while he went to effect repairs to another. At that moment the deceased took the fork lift truck and endeavoured with it to remove the pallet boards. In so doing he overshot the side of the quay and the machine with the deceased on it went down into the water, striking the side of the ship, and as a result he was drowned.

. . . .

If one goes back to one or two of the the leading authorities under the Acts of 1923 and 1925, the matter becomes reasonably clear. In *Wilsons and Clyde Coal Company, Ltd.* v. *M'Ferrin* and *Kerr or M'Aulay and Another* v. *James Dunlop & Co., Ltd.*, which were heard together and reported in [1926] A.C. 377, Viscount Dunedin dealt with the effect of Sect. 7 of the Act of 1923, It is unnecessary to read his speech in full, but I would refer to one or two passages. At the foot of p. 384 and the top of p. 385 of the report he said:

> . . . Injury must have occurred "arising out of and in the course of his employment." If he makes out the proposition that it did so, he succeeds; if he does not he fails. Now, it is obvious that one method which the employer resisting a claim had of showing that the injury did not arise out of his employment was to show that the workman was forbidden to do what, in fact, he did, and then came the distinction between the two classes of prohibition, which was laid down in [*Plumb* v. *Cobden Flour Mills Co.,* [1914] A.C. 62]; prohibitions which did and prohibitions which did not limit the scope of employment. The former class, which limited the scope of employment, if found to apply to the employment, formed a complete answer to the assertion that the accident arose out of the employment.

He then cited Sect. 7 of the Act of 1923, and at p. 386 he said that:

> The result of this section is, in my opinion, not doubtful. It does not either repeal or amend the radical provision of the principal Act, that the accident to entitle the workman to compensation must arise out of and in the course of his employment, but it does introduce a far-reaching, though artificial, consideration which prevents a certain class of evidence, available to show that the accident did not arise out of the employment, from being any longer in force.

That decision, which has often been cited in subsequent cases, was specifically referred to in *Thomas* v. *Ocean Coal Company, Ltd.*, [1933] A.C. 100. On pp. 128 and 129, Lord Russell of

Killowen referes to Viscount Dunedin's speech. He points out that apparently in argument it had been contended that Viscount Dunedin's remarks had a much wider significance than was at one time thought. Lord Russell of Killowen goes on and says:

> The general words used by Lord Dunedin cannot therefore bear their full signification. Indeed, if in all cases before a claimant could claim the benefit of this remedial provision he had to prove that the accident did arise out of and in the course of the employment, it is difficult to see how an opportunity for "deeming" it so to arise could ever present itself. Later portions of Lord Dunedin's speech make his meaning clear. He limited the operation of S. 7 by saying that notwithstanding that section it was still open to the employer to show that the accident did not arise out of the employment by showing "that the workman was doing something which was not his employment," or "doing something different in kind from anything he was required to do." If that were shown then, he said, the case never came within s. 7 at all.

Reference has also been made to the case of *Noble* v. *Southern Railway Company,* [1940] A.C. 583, where Viscount Maugham, at p. 591, said that the proper approach was

> . . . to answer the following questions:—
> First, looking at the facts proved as a whole, including any regulations or orders affecting the workman, was the accident one which arose out of and in the course of his employment?
> Secondly, if the first question is answered in the negative, is the negative answer due to the fact that when the accident happened the workman was acting in contravention of some regulation or order?
> Thirdly, if the second question is answered in the affirmative, was the act which the workman was engaged in performing done by the workman for the pusposes of and in connection with his employer's trade or business?

From the guidance given in those cases, it seems to me that the first question that the Deputy Commissioner really had to ask himself was whether the act in question, the driving of this fork lift truck, whether prohibited or not, was different in kind from what he was employed to do. If it was, then the effect of Sect. 8 could not be to bring it within the scope of the employment.

In the present case, this man was found to be a hooker on, and indeed when one realises that he was a hooker on, one understands the evidence which was given before the local appeal tribunal, that it was his job to have these pallet boards removed; in other words it was no part of his job to remove them manually. Further, the driving of the fork lift trucks was entrusted to special drivers. Accordingly, as it seems to me, there was a ground for coming to a conclusion that really his job was quite a different job, albeit they were members of the same gang, to those who were entrusted with the task of driving these fork lift trucks.

In my judgment, the Deputy Commissioner in par. 18 has not misdirected himself; he is there saying, having heard the evidence, and I imagine the most important evidence was that of the foreman stevedore, as to the duties of the various members of the gang, he finds that it was not within the scope of the deceased's employment that he should drive a forklift truck.

It is true that the Deputy Commissioner goes on after that to refer to the fact that it may well be that unauthorised persons had done so in the past but would have been stopped as soon as they were seen. In that passage as it seems to me, all that the Deputy Commissioner is doing is to meet an argument which has been raised before us, and which no doubt was raised before him, that these were men in a gang engaged on what one might call interchangeable jobs, and he is there meeting that argument by saying in effect there is no evidence that they were interchangeable; far from that, if one person unauthorised to drive a fork lift truck was found doing so, he would be stopped.

Mr. Stocker has argued with force that these men were members of a gang engaged quite generally on loading this ship, and that it is wrong to look upon them as having separate jobs in the sense of one man being hooker on, one man being a fork lift truck driver and so on.

It may well be that there are such cases, and indeed Viscount Dunedin himself in *Wilsons and Clyde Coal Company, Ltd.* v. *M'Ferrin, sup.,* dealt with that at p. 390. He said, in dealing with a fireman engaged on shot firing and others with him, this:

> . . . The learned counsel for the appellants urged that this was an operation which was being conducted by three men, and that, if one did something out of his ordinary appointed task, none the less he was working within the scope of his employment. . . .

Then Viscount Dunedin goes on:

. . . There might easily be figured cases where such an argument would prevail. In some classes of work a certain interchange would be innocuous. All depends on the facts, but the facts here show undeniably—and so the arbitrator who is the judge of fact has found—that this was not in the proper sense of the word a joint operation. . . .

In the present case the Deputy Commissioner heard the evidence, and he has in effect found that the jobs of the men in the gang were not interchangeable, at any rate between the hooker on and fork lift truck driver. For my part I cannot say, this not being an appeal, that he must have erred in law in coming to that decision.

Finally Mr. Stocker submits, and it is a submission which I think he would put in this way: he would if necessary submit that really this Court in construing Sect. 8 of the Act of 1946 ought to treat itself as not bound by authorities and interpretations given to Sect. 1(2) of the Workmen's Compensation Act, 1925. For my part I find it impossible to do other than approach the construction of Sect. 8 in the light of the decisions on the earlier Act. The wording, as I have said, is not only clearly based on the earlier Act, but embraces patently as it seems to me the interpretation put upon the sub-section by the House of Lords in many of the earlier cases.

Ashworth and Widgery J.J. delivered concurring judgments.

Travelling

R(I) 42/56

. . . .

7. The deceased was employed as a farm worker, on the farm of B. He lived in a tied cottage on the farm. The farm lands are intersected by a public road. Part of the farm including the steading, lies on one side of this public road, while the rest of the farm including the tied cottages, lies on the other. From the steading to the public road there is a service road. From the cottages to the public road there is a service road. These two service roads join the public road on opposite sides, and nearly opposite to each other. The natural and normal route for a person who has been working at or near the steading and who wishes to go to the cottages, is to follow the service read leading from the steading, cross over the public road, and take the other service road to the cottages.

8. The farm workers work both in the morning and in the afternoon, with a dinner break extending normally from 11.30 or 11.45 a.m. until 1 p.m. On the day of the accident the deceased was on his way from the place where he had been working (somewhere near the steading) to his cottage, for dinner. The distance in question is something like 1,000 yards; possibly 10 or 15 minutes' walk. A tractor belonging to the employer and driven by a fellow-worker was going from the neighbourhood of the steading to the cottages. The deceased got a lift on this tractor. The tractor was not adapted for the carrying of passengers, but the deceased stood on the drawbar, where (it is said) he was able to hold on to a rail and to the drivers' seat. There were also some children on the tractor. The tractor went along the service road from the steading to the public road (a distance of several hundred yards), crossed over the public road, and entered the service road leading to the cottages. At a very short distance along the service road the deceased fell from the tractor and sustained fatal injuries. The time of the accident was 12 o'clock.

9. It is a matter of express admission by the representative of the insurance officer that (1) the *locus* of the accident was within the perimeter of the farm, and (2) the deceased had implied permission from his employer to travel to the cottage on the tractor.

10. The first question for determination is whether—apart from the special provisions of Section 9[7] of the Act—the accident arose out of and in the course of the deceased's employment. It was submitted for the insurance officer that the deceased's place of work on the day in question was at a part of the farm near the steading; that in leaving his work to go home for his mid-day meal the deceased was disentangling himself from his work; that some reasonable latitude of distance should be allowed before he should be held so to have disentangled himself; but that by the time he reached the public road disentanglement was complete; nor could it be said that in completing the journey to his cottage to have his dinner the deceased re-entered the ambit of his employment albeit he had entered again the confines of the farm lands. Reference was made to a number of authorities under the Workmen's Compensation Acts, and to various Commissioners' decisions, including R(I) 9/51, R(I) 79/51, R(I) 1/53, R(I) 27/54 and R(I) 61/51.

11. As against this, it was pointed out that the accident which befell the deceased did not occur upon the public road, and thus did not represent a risk to the general public; that having regard

---

[7] See, now, the Social Security Act 1975, s. 53.

to the deceased's duties and responsibilities the ambit of his employment extended over the whole territory of the farm; and that on entering the service road leading to the cottages he re-entered the sphere of his employment.

12. I feel that in this chapter of the law, in which very subtle distinctions have been drawn, attempted assimilation of the circumstances of the accident under review with those of other cases in the reports, if carried too far, becomes merely perplexing. Nor—as was pointed out in the course of the argument—is it always satisfactory to apply to conditions of farm work *dicta* pronounced in relation to factory conditions. As I see it, however, the deceased's place of work (as that term is generally used) was at a part of the farm near the steading; and I refer, on this point, to Decision R(I) 7/52, paragraph 9(1). He left that place after the forenoon spell of work ended, to go for his meal. Primarily, at least, that journey was for his own purposes, rather than on his employer's business: compare Decision R(I) 1/53. It would not be reasonable to hold that as soon as he left the actual site of his labours he emerged from the ambit of his employment. Some extension must be allowed to cover his departure from his actual place of work. But the line must be drawn somewhere. I do not think it can be extended, consistently with principle of precedent, beyond the public road. In my judgment—apart from the effect of Section 9 of the Act—the deceased had left his sphere of his employment at a point in his journey before the accident occurred; and he had not re-entered it. Accordingly the accident did not arise in the course of his employment.

13. It remains to consider the effect of Section 9 of the Act, which is in the following terms—

> "9.—(1). An accident happening while an insured person is, with the express or implied permission of his employer, travelling as a passenger by any vehicle to or from his place of work shall, notwithstanding that he is under no obligation to his employer to travel by that vehicle, be deemed to arise out of and in the course of his employment, if—
>
> (a) the accident would have been deemed so to have arisen had he been under such an obligation; and
> (b) at the time of the accident, the vehicle—
>
>> (i) is being operated by or on behalf of his employer or some other person by whom it is provided in pursuance of arrangements made with his employer; and

(ii) is not being operated in the ordinary course of a public transport service.

(2). In this section reference to a vehicle includes references to a ship, vessel or aircraft."

14. This section has no counterpart in the Workmen's Compensation Acts. Under the Workmen's Compensation Acts, an accident to a workman travelling to or from work on a train (or other transport) in consequence of his employment was held not to arise in the course of his employment if the workman was under no obligation or duty to use that train—*Hewitson* v. *St. Helen's Colliery Co., Ltd.* (1923) 16 B.W.C.C. 230. The effect of Section 9 is that the absence of any obligation or duty to travel on the vehicle concerned is not, by itself to take the accident out of the category of industrial accidents, if all other conditions of an industrial accident are fulfilled. The representative of the insurance officer made two novel submissions as to the interpretation of Section 9. He submitted that a "vehicle" within the meaning of the section is limited to "vehicle appropriate for the carrying of persons," and that travelling "as a passenger" excludes cases where the employee is being conveyed on a part of a vehicle not intended for the carriage of passengers. The latter proposition receives support from a passage in MacGillivray's Law of Insurance, 4th ed., at paragraph 1514, which is based on three American cases there cited. But I am not prepared to accept it in relation to Section 9 of the Act. "Vehicle" is not exhaustively defined in Section 9. In ordinary usage the word imports a means of conveyance, whether of passengers or of goods, and I find no warrant for restricting it, as used in Section 9, to a means appropriate to the conveyance of passengers only. It might indeed be forcefully argued—having regard to the derivation and dictionary definition of the word—that a vehicle is something which *carries* and not something which *draws*; and that accordingly a tractor is not a vehicle. I think, however, that nowadays a tractor would be spoken of as a vehicle. At any rate it has so been regarded by the legislature. Thus the old-fashioned road locomotive or "traction engine" was regarded as a vehicle in the Locomotives on Highways Act 1896 and the tractor is treated as a vehicle in the Road Traffic Act 1930. For aught that I know there may be types of tractors which are designed to accommodate a passenger or a load. On the whole matter I am not prepared to hold that a tractor is not a vehicle within the meaning of Section 9 of the Industrial Injuries Act. Nor can I find any warrant for the suggestion that a passenger is not travelling "as a passenger" if he occupies some part of a vehicle not designed

for the carriage of passengers. It may be, of course, that in certain circumstances a workman who travelled on some obviously unsuitable part of a vehicle might be deprived of the benefit of the Act, on the principle of *Stephen* v. *Cooper* (1929) 22 B.W.C.C. 339 (as explained in the House of Lords in *Harris* v. *Associated Portland Cement Manufacturers* (1938) 31 B.W.C.C. 434, at page 438); but in the present case it was not contended before me that the claimant's action in travelling on the drawbar of a tractor amounted to "a foolhardy act of bravado" as in the case of *Stephen* v. *Cooper* (above), nor—in view of the evidence in the case—would I have accepted such a submission if it had been made. It was not disputed that if the tractor was a vehicle, and if the deceased was travelling by it as a passenger, all the other conditions of Section 9 of the Act were satisfied.

15. In the proceedings before the local appeal tribunal there seems to have been some discussion as to the meaning of that part of the subsection which runs as follows—"in pursuance of arrangements made with his employer," and Decision R(I) 67/51 (in which the meaning of that phrase was discussed) was referred to. At the oral hearing of the present appeal I asked the representatives of both parties whether it was contended that the phrase "in pursuance of arrangements made by the employer" qualified the whole of the sentence of which it forms part, or merely that portion which begins "or some other person by whom it is provided." Both were agreed that the phrase qualified only the latter portion of the sentence. In other words, if the vehicle is being operated by or on behalf of the employer, no question arises as to "arrangements made with his employer." This accords with my own view of the subsection.

16. In the result I hold that by virtue of Section 9 of the Act, the relevant accident is deemed to have arisen out of and in the course of the deceased's employment and I uphold the decision of the tribunal.

. . . .

Emergencies

R(I) 6/63

. . . .

2. In the course of his employment as a milk roundsman, the claimant was delivering milk at houses in a road from a van parked in the road. He picked up some bottles of milk from the van and started towards a bungalow on the opposite side of the road in

order to deliver milk there, when he noticed that the bungalow, in which there were children, was on fire. He immediately put down the milk bottles and ran to the back of the bungalow and unsuccessfully tried to get in to rescue the children. He then returned round the side of it past a window. Whilst he was doing so there was an explosion in the bungalow and he was injured by flying glass from the widow. In spite of his injury he continued to try to get into the bungalow but without success. The question for decision is whether this was or is deemed to have been an industrial accident.

3. The evidence on two points is not very clear. My findings on them are that (in accordance with the finding of the local appeal tribunal, who had the advantage of hearing the claimant himself and his solicitor) the place where the claimant put down the bottles was either on the highway or on the van parked on it, and that at the moment of the accident the claimant was on the bungalow premises.

. . . .

5. Section 10 of the Act[8] provides as follows:—

> "An accident happening to an insured person in or about any premises at which he is for the time being employed for the purposes of his employer's trade or business shall be deemed to arise out of and in the course of his employment if it happens while he is taking steps, on an actual or supposed emergency at those premises, to rescue, succour or protect persons, who are, or are thought to be or possibly to be, injured or imperilled, or to avert or minimise serious damage to property."

6. In my judgment it is necessary to consider in this case whether the claimant is entitled to benefit either irrespective of section 10 or by virtue of section 10.

7. There was no provision of general application similar to section 10 in the Workmen's Compensation Act, 1925, though there was a much restricted provision relating to rescues in coal mines in section 34 of that Act, which replaced section 110(2) of the Coal Mines Act, 1911. Nevertheless the courts in a number of cases held that, although as a general rule a workman had no title to compensation in respect of an accident caused by an act beyond the sphere of his employment, there was an exception to this rule where the accident happened to him whilst engaged in his employment and on his employers' work, if he voluntarily did upon an

---

[8] See, now, the Social Security Act 1975, s. 54.

emergency an act in the interests of his employer outside the scope of his ordinary employment (see Willis Workmen's Compensation, 37th Edition, pages 74–75). This doctrine has been applied by the Commissioner under the 1946 Act (see *e.g.* Decision R(I) 63/54).

8. In my judgment the present claim cannot succeed on this basis. No doubt the employer would have approved the claimant's action, as everyone else would, but in my judgment it cannot be said in a fair sense that the claimant was acting in the interests of his employer; he was acting in the interests of the occupiers of the bungalow and their children.

9. It is therefore necessary to consider whether apart from the above doctrine, the claimant can succeed by virtue of section 10. That section does not provide, as does section 2 of the Family Allowances and National Insurance Act, 1961, that an accident arising in the course of the employment shall in certain circumstances be treated as arising out of it; nor does it provide that an accident which arises out of it shall be deemed to arise in the course of it. Its effect is that, if the necessary conditions are fulfilled, an accident is deemed to arise both out of the employment and in the course of it. If therefore conditions in section 10 are fulfilled, it would be no answer to the claim to say that apart from section 10 the accident either would not arise in the course of the employment or would not arise out of it, or both. Section 10 confers rights on claimants over and above those which they would have without it under section 7, and it does not deprive them of any of those rights.

10. It is a curious fact that, during all the years in which section 10 has been in force, it appears never to have been subjected as a whole to close analysis in any reported decision, and there appears to be no reported case in which a claim under it has succeeded. I am indebted to the local appeal tribunal, who reluctantly disallowed the claimant's appeal for the clarity with which they have recorded the evidence and their findings and reasons. I am also indebted to the insurance officer now concerned with the case for his written submission and also to his legal representative, who appeared at the oral hearing before me, for having analysed the matter so carefully. They contend, as a result, that the claimant is entitled to succeed under section 10. Having considered their arguments I feel able to take a different view of the matter from that taken by the tribunal.

11. On certain points I feel no difficulty. In my judgment the word "premises" includes (in this case) not only the bungalow but also any land attached to it and forming one enclosure with it, which is often referred to by lawyers as the curtilage. But the word

"premises" cannot include a highway. This was so under the Workmen's Compensation Acts (*Andrews* v. *Andrews & Mears* [1908] 2 K.B.567, 1 B.W.C.C.264), and it is so under the 1946 Act (Decision R(I) 52/54, paragraph 9). So far as the accident is concerned, however, it is sufficient for the claimant's purpose if it was "in or about" the premises. This includes a place close to them (see *Andrew's* case above and other decisions under section 6(4) of the Workmen's Compensation Act, 1925). In my judgment the claimant was "in or about" the premises when he put down the bottles, and he was on them when the accident happened. There was manifestly an actual emergency on the premises, and in my judgment the claimant, by hurrying round the bungalow to rescue the children, was taking steps to rescue persons imperilled. The section does not require that he should have been actually rescuing them or actually averting serious damage to property.

12. The question still remains however whether at the time it could be said: "These are premises at which he is for the time being employed for the purposes of his employer's trade or business." I have felt great doubt and difficulty about this question, but on the whole I have come to the conclusion that it can be answered, as the insurance officer now concerned with the case submits, favourably to the claimant.

13. The first effect of section 10 is to extend the insurance to cover a person who, whilst working, for example, in his employer's factory, takes steps upon an emergency there to rescue anyone whether employed there or not, or to protect property whether it belongs to the employers or not. This is an extension of the law as it existed before the Act and was reproduced by section 7. The words "for the time being" extend it in another way. For example, if a painter is employed to paint the house of a customer of his employer, the house is premises at which the painter is for the time being employed, even though he may in general be employed elsewhere. The fact that he is employed there only temporarily does not matter. The premises in section 10 are not limited to premises owned or occupied by the claimant's employer. I think that the time referred to must be that of the accident. But in my judgment if a person working on the premises breaks off his work on becoming aware of an emergency he does not thereby cease to be employed "at" those premises, even if he goes out into the street to effect the rescue, and even though apart from section 10 the course of his employment might be temporarily interrupted. If it were otherwise, the words "or about" would be ineffective.

14. Once it is seen that the words "for the time being" includes a temporary worker on premises, in my judgment it can make no

difference whether he works for a short or a long time. If (to take again the example of the painter) his foreman visits the house for five minutes to inspect the work, the house is during those five minutes premises at which the foreman is for the time being employed for the purposes of his employers' trade. And if the postman or the milk-roundsman is *on* the premises for only a few seconds for the purposes of his work, similarly the house is in my judgment premises at which he is employed. There is a distinction in degree but not in kind between these various cases.

15. I have no doubt therefore that, if the claimant had entered the premises carrying the bottle to deliver them and had put them down on the premises, they would have been premises at which he was employed for the purposes of his employer's trade. The question is whether, since in fact he put them down before entering, they were not such premises. (The same question could arise with the painter if he detected the emergency before reaching the premises to start work.) Must it be held that because the claimant entered the premises for the purpose of dealing with the emergency and not for the purpose of delivering milk, at any rate immediately, he cannot benefit from the section?

16. In my judgment this would be taking too narrow a view of the section. The words "employed" and "employment" are not defined in the Act. The conception of employment *at* a place suggests a duty to work there, but in ordinary language a person can clearly be employed at premises even when he is not actually working on them. In this case there was an unusual combination of circumstances. It was the claimant's duty to deliver milk to the bungalow. He had decided to deliver it there next before going on to any other premises. In order to do so he had picked up the bottles from the van in the road outside the bungalow and had actually started to go towards the bungalow to deliver them. He put them down only because of the emergency. I have found the case difficult, but, taking into account what appear to be the general objects of the section, I have reached the conclusion that, even without giving an extended meaning to the word "at", it can in the special circumstances be held that the bungalow premises were premises at which the claimant was at the time of the accident for the time being employed for the purposes of his employer's trade. His claim therefore succeeds, and he is entitled to the declaration which he claims that the accident was an industrial accident.

Disablement Benefit

R(I) 3/76

. . . .

2. I granted to the claimant leave to appeal from the above-mentioned decision and directed an oral hearing which has now taken place. The claimant attended and was represented by Mr. John Ryman, M.P. whose constituent she is. The Secretary of State was represented by Mr. Malik of the solicitor's office of the Department of Health and Social Security.

3. The claimant is a single woman aged 50 and is a civil servant. On 6th February, 1974 she hurt herself in an incident which has been held to be an industrial accident. She hit the side of her face on a filing cabinet drawer and incurred a retinal detachment in her left eye. An operation to fix the retina in that eye was performed on 13th February 1974.

4. In connection with the claimant's claim to disablement benefit a report was obtained from Mr. A. L. Crombie, the consultant ophthalmologist at the hospital where her operation had been performed. Mr. Crombie stated in his report, writted on 27th August 1974, that the retina of the claimant's left eye was flat "following her successful operation", and that her main complaint at that time was of facial pain "which may be related to her operative treatment". The report concludes as follows:—

> "The diagnosis in her case therefore is a retinal detachment occurring in someone with a high degree of myopia following trauma. In my opinion there is certainly a connection between the trauma which she suffered and subsequent onset of her detachment although in a high myope there is a pre-disposition to detachment in any case.
> The prognosis for the left eye is difficult to ascertain as she may well redetach and she may also suffer a detachment in her right eye if trauma is sustained."

5. The claimant attended her first medical board on 15th October, 1974, when Mr. Crombie's report formed part of the medical evidence. The board found partly due to the accident and partly to a pre-existing congenital defect, injury or disease: "Injury to left eye with detached retina site of pre-existing myopia". And they described the effect of the relevant loss of faculty as: "Some loss of vision in left eye". They assessed the claimant's disablement at 5 per cent, which they arrived at by means of a gross assessment of 10 per cent and a deduction by way of offset of 5 per cent. It is not absolutely clear how the board justified the offset but it is

likely that they did so on the ground that the claimant had a predisposition to retinal detachment because of myopia. Their net 5 per cent assessment of the claimant's disablement was provisional and for the period from the end of the injury benefit period (6th August, 1974) to 6th August, 1975.

6. The claimant wished to appeal from the medical board's decision and, as she had no legal right to do so, the Secretary of State exercised her power to refer a case to a medical appeal tribunal. Accordingly, the claimant's case came before the medical appeal tribunal of 28th January, 1975 on the Secretary of State's reference.

7. The medical appeal tribunal did not confirm the decision of the medical board of 15th October, 1974 but in effect awarded to the claimant an assessment of 7 per cent from the end of the injury benefit period for life. They arrived at that percentage by means of a gross assessment of 12 per cent from which they made an offset of 5 per cent. They gave their reasons as follows:—

> "We have noted the report of Mr. Crombie dated 27th August, 1974 and having examined the claimant, we find no significant change in her condition since that report was prepared.
> We have heard the S. of S. submission and consider that in view of the high degree of probability of spontaneous retinal detachment in this case an offset is justifiable.
> In our view however the claimant is slightly under assessed and we assess at 12 per cent with an offset of 5 per cent—making 7 per cent net to 6.8.75, followed by 12 per cent offsetting 5 per cent for life."

8. The claimant and her association challenge the offset made by the medical appeal tribunal and have based their reasons for seeking leave to appeal, and for appealing, on the submission made to the tribunal by the Secretary of State's representative. They maintain that the tribunal should have acted in accordance with his submission that no offset should be made because of a likely predisposition to illness or injury, including a predisposition to retinal detachment. The chairman of the medical appeal tribunal also presided over the tribunal who heard the first application for leave to appeal and understood the claimant and her association to be asserting that the tribunal of 28th January, 1975 erred in failing to accept the view of the Department of Health and Social Security on a point of medical opinion. I do not think that the submissions made by the claimant and her association should be so read. I think that they intended to submit that the error consisted in failing to accept the submission of the Secretary of State's

representative on a point of law; although, not being trained lawyers, they phrased their submissions in a manner which left them open to the interpretation placed on them by the chairman. 9. I granted leave to appeal in this case because I considered it arguable that the medical appeal tribunal had failed to apply correctly the statutory provisions authorising an offset. In addition, I requested that the person who represented the Secretary of State at the medical appeal tribunal's hearing provide a statement of the submission which he made to them. In answer to this request, the representative has provided an excellent statement which is now included in the case papers. While he may not have made his submission in the neat form of his written statement, it is clear that he addressed the tribunal, and there was a discussion, on the law dealing with offsets. The following is extracted from the representative's written statement (the underlining being inserted by me):—

"3. As regards myopia I have been advised that the consensus medical view is that a person who is suffering from myopia . . . is at greater risk of suffering a retinal detachment than one whose eyesight is normal. Also, that the degree of risk is in direct proportion to the degree of myopia present. Thus for a person with a high degree of myopia, there is a high degree of probability that the retina will detach without the intervention of an industrial accident, though it cannot be maintained that every person who suffers from myopia will suffer a detached retina. I have been advised that, in cases of myopia where it has been accepted that an industrial accident precipitates a detached retina, I should not look for an offset for a predisposition to detachment (since disability and not predisposition to disability is the basis for offset); but that the assessment of a claimant's visual acuity is a matter solely for the Medical Appeal Tribunal, . . . and that the Tribunal may decide to make an offset if the circumstances so require: Indeed, if a Tribunal was satisfied that, because of myopia, retinal detachment would probably have occurred by a certain date even if the accident had not happened, I understand that it would be legitimate . . . for it to find no remaining loss of faculty due to the relevant accident after that date.

4. I do not now recall the exact terms in which I addressed the Tribunal, but my remarks were based on the above

advice. However, in the course of the discussion initiated by one of the medical members on the "offset"
question I referred to the statutory provisions set out
in regulation 2(2) and (3) of the National Insurance
(Industrial Injuries) Benefit Regulations which appear
for convenience's sake on pp. 36–37 of the Handbook
fo Industrial Injuries Medical Boards and to paragraphs
49 and 50 which contain guidance in the interpretation
of these provisions . . ."

10. The underlined sentence in that extract is a submission of
law and is unquestionably correct. The paragraphs of the regulations referred to in the extract have now been replaced, but without
substantive amendment, by paragraphs (2) and (3) of regulation
2 of the Social Security (Industrial Injuries) (Benefit) Regulations
1975 [S.I. 1975 No. 559], which are reproduced below. I need not
reproduce the passages referred to from the Handbook. I have
read them and they seem to me to be free from error.

11. The above-mentioned paragraphs (2) and (3) of regulation
2 read as follows:—

"2(2) When the extent of disablement is being assessed for
the purposes of section 57, any disabilities which,
though resulting from the relevant loss of faculty, also
result, or without the relevant accident might have
been expected to result, from a cause other than the
relevant accident (hereafter in this regulation referred
to as "the other effective cause") shall only be taken
into account subject to and in accordance with the
following provisions of this regulation.

(3) Any assessment of the extent of disablement made by
reference to any disability to which paragraph (2)
applies, in a case where the other effective cause is
a congenital defect or is an injury or disease received
or contracted before the relevant accident, shall take
account of all such disablement except to the extent
to which the claimant would have been subject thereto
during the period taken into account by the assessment if the relevant accident had not occurred."

12. I discussed the interpretation of those paragraphs (in their
pre-1975 form) in the recent Decision R(I) 13/75, and I shall refrain
from repeating here the authorities cited in that decision. The
points of interpretation which are material to the present decision
are the following:—

(a) The expression "loss of faculty" used in paragraph (2) means a cause of disability and is used in the medical sense of loss of power or function of an organ of the body; "disability" means inability to do something which persons of the same age and sex and normal physical and mental powers can do; "disablement" means a collection of disabilities, that is to say the sum total of all the relevant disabilities found present in a given case.

(b) Paragraph (3) contains the provision authorising an offset and only comes into play if paragraph (2) applies. This only happens if the disability under consideration has a dual causation, the relevant loss of faculty and another cause referred to as "the other effective cause"; and this must be "a congenital defect or . . . an injury or disease received or contracted before the relevant accident".

(c) An offset is only authorised in respect of a disability, not in respect of a cause or potential cause of disability.

13. Mr. Ryman submitted to me that the medical appeal tribunal appeared to have accepted Mr. Crombie's report but in making an offset gave a decision which was inconsistent with his views. Mr. Ryman asserted that there was no evidence to support the making of an offset. I am unable to accept these submissions, in which it seems to me that there is a tendency to treat the medical appeal tribunal as if it were a Court of Law. In my view, there is nothing in the tribunal's decision inconsistent with Mr. Crombie's report. The question is whether, accepting his report, the law authorises an offset. At the same time, I have to emphasize that the tribunal would not have erred in law if they had totally rejected Mr. Crombie's views.

14. In a written submission made after I had granted leave to appeal, and also through Mr. Malik at the hearing of this appeal, the Secretary of State submitted that the decision of the medical appeal tribunal is erroneous in point of law because it fails sufficiently to comply with the statutory requirement that the tribunal must record a statement of the reasons for their decision: regulation 23(1) of the Social Security (Determination of Claims and Questions) Regulations 1975 [S.I. 1975 No. 558]. The contention, as expressed in the written submission, is that the "MAT in making a similar offset [i.e. similar to that made by the medical board of 15th October 1974] have justified it on the grounds of "the high degree of probability of spontaneous retinal detachment" without making it clear whether or not they regarded myopia as a pre-

existing condition amounting to a disability and hence the other effective cause".

15. I have consulted three medical dictionaries on the meaning of the term "myopia" (Dorland 24th edition, Blakiston 2nd edition, and Levitt 1966) and have ascertained that it means and is sometimes called nearsightedness. I understand that it is caused by the lens of the eye having an abnormal refractive power, usually due to the eye-ball being too long from front to back, whereby the focal image is formed in front of, instead of on, the retina. It is not an easy word to control because it may be used to describe the shortness of sight, or the abnormal refractive power of the lens of which the shortness of sight is the symptom, or perhaps the malformation of the eye-ball which causes that abnormality, or a combination of these.

16. Plainly, the nearsightedness from which a myopic person suffers is a disability. I find it difficult to regard as a disability his proneness to detachment of the retina. This proneness is, in my view, not a disability; it is a threat of disability. However, it may be the cause of disabilities, for example by preventing or inhibiting the myopic person from undertaking activities normal for a person not threatened with retinal detachment.

17. I have come to the conclusion that I should accept the Secretary of State's submission but for a reason somewhat different from that advanced on her behalf. It is there suggested that the tribunal might have regarded "myopia as a pre-existing condition amounting to a disability". I am uncertain what this means. If "myopia" is used to describe the underlying condition causing the claimant to be short-sighted, then I think that it corresponds with the expression "loss of faculty" used in the Act and regulations. On the other hand, if "myopia" is used to describe the shortsightedness from which the claimant suffered before her accident, then it was a disability. Possibly the submission proceeds from the point of view that "loss of faculty" and "disability" express overlapping concepts. It has been said that the concepts underlying these expressions may overlap, but the statute envisages them as separate: see the speech of Lord Simon of Glaisdale in *Hudson* v. *Secretary of State for Social Services, Hudson* v. *Same* [1972] A.C. 944 at p. 1019 G (also the Supplement to the Commissioner's reported Decision R(I) 3/69 at p. 214 D). Accordingly, it is wise, if possible, to keep them separate. I do not see how the underlying condition can amount to a disability. In my view it is a cause of one or more disabilities, but not itself a disability.

18. On the other hand I do not think that the medical appeal tribunal have succeeded in making their reasons for the offset

clear. It is out of the question that they overlooked the legal principle that an offset is authorised only for a disability, because they discussed that very point with the Secretary of State's representative. Yet they have not explained how, in their view, the "high degree of probability of spontaneous retinal detachment" can constitute a disability. I consider that by using this phrase without explanation they have failed to give their reasons as required by the regulation referred to in paragraph 14 [above].

19. There was some controversy at the hearing of this appeal whether "myopia" ought to be regarded as a congenital defect. Mr. Ryman pointed out that "congenital" normally means "born with", or "present at birth", and indicated that the claimant was not born with myopia. As at present advised I see no reason to alter the view which I expressed in paragraph 22 of the Decision R(I) 13/75 that in the above-mentioned regulation 2(2) "congenital" should receive a rather more extensive meaning than that advocated by Mr. Ryman: cf. the reported Commissioner's Decision R(I) 9/65, where it was held that "congenital defect" included a genetically determined condition. However, this is a controversy which it is unnecessary to resolve in the present case. If the claimant's myopia was not a congenital defect, then it was a disease within the meaning of the regulation. The Shorter Oxford English Dictionary gives as the second meaning of the word "disease": "A condition of the body, or of some part or organ of the body, in which its functions are disturbed or deranged".

20. Finally, it seems to me that there is another reason for finding an error of law in this case. The claimant has persistently complained of facial pain and did so to the medical appeal tribunal on 28th January, 1975. The tribunal did not deal with this complaint, and I think that the claimant was entitled to have it determined by the tribunal whether or not the condition of which she complained constituted or brought about a disability, whether such disability is attributable to the accident, and if so at what percentage the tribunal rated it.

SPECIAL HARDSHIP ALLOWANCE

(See, now, the Social Security Act 1975, s. 60.)

Regina v. Deputy Industrial Injuries Commissioner, Ex p. Humphreys [1966] 2 Q.B. 1. (C.A.)

LORD DENNING M.R. Jack Humphreys is a ripper who worked underground in a colliery near Wrexham. On 16th September,

1959, a piece of stone lacerated his right leg and tore the Achilles tendon. It was an industrial accident such as to entitle him to the benefits provided by the National Insurance (Industrial Injuries) Act, 1946. He received injury benefit for three and a half months, and he has since received disablement benefit. Disablement benefit is based on his disability, and not on his loss of earnings. Any insured person gets disablement benefit so long as he is disabled, even though he is back at work and has lost nothing.

Jack Humphreys claims also a special hardship allowance. This is an allowance made to a man to compensate him for reduced earning capacity. Jack Humphreys claims that his earning capacity is reduced. He can no longer do his regular work as a ripper. He has a sensitive scar which prevents him wearing suitable boots. So he cannot do any heavy manual work. He can do work as a welder-burner, but this work does not command as high wages as a ripper. So he is suffering, he says, loss of earnings and is entitled to a special hardship allowance.

He would clearly have had a good claim if he had stayed at Wrexham and never moved from that area. He would have got a special hardship allowance. But a complication arises because in July, 1960 (10 months after his accident), he went to Doncaster to find suitable work. His wife's grandparents lived there. He found work there as a welder-burner and took his wife and two children over there. They all stayed with his wife's grandparents, for there was no other accommodation there. But after twelve months difficulties arose which made him reconsider the position. And a council house became available at Wrexham. So he brought his family back to Wrexham and has lived there ever since. At first he could not get any work on his return, but he has got it now.

Now the point is this: the wages in the Doncaster area are a good deal higher all round than they are in the Wrexham area. We have not got exact figures, but to illustrate the point I will take imaginary figures for 1963. In Wrexham Jack Humphreys would have got £17 13s. as a ripper, and £16 as a welder-burner. In Doncaster he would get £19 as a ripper, and £17 13s. as a welder-burner. So by going over from Wrexham to Doncaster, he would get the self-same amount in money in Doncaster (as a welder-burner) as he would as a ripper in Wrexham. But he is undoubtedly worse off as a disabled man than if he were able-bodied. He cannot earn so much in either place. Yet the deputy commissioner has held he is not entitled to a special hardship allowance. Jack Humphreys claims that the decision is erroneous in law on the face of it, and challenges it by certiorari.

The solution depends on the true construction of section 14 of the Act of 1946, as amended. I would introduce it by making a few fairly obvious definitions. What is meant by "his regular occupation"? It means, I think, his occupation as a ripper. *Not* as a ripper at Wrexham or at any place in particular. *Nor* as a ripper at the time of the accident. But simply his occupation as a ripper.

With this introduction, I will go through section 14. It is plain that Jack Humphreys can satisfy section 14(1)(*a*). As a result of his damaged ankle he was incapable "of following his regular occupation" as a ripper; and he was likely to remain permanently incapable of following that occupation. It is plain also that Jack Humphreys can satisfy section 14(1)(*b*). As a result of his damaged ankle, he was incapable of following "employment of an equivalent standard" which was "suitable in his case." Owing to his damaged ankle he was not capable, either at Wrexham or at Doncaster, of doing work which would bring him in wages equivalent to those of a ripper. The only employment at either place which was "suitable to his case" was employment as a welder-burner. That employment would not, at either place, bring him in wages equivalent to those of a ripper. At each place a welder-burner earned less than a ripper.

Seeing that Jack Humphreys can satisfy section 14(1)(*a*) and (*b*), the amount of the increase is to be determined under section 14(4). It is to

"be determined by reference to the beneficiary's probable standard of remuneration . . . in the insurable employments, if any, which are suitable in his case and which he is likely to be capable of following"

as compared with his probable standard of remuneration in his regular occupation. Now there was one insurable employment which was suitable in his case and which he was likely to be capable of following. It was employment as a welder-burner. To apply subsection (4), you must compare his probable wages as a welder-burner with his probable wages as a ripper. If the scale of wages is higher in one part of the country than the other, you must take the comparison at the place where he is living. You must compare like with like. If he is living at Wrexham, you must consider what his probable wages would be there as a welder-burner as compared with his wages there as a ripper. If he is living at Doncaster, you must consider what his probable wages would be there as a welder-burner as compared with his wages there as a ripper.

All this seems so plain on the wording of section 14 that I begin to wonder why the case has caused so much trouble. I think it derives from a mistaken view of the words "his regular occupation." That does not mean his occupation at the time and place of the accident. It means his ordinary kind of work when he was able-bodied, before he was disabled, no more and no less. After the accident, employment "suitable in his case" does not mean suitable at any place in England. It means simply the kind of work he is now capable of doing after the accident, suitable to his capacity, no more and no less, at the place where he is living.

When this interpretation is adopted, the case presents no difficulty. If his capacity to earn is reduced by his disability, he gets a special hardship allowance, no matter whether he is at Wrexham or at Doncaster. I would allow the appeal accordingly.

Davis and Salmon L.JJ. delivered concurring judgments.

Regina v. National Insurance Commissioner, Ex p. Mellors [1971] 2 Q.B. 401 (C.A.)

Lord Denning M.R. Mr. Samson Mellors has been in the coal mining industry all his working life. On October 27, 1961, he was working at the coal face as a chargeman ripper. A stone flew out and struck his left eye. His sight was so affected that he could not work underground any more. After a few months he was able to do work on the surface. Since October 1965 he has been employed at the same mine as a driver in the "plant pool."

His disablement by reason of defective vision has been assessed at 12 per cent. So he gets a disablement pension irrespective of what he earns. But he now claims a special hardship allowance under section 14 of the National Insurance (Industrial Injuries) Act 1965. The question is: how is it to be assessed?

The facts about his earnings are these: in his old occupation as a chargeman ripper he worked a total of 36¼ hours a week, with no overtime. His earnings were £28 1s. 9d. a week. In his new occupation as a driver in the plant pool he worked about 65 or 66 hours a week, of which about 41 hours were basic and 24 or 25 hours overtime; and his earnings were £26 19s. 2d. a week. So he had to work nearly twice as many hours, and yet he was still £1 2s. 7d. below his previous earnings. It sounds very long hours, but the explanation is that in the "plant pool" drivers may be "standing by" for long periods and only fully stretched for short periods.

A similar situation has arisen on several occasions. The commissioners have differed in opinion about it. So the chief commissioner appointed a special tribunal of three commissioners to determine it. They determined that his special hardship allowance should be 23s. a week, which was roughly the difference between his earnings before the accident (£28 1s. 9d.) and his earnings after it (£26 19s. 2d.). The special tribunal gave him no addition because of the extra long hours he had to work. He says that that was erroneous. He says that, as he had to work nearly twice as long, he ought to be granted the maximum special hardship allowance of £3 7s. He appealed to the Divisional Court under the familiar machinery of certiorari. Lord Parker C.J. and Ashworth J. dismissed his appeal [1970] 2 W.L.R. 1208, but Donaldson J. dissented. Now he appeals to this court. The case depends on the proper construction of section 14 of the National Insurance (Industrial Injuries) Act 1965. It deals with cases where a man suffers financial hardship as a result of his injury. It provides that his disablement pension can be increased. Section 14(1) specifies the circumstances in which he becomes *entitled* to an increase:

> "(1) The weekly rate of a disablement pension shall, . . . be increased by an amount not exceeding the appropriate amount . . . if as the result of the relevant loss of faculty the beneficiary—(*a*) is incapable and likely to remain permanently incapable of following his regular occupation; and (*b*) is incapable of following employment of an equivalent standard which is suitable in his case, . . ."

It is agreed that Mr. Mellors satisfies those entitlement provisions. He is incapable of his previous work, and also of any new work which brings him in the same wages. "Equivalent standard" means an equivalent standard of remuneration.

The question in dispute is the quantification of the amount. That is dealt with by subsection (6), which says:

> ". . . an increase of pension under this section shall be payable for such period as may be determined at the time it is granted, but may be renewed from time to time, and the amount of the increase shall be determined by reference to the beneficiary's probable standard of remuneration during the period for which it is granted in the insurable employments, if any, which are suitable in his case and which he is likely to be capable of following as compared with that in his regular occupation within the meaning of subsection (1) of this section."

It is quite plain that a comparison has to be made between two "standards of remuneration." Of course, you must compare like with like. That is essential for any fair comparison: see *Reg.* v. *Deputy Industrial Injuries Commissioner, Ex parte Humphreys* [1966] 2 Q.B. 1. So we must see what is meant by "standard of remuneration".

One thing is clear. "Standard of remuneration" is different from "rate of remuneration". When you speak of "rate of remuneration" you mean a rate per hour or per shift, such as 8s. an hour or £2 a shift. But when you speak of "standard of remuneration," you use the word "standard" in the same sense as in the phrase "standard of living." It means the level of remuneration which a man earns week by week or month by month, as the case may be.

Another thing is clear. "Standard of remuneration" is different from "average weekly earnings". Under the old Workmen's Compensation Act 1925 you had to take the man's total earnings over the year and then divide them by 52 in order to get the weekly average. That was not altogether satisfactory, especially when wages are very variable. So instead, in this Act, we are to take the "standard of remuneration". It is usually a weekly standard. The Act itself shows it. It prescribes the maximum allowance as £3 7s. a week.

In these circumstances I think that the comparison required by section 14(6) is to be taken in this way: On the one side you find the level of remuneration which would probably have been received by the man in his regular occupation in a normal working week if he had not been injured. On the other side, since the accident, you look at the level of remuneration which he is probably capable of receiving in a normal working week in employment which is suitable in his case.

In making the comparison, you look at the financial remuneration for a normal working week. You do not look at the conditions of the work. You do not look to see whether it is a high rate per hour because it is hazardous (underground in a mine), or a low rate because it is safe (on the surface): nor whether the work is burdensome or easy; light or heavy; long hours or short hours: paid by the hour or by the piece: paid extra for overtime, or not. None of these things comes into the calculation. The only thing that matters is the level of remuneration which week by week he would probably have been receiving if he had not been injured, compared with what he is probably capable of receiving after the accident. Of course in the same neighbourhood.

Mr. Turner-Samuels submitted that the comparison ought to be made by establishing what he called a "common time basis." By which I understand him to mean that, in ascertaining the standard of remuneration, you must take the same time, *i.e.,* the same number of hours each week, before and after the accident. Thus, in this case he was working 36¼ hours per week before the accident. So you must compare it with 36¼ hours after the accident. The money basis may vary, but however it is expressed, it comes to this: you take the same number of hours of work before and after the accident. An argument on these lines (with variations) appealed to the chief commissioner in the two cases numbered C.I. 18/68 and C.I. 29/68 and appealed to Donaldson J. in this case [1970] 2 W.L.R. 1208, 1215. But I cannot accept it. It looks to me very like saying that "standard of remuneration" equals "hourly rate of remuneration". That is wrong. I prefer the reasoning of the tribunal of three. They held that the standard of remuneration meant the level of remuneration.

It is interesting to notice that as long ago as 1949 the deputy commissioner gave this meaning to the "standard of remuneration". He said in C.W.I. 17/49 (K.L.):

". . . I think that 'standard of remuneration' is intended to denote a certain scale of pay—not a rate in the sense above mentioned, but the actual amount received, or expected to be received, in respect of a given period, which may be expressed for convenience in terms of a weekly or other periodic average."

On this interpretation of "standard of remuneration" I think the tribunal here were right in taking the pre-accident standard as £28 1s. 9d., and the post-accident standard as £26 19s. 2d., and fix the award "by reference to" it at 23s.

I ought to mention the "part-time" cases which have given rise to some difference between the commissioners. I think that part-time employment falls into a special category of its own. The decision of R(I) 10/66 is wrong. But the decisions in R(I) 6/68 and R(I) 7/68 are correct. They are to be explained on the basis that, in the case of part-time work, you look to the probabilities. The word "probable" is used in section 14(6). If it is "probable" that the man or woman will work part-time after the accident, as he did or she did before, then you make the comparison by taking the part-time level of remuneration before and after.

So we look at the remuneration probably receivable for a normal working week if he had not been injured, and as it is now after he has been injured. If the man gets more, then he gets no hardship allowance at all: if he gets less, as in the present case, then the hardship allowance is assessed "by reference to" the difference. It need not be exactly in accordance with the difference. But the difference is the starting point. And it must not exceed the maximum £3 7s. That is how the tribunal determined the case. They awarded 23s. I think they were quite right, and I would dismiss the appeal.

Prescribed Diseases

R(I) 15/75 (T)

. . . .

4. [Regulation 2(d) of and Schedule 1 to the Social Security (Industrial Injuries) (Prescribed Diseases) Regulations 1975 (S.I. 1975 No. 1573 as amended)] provides that occupational deafness should be prescribed in relation to all . . . persons who have been employed—

> (i) in insurable employment at any time on or after the appointed day [*i.e.* 5th July, 1948]; and
> (ii) for a period or periods (whether before or after the appointed day) amounting in the aggregate to not less than 20 years;

in one or more of the occupations set out in the second column of paragraph 48 of Part I of the First Schedule to these regulations.

The occupations set out in the second column of paragraph 48 of the Schedule referred to are—

"Any occupation involving:

> (i) the use of pneumatic percussive tools or high-speed grinding tools in the cleaning, dressing or finishing of cast metal or of ingots, billets or blooms; or
> (ii) the use of pneumatic percussive tools on metal in the ship-building or ship repairing industries, or
> (iii) work wholly or mainly in the immediate vicinity of drop-forging plant or forging press plant engaged in the shaping of hot metal."

5. The issue for determination of this appeal is whether the claimant's occupation is included amongst those described in the above quotation. This issue raises a problem of construction of the words "occupation involving the use of . . . tools". The insurance officer has throughout maintained that those words only apply to a person who himself uses the tools referred to, and in the recent unreported Decision C.I. 10/75 a Commissioner has so held. On the other hand, the claimant has maintained the contrary and

in a carefully reasoned decision the local tribunal have accepted the argument advanced on his behalf.

6. The claimant, who appeared before us wearing a hearing aid, proved to be an excellent witness and we accept his evidence without reservation. He has been employed since 1946 by a company whose business includes the manufacture and repair of ships propellers, and has always been employed in the shop where new propellers are finished. He was a charge hand for two years, a foreman for one year, and has since been and still is a superintendent. The new propellers enter the shop in the form of metal castings, and go through all the processes required for finishing them. The claimant described these processes to us; pneumatic hammers are used in more than one process and high speed grinding tools in another. There is no doubt, therefore, and we find as facts, that in the shop where the claimant has worked for 29 years pneumatic percussive tools and high speed grinding tools are used in the dressing and finishing of cast metal.

7. It is no part of the function of the claimant, as the superintendent, himself to use pneumatic hammers or grinding tools. When asked whether he ever did so in order to demonstrate to another employee how the work should be done, or for any similar instructional purposes, he said that he did not. He had occasionally used a grinding machine when a rushed job had to be dealt with, but officially he was not supposed to do so; and he doubted whether he had worked a grinding machine himself more than a dozen times in 20 years. His functions consist of supervising the work of the other employees working in the same shop as himself. He has to mark with chalk on the metal castings the areas where the hammers are to be directed, to ensure that the propellers are properly "pitched" for boring and are properly balanced, and to make the final checks on the accuracy of the work done. While he does not use any percussive implement or high speed grinding tool himself, his work requires that he often stands alongside an employee who does. He told us that from the point of view of his exposure to noise the worst part for him is the finishing process known as "fullering". During that process he stands within a foot of an employee wielding a pneumatic hammer, and examines and touches the propeller being worked on. His functions may be summed up by stating that he examines the job while work is being done on it and is responsible for the finished article.

8. The shop where the claimant works is so noisy that the employees who work there, other than supervisory staff, are organised in gangs of three so that they may have some respite from the noise. Each member of the gang works in the shop for

half an hour and then withdraws to a rest room for a quarter of an hour. Consequently each member of the gang works in the shop for two-thirds of his working time. On the other hand, the claimant spends 90 per cent of his working time in the shop. There are six gangs at work in the shop and consequently, even if employees whose work is receiving the claimant's attention are not using a hammer or grinding tool, members of other gangs are likely to be doing so.

9. In our view, there can be no doubt that the occupation of any one of the claimant's fellow employees who is required to use a pneumatic hammer or a grinding machine falls within the description of sub-paragraph (i) quoted in paragraph 4 above. It is not necessary for us to decide whether it also falls within sub-paragraph (ii). On the other hand, we find that the claimant's occupation does not require him personally to use any of the tools referred to, and also that he has not in fact done so save to a negligible extent.

10. Arguments very similar to those addressed to us were presented to the learned Commissioner who decided the Decision C.I. 10/75. In the case with which he then dealt the claimant was a welder-burner employed in the shipbuilding industry, in which skilled workers work in gangs consisting of one tradesman of each of several categories. The claimant in that case did not himself use a pneumatic percussive drill, but worked in the presence of another member of his gang who did so, and sometimes worked in a confined space in which a total of three gangs might be working. The Commissioner rejected the argument that occupational deafness was prescribed for the then claimant because the statutory language was satisfied if it was found that the claimant worked as a member of a gang one of whom used the offending tools. In the learned Commissioner's view, there was a strong context in the 1959 regulations, as amended by the amending regulations, which compelled him to hold that the words "occupation involving the use of percussive pneumatic tools on metal. . . ." were only apt to cover persons who themselves use the defined tools.

11. In his argument on behalf of the claimant, Mr. Cohen contended that, given a literal interpretation, the crucial words in the amending regulation ("Any occupation involving the use of . . .") include the claimant's occupation, because the claimant is involved in a process of which the use of the specified tools is an essential feature. He contended alternatively that if the critical words are thought to be ambiguous, then the right way to resolve the ambiguity is to give them an interpretation consistent with the intention of the legislature. And in order to ascertain that intention, Mr.

Cohen referred us to paragraphs 55, 83 and 85 of the report published in 1973 of the Industrial Injuries Advisory Council on "Occupational Deafness" (Cmnd. No. 5461).

12. Mr. Cohen's argument, which he had presented to the local tribunal, can perhaps, best be summed up by a paragraph taken from the tribunal's grounds of decision. The paragraph reads as follows:—

> "It is our considered opinion that the words "involving the use of" in the present context are ambiguous in that they are capable of being interpreted in either of the two ways before mentioned and that in deciding upon the correct interpretation we must look to the intention behind the regulation. In our view the purpose of the regulation was to provide the appropriate benefit for those who became subject to occupational deafness as a result of not less than 20 years' insurable employment in an occupation in which that disease was caused by one of the prescribed processes without distinction between those who performed different tasks in furtherance of that process."

13. Mr. Cohen sought to distinguish the present case from that dealt with in the decision C.I. 10/75 on the ground that the claimant in that case had not been a person engaged upon a process which involved the use of percussive tools, but had simply been a fellow employee of the person who used such a tool and had to stand by while the tool was used. The present claimant, so Mr. Cohen argued, was engaged upon the process which required the work of other employees to use the defined tools.

With respect to Mr. Cohen, we do not consider that his suggested distinction is a valid one. The claimant whose case was considered in Decision C.I. 10/75 was just as much engaged upon a process as the present claimant. We do not doubt that when men are organised for work in gangs, each member of the gang being skilled in a different trade, that is done for the purpose of producing an end product; and the work of producing that end product is a process. In our view, therefore, if Mr. Cohen's argument is right then the decision in C.I. 10/75 must be wrong. Of course, we should not shrink from holding that decision wrong if Mr. Cohen's argument convinced us.

14. Unfortunately, we are unable to accept Mr. Cohen's argument. We have to reject it for the reason which caused the author of C.I. 10/75 to reject the similar argument addressed to him. The context of the 1959 regulations as amended, and now of the 1975 regulations, is too strong to admit of any interpretation other than

the strict one adopted by him; that is to say that occupational deafness is only prescribed in relation to persons who themselves use the defined tools. We cannot do better than quote paragraphs 11 and 12 of his decision with which we wholly agree. They are as follows:—

"11. So far as relevant to this part of the case, occupational deafness is prescribed in relation to persons employed in an "occupation involving the use of percussive pneumatic tools on metal . . ." (see paragraph 48(ii) of Part I of the First Schedule to the Prescribed Diseases Regulations, read in conjunction with regulation 2(d)). In my judgment these words on their true construction are only apt to cover persons who themselves use the tools. They do not cover persons who do not themselves use them but work in the vicinity of those who do. This view seems to me assisted by paragraph 48(iii) of Part I of the First Schedule which makes special provision for persons who work in the immediate vicinity of particular types of noisy plant. Again, and perhaps more cogently, it is indicated by the descriptions in the First Schedule of other prescribed occupations. Thus the first 5 occupations described in Part I thereof are those "involving the use or handling of, or exposure to the fumes, dust or vapour of" various noxious substances. And the next 10 occupations are described in similar terms subject to immaterial variations of languages. Paragraph 6 of Part II is concerned with "any occupation involving the grinding of mineral graphite, or substantial exposure to the dust arising from such grinding". Similarly, paragraph 8 is concerned with "any occupation involving the use, or preparation for use, of a grindstone, or substantial exposure to the dust arising therefrom".
12. In the light of the above description I conclude that if the draftsman had wished, in dealing with occupational deafness, to cover occupations involving exposure to noise as a result of working in close proximity to percussive tools in use, he would have specifically so provided. For a distinction is clearly and consistently drawn throughout the Schedule between a person's use or handling of an instrument or substance and his exposure to injurous results arising from such use or handling by another. Where it is desired to cover occupations involving such exposure, specific provision to that effect is made."

15. Mr. Jones as well as Mr. Cohen referred us to the report of the Industrial Injuries Advisory Council, and we have read this

report with interest. Mr. Cohen argued that the emphasis of the report is on processes, and suggested that paragraph 55 indicates that the Council were treating "occupations" and "processes" as practically synonymous terms. We agree that the council were concerned to identify the processes in which are to be found the highest noise levels—see paragraph 85 of their report. We do not, however, agree that they confused the two terms "occupations" and "processes". However that may be, it is a dangerous proceeding to search through the report for pointers to the meaning of words and phrases used in the amending regulations. We consider that the local tribunal may have fallen into error by some such proceeding. In the extract from their decision quoted in paragraph 12 above, they refer to "prescribed processes". But there were no prescribed processes in the amending regulations; there were only prescribed occupations.

16. On the other hand the report does show the motives which prompted the Council to make their recommendations. In our view these are two-fold. The Council wished to recommend that a start should be made on providing insurance cover to persons at risk of occupational deafness. But secondly they intended that the cover provided in the first place should be severely restricted, so as to avoid overstraining existing audiological services—see paragraphs 83 to 86 and 90 to 92 of the report. In so far as it is possible to rely on the report at all to show the underlying purpose of the amending regulations, then we consider that the only passage which is valuable from this point of view is in paragraph 93 of the report, which is the paragraph containing the Council's recommendations. The second recommendation reads: ". . . the occupational cover to be defined by reference to the limited number of processes recommended in paragraph 85; . . .".

17. As to the argument that the passage which it is necessary for us to construe is ambiguous, and the ambiguity should be resolved by reference to the underlying purpose of the amending regulation, we fully accept that it is a well established principle of the construction of statutes and statutory instruments that an ambiguity may be resolved by reference to the purpose of the relevant legislation. However, in our view read in their true context the crucial words which we have to construe are not ambiguous. We consider that the decisive factor in the determination of this appeal is that those words "Any occupation involving the use of . . ." must have the same meaning throughout Schedule 1 of the 1975 regulations (formerly throughout the First Schedule to the 1959 regulations). In our view, acceptance of the argument advanced on behalf of the claimant would have the results that those words

would receive an extended meaning in relation only to prescribed disease No. 48.

18. With regret, therefore, we are driven to the conclusion that it is our duty to allow this appeal.

REASONS OF MR. J. S. WATSON, Q.C.

19. I agree with the facts as they have been set out and I also agree that the occupation to be considered is that which comes within sub-paragraph (i) in the second column of paragraph 48 of the Schedule. I have, however, reached a different conclusion on the construction of paragraph 48 and respectfully dissent from the decision of my colleagues. I appreciate that the Industrial Injuries Advisory Council (Cmnd. No. 5461) recommended restrictions on the occupations and processes for which occupational deafness should be prescribed but they did not specifically recommend the identification of workers to be covered. At the end of paragraph 85 of their report they stated—

> "Problems are bound to arise as regards the precise definition of the processes and the identification of the workers involved, and these will need to be carefully examined."

Such recommendations do not, however, assist on questions of construction and I do not understand my colleagues to suggest that they do.

20. Part I of the First Schedule to the Prescribed Diseases Regulations, 1959, covers a great variety of diseases, 48 in number, most of them completely diverse in character and in their effects on the health of the worker, from the industrial use of substances, minerals and metals, also animals and their carcases, and the adverse effects of fumes, vapours, dust, liquids, heat, radiation, contact etc. These cannot be regarded as analogous to the use of tools. Prescribed Disease No. 48 (to which I shall refer as P.D. 48) provides for occupational deafness resulting from the effects of exposure to noise. The risk does not arise from the tools themselves but solely from the noise they make when in use. The risk is entirely different from that arising from other processes listed in the Schedule. Noise is the mischief and in the nature of the occupation it would be inappropriate to import such words as "handling", "exposure to" or "contact with" the tools. Handling of tools would be inapt since tools which are not in use are inert and do not create noise. The addition of occupational deafness to the Schedule is unique as indeed are some of the other diseases.

It is not possible to draw a comparison between many of the diseases and I am not persuaded that the nature of the occupation and the word "use" in relation to one disease is an infallible guide to the use of that word in every other context in the Schedule. In view of the difficulty of definition in the particular circumstances of noise, different in concept from the diseases resulting from other occupations, it would not have been difficult to devise a form of words which would have indicated that only the user of the tool is intended to be covered by sub-paragraphs (i) and (ii). If in the First Schedule the word "use" is limited to the worker who personally uses the substances etc. it does not follow that the same applies to a tool.

21. The provisions of the industrial injuries legislation are for the benefit of the worker; they are the successors to the Workmen's Compensation Acts. They should be given a beneficial construction and, where permissible, a wide rather than a narrow construction and construed not in a technical but in a popular sense. (Compare *Lysons* v. *Knowles* [1901] A.C. 79, Lord Halsbury L.C. at p. 84/85; *Smith* v. *Coles* (1905) 2 K.B. 827, Romer L.J. at p. 830/31. Workmen's Compensation Acts ought to be construed not in a technical but in a popular sense; *Ball* v. *Hunt* [1912] A.C. 496, Lord Loreburn L.C. at p. 499; *Tannoch* v. *Brownieside Coal Co. Ltd.* [1929] A.C. 642, Lord Atkin at p. 648).

22. It does not follow that the same words are to be given the same construction because they are in the same Act or Schedule. In *Martin* v. *Lowry, Martin* v. *Inland Revenue Commissioners* [1926] 1 K.B. 550, Atkin L.J. (as he then was) said at p. 561—

> "If one could adopt as a rigid canon of construction an assumption that in any statute the same word is always used with the same meaning, one's task would perhaps be easier: but it is plain that the assumption is ill-founded: and particularly so in regard to the Income Tax Acts. We must have regard to the context."

In *Maddox* v. *Storer* [1963] 1 Q.B. 451, Lord Parker C.J. was dealing with the word "adapted" in section 24 of and the First Schedule to the Road Traffic Act 1960. He said at p. 455—

> "They (the justices) proceeded on the principle, a perfectly correct principle in most circumstances, that where you find a word used in many parts of a statute or, indeed, in a section or, as here, in a Schedule, you would expect Parliament to intend the same meaning whenever that word is used . . .
> . . . .
> As I have said, the principles upon which they approached

the matter are in general correct, but in my judgment even where the same word does occur in the same section or the same schedule the context must govern the true meaning."

The other members of the court agreed.

In *Gardiner* v. *Admiralty Commissioners* [1964] 1 W.L.R. 590, Lord Guest said at p. 594/5—

"There is no principle which would compel a court to restrict general words to be found in one section by a limitation to be found in other surrounding sections dealing with different matters."

See generally Halsbury's Laws of England, 3rd Ed. Vol. 36, page 396, paragraph 595, and *In re Smith, Green* v. *Smith* [1883] 24 Ch. D. 672, North, J. at p. 678.

23. Those principles apply with perhaps even greater force in the case of a statutory instrument which, in a Schedule, lists 48 diseases of the most diverse kind and it is appropriate to consider the particular context of each disease in construing the language. One has to consider the object of the provisions and the mischief which it is intended to cover (Compare *Coliman* v. *Roberts* [1896] 1 Q.B. 457, Lindley L.J. at p. 459). The Shorter Oxford English Dictionary gives one meaning of the word "involve" as "to include; to contain, imply", and the primary meaning of "use" as "Act of using or fact of being used". Reading the "nature of occupation" in the context of P.D. 48 as a whole, a narrow construction of the words "Any occupation involving the use of . . . tools . . ." confining it to the actual user of the tool, would provide cover for fewer workers than does sub-paragraph (iii). I appreciate that in the processes included in sub-paragraph (iii) no person actually uses the plant in the narrow meaning but I think the language of sub-paragraph (iii) assists in giving a wider meaning to the language in sub-paragraphs (i) and (ii) and construing "use" to include the fact of use. It may be that in some instances tools, as described, are automatic and are used by the operator simply pressing a button or moving a lever. "Use", if given a restricted meaning, would presumably refer to manually operated tools which the user holds.

24. I resile from a construction of the language of sub-paragraphs (i) and (ii) which gives cover to a more limited class of worker employed than is provided by sub-paragraph (iii). There can be no doubt that the claimant would have been included if the process had happened to fall within sub-paragraph (iii). The claimant's occupation involved his being exposed to the noise of the use of

the tools to as great an extent as the users of the tools and, indeed, he spent 90 per cent of his working time subject to such exposure whereas the users of the tools spent only two-thirds of their working time (see paragraph 8 above). As superintendent his work was concerned with the cleaning, dressing and finishing of cast metal in the shape of ships' propellers. His task was to ensure that the specification was accurately followed which, in the circumstances which he described and which were not disputed, could not be done without the use of the specified tools. He and the operators worked in unison, one being as indispensable as the other; the claimant's work was so closely associated with the use of the tools as to be involved in their use.

25. I think one is assisted to adopt a wide construction of "involving the use of . . . tools" as this affords comparable cover to that provided by sub-paragraph (iii) and provides similar cover under all three sub-paragraphs: such a construction does not cut down the cover provided by sub-paragraphs (i) and (ii) in relation to the cover provided by sub-paragraph (iii). I see no reason to adopt a narrow and restricted construction. In a popular sense the words "Any occupation involving the use of . . . tools" connotes both the act of use and the fact of use.

26. In my opinion, in the ordinary and popular meaning of the language, the claimant's occupation involved the use of the specified tools and the disease of occupational deafness is prescribed in relation to him in terms of sub-paragraph (i) of P.D. 48. I would have dismissed the insurance officer's appeal.

CHAPTER 7

BENEFITS IN GENERAL

A CLAIMANT satisfying the conditions of entitlement to benefit under the Social Security Act 1975 will, on a proper claim, receive that benefit at a rate initially fixed by reference to schedule 4 to the Social Security Act 1975 (except in the case of supplementary benefits, family income supplement and child benefit), as amended by subsequent up-rating orders, now on an annual basis. This initial determination will need to be varied in many cases, however, by reason of special considerations applicable in a particular case. Sometimes, the rate of benefit is reduced, as in the case of certain hospital in-patients; sometimes it is increased, most commonly where provision has to be made for certain classes of dependents: sometimes it may turn out that a benefit paid should not have been paid, in which case, its repayment may be required and an offender prosecuted.

REDUCTION OF BENEFIT

Hospital In-patients

The Social Security (Hospital In-Patients) Regulations 1975 (S.I. 1975 No. 555), as amended, provide for reduction of the *personal* element in benefit (*i.e.* normally not of any increase payable for dependants) where the beneficiary is receiving "free in-patient treatment." The reduction does not take effect immediately and varies according to the duration of treatment in a hospital or similar institution. Part of the benefit retained may become payable to the beneficiary when discharged by and with the approval of a duly authorised or empowered person and when no longer receiving free in-patient treatment (regulation 15).

R(S) 12/56

. . . .

3. The claimant was a certified mental patient in a hospital from the 6th June, 1951 to the 31st March, 1956 and, . . . a certain part of the sickness benefit which would otherwise have been payable to him was accumulated and withheld from him. Pursuant to the provisions of that regulation, that sum is not payable to him "unless and until the beneficiary" (which means the claimant) "is discharged from the hospital or similar institution by and with the approval of a person authorised or empowered to discharge him."

4. On the 31st March, 1956 the claimant escaped from the hospital.

277

5. It is provided by the Lunacy Act 1890, Section 85, as amended by the National Health Service Act 1946, Section 50 and the Ninth Schedule, Part 1, that "If any person detained as a person of unsound mind under this Act escapes, he may, without a fresh order and certificate or certificates, be retaken at any time within fourteen days after his escape by the manager of the institution for persons of unsound mind or the person in charge of the hospital or part of the hospital designated for the purposes of section twenty of this Act in which he was detained, or any officer, or servant thereof respectively, or by the person in whose charge he was as a single patient, or by anyone authorised in writing by such manager, or person."

6. The claimant was not retaken within fourteen days of his escape and the physician superintendent of the hospital certified on the 19th April, 1956 that the claimant was discharged on the 14th April, 1956. The secretary of the hospital management committee reported on the same day that the claimant having escaped from the hospital on the 31st March, 1956 was discharged according to law fourteen days after that date.

7. The acting physician superintendent of the hospital further stated on the 28th June, 1956 in answer to an inquiry that the claimant was not discharged with the approval of the superintendent.

8. The claimant has contended that since the medical superintendent of the hospital had no alternative other than to treat him as discharged he must be regarded as having been discharged by and with the approval of a person authorised or empowered to discharge him, or, alternatively, that those words have no application to the circumstances of his case since after the 14th April, 1956 the medical superintendent had no status in relation to the claimant.

9. I cannot agree with those contentions. The section of the Lunacy Act, 1890 which I have set out above precludes the hospital authorities from retaking the claimant, but that does not mean that he was discharged from the hospital with the approval of a person authorised or empowered to discharge him. The fact that the superintendent of the hospital has no power to take the claimant back into the hospital does not mean that he approved the claimant discharging himself.

10. The Commissioner has already held, in Decision R(S) 1/54 (which dealt with the case of a claimant who had been detained in a mental hospital pursuant to a reception order made under Section 16 of the Lunacy Act, 1890 and had been discharged on the direction of his father who was the person on whose petition

the reception order was made held) that the only person who could be said to be authorised or empowered to discharge patients from the hospital was the medical superintendent or other officer who was authorised or empowered to discharge patients by the committee or other authority in control of the hospital. No such person has approved the discharge of the claimant.

11. A majority of the local tribunal, the chairman dissenting, allowed the claimant's appeal on the ground that the failure of the hospital authorities to take steps to retake the claimant within the period of fourteen days from his escape and their admission that he was discharged according to law thereafter established that the claimant was discharged with their approval. With all respect to the members of the local tribunal who took this view, I cannot agree. Even if there were evidence (which there is not) that the hospital authorities took no steps to retake the claimant, it would prove no more than at the highest they consented to his escape, but consent and approval are quite different attitudes of mind. A man may consent to that which he does not approve, and the acting physician superintent has stated in terms that the claimant was not discharged with the approval of the superintendent.

. . . .

Overlapping Benefits

(See now the Social Security (Overlapping Benefits) Regulations 1975 (S.I. No. 554).)

R(S) 9/58

. . . .

2. The claimant is a married man with three children, whose wife (it appears) had left him. He sent for his mother (M.L.) to keep house for him and to help him look after the children. She arrived on the 6th January, 1958. She had no home of her own, and the arrangement whereby she came to live with the claimant was expected to last indefinitely. She was, and continued to be, in receipt of a retirement pension of 50s. 0d. a week. On the 17th January, 1958 the claimant fell ill, and he remained incapable of work until the 4th March, 1958. He claimed sickness benefit, with an increase in respect of children, and also with an increase in respect of M.L. It is with the latter increase that the present appeal is concerned.

. . . .

The general effect of the regulation is to provide for the adjustment or elimination of dependency benefit in cases where personal benefit is payable. The "personal benefit" concerned include "any personal benefit under the [National Insurance] Act": that is to say they include the retirement pension which M.L. is receiving. The increase of sickness benefit claimed in respect of M.L. is a "dependency benefit". Shortly put, and subject to various qualifications, the regulation provides that dependency benefit shall not be paid in respect of a person who is in receipt of personal benefit equal to or exceeding the rate of dependency benefit which would otherwise be payable in respect of that person. In the present case, M.L.'s personal benefit is equal to or exceeds the rate of dependency benefit which is being claimed in respect of her. *Prima facie* therefore, the regulation applies in the present case. There is an exception in the case of "a person who is employed by, but is not residing with, the beneficiary": but as M.L. is residing with the claimant, this exception does not apply. In the circumstances, therefore, no dependency benefit in respect of M.L. is payable.

Earnings

Earnings are relevant to entitlement to benefit in a number of ways. In some cases, earnings above a stated level are necessary in order to confer title to benefit; in others, they result in disentitlement. The context in which relevance of earnings is most familiar is that of the "earnings rule" according to which benefit decreases proportionately as earnings increase above the statutory maximum for entitlement to full benefit, *e.g.* in the case of retirement pensions. In all these cases, determination of "earnings" is, of course crucial.

Social Security Benefit (Computation of Earnings) Regulations 1974 (S.I. No. 2008), regs. 2–4

Calculation and estimation of amount of earnings

   . . . .

   2.—(1) . . .

(2) The amount of a person's earnings for any period to be taken into account shall be the whole of his earnings for that period except in so far as regulations 3 and 4 below provide that no account shall be taken of certain payments or perquisites and that certain payments shall be deducted.

(3) Except in relation to earnings which fall to be calculated in

accordance with regulation 5 or regulation 7 below, if a person has earnings which do not consist of salary, wages, fees or other payments related to a fixed period or if his earnings from any employment for any period are not immediately ascertainable, the determining authorities shall calculate or estimate the amount of those earnings, for any day or week on or in which that person is following the employment from which they are derived, as best they may having regard to the information (if any) available to them and to what appear to them to be the probabilities of the case.

Payments to be disregarded

3.—(1) Except in relation to earnings which fall to be calculated in accordance with regulation 5 or regulation 7 below, in calculating or estimating the amount of a person's earnings for any period no account shall be taken—

(*a*) for the purpose of any provisions of the Acts and of any regulations made under them which relates to benefit under the Acts, of the value—

(i) up to 15 pence for each working day, of meal vouchers supplied to him which are not transferable and are valid only for meals;

(ii) of meals provided for him at the place of work;

(iii) of accommodation in which he is required to live as a condition of his employment; and

(iv) of food or produce provided for his personal needs and those of his household;

(*b*) for the purposes only of section 23, 26, 34 and 35 of the 1973 Act[1], of any sums of money not exceeding £10 in the aggregate, or of the first £10 of any sums the aggregate of which exceeds that amount, and of any remuneration in kind, if those sums are or (as the case may be) that remuneration in kind is paid by the employer in December of any year by way of Christmas bonus.

(2) A sum shall not be treated as paid to a person by way of Christmas bonus within the meaning of paragraph (1)(*b*) of this regulation if—

(*a*) it is one of a series of sums paid to him at intervals of less than one year; or

---

[1] *I.e.* provisions relating to retirement pensions and increases of benefit for a spouse: see, now, the Social Security Act 1975, ss. 27–30, 45.

(*b*) it is received by him by way of payment for work done and either accrues to him as overtime or incentive payment or is otherwise directly related to his hours of work or to the amount of work performed by him.

Deductions to be made

4. Except in relation to earnings which fall to be calculated in accordance with regulation 5 or regulation 7 below, in calculating or estimating for the purposes of any provision of the Acts and of any regulations made under them which relates to benefit the amount of a person's earnings for any period, there shall be deducted from the earnings which he derives from employment in that period—

(*a*) any contribution payable under Part I of the 1973 Act or any scheme made under the National Insurance (Industrial Injuries) Act 1965(a)—

   (i) which his employer pays or is liable to pay on his behalf and the amount of which the employer deducts from a payment of his earnings from that employment; or

   (ii) which is duly paid by him otherwise than as a secondary Class I contributor and which either is so paid in respect of any period falling wholly or partly within that period or is fairly attributable to that period or any part of it;

(*b*) expenses reasonably incurred by him without reimbursement in respect of—

   (i) travel between his place of residence and his place of work and travel which he undertakes in connection with and for the purposes of that employment;

   (ii) premises (other than premises in which he normally resides), tools and equipment reasonably required by him for the purposes of that employment;

   (iii) protective clothing reasonably required by him for the purposes of that employment (including the laundering and cleaning of such clothing) and excessive wear and tear of his clothing attributable to the conditions and circumstances of that employment;

   (iv) subscriptions paid by him to any association of employed persons or other association or body to which, having regard to the nature or objects of the association or body and the nature and circumstances of that employment, it is reasonable for him to subscribe;

(v) the making of reasonable provision for the care of another member of his household because of his own necessary absence from home to carry out his duties in connection with that employment; and

(vi) the cost, up to 15 pence, of each meal taken during the hours of that employment for which no meal voucher has been provided; and

(*c*) any other expenses (not being sums the deduction of which from wages or salary is authorised by or under any enactment) reasonably incurred by him without reimbursement in connection with and for the purposes of that employment.

R(P) 9/56

. . . .

3. The claimant was entitled to 7/8ths of the profits of the partnership business and the son-in-law to 1/8th. Shortly before the claimant attained the age of 65 he received from the local insurance office a form of application for a retirement pension and was informed that he should call at that office, if he required any advice. He did so and asked the official whom he saw there whether it would be all right for him to work for, say, "a couple of hours a day and draw a wage of £2 a week," even though he claimed a retirement pension. He was told that that would be in order. He also inquired whether he would be required to pay insurance contributions and he was told that he would be. He says that he mentioned the fact that he was a partner in a small business, but that no mention was made of the profits of the business, nor was any inquiry made by the official whom he interviewed with reference to them. The claimant's reference to a "wage" had been liable to mislead, for sums received weekly by a partner in a business are not a wage, but a payment on account of profits. After that interview the claimant claimed a retirement pension, which was awarded to him, and the claimant has stated that he did not declare his earnings because he did not receive a "wage" exceeding £2 a week. He has admitted that his profits exceeded £5 a week throughout the period from the 5th June, 1952 to the 21st September, 1955 during which he drew his pension.

. . . .

5. The first question which falls for decision in this appeal is whether the claimant's right to payment of the retirement pension was extinguished by the amount of his earnings . . . On the facts of this case, it is clear that, if the profits which the claimant received

from the business in which he was a partner are to be included in his earnings, the claimant's right to payment of his retirement pension was extinguished.

6. The claimant has contended that the profits which he received from the partnership business should be treated as if they were dividends payable in respect of shares in a company. He has contended that they were the proceeds of an investment and not earnings. He has stated that he goes to the business premises only from 11.30 a.m. to 1 p.m. daily, and takes the cash takings to the bank. He spends the rest of the time, according to him, in conversation on general topics. He goes on holiday for at least three months a year. His son-in-law runs the business. He had to concede, however, that for the purpose of income tax he had treated the profits which he received as part of his earned income and it appears to me quite clear that the profits of the partnership business are just as much the earnings of the partners as the profits of a business carried on by a single person are his earnings. They are to be distinguished from dividends on shares in a limited company. A shareholder is under no liablity for the debts of the company. A partner is liable for the partnership's debts. A shareholder has no executive authority in the conduct of the business of the company. A partner has.

7. "Earnings" . . . which have to be taken into account are "the net remuneration or profit derived by the person from any occupation or occupations". . . . [2] It is impossible to say that the claimant had no occupation, even though the work he performed was very little, or that he derived no profit from it. It follows that as the claimant's profits (apart from his so-called "wage") exceeded £5 a week they were sufficient to extinguish his right to the payment of the retirement pension which he received during the period named at the head of this decision. . . .

. . . .

R(G) 1/60

. . . .

2. . . . The claimant . . . owns a large number of shares in the company and had lent the company considerable sums of money, which were still owed to her. In those circumstances an agreement was entered into between herself and the company on the 4th

---

[2] See, now, the Social Security Benefit (Computation of Earnings) Regulations 1974, (S.I. 1974 No. 2008), reg. 1(2): "'earnings' means earnings derived from a gainful occupation."

October 1958, by which her services were retained as a consultant to the company. She was to be paid an annual salary of £350 with effect from the 1st September 1958, so long as no dividend was paid by the company upon its ordinary shares, but, if a dividend was paid, her salary was to be reduced by the amount of the dividend paid on the shares which she held. Under the terms of the agreement she was required to devote such time and attention to the business of the company as the directors of the company for the time being considered desirable. No dividend has been paid since the agreement came into force.

. . . .

3. The claimant is an invalid and the directors of the company have not required her to perform any services. Her salary is paid after deduction of income tax and she has returned the sum so received as earned income for the purposes of the Income Tax Acts, but she claims that the sums so received are not "earnings" within the meaning of the National Insurance Acts. They are such earnings, however, if they are remuneration which she derives from an occupation. . . .

. . . It seems to me that a person appointed as consultant to a company cannot be said to have no occupation, nor can it be said that the claimant's remuneration is not remuneration derived by her from that occupation. No doubt, it is a curious arrangement by which the claimant's remuneration would decrease in proportion as the company prospered under her advice, if she gave any, but that cannot, it seems to me, affect the question.

. . . .

R(G) 7/62

. . . .

8. The wording of regulation [4, above[3]] makes it obvious that a widow who goes out to work, and who incurs expense in doing so, may not be entitled to deduct every such expense, even though she is in fact out of pocket to that extent. This may seem hard: but the regulation expressly provides that what she is entitled to deduct is restricted to "reasonable" expenses. In a number of Decisions the Commissioner has taken the view that it is not "reasonable" to allow an expense which has been incurred merely for convenience or comfort. Thus in early Decision C.G. 114/49 (reported), relating to a widow with a young child who had to have her child

---

[3] Regulation 4, above is couched in narrower terms than that considered in *R(G)* 7/62 but the decision in that case is of assistance in interpreting the present regulation 4.

minded when she was at work, the Commissioner allowed as a reasonable expense the cost of having the child minded, but disallowed as unreasonable the expense incurred by the claimant for having her dinner cooked for her. He said—"The expense in question is not one normally incurred by those earning small wages, and I can find no such exceptional circumstances in this case as would justify me in saying that it is any more than an expense incurred by her for her convenience or comfort. I am not prepared, therefore, to accept that it is a reasonable expense. . . . " In the more recent Decision R(G) 1/56 the Commissioner again applied this limitation. The claimant in that case worked and earned £7 15s. 0d. a week. She had one child, apparently of school age, and she employed a woman to look after the child, cook and do general housework, for a total cost of £3 18s. 11d. a week. The Commissioner considered this an unreasonable expense. He said—"A reasonable person earning no more than £7 15s. 0d. a week would not incur an expense of £3 18s. 11d. a week for the purpose of having her child looked after during her absence at work." The Commissioner restricted the deductible expense to the figure of 30s. 0d. a week *plus* 3s. 11d. insurance. The reasoning of the Commissioner shows that in that case he regarded the ratio of expenses to gross earnings as of materiality in determining what was "reasonable", and in that case the expenses amounted to almost exactly half of the gross earnings. But I feel sure that the Commissioner did not intend thereby to impose a general formula based on a specific arithmetical ratio. I am clearly of opinion that, while consistency of standards is to be aimed at, what is reasonable in any given case falls to be determined according to the circumstances of that case.

9. I accept in the present case that in the circumstances in which the claimant was placed, the hiring of domestic assistance to the extent of about 12 hours a week was *necessary*: in the sense that she could not (except possibly for short periods) have carried on her job with less assistance than that. This was her evidence, and, as already stated, the insurance officer's representative did not dispute her evidence. There is no evidence that the wage rate paid was excessive. The expense of 30s. 0d. *plus* 7s. 2d. insurance was thus, on the evidence, *necessarily* incurred. There may no doubt be cases in which an expense which was *necessarily* incurred may nevertheless by properly characterised as *unreasonable*. Such cases are probably, in my opinion, exceptional. In my view an expense proved to have been incurred in order to enable a widow to go to work, and proved to have been necessarily incurred, should not readily be characterised as unreasonable: for so to characterise

such an expense may come near to implying that the widow should not have taken up employment but should have stayed at home. That is not, in my view, a proper concern of the determining authorities. It is not established, in the present case, that by adopting the course which she did the claimant was improving her standard of living beyond that which had been customary for her. During her husband's lifetime, although admittedly conditions were then different and a precise comparison is not possible, she had domestic assistance from time to time. What happened was that, having to reorganise her affairs because of her husband's death, the claimant fully considered the alternatives open to her, and went back to her former employment, fully realising that she would have to incur the expense of paid domestic help, in order to be able to do so. Although in this case the ratio of expenses to gross earnings is fairly high (very nearly one-third) it does not strike me as unreasonable in the circumstances. I therefore hold that all four items of claim, amounting in all to £2 5s. 2d., constitute reasonable expenses incurred by the claimant in connection with her employment. They may legitimately be deducted from her gross wage of £7 0s. 0d. in order to arrive at her net earnings, which are thus £4 14s. 10d. Since this net figure does not exceed the limit of £5 0s. 0d. a week, benefit does not fall to be reduced in respect of these earnings.

. . . .

R(P) 1/66

. . . .

4. . . . . I have been referred to Decision C.G. 114/49 (K.L.) in which the learned deputy Commissioner construed the words "in connection with"[4] as meaning "in consequence of" rather than "for the purposes of". With respect to the learned deputy Commissioner, it is a well established canon of construction that courts and tribunals in construing words in a statute should not substitute other words for the plain and unambiguous words of the statute: the same rule applies in relation to a statutory regulation. As I understand the regulation, the expenses are related to the person, that is to the particular individual concerned and not to an abstract ordinary reasonable person, and the expenses incurred by the person concerned must be in connection with the employment; they must also be reasonable expenses. The words must be read together so that the expenses must be reasonable not only in relation to the subject matter of the expenditure and the amount

---

[4] See Regulation 4, above.

spent on it but also in connection with the employment. It seems to me to be unnecessary to attempt further elaboration of the words as the general principle to be applied is apparent and the remaining question is one of fact and of degree, namely whether expenses claimed in certain circumstances fall within or outside the words of the regulation.

. . . .

8. . . . I have come to the conclusion that, having regard to the claimant's health, it is reasonable that he should return home for his midday meal. That he has to do so is necessary because of the state of health of the individual claimant, and, in my judgment, the words "incurred by the person in connection with the employment" are wide enough to cover reasonable expenses incurred in making a return journey home at midday for the purpose of taking a meal which is necessary or desirable in the interest of a claimant's state of health. It might be otherwise if, for example, the mileage involved was considerable or the means of transport unduly expensive. The question is, in my view, one of fact and of degree and in this instance I consider that the claimant has brought the expense incurred within the ambit of the words used in the regulation.

. . . .

INCREASE OF BENEFIT

Increase for Dependants

Sections 41–49 and 64–66 of the Social Security Act 1975 provide for benefit to be increased in the case of certain classes of dependant if certain conditions are satisfied. The four classes of dependant are:

1. Children;
2. Spouses;
3. Prescribed relatives;
4. Female persons having care of the beneficiary's children ("housekeepers")

Whether, in any given case, an increase is payable may depend upon whether the beneficiary is living with or residing with the dependant, whether or not he is contributing towards the cost of providing for the dependant at the statutory rate, or wholly or mainly maintaining the dependant, whether the dependant is capable of self-support etc. Here, as elsewhere in the social security system, whether or not parties are validly married may be crucial.

Marriage

R(U) 1/68

. . . .

10. English law frequently recognises the validity of a monogamous marriage celebrated in foreign territory notwithstanding that its own requirements are not satisfied. Particularly is this the case where the law of the territory where the marriage occurred regards the marriage as valid and the parties to it were domiciled there when it occurred. Whether Indian law recognises the marriage between the claimant and M. as valid is, therefore, a material consideration. It is, however, necessary to know what were their respective domiciles and ages at the date of the marriage. There is no doubt that it was a monogamous marriage.

11. The insurance officer was unable to obtain adequate evidence of the domiciles or ages of the claimant and M., but she did obtain from the claimant what purported to be a copy in the English language of a marriage contract between himself and M. dated 26th August, 1934. This document was submitted to Mr. S. P. Khambatta, Q.C., an expert in Indian law, with instructions to advise whether Indian law would recognise the marriage as valid on the assumptions that both the claimant and M. were domiciled in India at the time and were over 16 years of age. Mr. Khambatta advised that Indian law would recognise the marriage as valid if it was valid according to the usages of the Jews. Accordingly, it became necessary to obtain an opinion from an expert in Jewish usages, and, on my direction, the case was referred to the Beth Din in London for their opinion on the two questions (i) whether the marriage contract showed that the marriage ceremony was valid in accordance with the usages of the Jews, and (ii) what were the minimum ages of marriage under Jewish law at the material time. On this occasion the claimant produced the original marriage contract, which was submitted to the Beth Din; it is in Hebrew with an English translation on the reverse, and both the Hebrew and English texts bear the attested signatures of the bridegroom, the bride and the celebrant. The Beth Din replied in a letter written by their secretary in which it was stated that the marriage contract evidenced a marriage ceremony in accordance with the traditions and usages of the Succath Shlomo Synagogue; the question concerning the minimum ages was not answered.

12. On the basis of the material described in the foregoing paragraph the insurance officer submitted that the claimant's marriage to M. should be accepted as valid for the purposes of the National Insurance Act 1965. But such material would, in my view,

be inadequate to support the submission if it was all upon which reliance could be placed. The domiciles and ages of the claimant and M. have been assumed and not proved. Furthermore, the reply received from the Beth Din is very guarded and conveys to my mind that the Succath Shlomo Synagogue is a Jewish sect having unorthodox traditions and usages. Whether or not Indian law would recognise the validity of the marriage might, therefore, depend on what those traditions and usages are.

13. Fortunately, however, the situation arising from the inadequacy of the evidence is covered by a principle of English law which, in my view, is applicable to this case. The principle is that, in civil proceedings, where the usual evidence of a valid marriage is not forthcoming or is not readily available, everything necessary for the validity of the marriage will be presumed once it is proved that there was a ceremony of marriage and that such ceremony was followed by cohabitation. If these facts are proved the burden of disproof of the validity of the marriage lies upon the person asserting its invalidity—see *Spivack* v. *Spivack* (1930) 46 T.L.R. 243.

14. The marriage contract, the letter from the Beth Din and the claimant's own evidence establish beyond doubt that there was a ceremony of marriage between him and M.; and his evidence that it was followed by cohabitation. Therefore, in accordance with the above-mentioned principle, the burden of disproving the validity of the marriage lies on the claimant. This burden he has not sustained, because he has produced no evidence disproving the validity of the marriage. As to his assertion that he was advised by a solicitor of the invalidity of the marriage under English law, this is not evidence of such invalidity. It is merely evidence that a solicitor formed an opinion upon the very question I have to decide, on factual instructions and for reasons of which I am totally uninformed. I could not be influenced by such an opinion unless its purport were submitted to me in the form of a reasoned argument; and this has not been done. I hold, therefore, that under English law the claimant's marriage to M. must be presumed to be valid, and accordingly that it is valid for the purposes of the National Insurance Act 1965.

15. It follows that the claimant was entitled to the increases of unemployment benefit that were paid to him in respect of M., A. and S. for the relevant periods, and therefore that he was not overpaid the amount of such increases.

. . . .

R(G) 2/70

. . . .

3. In 1946 the claimant's marriage to one B. was dissolved, and, on decree absolute, marriage became possible for the claimant and Mr. E. with whom she was then cohabiting as his wife. Their relatives and their circle of friends thought that they were married. Mr. E. had an army friend, one McQ., who, after some discussion, lent himself to an arrangement whereby the claimant and Mr. E. should visit him at A. [a town in England] where he lived, ostensibly for a short holiday, but really for the purpose of getting married without the family knowing. The visit (which was the claimant's second visit to A.) took place as arranged. The claimant, with Mr. E., arrived about 9 a.m. on Saturday 12th July, 1947 at some address in A. They had a "special licence" and the claimant took her divorce documents with her. A person, whom the claimant thought was and describes as being "the Registrar" married them. They signed a book; they were given a copy of what the claimant took to be the marriage certificate, and all these transactions at the ceremony took place in the presence of McQ. and a lady friend of his, and both acted as witnesses. The claimant says that on leaving the room where the ceremony had taken place she recollects seeing two soldiers and two ladies in the waiting room, and one of the men remarked "That didn't take long you've only been ten minutes." The claimant and Mr. E. returned home. They lived together in England until his death on 9th May 1968, known and universally accepted as a respected married couple, to whom two children were subsequently born on 12th June, 1951 and 13th August, 1960. The marriage certificate was retained by Mr. E. and kept with his papers. On an occasion some years later, when the claimant, as a result of some difference was contemplating leaving him, Mr. E. destroyed the certificate in a symbolic gesture, no doubt to indicate that the marriage was ended. The parties, however, composed their differences, and never separated.

. . . .

9. The general tendency of the law as it has been developed has been to preserve marriages where the ceremonial aspects were in order. In *Collett* v. *Collett* [1968] P. 482 at p. 492 Ormrod J. said "In my judgment, the principle which emerges from the corpus of legislation regulating the formation of marriages in England and from the reported cases arising therefrom, is that if a ceremony of marriage has actually taken place which, as a ceremony, would be sufficient to constitute a valid marriage, the courts will hold the marriage valid unless constrained by express statutory enactment

to hold otherwise." Applying that principle to this case the situation would appear to be as follows.

10. Section 42 of the Marriage Act 1836, in force in 1947 provides that in certain events, if any person shall knowingly and wilfully intermarry under the provisions of the Act, the marriage of such persons shall be null and void. An example of such events is a marriage in the absence of a registrar or superintendent registrar. The evidence, however, being that the claimant acted *bona fide* throughout in the belief that she was being validly married, section 42 of the Marriage Act 1836 would not, of itself, make void that which occurred on 12th July, 1947, if it were otherwise a valid marriage. The section only made void marriages unduly solemnised with the knowledge of both parties. As a ceremony, the events which occurred on 12th July, 1947 would have satisfied the essential requirements of a marriage *per verba de praesenti* before the passing of Lord Hardwick's Marriage Act 1753 (26 Geo. 2 c. 33), but not afterwards; and in any event the interchange of consents was not made in the presence of a priest episcopally ordained. That require-ment for a common law marriage in England was laid down by *R.* v. *Millis* (1844) 10 Cl. and Fin. 534. It seems to me, on the evidence as to what took place, that the "marriage" was not celebrated in an authorized mode in a stipulated place by a proper officiant, and that it was void *ipso jure*. Nor do I consider that it was a ceremony such that it would be right to deal with the matter on the basis that there was doubtful or inconclusive evidence of a ceremony of marriage imperfectly performed, to which, there being cohabita-tion thereafter, the presumption of validity, referred to hereafter, attached. In my view the submission made to the local tribunal, that what took place was not a ceremony of marriage properly so called, was correct. As I see it, if the claimant was not married by the ceremony of 12th July, 1947 she was not married at all, and with regret, I have felt obliged to come to the conclusion that she was not so married.

11. It would not, however, be right to part with this aspect of the case without referring to *Re Shephard. George* v. *Thyer* [1904] 1 Ch. 456. There the parties gave evidence that the only ceremony of marriage through which they went took place in France. The case was argued and decided on the basis, accepted by the learned judge, that expert evidence showed that the ceremony could not have been valid, and it was submitted that if the parties were not married by that ceremony they were not married at all. Never-theless, from the parties' long cohabitation after the ceremony, a marriage was presumed. I regret that I do not find any great assistance in the case. It is clearly unsupported by *Sastry Velaider*

Aronegary v. *Sembecutty Vaigalie* (1881) 6 App. Cas. 364 which it purports to follow, and where the decision depended upon a ceremony of marriage, *prima facie* valid. If the only marriage ceremony which the parties claim to have gone through is invalid, the whole force of any presumption in favour of their marriage is destroyed, and it is impossible to treat an invalid marriage as presumptive evidence of a valid marriage. An explanation of *Re Shephard*, to be found in the books, is that the learned judge must have rejected the evidence of the parties as to what occurred in France. But the claimant's evidence in this case is quite clear, and was accepted, and I feel unable (with respect to the learned judge) to follow *Re Shephard*, which was undoubtedly decided as a hard case. And hard cases are, I think, to be cautiously regarded. Where there is evidence that the marriage asserted can only derive from a particular ceremony having validly taken place, it seems to me that the formal validity of that ceremony is unaffected by the fact of cohabitation thereafter. If such cohabitation is relevant, it may have reference to the possibility that the parties thought they were married, and validly married. But it has no bearing on the validity of the ceremony itself.

12. In the event that it may be desired to take this case further. I have thought it right to deal now with aspects of the case which have hitherto not arisen for consideration in this decision, and which, if I am right in my views and conclusions on the ceremony, do not arise.

13. The local tribunal applied the principle that where there is doubtful or inconclusive evidence of a ceremony of marriage having been performed, possibly imperfectly, and cohabitation thereafter, the validity of the marriage will be presumed in the absence of evidence to the contrary. *Russell* v. *Attorney-General* [1949] P. 391; *Piers* v. *Piers* (1849) 2 H.L. Cas. 331. On the evidence they accepted, this could only have application to the ceremony, as described by the claimant, occurring on 12th July, 1947; and if I am correct in my view of the ceremony, there was, I think, no room for the application of any such principle and presumption to save the invalid ceremony. I do not see how the presumption could have been invoked save in respect of some ceremony at an unidentified and unidentifiable register officer, and this would have involved rejecting the claimant's evidence. The claimant might in fact be mistaken in her unshaken belief that she was married at A., but there is nothing in the evidence which would justify this view of the matter, or which tends to show that a theory of mistake would be any more than mere speculation.

14. The presumption having been applied (as I think wrongly) to the ceremony at A. as described by the claimant, it was argued, and repeated before me in argument, that evidence sufficient to rebut the presumption could be found in the fact that no record could be traced in the general registers or recorded entries of marriages at the register office at A. relating to the ceremony. The claimant relied upon *Re Taplin, Watson* v. *Tate* [1937] 3 All E.R. 105 as showing that the absence of registration was, in the circumstances, insufficient to rebut the presumption, not being "most cogent" evidence.

15. But the parties on the evidence did not marry at the register officer at A. at all. The significance of the fact that no record can be found when registration is in force, can only arise in respect of a marriage alleged to have been duly celebrated where the particulars known are precise enough to have enabled searches to be made to find the record if it exists. If the particulars are imprecise, and the place of ceremony unknown, it is not possible to say that the absence of any record is of significance, because the searcher does not know where to look for the record, which may exist. The evidence showed that the ceremony did not take place at the register office at A.; it is not suprising that searches for a record of the marriage having taken place there revealed nothing. To my mind the absence of any record of the claimant having been married in the register office at A. is corroboration—if corroboration be needed—of the claimant's evidence that the ceremony did not take place there.

16. The claimant and Mr. E. became the parents of children born on 12th June, 1951 and 13th August, 1960. Certificates of birth are admissible on the question whether parties, the parents, were married. *Re Stollery. Weir* v. *Treasury Solicitor* [1926] Ch. 284; *Re Peete (Decd.) Peete* v. *Crompton* [1952] 2 All E.R. 599. The parties were registered as the parents, the claimant being the informant, her name and maiden surname being given, in each case, as "P.M.E. formerly B." Her maiden surname was "R." as appears from the certificate of her marriage to "B." on 28th May, 1938. Inasmuch as on 28th October, 1946 she had given birth to a child by Mr. E. which she registered on 11th November, 1946, giving her name and maiden surname as "P.M.E. formally B.", I would not attach any real weight to the certificates if they were relevant, on the facts of this case, to assist in supporting a presumption of validity.

17. The standard of proof required to rebut the presumption to which I have referred in paragraph 14 has been variously described. In *Re Taylor, Decd. Taylor* v. *Taylor and Anor* [1961] 1 W.L.R.

9, where there was no evidence of any marriage, the standard was "clear proof". In *Mahadervan* v. *Mahadervan* [1964] P. 233 at pp. 244–246, proof beyond reasonable doubt was said to be the requirement. Notwithstanding the subsequent case of *Blyth* v. *Blyth* [1966] 1 All E.R. 524, from which it might be argued that the standard of proof required to rebut the presumption of formal validity of a marriage ceremony is no more than the standard of probability, I think that the standard of proof is that of proof beyond reasonable doubt. This is supported by *Mahadervan* v. *Mahadervan* and, as appears to me, by the cases discussed in the report of that case at the pages to which I have referred.

18. If the evidence had established a ceremony of marriage to which the presumption of validity arising from cohabitation thereafter could have been applied, my view would have been that the presumption prevailed notwithstanding the absence of any record, and I would have endorsed the decision of the local tribunal in this respect.

19. My decision is that the marriage between the claimant and Mr. E. is not established and cannot be presumed.

. . . .

"Spouse"

R(S) 9/61

2. On the 19th February, 1958 the claimant's wife obtained a separation order against him. This gave here the custody of Philip and ordered the claimant to pay through the Court 5s. weekly towards the maintenance of his wife and 10s. weekly towards the maintenance of Philip. There were also divorce proceedings: on the 16th July, 1958 a decree nisi was pronounced and on the 16th October, 1958 it was made absolute. The result was that the claimant's wife became his ex-wife. But the separation order remained in force.

3. On the 30th September, 1959 the claimant was admitted to hospital, where he remained for the rest of the period in paragraph one above, during which he was incapable of managing his own affairs; they were looked after by his sister with the help of their father.

4. The question arising for decision in this case can be stated very simply, though it arises under some complicated statutory provisions. It is whether during that period contributions to the cost of providing for Philip were being made by or on behalf of the claimant at a weekly rate of not less than 15s.

L

. . . .

6. The local tribunal by a majority decided in favour of the claimant, relying on regulation 5D of the National Insurance (General Benefit) Regulations, 1948 [S.I. 1948 No. 1278], ("the 1948 regulations") which was added by the National Insurance (General Benefit) Amendment Regulations, 1957 [S.I. 1957 No. 1888] regulation 4. Regulation 5D(1) provides as follows:— "Subject to the provisions of this regulation, any sum or sums paid by a person by way of contribution towards either or both of the following, that is to say, the maintenance of his wife and the cost of providing for one or more children, being children to whom this regulation refers, shall be treated for the purposes of section 5 and subsections (3) and (4) of section 6 of the Act of 1957 and subsection (1) of section 24 of the Act as such contributions, of such respective amounts equal in the aggregate to the said sum or sums, in respect of such of the persons hereinafter mentioned, that is to say, his wife or any child or children to whom this regulation refers, as may be determined by the determining authority so as to secure as large a payment as possible by way of benefit in respect of dependents."[5] If, therefore, this regulation applied in the circumstances of the present case the local tribunal were entitled and indeed bound to allocate 15s. weekly to Philip and to award the claimant the increase. The chairman of the local tribunal, however, dissented on the ground that the regulation only applies to a wife and not to an ex-wife; and the insurance officer now concerned with the case submits that this view of the matter is correct.

. . . .

8. As a general rule the word "wife" in the . . . Acts and regulations does not include an ex-wife but means a woman who at the relevant time is married and whose marriage still subsists (to whom I will refer as a wife in the strict sense). In my judgment it would be impossible to give any wider meaning to the word "wife" in section 24 of the Act. Prima facie therefore one would expect the same word to have the same restricted meaning in regulation 5D, especially as words in the regulations are, unless the context otherwise requires, to have the same meanings as in the Act (regulation 1(2) of the 1948 regulations). At first sight the reference in regulation 5D to section 5 of the 1957 Act might be thought to create a difficulty, since the woman affected by that section is not a wife in the strict sense, but a woman whose divorced husband has died, which might be thought to suggest that "wife" in regulation 5D

[5] See, now, the Social Security Benefit (Dependency) Regulations 1977 (S.I. 1977 No. 343), reg. 3

should be given a more extended meaning. On the other hand it would be extraordinary if the same word "wife" in regulation 5D had different meanings according to the section for whose purposes it was being applied.

9. Having fully considered the matter I am satisfied that the word "wife" in regulation 5D means a wife in the strict sense, and that any apparent conflict is resolved by the words in regulation 5D "either or both of the following". I think that the effect is that for the purposes of section 5 of the 1957 Act payments for children (but not for a wife, since there is no wife) are to be treated as regulation 5D provides; whilst for the purposes of the other sections referred to in the regulation payments for the wife and children or child (or any combination of them) are to be so treated.

. . . .

"Prescribed Relative"

C.S. 2/48(K)

1. My decision is that from and including 5th July, 1948, an increase of sickness benefit is not payable to the beneficiary in respect of his housekeeper.

2. It is not contended that she has the care of any "child" within the meaning of the Family Allowances Act, 1945, and accordingly, by reason of the definition of "child" in the National Insurance Act, 1946, Section 78(2), it is clear that the beneficiary cannot establish a right to increase of benefit under Section 24(2)(*c*) of that Act.

3. The Local Tribunal allowed the claim under Section 24(2)(*b*). That would apply if the housekeeper were "such other relative as may be prescribed". The prescribed relatives will be found by reference to Regulation 11(1) and Schedule I to the National Insurance (Unemployment and Sickness Benefit) Regulations, 1948 [S.I. 1948 No. 1277].[6] She is not one of the relatives so prescribed.

4. The Local Tribunal refer to Section 24(4),[6] which provides that "relative" includes a person who would be a relative if some person born illegitimate had been born legitimate. The argument appears to be that, if the children of the beneficiary and his housekeeper had been born legitimate his housekeeper would have been his wife. One of the answers to that contention is that a wife

---

[6] See, now, the Social Security Benefit (Dependency) Regulations 1977 (S.I. 1977 No. 343), reg. 9, Sched 1.

L*

is not one of the relatives prescribed for the purposes of Section 24(2)(*b*). She is not mentioned in Schedule I to the Regulations above referred to. In the case of a wife, title to increase of benefit in respect of her would arise under Section 24(1).

5. The beneficiary has, therefore, failed to establish any right to increase of benefit in respect of his housekeeper, and I allow the Insurance Officer's appeal.

"Housekeepers"

C.U. 257/50 (KL)

. . . .

2. Before he became unemployed and thereafter the claimant and his two children were boarders in the house of Mrs. F.D., paying £3 a week in respect of board and lodging for himself and them. On becoming unemployed he claimed an increase of benefit in respect of Mrs. D on the ground that she looked after his children. He did not, however, allege that he "employed" her in that or in any other capacity and indeed stated that he did not, and the ground of his appeal against the decision of the local Insurance Officer disallowing the increase claimed—as stated by the claimant himself—was that "Mrs. D.'s income does not exceed £1 apart from what I give her for me and my family's assistance". The further information considered by the local Insurance Officer and the Local Tribunal showed that Mrs. D., who is the tenant of the house, has an income of 17*s* 6*d*. a week apart from any profit derived from the £3 a week paid by the claimant, and that she looks after the children while he is at work but receives no additional payment from him. The claimant did not attend the hearing before the Local Tribunal, but on the information before them they allowed the increase of benefit claimed on the ground—as stated in their statement of grounds of appeal—that:—

> "Mrs. D is employed by the applicant as a woman looking after his two children and 16*s*. per week out of the £3 paid to her is attributable to that service".

3. I am, however, unable to affirm that decision, as it is not justified by the provisions of the National Insurance Act and regulations applicable to the claim—Section 24 of the Act and

Regulation 12 of the National Insurance (Unemployment and Sickness Benefit) Regulations, 1948 [S.I. 1948 No. 1277].[7] As the members of the Local Tribunal appreciated, the claim could not succeed unless the conditions required in such a case under the provisions of Section 24(2)(*c*) and Regulation 12(1)(*a*) were satisfied, and on the evidence it is clear that the conditions were not satisfied under either alternative. For Mrs. D. is not wholly or mainly maintained by the claimant as Regulation 12(1)(*a*) would require, and she is not "employed by him in an employment from which her weekly earnings . . . are not less than 16*s*.". The relationship between the claimant and Mrs. D. is that of boarder and landlady, although it is unnecessary for the purposes of the present case to decide the question. I am inclined to doubt whether the occupying owner or tenant of a house *is within the meaning of Regulation 12(1)(a)* "residing with" a man living as a lodger or boarder in her house. But, on the assumption that Mrs. D. was so "residing with" the claimant, the evidence gives no support for the view that she was wholly or mainly maintained by him as required by Regulation 12(1)(*a*). On the contrary, it would appear that she maintained herself out of her income of 7*s*. 6*d*. a week "compensation" and 10*s*. pension and the profit or "earnings" derived from the payment of £3 a week received from the claimant for board and lodgings and for her services in looking after his children.

4. As regards the conditions required under Regulation 12(1)(*b*), the only capacity in which I could hold that Mrs. D. was "employed by" the claimant was as a person "who has the care of" his children, but to satisfy the conditions of the regulation her weekly earnings *from her employment by the claimant* required to be not less than 16*s*. That condition, in my judgment, cannot be held to be satisfied by regarding the whole services of Mrs. D. as rendered in the capacity of an employee of the claimant and, on the assumption that it might be satisfied if a sum of 16*s*. a week could be regarded as a reasonable payment for taking care of the children. I am unable in the circumstances of the case as disclosed in the information before me to regard 16*s*. as a reasonable appropriation out of the total weekly payment of £3.

. . . .

---

[7] See, now, the Social Security Act 1975, ss. 44, 46; the Social Security (Dependency) Regulations 1977, (S.I. 1977 No. 343), reg. 10.

C.S. 726/49 (KL)

. . . .

2. The claimant employed Mrs. A. at 16*s*. 6*d*. a week to come to his house daily (including Sundays) from 9 a.m. until 2.30 p.m. or 2.45 p.m. to carry out household duties, and, as he alleges, to have care of his child, now aged 12.

3. Before he became incapable of work he was in full-time employment, and has since resumed it.

4. His child gets her own breakfast before going to school. She returns to dinner in the middle of the day, and Mrs. A. prepares it for her. Mrs. A. also washes the child's cloths, and buys them. As part of the housework, presumably, Mrs. A. cleans the child's bedroom and makes the child's bed. The child gets her own evening meal, and lays it for the claimant.

. . . .

7. The fact that a particular child does not need much care, because of personal aptitude to look after himself or herself, does not seem to me to preclude a person from being spoken of as having the care of a child. This is consistent with a decision of the Umpire under the former Unemployment Insurance Acts, in which he held that a claimant was entitled to an increased rate of unemployment benefit in respect of a housekeeper on the ground that she had care of his dependent child on those days of the week on which the child was a dependent child although the child was aged 15 and was working on the other days of the week. (See Decision No. 11118/34.) Further, since a child may continue to be a child of the beneficiary's family until 31st July following his or her 16th birthday, if working as an "apprentice" within the meaning of the Family Allowances Act 1945, it is clear that some of the children to be taken into account will need relatively little care.

8. I think it is also clear that "care" does not mean "exclusive care". The Umpire under the former Acts referred to above drew a distinction at one time between "assisting in the care of" and "has the care of". (See Decision No. 18230/30.) But he later rejected this distinction. (See Decision No. 10914/31.) I feel satisfied that no such distinction was intended in the present Act, and this is confirmed by recollecting that the "female person" spoken of in Section 24(2)(*c*) referred to above may be, as in this case, one who is not resident with the claimant and his child.

9. It was submitted by the Insurance Officer that "care" meant "main care", that is to say, that the care which devolved on the "female person" referred to in the National Insurance Act 1946, Section 24(2)(*c*) must exceed the care retained by the claimant, and that in this case the claimant had the main care of his daughter.

10. It does not seem to me, however, that care of a child is susceptible of division in that way. Clearly, a comparison of the number of hours during which a claimant and the "female person" are normally in the house concurrently with the child would not be the test. The female person might perform those duties for a child, with which a child needs assistance, in comparatively few hours out of the 24 hours of the day. As the child grows older the child's needs in this sense would decrease.

11. In the case of an older child, the child might need little more than the general supervision of a parent. In such a case no "female person" could be brought within the provisions of the Section 24(2)(c) while the child is living with the parent. But I think that a female person may be said to have "the care of a child", if to a substantial extent she performs those duties for a child, with which a child needs assistance because he or she is a child, or exercises that supervision over a child which is one of the needs of childhood.

12. In the present case, the cooking of her midday meal is one of the duties referred to above. So, too, the cleaning of her bedroom may, I think, be included, and clearly the washing and buying of her clothes should be. Those are the chief matters with which this child of 12 needs assistance. No doubt she also needs general supervision, but what Mrs. A. does for her constitutes a substantial part of the care of the child.

. . . .

Residence With

R(S) 10/55

. . . .

2. The claimant who had lived with his mother in Italy, came to the United Kingdom on the 28th September, 1951. He stated in December, 1954 that he had no intention of returning to Italy, that his mother was still in Italy and that it was not intended that she should come to the United Kingdom. He has explained that she has a son of 14 and a daughter of 11 and that he could not afford to bring them to the United Kingdom or maintain them here. He became incapable of work on the 24th September, 1954 and has claimed sickness benefit, together with an increase in the rate of that benefit in respect of his mother.

. . . .

8. The question whether two persons not in fact living together may be treated as still residing with one another, . . . has been

discussed in numerous Commissioner's decisions. For example, in Decision R(P) 7/53, which was dealing with persons in hospital, it is said "In Decision C.P. 84/50 (not reported) the Commissioner said: 'A period of absence which has lasted for more than a year, and of which there is no reasonable prospect of its coming to an end, cannot, I think, be spoken of as 'temporary'. If a man left home, and if it was ascertained after more than a year had elapsed that there was still no prospect of his return, he would not be said to be temporarily absent'". In Decision R(P) 5/54, after quoting this passage, the Commissioner proceeds: "In some cases the evidence that there is no prospect of the claimant's return home is medical evidence that she is unlikely to be fit to be discharged. That is not the case. The medical evidence is that she is fit to be discharged from the hospital where she now is and has been fit to be discharged for many months past. Yet she has not returned home and there is no evidence that she will do so at any ascertainable future date." In that case, the Commissioner held that the claimant was no longer residing with her husband.

9. It is true that in Decision C.S. 185/50 (reported) a man, who had been sent to prison for a term of three years, was held to be residing with his wife on the ground that his absence from home was temporary . . . but in that case the term was no more than three years and its maximum duration was known. It was also recorded in that case that, in an unreported decision C.S. 31/48, the absence of a man who had been sent to prison for five years was not temporary because his absence from the place of residence he shared with his wife had a quality of permanence, or a settled character, which could more fittingly be described as a change of residence than as a "temporary absence", in the sense in which that phrase is used, having regard to its context.

10. Reviewing these decisions and applying them to the facts of the present case, I do not think that the claimant could be said to have his mother residing with him on the 24th September, 1954. He had not shared a common home with her since September, 1951. He had no present intention in December, 1954 of resuming residence with her and the time when he would do so was uncertain. His landing permit had already been extended to September, 1955 and there was no prospect of his mother coming to this country to live with him before that date for reasons which he gave. It was not even certain that they would live together after September, 1955 or that he would then return to Italy. I appreciate that he told the local tribunal that his work permit might be revoked on account of his illness, but it had not been. There was no evidence that the claimant intended to return to Italy before he had to do

so on account of being unable to obtain an extension of his permit to stay in this country, or of his work permit being revoked.

. . . .

Contributing Towards the Cost of Providing for; Maintaining

R(S) 7/58

. . . .

2. At the time to which this appeal relates, the claimant, her child, her mother and her brother lived together. The claimant received at the time to which this appeal relates £2 12s. 6d. a week from the Air Ministry by reason of the service of her husband in the Royal Air Force. He did not live at home owing to his duties. On inquiry of the Air Ministry it has been explained that this sum is made up of 35s. a week marriage allowance payable by the Ministry in respect of the claimant and a qualifying allotment of 17s. 6d. a week deducted from her husband's pay . . . .

3. The claimant's mother and the child make no contribution to the family fund, from which the household is maintained, but the claimant's brother contributes £5 a week. The claimant, when not incapable of work earned £2 17s. 6d. a week and the contribution which she made to the family fund, if the £2 12s. 6d. a week received from the Air Ministry is treated as part of her contribution, amounted in the aggregate to £5 10s. a week. In any event, the family fund amounted in the aggregate to £10 10s. a week and, applying the family fund principle, the unit cost of maintenance of the household was, therefore, £3 a week for each adult and £1 10s. a week for the claimant's child.

4. The local tribunal, having treated the whole £2 12s. 6d. a week contributed by the claimant's husband as a contribution to her maintenance regarded her own contribution to her own maintenance as 7s 6d. a week and the balance of her contribution of £2 17s. 6d. a week derived from her earnings as contributed by her to the maintenance of her mother and her child. On that footing, she was contributing £2 10s. a week to their maintenance as contrasted with her brother's £2 a week (their respective surpluses over the unit cost of maintenance of £3 a week). Consequently the tribunal held that the claimant was mainly maintaining her mother and entitled to the increase of benefit claimed.

5. The local tribunal had had cited to them Decision C.U. 544/50 (reported). That decision dealt with a claim by a non-resident husband for an increase in the rate of his unemployment benefit

in respect of his wife, to whom he contributed 20s. a week, as well as 15s. a week in respect of his three children, under a Court order. In that case, it was held that the whole 20s. a week so contributed by the claimant for his wife's use must be allocated to her maintenance and not thrown into the family fund.

6. The Commissioner added "even where there is no express allocation of the non-resident's contribution (either legally binding or voluntary) there may be cases where it would be right to treat his contribution as allocated to one resident only; e.g. where the contribution is made by a non-resident husband whose wife is living with her own relatives or friends with whose maintenance the husband is not concerned it would usually be right to treat the husband's contribution as made for the maintenance of the wife only."

7. Inasmuch as the 35s. a week received by the claimant is an allowance payable to her by reason of her husband's service in the Royal Air Force and his marriage to her, and inasmuch as no allowance is payable is respect of the child, it seems to me that, to that extent at any rate, the decision of the local tribunal is correct. The sum of 35s. a week is as much allocated to her maintenance as if it were paid under a Court order. So far as the 17s. 6d. a week qualifying allotment deducted from the pay of the claimant's husband is concerned, it may be that that sum should be regarded as not the subject of any express allocation, but if so, applying the principle laid down in Decision C.U. 544/50 (reported) referred to above, I think that it should be treated as allocated equally between the claimant and her child (if not regarded as allocated to her alone) and I do not think that it can reasonably be regarded as allocated to the family fund without distinction of persons, inasmuch as the family includes the claimant's mother and brother, two persons with whose maintenance the husband would not be concerned. The claimant's mother it will be remembered has her own son living in the household.

8. If the 17s. 6d. a week is so allocated equally between the claimant and her child, the share of each will be 8s. 9d. a week. Thus, the cost of her maintenance will have been provided by her husband to the extent of 43s. 9d. a week.

9. Thus, the claimant will need to provide only 16s. 3d. a week from her earnings for her own cost of maintenance, and she will have £2 1s. 3d. a week available to contribute towards the cost of maintenance of her mother and child as against her brother's £2 a week. Though on this reasoning her excess is much less than it was on the basis of the decision of the local tribunal, she is still able to show that she is mainly maintaining her mother and her

claim for an increase in the rate of her sickness benefit in respect of her mother succeeds.

. . . .

R(S) 3/74

. . . .

2. Some years ago the marriage of the claimant and his former wife was terminated by divorce. They had two children. Throughout the period with which we are concerned in this appeal the children were always living with their mother and not with the claimant, the claimant was under a legal duty pursuant to a Justices' order to pay his former wife £3 weekly towards the maintenance of the two children and the claimant was remarried and living with his present wife.

3. Since August 1968 the claimant has been continuously incapable of work. Down to 22nd September, 1971 after which date invalidity benefit was introduced he was in receipt of sickness benefit together with an increase for his present wife and increases for the two children.

4. One of the conditions of title to an increase of either sickness or invalidity benefit in respect of children not living with the beneficiary is that contributions to the cost of providing for the children in question are being made at a weekly rate not less than that of the amount of the increase . . . Where however contributions to that extent are not being made the condition can be deemed to be satisfied if the beneficiary signs an undertaking to make such contributions and in fact does so[8] . . . . In August 1971 a form completed by the claimant showed that he was not contributing quite enough to give him title to an increase of sickness benefit in respect of the children. Accordingly on 3rd September, 1971 he signed an undertaking under regualtion 9 and, increased the rate of his contributions.

5. An increase of invalidity benefit in respect of children has always since its first introduction in 1971 been at a higher rate (£2·95 for an elder child and £2·05 for a second child) than an increase of sickness benefit for such children. Accordingly on 29th September, 1971 the claimant was notified by the Department of Health and Social Security that he must contribute £5 weekly. He did so with complete regularity paying £5 each week to the Court.

6. That was the situation in August 1972, by which time it had become known that by virtue of the National Insurance Act 1972

[8] See, now, the Social Security Benefit (Dependency) Regulations 1977 (S.I. 1977 No. 343), reg. 3.

("the 1972 Act") the rates of benefit including increases were to be raised to £3·30 for an elder child and £2·40 for a second child—total £5·70. The claimant's contribution of £5 was therefore now about to become insufficient.

7. This was a very serious pitfall for persons in the position of the claimant. The Department however in my judgment did all that they could reasonably have been expected to do to draw attention to the situation. In August 1972 a new order book covering 13 weeks was issued to the claimant. The orders dated for weeks down to 4th October, 1972 were for £15·30 as before. Those for the weeks starting on 5th October, 1972, the date on which the 1972 Act started to operate, were for £17·30. The instructions in the book, which the claimant was specifically warned to read, told him to report if any payment towards the support of a child fell below £2·95 a week, and a special form, BF 140 (1972) was sent to him setting out in detail the amount of the increases for a wife and children respectively. Unfortunately the claimant despite these warnings continued to send to the Court £5 weekly as before. From 5th October, 1972 onwards therefore he was drawing £5·70 for the two children, paying over only £5 of it, and not telling the Department what he was doing. This went on for some 19 weeks till February 1973 when the Department sent the claimant a form to complete and his letter replying to it disclosed the situation. In view of the terms of the letter the increase for both the children was stopped.

8. The insurance officer then reviewed the claimant's awards of the increase in respect of the younger child from 12th October 1972 to 14th February 1973. He decided that the increase had not been payable during that period and required repayment of £43·20 (18 weeks at £2·40).

9. Regulation 10 of the 1970 regulations[8a] so far as material provides as follows: "*Allocation of contributions for wife or children*:

> 10.—(1) Subject to the provisions of this regulation, any sum or sums paid by a person by way of contribution towards either or both of the following, that is to say, the maintenance of his wife and the cost of providing for one or more children, being children to whom this regulation refers, shall be treated for the purposes of sections . . . 42(1)(*b*) . . . of the Act as such contributions, of such respective amounts equal in the aggregate to the said sum or sums, in respect of such of the persons hereinafter mentioned, that is to say, his wife or any child or children to whom this regulation refers, as may be

---

[8a] See, now, the Social Security Benefit (Dependency) Regulations 1977 (s. 1. 1977 No. 343), reg. 3.

determined by the determing authority so as to secure as large a payment as possible by way of benefit in respect of dependants...

(3) The children to whom this regulation refers are any children who, in the period for which the sum in question is paid by the person, either are included in that person's family or though not so included could have been treated under paragraph 3 of the Schedule to the Family Allowances Act 1965 as so included, or would have been, or could have been treated under that paragraph as, so included had the person contributed to the cost of providing for the child at a sufficient weekly rate: ....

10. The effect of the insurance officer's decision, which was affirmed by the local tribunal, was that although the claimant's weekly payments to his former wife had fallen short of the necessary amount by only 70p (i.e. £13·30 for 19 weeks) he had been required to repay £43·20 (i.e. 18 weeks at £2·40 weekly). He appealed to the Commissioner expressing his willingness to refund the £13·30 but submitted that he was not bound to repay more.

11. When the papers first came before me I noticed that they contained no reference to regulation 10. In a recent case however, which was the subject of my Decision C.U. 1/74 (not reported), where the facts were somewhat similar, the insurance officer had in favour of the claimant "spread" parts of the payments forward to later weeks. In another case on Commissioner's file C.S. 229/73, which is pending before me, where there is only one dependant concerned, the insurance officer has spread the payments made not only forwards but also backwards and where there was a balance of less than £2·95 had carried it forward as an outstanding balance relying on regulation 10 as authority for doing so. As it appeared to me that the treatment which the claimant was receiving differed from that received by others I directed an oral hearing of the present appeal with a view to a full discussion of the matter. Unfortunately the claimant, who had not attended the hearing before the local tribunal, did not attend the hearing before me.

12. In paragraph 25 of Decision C.U. 1/74 I suggested a manner of describing two possible views as to the operation of regulation 10. If, as is commonly done in these cases, one sets out a succession of dates in one vertical column and a series of contributions opposite to them in an adjoining column and pictures the beneficiaries alongside each payment, one can think of the regulation as requiring an allocation of a sum paid on a particular date as between various beneficiaries i.e. a horizontal allocation, or an

allocation of all or part of a payment made on a date to either a later or an earlier period i.e. a vertical allocation down or up. Nobody doubts that the regulation permits and indeed requires horizontal allocation. The question for decision is whether it permits vertical allocation either downwards only or upwards only or both.

13. In paragraphs 24 and 25 of Decision C.U. 1/74 I explained that regulation 10 replaces regulation 5D of the National Insurance (General Benefit) Regulations 1948 [S.I. 1948 No. 1278], regulation 5D having been inserted into those regulations by the National Insurance (General Benefit) Amendment Regulations 1957 [S.I. 1957 No. 1888] regulation 4. That insertion resulted from the consideration of the whole question of dependency by the National Insurance Advisory Committee whose report dated 18th July 1956 on the "Question of Dependency Provisions" is Cmd. 9355. The Committee's discussion of the problem in paragraph 63 of the report makes clear that they had in mind what I have described as horizontal allocation, but there is nothing in the report that suggests to me that they were contemplating vertical allocation either upwards or downwards. The Committee's recommendation in paragraph 64, repeated in paragraph 93, sub-paragraph 11(iii) reads as follows: "Provision should be made for a general contribution by the claimant towards the maintenance of his children, or wife and children who are not living with him, to be deemed to be allocated between them in such a way as to secure title to the maximum total amount of dependency benefit."

14. In paragraph 25 of Decision C.U. 1/74 I referred to arguments which might be used in support of the view that regulation 10 provides for vertical as well as horizontal allocation. At the hearing of the present appeal before me however Mr. Nathoo of the solicitor's office of the Department of Health and Social Security representing the insurance officer submitted that regulation 10 does not provide for vertical allocation at all, but that irrespective of regulation 10 a single payment may be treated as covering a future period longer than a week if that is what in fact was intended.

15. I have no doubt that Mr. Nathoo's second submission is correct. Where for example, as in the case the subject of Decision C.U. 1/74, the claimant has been contributing to the support of his children a regular sum paid at the beginning of each month to cover that month, the statutory authorities will readily accept that, quite apart from regulation 10, the payment is to be treated as covering that month. (In view of the purpose of contributions to the support of children payments in arrear may be in a very

different position.) In the present case I do not feel justified in reaching any conclusion other than the regular weekly payments of £5 made by the claimant were intended to cover one week and no more and must be treated as doing that.

16. On Mr. Nathoo's first point, after full consideration I am persuaded that his argument is correct. Where regulation 10(1) is referring to the plural it does so expressly, yet the end product of the operation is "to secure as large a payment as possible by way of benefit". The words "equal in the aggregate" do not suggest to me that carrying forward a balance is contemplated. Horizontal operation only is consistent with the apparent intentions of the National Insurance Advisory Committee. Any other would result in administrative complications. It would be necessary to keep a running account of payments made, and if the unit of time for this purpose is a day and not a week, as it is for most purposes of sickness or invalidity benefit the complications would be greatly increased. The allocation most advantageous to the claimant in respect of two weeks might be different if there were title for a third week. The remainder of the regulation is completely consistent with an intention to provide for only horizontal allocation. On the whole I am driven to the conclusion that it does no more. The result in the claimant's case is that his payments during the relevant period entitled him to the increase in respect of one child but not in respect of the other child for any part of that period.

17. It follows in my judgment clearly that the claimant's award must be reviewed and revised both under section 72 of the Act because there was a relevant change of circumstances, namely that the claimant was no longer contributing enough, and also under regulation 9.

18. The final question is whether and to what extent the claimant must be required to repay. Section 81 of the Act requires repayment of any benefit to the extent to which it would not have been payable if my decision had been given in the first instance, unless the claimant shows that he throughout used due care and diligence to avoid overpayment. In view of his disregard of the warnings sent to him in 1972 I find it impossible to hold that he throughout used due care and diligence. He must therefore be required to repay. Moreover in view of the wording of section 81 I have no power to limit the requirement to the £13·30; my duty is to require repayment of the whole £43·20. I have therefore made the decision in paragraph 1 above (*cf.* Decision R.U. 11/71, paragraph 6).

Incapacity for Self-support

R(S) 2/56

. . . .

2. The claimant became incapable of work on the 7th April, 1955 by reason of a compound comminuted fracture of the left leg. He claimed and was paid sickness benefit, including an increase in the rate of that benefit in respect of his wife and two children. On the 13th May, 1955 the claimant informed the local insurance office that on the following Monday, the 16th May, 1955, his wife was commencing work at a wage of approximately 35s. a week.

3. From that date, therefore, the claimant would no longer be entitled to an increase in the rate of his sickness benefit in respect of her, unless he was incapable of self-support. . . .

4. "Incapable of self-support" is defined [in the Social Security Act 1975, schedule 20] which provides: "a person shall be deemed to be incapable of self-support if, but only if, he is incapable of supporting himself by reason of physical or mental infirmity and is likely to remain so incapable for a prolonged period."

5. At the time when the local insurance officer had to determine the question whether the claimant was entitled to an increase in the rate of his sickness benefit in respect of his wife for the period named at the head of this decision, he had before him a letter from the claimant, explaining that he had a steel plate joining the bone of his leg together, and a statement by him that he would be away from work for approximately five or six months, "according to the hospital." A certificate from the hospital dated the 3rd June, 1955 stated that the claimant was likely to be disabled for a further period of about ten weeks from that date. . . .

. . . .

9. . . . the insurance officer now . . . contends that, since the question whether a claimant is entitled to sickness benefit has to be looked at by reference to each day in respect of which the claim is made, it is necessary to inquire whether on the 16th May, 1955 and each day thereafter he was incapable of self-support. (With that proposition I agree.) As the claimant has to show . . . that he is likely to remain incapable of self-support for a prolonged period it is necessary to determine in respect of the 16th May, 1955 and each day thereafter whether on that day he was likely to remain incapable of self-support for a prolonged period. The Commissioner had already held in Decision C.S. 343/49 (reported) that a period must have lasted, or be expected to last, for some months before in the normal use of language it could be spoken of as a prolonged period, and, in Decision C.S. 288/50 (reported),

that a period of which it could not be said that it was likely to last for six months would not normally be spoken of as a prolonged period.

10. The insurance officer contended, therefore, that in the absence of evidence justifying a finding that the claimant, on the 16th May, 1955, was likely to remain incapable of self-support for a further six months, the claimant could not be held on that day to be incapable of self-support. There was now evidence that the claimant had remained incapable of work up to the present date and would remain so until at least the 16th December, 1955. In those circumstances the insurance officer conceded that, following Decision C.S. 288/50 (reported) referred to above and R(U) 16/51, subsequent events might be taken into account by an appellate tribunal in determining probabilities at a past date and that the claimant had now been shown to have been likely to remain incapable of self-support for a prolonged period on each day within the period to which this decision relates. He asked, however, for guidance as to the correct date from which the prolonged period of incapacity for self-support ought to be calculated.

11. It is clear that in Decisions C.S. 343/49 (reported) and C.S. 288/50 (reported) the Commissioner assumed that it was the whole period of the claimant's incapacity which had to be taken into account, but the insurance officer submitted that the question now in issue had not arisen in the cases to which those decisions related because the Commissioner had decided that the whole period of the claimant's incapacity was not a prolonged period.

12. If I were to adopt the insurance officer's contention as to the meaning of the words "is likely to remain incapable of self-support for a prolonged period," it would produce the anomalous result that, no matter how long the claimant's incapacity had lasted, when he had reached the stage in his recovery at which it was no longer possible to hold that he was likely to remain incapable of self-support for a further six months, the claimant would no longer be "incapable of self-support" for the purposes of a claim for an increase in the rate of his sickness benefit. Such an anomalous result renders it necessary to examine the validity of the insurance officer's argument with great care.

13. I do not think that the words in question drive me to such a result. It seems to me quite reasonable to speak of a man whose period of incapacity looked at as a whole is likely to be a prolonged one as a person who is likely to remain incapable for a prolonged period. It is obviously the gravity of the claimant's incapacity calculated by reference to its probable duration that is the significant matter to which the Act is designed to draw attention.

14. There is no definition in the Act of the words "a prolonged period." The need to prove its duration for six months derives from Commissioner's decisions and those decisions were given on the assumption that it was the whole period of incapacity which had to be looked at. The Act does not say that the claimant has to prove that he is likely to remain incapable of self-support for a further prolonged period beyond the day to which the claim relates.

15. It has to be remembered that Section 24(1)[9] contemplates the payment of an increase in the rate of sickness benefit "for any period" during which the claimant is residing with or is wholly or mainly maintaining his wife, provided that her earnings do not exceed a named sum and that the amendment introduced by the National Insurance Act, 1951 fixed a higher named sum "for any period during which the beneficiary is residing with his wife and is incapable of self-support." The decision of the question whether the claimant is residing with his wife makes it necessary to have regard to their past conduct as well as their apparent future intentions. So, too, it seems to me that the legislature, in requiring the claimant to prove that he is incapable and likely to remain so for a prolonged period, contemplated that, in judging whether the period was a prolonged one, the past would be taken into account as well as the future.

. . . .

Repayment of Benefit Overpaid

Social Security Act 1975, s. 119 (2)

A decision given on appeal or review shall not require repayment of benefit paid in pursuance of the original decision in any case where it is shown to the satisfaction of the person or tribunal determining the appeal or review that in the obtaining and receipt of the benefit the beneficiary, and any person acting for him, has throughout used due care and diligence to avoid overpayment.

R(U) 7/64

. . . .

3. The claimant was in receipt of unemployment benefit, together with an increase of benefit for his wife, during 1961 for the following periods (all days included), that is to say, from the 8th to the 21st August; from the 28th August to the 4th September;

---

[9] See, now, the Social Security Act 1975, s. 44.

and from the 20th September to the 25th October. In 1962 he was again in receipt of unemployment benefit, together with an increase for his wife, from the 30th April to the 30th May; from the 11th to the 30th June; and from the 9th to the 21st July.

4. The first claim for an increase of benefit relevant to those periods was made on the 16th August 1961, in respect of a period beginning on the 8th August, when it was stated that the claimant's wife was earning £2 a week. A further claim, giving similar information, was made on the 3rd May, 1962 and was renewed on the 12th June, and again on the 9th July, 1962. It subsequently transpired however that the claimant's wife, who was employed as a cleaner at a club, had had an increase of wages on the 16th June, 1961 and that at all material times after that date her weekly earnings had exceeded 40s. a week.

5. The matter was further investigated and in the result the decisions by which the claimant had been awarded an increase of unemployment benefit for his wife were reviewed by the insurance officer under regulation 18(1)(*a*) of the National Insurance (Determination of Claims and Questions) Regulations, 1948 on the ground that those decisions had been given in ignorance of the material fact that the claimant's wife was in receipt of earnings in excess of 40s. a week. I am satisfied that those decisions were properly reviewed and that the insurance officer's decision that the claimant was not entitled to an increase of benefit for the periods mentioned above was correct.

6. On appeal the local tribunal, before whom the claimant attended, found that the claimant was unable to read and write, that the claim forms (which I assume means the forms on which the increase of benefit was claimed) were filled in and completed and signed by the claimant's wife, the contents of the forms not being wholly known to the claimant, and that he reported the fact of his wife's increase in wages to the local employment exchange as soon as he knew of it. On those findings the tribunal decided as follows: "Overpayment of benefit proved (£29 1s. 4d.) but repayment not required as due care and diligence proved to our satisfaction in this particular case." The grounds for that decision were recorded as follows: "We accept claimant's evidence."

7. The local tribunal had the advantage of seeing the claimant and hearing his evidence and I see no reason for not accepting their findings of fact; nor have I any doubt that in deciding not to require repayment of the amounts overpaid the tribunal were rightly influenced by the fact that the claimant is illiterate. But, in coming to that decision, they failed to give full effect to the provisions of section 9(1) of the Family Allowances and National

Insurance Act, 1961, by which it is provided that where benefit is (or has before the coming into force of the section been) paid in pursuance of a decision which is revised on a review, the decision given on review *shall* require repayment to the fund of any benefit overpaid, unless it is shown to the satisfaction of the person or tribunal determining the review that in the obtaining and receipt of the benefit the beneficiary, "and any person acting for him", has throughout used due care and diligence to avoid overpayment.

8. It is, in my opinion, clear from the tribunal's findings of fact that the claim forms were filled in and completed and signed by the claimant's wife, that she was a "person acting for him" within the meaning of section 9(1), and it is not therefore sufficient merely to be satisfied that the claimant had throughout used due care and diligence to avoid overpayment. It is necessary also to be satisfied that his wife used due care and diligence to avoid overpayment and, although it is no doubt understandable that the claimant himself may not have been aware of the amount his wife was earning, she must have known that she was earning more than £2 a week when she completed the claim forms. In those circumstances I find it impossible to be satisfied that it can be said that in the obtaining and receipt of an increase of unemployment benefit for his wife any person acting for the claimant used due care and diligence to avoid overpayment.

9. I therefore have no alternative but to require repayment to the fund of the amount overpaid to the claimant by way of such an increase.

. . . .

Social Security Act 1975, s. 146(3)

If a person—

. . . .

(c) for the purpose of obtaining any benefit or other payment under this Act, whether for himself or some other person, or for any other purpose connected with this Act—

(i) knowingly makes any false statement or false representation, or

(ii) produces or furnishes, or causes or knowingly allows to be produced or furnished, any document or information which he knows to be false in a material particular,

he shall be liable on summary conviction to a fine . . . or to imprisonment . . . or to both.

Tolfree v. **Florence [1971] 1 W.L.R. 141 (D.C.)**

LORD PARKER C.J. This is an appeal by way of case stated from a decision of South West London quarter sessions, who quashed a conviction by the Sutton magistrates' court of Mr. Tolfree for an offence contrary to section 93(1) of the National Insurance Act 1965. That subsection, so far as it is material, provides as follows:

"If any person . . . (*c*) for the purpose of obtaining any benefit or other payment under this Act, whether for himself or some other person, or for any purpose connected with this Act—(i) knowingly makes any false statement or false representation . . . he shall be liable on summary conviction to a fine . . . "

The short facts here are that on January 20, 1969, Mr. Tolfree made an application filling up the requisite forms for sickness benefit. He enclosed a medical certificate of that date, stating that he would be incapacitated for work for seven days from Saturday, January 18. As a result of considering that application, the Department of Health and Social Security issued a sickness benefit postal order for £12 17s. 10d. On January 25, Mr. Tolfree produced that postal order at Sutton Post Office, asking for payment. The postal order stated that the sum of £12 17s. 10d. was for sickness benefit to cover the period January 18 to January 25 and before he could get his money, he had to sign the postal order under the words: "Received the above sum to which I am entitled." As a result of signing that, he received the payment of £12 17. 10d. In fact he had worked on January 23 and 24 and was accordingly not entitled to the full sum of £12 17s. 10d.

It was in those circumstances that the information charged Mr. Tolfree with having on January 25, 1969, at Worcester Park, for the purpose of obtaining for himself sickness benefit under the National Insurance Act 1965, knowingly made a false representation that he was entitled to sickness benefit of £12 17s. 10d. whereas he was not so entitled as on January 23 and 24, 1969, he had been working for District Plant Services.

Quarter sessions in quashing the conviction, appeared to have read the subsection in such a way as to provide that the obtaining was not an obtaining of payment, but obtaining of the decision to make the payment; accordingly they said that the decision to make the payment was made on the representation, then perfectly truthful, of January 20.

In my judgment, however, quarter session were wrong. A proper reading of section 93(1) shows that the false representation in question is for the purpose of obtaining any benefit or other payment. In that context "benefit" clearly means not the decision

M

to pay the benefit, but the payment of the benefit. That payment he could not get without filling up the receipt form on the postal order "Received the sum in question, to which I am entitled." That was a false representation; accordingly a prima facie case was made out.

. . . .

CHAPTER 8

GENERAL DISQUALIFICATIONS

SECTION 82 of the Social Security Act 1975 and regulations made thereunder provide for a person to be disqualified for benefit under that Act on certain grounds. The commonest ground is failure to make a claim within the prescribed time limits. Most difficulty has been occasioned by section 82(5) which provides:

Except where regulations otherwise provide, a person shall be disqualified for receiving any benefit, and an increase of benefit shall not be payable in respect of any person as the beneficiary's wife or husband, for any period during which the person—

(a) is absent from Great Britain; or

(b) is undergoing imprisonment or detention in legal custody.

ABSENCE

C.U. 28/49(KL)

. . . .

4. The Local Tribunal in my opinion misread the subsection. They thought "that person" ["the person" in s. 82(5) above] related only to the beneficiary. It does refer to the beneficiary so far as the beneficiary's own benefit is concerned; but, so far as an increase payable in respect of his wife is concerned, it relates to his wife.

. . . .

R. v. National Insurance Commissioner, Ex p. McMenemey R(S) 2/69 (appendix)

THE LORD CHIEF JUSTICE: . . . The Regulations [see, now, Social Security Benefit (Persons Abroad) Regulations 1975 (S.I. 1975 No. 563), reg. 2(1)(b)] provided that a person shall not be disqualified for receiving sickness benefit by reason of being temporarily absent from Great Britain for the specific purpose of being treated for incapacity which commenced before he left Great Britain . . . .

. . . where a person goes abroad merely for the purposes of rest and freedom from worry in order to allow nature to continue the cure and recovery . . . he is not going for the purpose of being treated. . . .

R(S) 1/75

. . . .

5. The facts are as follows. The claimant is employed in the B.B.C. as a studio manager. She told me that this involves some physical effort, and requires her to be on her feet much of the day. She worked up to and including 5th November, and on the following day left Great Britain by air for Ethiopia on a package tour holiday scheduled to last three weeks. She was examined by a gynaecological surgeon on 30th October. He advised her that she was pregnant. This advice was based on a urine test, and on the fact that her last menstrual period started on 20th September. In a written statement he says that it was not possible for him at that time to determine the site of the pregnancy, although subsequent events have established that it was an ectopic (tubal) pregnancy. I deal further with this below.

6. The claimant took off from London airport on the afternoon of 6th November. After an intermediate stop at Rome her plane took off for Addis Ababa at 8.45 p.m., and shortly afterwards she developed symptoms which were correctly diagnosed by a doctor on board as a ruptured ectopic pregnancy. On reaching Addis Ababa she was immediately admitted to hospital, where an operation was successfully performed. She returned to Great Britain on 27th November, which was the date originally scheduled. She was continuously in receipt of medical treatment while in Ethiopia.

7. I had written medical evidence as to the nature of an ectopic pregnancy, which I think it best to quote verbatim:—

> "In a normal pregnancy the ovum (egg) travels from the ovary along the fallopian tube to the uterus (womb) and is fertilized at some time during that journey and eventually implants into the lining of the uterus where it will develop into a foetus and, eventually, a viable child.
>
> In an ectopic pregnancy the fertilized ovum implants at some anatomical site other than the lining of the uterus. The commonest place for this abnormal implantation is the fallopian tube but occasionally it may be in the ovary itself. During the development of the ovum to become a foetus the usual tests for pregnancy would be positive but they would not indicate the location of the foetus and therefore it would not be possible to diagnose the presence of an ectopic pregnancy, as opposed to a normal one, by that examination. As the implanted foetus

develops it increases in size and eventually a stage is reached when the ectopic pregnancy ruptures and there is abdominal pain, shock, internal haemorrhage and a minor discharge of blood from the uterus through the vagina. This complication usually occurs between the fourth and sixteen weeks of pregnancy and is commonly the time that the ectopic pregnancy is first diagnosed. By ordinary physical examination and by the usual laboratory tests for pregnancy it would be highly improbable that an uncomplicated ectopic pregnancy could be diagnosed at five weeks. When the ectopic pregnancy ruptures, an emergency operation is essential within the next few hours to prevent death from exsanguination.

From the foregoing it is medically reasonable to say that neither the claimant nor her doctor would have been aware that her pregnancy was an ectopic one, before she boarded the plane. If it was known that she had an ectopic pregnancy, even though it had not ruptured, the appropriate medical advice would have been for immediate admission to hospital as an emergency and for a pre-emptive operation to be performed to remove the ectopic pregnancy before it ruptured. If this had occurred the claimant would of course have been in hospital and incapable of work for the period of the operation and subsequent convalescence. It is medically reasonable to state that the claimant was pregnant when she boarded the aeroplane on November 6 and that this was by reason of an unsuspected ectopic pregnancy. The diagnosis of the ectopic pregnancy was, as is common, made when the complication of rupture of the ectopic pregnancy and internal haemorrhage occurred during the flight."

8. I have to determine in the light of the above whether . . . the claimant's absence from Great Britain from 7th to 26th November was for the specific purpose of being treated for incapacity which commenced before she left Great Britain. The word "incapacity" must be construed in the context of the National Insurance Statutes. In this connection it is relevant to bear in mind that the claimant's title to sickness benefit for each day in the above period is conditional on its being shown that it was a "day of incapacity for work"[1] . . . . It is also relevant to bear in mind[2] . . . that a day shall not be treated in relation to any person as a day of incapacity for work unless on that day "he is . . . incapable of work by reason of some specific disease or bodily or mental disablement". It

---

[1] See, now, the Social Security Act 1975, s. 14(1)(*b*), *ante*, p. 1.
[2] See, now, *ibid*. s. 17(1)(*a*)(ii), *ante*, p. 2.

follows that "incapacity" . . . means incapacity for work by reason of a specific disease or bodily or mental disablement.

9. Throughout her stay in Ethiopia the claimant was incapable of work by reason of bodily disablement attributable to a ruptured ectopic pregnancy and surgery consequent thereon. Furthermore, she was receiving treatment therefor. The first question I have to determine is whether she was absent from Great Britain for the purpose of receiving such treatment. In a number of cases the Commissioner has pointed out that the language . . . is not restricted to persons who leave Great Britain with the specific purpose or intention in mind of receiving treatment. He has said (see, for example, Decision C.S. 1/71 unreported) that the language is apt to cover a person who is obliged while absent from Great Britain to obtain treatment for some incapacity which commenced before he left, notwithstanding that he did not leave for that purpose. An obvious example of a case of that kind would be where a person leaves Great Britain for a short convalescent holiday, but is compelled to prolong his stay abroad as a result of the worsening of the condition which was incapacitating him for work when he left. That is not the present case, for the claimant returned to Great Britain on the day she had planned. On the other hand it is fair to say that she left Great Britain for the purpose of a holiday in Ethiopia, and that that purpose was frustrated before she got there. No doubt when her symptoms manifested themselves she would have preferred to return home for treatment, but that was impossible for it was vital for her to undergo an immediate operation. She had no alternative but to stay in Ethiopia until convalescent. In my judgment it is possible to say in these circumstances that she was absent from Great Britain for the purpose of receiving treatment.

10. The next question is whether she was receiving treatment for incapacity which commenced before she left Great Britain. This is more difficult. To answer the question affirmatively I must, bearing in mind the meaning of the word "incapacity", be satisfied that when she left Great Britain on 6th November she was incapable of work by reason of the bodily disablement for which she received treatment in Addis Ababa. In my judgment she was not so incapable. I accept, as the claimant pointed out in the course of an attractive argument on her own behalf, that when she left Great Britain she was in the fifth or sixth week of an abnormal pregnancy which, had it been diagnosed, would have led to an immediate operation. I also accept that the pregnancy was liable to rupture at any time, with severely disabling results. But her gynaecological consultant failed to diagnose the ectopic pregnancy when he

examined her on 30th October, and the medical evidence establishes that it is highly improbable that such pregnancy could be diagnosed at five weeks. Furthermore the claimant worked up to and including 5th November, and I have no reason to doubt that she would have gone to work on the following day if her tour had been scheduled to start on 7th November. It seems to me that the claimant was not incapable of work by reason of bodily disablement until the ectopic pregnancy actually ruptured on the evening of 6th November while she was in flight from Rome to Addis Ababa. Until then, as is evidenced by the fact that she worked up to and including 5th November, there was no disablement which rendered her incapable of work. An alternative, but in my judgment equally correct way to put it, is that the claimant's absence in Ethiopia was for the purpose of receiving treatment for a ruptured ectopic pregnancy, and that the rupture occurred after she had left Great Britain.

11. To sum up, a person is not in my judgment to be regarded as incapable of work by reason of bodily disablement merely because she suffers from an undiagnosed and symptomless, albeit potentially dangerous condition, which does not in fact prevent her from working.

12. Both the claimant and the insurance officers' representative drew my attention to a number of Commissioner's decisions. The only ones which seem to me at all close to the point which I have been discussing were Decisions C.S. 317/45 (K.L.) and R(S) 10/51. I respectfully find the reasoning of both these decisions a little difficult, but in any case they are distinguishable on their facts. They were both concerned with persons who received treatment while absent from Great Britain for conditions which had been diagnosed before they left on the basis of symptoms which had already manifested themselves.

. . . .

R(S) 23/52

. . . .

4. As has been decided in Decision C.P. 93/49 (reported), a British ship on the high seas is not a part of Great Britain, and *a fortiori* a British ship in the territorial waters of another state is not a part of Great Britain. Even, therefore, if I could treat the claimant as if he were still on board his ship throughout the period from the 3rd to the 16th November, 1951, he would not thereby escape the disqualification imposed by Section 29(1)(*a*) referred to above.

. . . .

R(S) 1/78
. . . .

Preliminary question of jurisdiction

6. At the outset of the consideration of this appeal I have been confronted with a point suggested by two recent decisions of the Employment Appeal Tribunal which at first sight suggest that the statutory authorities (the insurance officer, the local tribunal and the Commissioner) have no jurisdiction to adjudicate on question of European Community Law. In the two cases to which I refer (viz. *Amies* v. *Inner London Education Authority* [1977] 2 All E.R. 100 and *Snoxell and Davies* v. *Vauxhall Motors Ltd* to be reported in [1977] 1 C M L R 487), a claim for equality of treatment made to an industrial tribunal and heard on appeal by the Employment Appeal Tribunal was framed under both domestic legislation and Article 119 of the Treaty of Rome. In relation to the latter it was held, in each case, that industrial tribunals and the Employment Tribunal were pure creatures of statute with no powers other than those conferred on them by statute, and that the tribunals could exercise no other powers than those conferred on them, and so cannot adjudicate on a claim under Article 119 of the Treaty of Rome. Such a claim would have to be made in the High Court.

7. Does this mean that the statutory authorities under the Social Security Act, who are equally creatures of statute, have no jurisdiction to deal with points of European Community Law? I have reached the conclusion that that is not the effect of the two decisions I above referred to. If an Act of even the British Parliament introduced some new benefit without prescribing a means by which it could be claimed, either expressly or by incorporating in into the Social Security Act, the statutory authorities would have no jurisdiction to adjudicate on it, however similar it might be to benefit on which they had authority to adjudicate; and the claimant would be left with his remedy, if any, in the courts. I interpret the two decisions as giving the same effect to such a provision where it is contained in the Treaty of Rome or in European secondary legislation. On the other hand where an Act of Parliament makes some provision (not necessarily in an Act relating specifically to Social Security) which affects the title to any benefit on which the statutory authorities have jurisdiction to adjudicate they must give effect to it, as they give effect, for instance, to the Nullity of Marriage Act 1971 (see Decision R(G) 2/73). It seems to me therefore that the statutory authorities are bound (by section 2(1) of the European Communities Act 1972) to give effect to such provisions of European Community Law as "are without further enactment to be given legal effect" and bear on the decision on

questions (such as the present) on which they have jurisdiction to adjudicate.

The meaning of "worker" in Regulation 1408/71

8. I turn therefore to the question whether the claimant was at the material time a worker within the meaning of the EEC Regulation. On this point I have benefit of a very full and helpful submission, favourable to the claimant, of the insurance officer now concerned. The submission is based on an analysis of not only the decision of the European Court but also the opinion of the Advocate-General in the *Brack* case[3]; he submitted that the latter as well as the former was authoritative and I agree. I must regard the opinion of the Advocate-General, where it is not inconsistent with the decision of the Court itself, as highly persuasive and where adopted by the Court as constituting binding authority. (I would refer in this connection to a lecture by Mr. J. P. Warner QC, the British Advocate-General which is published in the 1976 volume of the Journal of the Society of Public Teachers of Law especially at pages 17–18).

9. The EEC Regulation contains two relevant provisions bearing on the meaning of the word "worker". In paragraph 1 of Annex V Point I (which is a part of the Annex relating specifically to the United Kingdom) there is a provision that all persons required to pay contributions as employed workers shall be regarded as workers for the purposes of Article 1(a)(ii) of the EEC Regulation. This seems prior to the *Brack* case to have been treated as an exhaustive definition, so that only those currently insured as employed persons were treated as workers. In the *Brack* case the European Court held that the definition was not exhaustive, so that a person may be a worker if he falls within any of the subparagraphs (i), (ii) or (iii) of the definition of "worker" in Article 1(a) of the EEC Regulation.

10. The questions referred to the European Court in the *Brack* case included questions relating to each of the three subparagraphs (i), (ii) and (iii). The Court did not find it necessary to answer the questions relating to subparagraphs (i) and (iii). As to subparagraph (i) I should hesitate to determine that a person not otherwise a worker was a worker within that subparagraph without a further reference to the European Court. That is not however necessary in the present case, as I have reached the conclusion in accordance with the submission of the insurance officer now concerned that the claimant was at all material times a worker within either subparagraph (ii) or subparagraph (iii).

[3] *Brack* v. *Insurance Officer (No. 2)* [1977] 1 C.M.L.R. 277.

11. Article 1(a) of the EEC Regulation so far as material is as follows:—

"For the purposes of this Regulation:
(a) "worker" means:
(i) . . .
(ii) any person who is compulsorily insured for one or more of the contingencies covered by the branches of social security dealt with in this Regulation, under a social security scheme for all residents or for the whole working population if such person:
—can be identified as an employed person by virtue of the manner in which such scheme is administered or financed, or
— . . .

(iii) any person who is voluntarily insured for one or more of the contingencies covered by the branches dealt with in this Regulation, under a social security scheme of a Member State for employed persons or for all residents or for certain categories of residents if such person has previously been compulsorily insured for the same contingency under a scheme for employed persons of the same Member State;"

The present claim extends over what I shall call "the first period", when the National Insurance Act 1965 was still in force in respect of which I am concerned primarily with subparagraph (ii) of the above definition; and over what I shall call "the second period" when the Social Security Act 1975 had come into force in its place, in relation to which I am concerned solely with subparagraph (iii).

The position during the first period (*24th March to 5 April 1975*)
12. In the *Brack* case the European Court ruled that a person who

(1) was compulsorily insured against the contingency of sickness successively as an employed person and as a self-employed person under a social security scheme for the whole working population; and
(2) was a self-employed person when the contingency occurred; but who
(3) could at the same time, and under the provisions of the same scheme, have [successfully] claimed sickness benefits in cash at the full rate only if there were taken into account

both the contributions paid by him or on his behalf when he was an employed person and those which he made as a self-employed person

constitutes, as regards British legislation, a "worker" within the meaning of Article 1(a)(ii) of Regulation No. 1408/71 for the purposes of the application of the first sentence of Article 22(1)(ii) [*i.e.* Article 22(1)(a)(ii)] of that regulation. It is clear from paragraph 27 of the judgment that this conclusion was based on an interpretation of the words "identified as an employed person by virtue of the manner in which such scheme is administered or financed" in Article 1(a)(ii). In relation to the first period the real question to be decided is whether the present claimant can be so identified; in other respects the facts do not materially differ from those in the *Brack* case.

13. On the basis of this judgment it was held in Decision C.S. 10/76 (to be reported as R(S) 2/77) that the claimant in the *Brack* case (whose claim for sickness benefit related wholly to a period before the Social Security Act 1975 came into force) was a worker for the purposes of Article 22 of the EEC Regulation. That claimant was at the date to which the claimant related a self-employed person who had attained pensionable age but had not retired, so that the rate of sickness benefit which he was claiming was (by section 19(3) of the National Insurance Act 1965) the same as the rate of pension that would have been payable to him if he had retired. Thus an award of sickness benefit was governed by the contribution conditions relevant to an award of retirement pension. It was clear that he could not have qualified for retirement pension and so could not have qualified for sickness benefit, at the full rate without taking into account his contributions over the whole period since 1948 which included employed person's contributions. If he had been under retirement age, so that the relevant contribution conditions had thus been those appropriate to a claim for sickness benefit, he would not (any more than the claimant in the present case) have had to rely on employed person's contributions to secure title to the benefit at the full-rate.

14. In the first period the claimant was insured as a non-employed person, having been previously insured first as an employed person and then as a self-employed person. Basically he was compulsorily so insured, but under regulation 5 of the National Insurance (Residence and Persons Abroad) Regulations 1948 as amended [S.I. 1948 No. 1275] payment of contributions was optional for any contribution week throughout which he was absent from Great Britain *i.e.* from the Monday following his departure. He in fact

paid his contributions down to the end of the first period in anticipation of his holiday, such payment being optional in respect of part of the first period. The European Court in paragraph 16 of their judgment in the *Brack* case made it clear that a person's insurance does not cease to be compulsory because of the fact that during certain limited periods, such as a stay abroad, payment of contributions is optional for him. It follows that during the first period the claimant was compulsorily insured within the meaning of Article 1(a)(ii) of the EEC Regulation. This conclusion is not in my judgment affected by the coincidence that from the start of the second period (which immediately followed) insurance as a non-employed person became optional by a change in the law.

15. The claimant's position during the first period was in some respects different from that of the claimant in the *Brack* case, but this does not in my judgment necessarily lead to a different conclusion. The claimant was at the material time within Article 1(a)(ii) a person compulsorily insured for one or more of the contingencies covered by the branches of social security dealt with in the EEC Regulations (*e.g.* under Article 4 death and old age as to which non-employed contributions were by section 18 of the Act contributions of the appropriate class). Admittedly the claimant had not reached pensionable age and under paragraph 1 of Schedule 2 to the National Insurance Act 1965 the contribution conditions relevant to a claim for sickness benefit were (1) not less than 26 contributions of the appropriate class paid and (2) not less than 50 contributions of the appropriate class or their equivalent paid or credited in the relevant contribution year, (which in relation to the whole of the first period was the 52 weeks 4th December, 1972 to 2nd December, 1973). The claimant made no employed contributions relvant to the fulfilment of condition (2) although he fulfilled condition (1) indifferently with employed or self-employed contributions.

16. If all the conditions laid down in the *Brack* case were necessary conditions then the claimant does not fulfil them and his claim in respect of the first period would fail. But I do not think that they are necessary conditions and I think that the reasoning in the judgment of the Court and in particular in the opinion of the Advocate-General in the *Brack* case supports this view. I do not think that it is possible for a person to be considered a worker in relation to any one particular contingency covered by the national insurance scheme without his being considered a worker for purposes of all such contingencies. In his opinion the Advocate-General ([1976] ECR at p. 1466) posed the following question: ". . . does the assimilation of a class of persons for all aspects of

a particular risk, for example, sickness, entail assimilation—and thus the application of Regulation No. 1408/71—as regards protection against all the other risks or contingencies from which all employed persons benefit?" In discussing this question he said "For my part, I would tend to accept the same solution for all the contingencies to which the regulation applies." I find nothing inconsistent with this in the judgment of the Court. I hold that it is sufficient to make the claimant identifiable "as an employed person by virtue of the manner in which [the British] scheme is administered or financed" and so as a worker during the relevant period if it can be shown that at that time he was insured against any contingency (not necessarily that which is the subject of the claim in question) in respect of which the contributions paid by him as an employed person affected the rate of benefit payable. He was insured against the contingency of old age, and should be regarded as so insured at the relevant time notwithstanding that the contingency insured against might never occur and could not possibly have occurred during the first period. The contribution conditions for pension were then the same as those considered in the *Brack* case, and though they were about to be altered on the coming into force of the Social Security Act 1975, the alteration was not such as to affect the reasoning. Thus in relation to the contingency of old age it was virtually certain that the claimant would be entitled either to the full benefit or to benefit at the highest rate to which his contributions of all classes entitled him only by taking into account his contributions as an employed person. He was thus at the relevant time a worker within Article 1(a)(ii).

Position during the second period (6 April to 13 May 1975)
17. I now come to the second period when the Social Security Act 1975 had come into force. This Act equally with the previous Acts has to be read as subject to the EEC Regulations, since under section 2(4) of the European Communities Act 1972 any Act then passed or then to be passed is to be read subject to the provisions of that section. The Social Security Act 1975 brought about the significant change that insurance as a non-employed person ceased to be compulsory and became voluntary (see section 1(2)) and on its coming into force the claimant ceased to be a person compulsorily insured and so ceased to be a worker within Article 1(a)(ii). On the other hand it seems clear that, provided he exercised his voluntary right to continue to be insured, he became a worker within Article 1(a)(iii) as being a person insured voluntarily for one or more of the contingencies covered by the branches dealt

with in the EEC Regulation who has previously been compulsorily insured for the same contingency under a scheme for employed persons.

18. I find on the question of fact that the claimant must be regarded at the relevant time as voluntarily insured. He had in anticipation of going abroad paid his non-employed contributions down to 5th April, 1975 even, though for the reason mentioned in paragraph 14 above he had an option to pay or not while abroad. He was, as the insurance officer now concerned submits, from 6th April, 1975 under regulation 9 of the Social Security (Credits) Regulations 1975 [S.I. 1975 No. 556] entitled to be credited with contributions during his incapacity and he must in my judgment be regarded as voluntarily insured during the second period.

Conclusion

19. I have thus decided that the claimant was throughout both the first and the second period for one reason or another a "worker" within the meaning of the EEC Regulation. His title to benefit is nevertheless subject to the satisfaction to a sufficient extent of the British contribution conditions, which by virtue of regulation 3 of and Schedule 1 of the Social Security (Short-Term Benefits) (Transitional) Regulations 1974 [S.I. 1974 No. 2192] continued broadly to be those in Schedule 2 to the National Insurance Act 1965 throughout the second period. Those conditions may be satisfied by contributions of whatever class the British legislation permits. The question of the extent to which they are satisfied if put in issue must be referred to the Secretary of State for Social Services for decision, but I think it likely that the matter can be agreed and I make no direction that it be referred unless it appears that a contribution question has arisen.

20. In substance therefore the claimant establishes that he was a worker within the meaning of the EEC Regulation throughout the relevant period and so escapes disqualification on the ground of absence abroad during that period. It begins to look as if it can be stated simply but at some risk to accuracy that a person who has once been compulsorily insured as an employed person or employed earner will remain a worker so long as he continues to be insured, (compulsorily or voluntarily) and whether as an employed person or earner or not. I regret that a statement of the rule as "Once a worker always a worker" is not accurate enough.

. . . .

DETENTION IN LEGAL CUSTODY

Regina v. National Insurance Commissioner, Ex p. Timmis, Cox and James [1955] 1 Q.B. 139

LORD GODDARD C.J.: [His Lordship considered first the case of Timmis. He referred to the facts and to section 24(1) of the Criminal Justice Act 1948, and continued:] The point that arises is whether or not Timmis, who is an insured person under the National Insurance Act, 1946, and who is now in a mental hospital, is entitled to receive sickness benefit under the provisions of that Act as a person who is sick and in hospital. For the present purposes I think that it is only necessary to consider section 29 of the Act of 1946, by reason of the provisions of which the commissioner has decided that Timmis is not entitled to receive benefit. [His Lordship read section 29(1) and continued:] The question is whether Timmis, being a person committed to an institution under section 24 of the Criminal Justice Act 1948, is a person undergoing detention in legal custody. It is to be observed that section 66 of the Act of 1948 provides: "Any person required or authorised by or under this Act to be taken to any place or to be kept in custody shall, while being so taken or kept, be deemed to be in legal custody; and a constable, while taking or keeping any such person as aforesaid, shall have all the powers, authorities, protection and privileges of a constable as well beyond his constablewick as within it." The only point on which I feel inclined to differ from the decision of the commissioner is that he seemed to think that section 66 was not conclusive of this matter. With all respect to the commissioner, I should have thought that it was clear, without any particularly subtle reasoning, that section 66 means that, if a person is committed to a hospital by virtue of the provision of section 24, which enables him to be taken by a constable or other person and there kept and detained, he is to be taken to be in legal custody.

Mr. Widgery submitted, with regard to the construction of section 29, that, as the words "penal servitude" and "imprisonment" precede the words "detention in legal custody," the legal custody that is referred to there must be punitive or corrective. It seems to me that the section means that a person is to be disqualified from receiving benefit while he is detained by reason of a legal proceeding or as the result of a court proceeding. He is in custody by virtue of the decision and order of a competent court, and one might read this section as saying that he is deprived of benefit during the time he is detained in legal custody, whether it is penal servitude, imprisonment or any other form of detention. To my mind, however, the matter is put beyond doubt by section 66 of the Act of 1948, which indicates that a person detained under section 24 of the Act is detained in legal custody. Here is a man brought before a court; the court finds that he committed the offence but that he was insane at the time. The offence was one which was punishable on summary conviction because it was a form of aggravated assault and, therefore, the court had power to deal with him without sending him to trial. It would be impossible to say that a person who is brought before a court of assize charged with murder or doing grievous bodily harm, and is found insane and ordered to be detained during Her Majesty's pleasure, is not in legal custody during the time that he is in Broadmoor. I see no difference between a person sent to Broadmoor by the order of assizes and a person sent to a mental institution for persons of unsound mind by order of the magistrates. The two things seem to me to be exactly the same.

I suggested during the course of the argument that one way of testing whether a person was in legal custody or not would be to see whether habeas corpus would lie. If habeas corpus were applied for on behalf of Joseph Timmis, the answer would be: here is the order of the magistrates under which he was committed to the custody of the keeper of the mental institution and, therefore, he is being kept in the mental institution in consequence of a lawful order. He is in legal custody and the court would be bound to refuse the order for habeas corpus. For these reasons I think it is clear that Timmis is in legal custody.

In the other two cases the court proceeded under the Mental Deficiency Act, 1913, the two persons being mental defectives. The only difference between the two cases is that Cox has been detained as a mental defective for some 30 years, and James has only recently been so detained. With all respect to Mr. Widgery's argument, I do not think that that makes any difference. The scheme of the Mental Deficiency Acts is that the court makes an order, if it sees fit, instead of sending a man who has committed an offence—and a mental defective is a person who in law is responsible for his acts and not in the same position as a person of unsound mind—to prison, sending him to a place where he will receive treatment. The order in the first instance will last only for a year, but provision is made by which the Board of Control can continue the order, and it is a continuance of the order under which he is sent which remains in force so long as the Board of Control keep it in force. I think, therefore, that it is in exactly the same position as any other order. It has not expired; it remains in force because it has been continued by lawful and statutory authority by the Board of Control. I can see no difference between persons who are detained under the Mental Deficiency Act and persons who are detained under section 24 of the Criminal Justice Act, 1948. In either case it seems to me that they are in legal custody, that is to say, they are detained under and by virtue of a legal proceeding. It is not necessary to consider, and I desire to say at once that this court is not deciding, a case where a summary reception order is made, which has nothing to do with a criminal offence. Whether there is any difference, I do not know. It is not for this court to give a decision in any case except the cases before them. These particular cases are cases where an order has been made by a court exercising criminal jurisdiction in accordance with criminal law, and for these reasons I think that the orders must be refused.

LYNSKEY J. I agree.

ORMEROD J. I agree.

R. (O'Neill) v. National Insurance Commissioner [1974] N.I. 76
. . . .
O'DONNELL J.: The applicant, Bernard O'Neill, an insurance officer appointed under the National Insurance Act, sought orders of certiorari and mandamus to remove a decision of a Tribunal of Commissioners, dated 12th April, 1973, into the Queen's Bench Division for the purpose of being quashed.

The said decision was given by a Tribunal of Commissioners consisting of Commissioners Blair and Reid on an appeal by William John Mulholland (hereinafter called "the respondent") against a decision of a local tribunal dated 8th August, 1972.

Counsel on behalf of William John Mulholland conceded that certiorari lay to remove and quash the said decision if it was considered that the Tribunal of Commissioners had erred in its findings.

The respondent was arrested on 9th August, 1971, in purported exercise of powers conferred by regulation 10 of the regulations made under the Civil Authorities (Special Powers) Act (Northern Ireland) 1922. On 14th September, 1971, an internment order was served on the respondent, and he was detained in Crumlin Road Prison. On 19th September, 1971, an order for removal and internment was made ordering the removal of the respondent to the Internment Centre, Long Kesh. This order was not served on the respondent but he was removed to Long Kesh and interned there until his release on 7th April, 1972, pursuant to an order made on

6th April, 1972. On 15th December, 1971, an insurance officer decided that the respondent was disqualified from receiving retirement pension as from 16th August, 1971, the first pension day after his arrest.

It was conceded that the respondent was entitled to be paid his retirement pension from 9th August until 15th September, the date on which the internment order was served on him, and the substantial issue was whether the respondent was disqualified from receiving his retirement pension from the period 15th September, 1971, until 6th April, 1972, the date of his release.

The applicant's contention was that the respondent was disqualified from receiving his retirement pension during the period of his internment. This contention was based on the wording of section 48 of the National Insurance Act (Northern Ireland) 1966, which provides:

"48(1) Except where regulations otherwise provide a person shall be disqualified for receiving any benefit, and an increase of benefit shall not be payable in respect of any person as the beneficiary's wife or husband for any period during which that person—

(a) is absent from Northern Ireland; or
(b) is undergoing imprisonment or detention in legal custody."

The applicant contended that the respondent while interned was "undergoing . . . detention in legal custody."

In a long and careful judgment the Tribunal of Commissioners held that the applicant while interned was not undergoing detention in legal custody, and accordingly held that he was entitled to his retirement pension during the period of his internment.

At first sight the words "undergoing . . . detention in legal custody" would appear wide enough to include detention under an internment order.

The words of section 48(1) are a substantial re-enactment of section 28 of the National Insurance Act (Northern Ireland) 1946. The only difference in the wording of the sections is that in section 28 the disqualification applies to a person—"undergoing penal servitude, imprisonment or detention in legal custody." This change was obviously brought about by the abolition of penal servitude. I do not think that the amendment was intended to change the meaning of the remaining words. Since 1946 Commissioners in England have given a restricted meaning to the words "undergoing . . . detention in legal custody."

In decision No. R(S) 20/53 a commissioner said—

"However the context in which the expression 'detention in legal custody' is used in section 29(1)(b) does indicate that it is not to bear its full meaning since this would have included the preceding terms 'penal servitude' and 'imprisonment' which would thus have been superfluous. It therefore follows (as was held in Decision C.S. 16/48 (reported)) that the expression must be taken to refer only to detention which has some connection with criminal proceedings."

In *Reg.* v. *National Insurance Commissioner* [1954] 3 All E.R. 292, Lord Goddard, at p. 294, said—

"It seems to me that the section means that a person is to be disqualified for receiving benefit while he is detained by reason of a legal proceeding or as the result of a court proceeding. That is what I think is meant by 'legal custody.' He is in custody by virtue of a decision and order of a competent court, and the section may be read, I suppose, as saying that he is deprived of benefit while he is detained in legal custody, whether it is imprisonment or any other form of detention."

The court in that case did not decide whether a detention order which had nothing to do with a criminal offence involved disqualification. The position as far as I can ascertain has remained the same since 1954, and it is of interest that the Ministry had made no attempt to deprive of benefit persons detained as involuntary patients in mental institutions.

After 1954 there were further decisions of Commissioners which maintained the earlier restrictions on the meaning of "undergoing detention in legal custody."

In decision No. R(S) 3/55 it was held that a young person who was detained in an industrial school for something which was not a criminal offence and transferred as a mental defective to an institution for defectives was not "undergoing . . . detention in legal custody," within the meaning of the National Insurance Act.

The position seems to be therefore that since at least 1954 the phrase "undergoing . . . detention in legal custody" has been interpreted in a restricted way, indeed in the 3rd ed Halsbury vol. 27, para. 1354, the categorical statement is made that "undergoing . . . detention in legal custody" means "detained by the order of a court exercising criminal jurisdiction in accordance with criminal law." Internment under the Civil Authorities (Special Powers) Act (Northern Ireland) 1922 is not detention by order of a court exercising criminal jurisdiction. In this context it is important to consider the proviso to section 1 of the Civil Authorities (Special Powers) Act (Northern Ireland) 1922—

"Provided that the ordinary courts of law and avocations of life and the enjoyment of property shall be interfered with as little as may be permitted by the exigencies of the steps required to be taken under this Act."

The words of this proviso are sufficient to indicate that internment was not intended to deprive a person of rights to benefit acquired under the National Insurance Acts.

While it is not conclusive, it appears incredible that the Ministry of Health and Social Services, who presumably promoted the National Insurance Act 1966, and who were aware of the decisions referred to earlier, would not have sought to amend the wording of section 48, if it was intended that the words "undergoing . . . detention in legal custody" should extend to all these cases where persons are detained and not merely those detained as a result of court orders.

This view is reinforced by the regulations made under the 1966 Act (S.R. & O. 1971 No. 190). Regulation 11 appears to me to contemplate a court appearance and court order in all cases. It would be anomalous in the extreme if a person remanded in custody, subsequently tried and convicted but not sentenced to imprisonment, borstal or detention under the Children and Young Persons Act 1968 should not be disqualified from receiving benefit in respect of his period in custody, but an unconvicted person detained on suspicion were to be disqualified. I do not think that social legislation should be construed so as to produce such a result unless the words of the statute clearly intend it. As I have indicated all the decisions suggest that the words of the statute in this case do not intend such a construction.

In my view the Ministry of Health and Social Services have clearly acquiesced in the restricted view of section 48 and I assume that they did so because they considered such a restricted interpretation to be correct.

If all the words of the subsection in question are to receive a meaning then "undergoing . . . detention in legal custody" must receive a restricted meaning, otherwise "imprisonment" and in the earlier statute "penal servitude" are superfluous.

Since I hold that the meaning of the words in the 1948 Act has not been affected by the removal of the words "penal servitude", I think that the learned Tribunal of Commissioners were correct in their approach to the interpretation of the subsection. It seems to be that in the 1948 Act "penal servitude" and "imprisonment" constitute a "genus", namely, custody imposed as a result of the order of a court exercising criminal jurisdiction. Applying the "ejusdem generis" rule I would therefore hold that "undergoing . . . detention in legal custody" must refer to a detention arising as the result of or by reason of an order of a court exercising criminal jurisdiction.

Accordingly I hold that the respondent while interned was not "undergoing . . . detention in legal custody." Even if the words "detention in legal custody" were not to receive the restricted meaning which I have indicated I consider that the proviso to section 1 of the Civil Authorities (Special Powers) Act (Northern Ireland) 1922 read in conjunction with section 48 of the National Insurance Act 1966, would operate to prevent the disqualification from rights to benefit enjoyed by him. If he is detained in legal custody, it is detention which shall not interfere with rights acquired by him.

I reject the argument of counsel for the applicant that because of the history of internment in Northern Ireland, the words should be construed differently here. Both the Northern Ireland and Imperial Statutes are virtually identical in wording, and identical in purpose, and to adopt a different construction would raise far more difficulties than it would solve. If the Legislature in Northern Ireland wish to adopt different practices, or different standards, from those in the rest of the United Kingdom, then they must do it by express words.

Counsel for the respondent argued that the internment of the respondent in Long Kesh was not valid because of the failure to serve a notice of transfer on him. I have not dealt with this argument since in the light of my decision it does not now arise, and since any decision on the point would have effect far outside the scope of this particular case.

. . . .

LATE CLAIMS

Social Security (Claims and Payments) Regulations 1975 (S.I. 1975 No. 560), reg. 13:

(1) . . .

    (*b*) if a person fails to make his claim for . . . benefit within the prescribed time, he shall be disqualified for the receipt of benefit to the extent specified . . .

(2) if in any case the claimant proves that there was good cause for the failure to make the claim before the date on which it was made, the prescribed time for making that claim

shall . . . be extended to the date on which the claim is made . . .

R(G) 2/74

. . . .

The claimant's husband died on 21st June, 1961, at which date she was aged 48. Widowhood is a contingency covered by the national insurance scheme, and she duly claimed widow's benefit. As she had not attained the age of 50 at the date of her husband's death, she was not under the legislation then in force entitled to a widow's pension, but only to a widow's allowance. That was payable, and paid, for the 13 weeks following the date of her husband's death.

2. Section 2 of the National Insurance Act 1970 effected a change in the law regarding entitlement to a widow's pension. Its effect, read in conjunction with subordinate legislation, was (i) that as the claimant had attained the age of 40 at her husband's death, she became entitled to a widow's pension with effect from 5th April, 1971; but (ii) that such entitlement was conditional on a claim being made.

3. It was not until November 1972 that the claimant became aware of the change in the law. What happened was that on 14th November, in anticipation of her 60th birthday, she submitted a claim for a retirement pension. Receipt of this claim drew the Department's attention to the fact that she was not drawing a widow's pension, and they told her that her claim for a retirement pension would be treated as a claim for a widow's pension. . . . If the claimant establishes that she had good cause for not claiming before 14th November, 1972, the effect of the statutory provision is that benefit is payable from the first pension pay-day following 14th November, 1971.

5. A majority of the local tribunal concluded that the claimant had failed to prove good cause as above, but gave no reasons for their conclusion. The dissenting member gave his reasons for reaching an opposite conclusion, and with these reasons I am in agreement.

6. In his submission to the local tribunal the local insurance officer pointed out that the claimant attributed her failure to make an earlier claim to widow's pension to the fact that she was unaware of her right to it, and he commented as follows:—

"The Commissioner has held on many occasions that a claimant's ignorance of the law and his rights and duties thereunder does not, in itself, constitute good cause for his failure to claim within the prescribed time. It is the duty of claimants who are ignorant of their rights to take reasonable steps to obtain the necessary information, for example, by enquiring at a national insurance office."

He added that in January 1971 the Department mounted an extensive publicity campaign (press, radio and television) to draw attention to the above change in the law.

The insurance officer concerned in the appeal to me adopts and endorses the local insurance officer's submission.

7. There are doubtless many cases arising out of a late claim for benefit in which the words quoted above are opposite. In the present case they seem to me wholly out of place. Whether a person has good cause for a late claim depends on the facts and circumstances of the particular case, and an *a priori* approach to the question—an approach which avoids considering the facts and circumstances but seeks to apply some fixed and automatic principle—can in many cases lead to injustice.

8. I am unable to understand how it can be suggested that the claimant ought to have made enquiries of the Department as to her revised rights under section 2 of the National Insurance Act 1970. When her husband died she claimed widow's benefit, and learned that her benefit rights were restricted to 13 weekly instalments of widow's allowance. It is not suggested that as a result of the publicity campaign in 1971 she became aware that she might have acquired additional rights, but nevertheless failed to ascertain what they were. I accept her evidence that the campaign passed her by. She told the local tribunal that she seldom watches television; that she listens mainly to music on the radio; and that she reads one provincial newspaper. I am not prepared to hold that her failure to note the information put out by the Department in its publicity campaign is inconsistent with her plea that she had good cause for her late claim.

9. This decision lays down no general principle, except that there is no automatic short cut to the determination of good cause cases: all relevant facts must be considered. I would particularly emphasise that I am not here concerned with a late claim for a new benefit. Section 2 of the National Insurance Act 1970 altered the conditions governing entitlement to a widow's pension, and it did this with retroactive effect. By that I mean that widows who had no right to a pension at their husband's death, and whose right to widow's benefit under the legislation in force prior to 5th April, 1971 had been completely satisfied, were, under the amended

legislation, given a right to claim further benefit as a result of having been widowed.

. . . .

Chapter 9

CHILD BENEFIT

Section 1 of the Child Benefit Act 1975 provides that "a person who is responsible for one or more children in any week . . . shall be entitled to . . . [child] benefit . . . for that week in respect of the child or each of the children for whom he is responsible. . . ." Section 2 provides that

"A person shall be treated as a child for any week in which—

(a) he is under the age of sixteen; or

(b) he is under the age of nineteen and receiving full-time education by attendance at a recognised educational establishment."

A person is responsible for a child in any week if:

(a) the child is living with him; or

(b) he is contributing to the cost of providing for the child at a weekly rate which is not less than the weekly rate of child benefit (Child Benefit Act 1975, s. 3).

"Child"

R(F) 4/62

. . . .

4. At the material time Irene was undergoing instruction at a secretarial school in a course described as "Dictaphone—Copy Typists' Course". . . . The hours of attendance at the course were from 9.15 a.m. until mid-day from Monday to Friday, five days a week, a total of 13¾ hours a week. Irene attended the course for those hours. She was not expected to do any homework in connection with the course. The Prospectus of the school describes the course as a half-day course. The curriculum of the course covered touch typing, dictaphone typing, stencilling and duplicating, business principles, and filing. The question is whether in attending that course for those hours Irene was, in the words of section 2(1)(b), "undergoing full-time instruction". That she was undergoing instruction is not disputed, but was it full-time instruction? Unless it was "full-time instruction", within the Act, Irene cannot be treated as a child for the purpose of the Act, and must

be excluded in considering the claimant's entitlement to family allowances.

5. The phrase "full-time instruction" is not defined in the Act or regulations and must therefore be given its natural and ordinary meaning. In my opinion the question whether instruction which a person is undergoing is "full-time", for the purposes of the Act, is a question of fact to be decided in the light of all the circumstances.

6. The local tribunal allowed the claimant's appeal holding that,

"The course envisaged an attendance of 13¾ hours each week by a pupil, and Irene regularly fulfilled this quantum of study and instruction."

The fact that Irene attended the secretarial school for the full hours of the course is, no doubt, a relevant fact, but it by no means answers the question whether she was undergoing full-time instruction. The question whether the instruction is full-time may, no doubt, present difficulty in border-line cases, but I do not regard this as such a case. In my opinion to describe instruction at the course in question during the hours 9.15 a.m. to mid-day, for five days a week, as being "full-time" instruction is a misuse of ordinary language. I repeat that I cannot regard this as a borderline case. I have no hesitation in holding that Irene was not, at the material time, undergoing full-time instruction.

. . . .

R(F) 7/64

(See, now, Child Benefit (General) Regulations 1976 (S.I. 1976 No. 965), reg. 6 which provides that in determining whether a person is receiving full-time education no account is to be taken of a period of up to 6 months of any interruption to the extent to which it is accepted that the interruption is attributable to a cause which is reasonable in the particular circumstances of the case.)

. . . .

3. Gregory was born in April 1947. During the summer term 1963 he was at a public school and was just 16. The claimant and her husband had decided that on leaving school he should become an apprentice with certain employers. But the employers required him to have passed certain "O" Level examinations (G.C.E.) which he was due to take in the summer term 1963. Accordingly at the beginning of that term the claimant and her husband visited the headmaster, and it was agreed that if Gregory passed the necessary "O" Levels he would leave at the end of the summer term, but if he was not successful he would return for the following term and try again in December. There was no question of his

staying on to try for "A" Levels. The results of the "O" Level examinations would not be known until September, but the headmaster was good enough to agree to leave the matter in the indefinite state indicated above, without requiring the parents to make a positive decision and give a definite notice.

4. In July Gregory sat for the "O" Levels. On the 17th July the claimant very properly notified the Ministry of Pensions and National Insurance that Gregory was not staying on at school after that term provided that he got his "O" Levels. The Ministry instructed her to send a short note stating the date when he last attended school, and on the 30th July the claimant sent them her family allowance book stating that Gregory finished school that day. The school report received at the end of term suggested that there was a very real doubt whether Gregory would pass, but no doubt his parents and the school authorities both hoped that he would. On the 6th September the results were published, and it was found that he had passed in four out of six subjects, including those required by the employers. On the 10th September he was interviewed by the employers and accepted as an apprentice, and he began his apprenticeship on the 23rd September, his earnings being insufficient to prevent him from being regarded as an apprentice for the purposes of the 1945 Act.

5. At the oral hearing before me of the claimant's appeal against the decision of the local tribunal affirming the decision of the insurance officer disallowing the claim for the period stated in paragraph 1 above, the claimant contended that Gregory had throughout been undergoing full-time instruction in a school and indeed was still doing so.

. . . .

9. In Decision No. 117 given on the 17th June, 1953 the Referee, who formerly dealt with these problems, had to consider a case somewhat like the present case. A boy had been attending a secondary modern school, and it was his parents' intention that he should leave at the end of the term on the 5th April, 1950, provided that he obtained suitable work. If he did not do so, he would return to school for the following term. In fact the claim was more than a year out of date and therefore failed at the outset on that ground. But the Referee went on to express (obiter) an opinion on the legal questions involved. He said:

> "The date when a child leaves school depends, in my view, on the intention of the parent or other person responsible for securing that the child receives efficient education. The provision in Regulation 17 of the Family Allowances (Qualifi-

cations) Regulations, 1946, to the effect that a child shall not cease to be treated as undergoing full time instruction in a school during any period when he would have been undergoing such full time instruction but for the occurrence of school holidays is only applicable, in my judgment, where the parent or other person responsible for securing that the child receives efficient education intends that the child shall return to school at the end of those holidays.

For the purposes of that Regulation there is, in my view, a difference between the case where the intention is that a child shall return to school next term unless some event happens, and the case where the intention is that a child shall leave school at the end of the term unless some event happens. Where it is the intention that the child shall return to school next term unless some event happens then, until that event happens or the intention is changed, the child may be treated in accordance with that Regulation as undergoing full time instruction in a school during the continuance of the school holiday. But where the intention is that the child shall leave school at the end of the term unless some event happens then, unless that event happens or the intention is changed, the child cannot be treated for the purposes of the Regulation as a person who would have been undergoing full time instruction in a school but for the occurrence of the school holidays.

In this appeal it is clear that [his] parents determined he should leave school at the end of the Easter term 1950 and not return unless he failed to obtain employment. That term ended on 5th April, 1950, and he did not fail to obtain employment. In my view therefore [he] left school on 5th April, 1950''.

10. There is a distinction between that case and this in that Decision No. 117 was clearly based on the assumption that it was the parents' intention alone which mattered on the question whether the boy returned to school the following term or not. Here we are dealing with a public school, where the matter is one for agreement between the school authorities and the parent. In applying that decision to the present case therefore one must substitute the mutual intention of the headmaster and Gregory's parents for the intention of the other boy's father.

11. At the oral hearing I was attracted by the view that it might be possible to say that this case was not covered by Decision No. 117 on the ground that it was just as true to say that the intention was that Gregory should stay at school unless he passed as it was to say that he should leave school unless he failed. On further

consideration I think that this view is not correct. It would apply equally to the situation which was the subject of Decision No. 117. I think that in using the word "intention" the Referee was not merely referring to a neutral assessment of what would happen in certain events but was including the wishes and plans of the boy's parent. In that case it was the wish of the parents, and in this case it was the wish of the parents and the school that the boy should leave school unless something happened to make that course inappropriate. It was this factor which enabled the Referee to decide whether the case fell on one or the other side of the line which he drew. I do not think that that case can be distinguished from this one. The question then is whether I ought to follow the opinion expressed in it, which appears to be the only recorded opinion on this subject. Regulation 17 was rewritten and remade shortly after Decision No. 117 had been given. The rule-making authorities did not consider it necessary to alter regulation 17(2)(a) so as to reverse the effect of the decision. I have no doubt that it has been acted on in very many cases since, and there is nothing in Decision R(F) 4/60 or in any other decision known to me to throw doubt on it. On the whole I have come to the conclusion that my duty is to follow it, and to hold that, since the plan was for Gregory to leave school unless he failed in his examination (which he did not), the school holiday period cannot be regarded as *his* holidays within the meaning of regulation 17(2)(a).

12. There is another way of looking at this matter. *Prima facie* a boy during holiday time is not undergoing full time instruction in a school. That is why it was necessary to make regulation 17(2)(a). It creates an extension of the phrase "undergoing full-time instruction". It is clearly for the claimant to show that she satisfies the conditions necessary for title to benefit. She must therefore show that the holidays were Gregory's holidays. But in my judgment this she is unable to do. At the very best the matter was left in doubt, and the doubt was not resolved in her favour when the examination results came out.

13. The result is that Gregory cannot be regarded as having been undergoing full-time instruction at any date after the 30th July.

. . . .

"living with"

R(F) 1/71

. . . .

2. The basic facts are as follows. The daughter was born in December 1951, and in 1968 she was attending a secretarial course

as a student. The grandmother had obtained employment. In the autumn of 1968 the daughter became pregnant, and this situation led to frequent and serious disagreements between the daughter and her parents over the future of the unborn child. The daughter wished the child to be adopted at birth, and made arrangements to this end with the local authority. The grandparents were not in agreement with this course, and planned to take the child themselves to be brought up as their own daughter, they assuming full responsibility so that the daughter could resume her life as an unmarried teenage girl, relieved of her parental responsibility towards the child.

3. In April 1969 the daughter ceased to attend her secretarial course. The grandmother gave up her own employment as a preliminary and necessary step to assuming the responsibility for her daughter's child, and the finance for all necessary things was provided by the grandparents. The child, a girl, was born on 16th July, 1969 and was taken home, with her mother, to the grandmother's house.

4. The daughter, on recovering from her confinement, resumed her teenage life. She resumed her secretarial studies, although at a different college, in September 1969, and in January 1970 became employed. So far as maintenance of the child is concerned no one, other than the grandparents, has ever paid anything. The daughter retains her earnings, and is herself maintained by her parents; she is encouraged to save part of her salary against the future.

5. As from the birth of the child the grandmother has brought it up as if it were a child of her own. The child's requirements in washing, feeding, clothing and the like were and are attended to by the grandmother. The grandmother fed the child at 6 a.m.; the grandfather undertook the responsibility if the child cried at night. The grandmother's other children regard the child as their sister, and the grandmother describes the relationship between the daughter and the child as sisterly, rather than maternal. I prefer to attach more weight to this than to any inference from the fact that it is said that the child regards the daughter as her mother. What matters is not what the child of twelve months may think, but what the daughter as a mother and parent does for her child.

. . . .

7. It is accepted that the child can be included in the claimant's family as a maintained child; it is accepted that the daughter is not contributing at the rate of 18s. a week. If, therefore, the child is "living with" her mother she cannot be treated as a member of

the same family as the claimant, and this is the point on which the appeal turns. . . .

8. The fact that the daughter and the child are living under the same roof is not decisive of the matter. The restatement of the test adopted by the Referee as set out in the Commissioner's Decision R(G) 4/62, reads as follows "Where a mother and child are living under the same roof, that is not conclusive evidence that the child is living with its mother for the purposes of section 3(2). It does however raise a very strong presumption that it is doing so and that there exists the normal relationship of parent and child. That presumption may be rebutted, but only by very clear and cogent evidence of the absence of the normal relationship. In this matter both maintenance and the exercise of parental control by a person other than the parent are factors to be considered. If the mother has intended to relinquish and has in fact relinquished her parental rights and has been relieved of her parental duties and obligations to such an extent that she and the child cannot be said to be in the relationship of parent and child, the presumption may be held to have been rebutted."

9. I think it right to point out the emphasis which the above passage places on the retention or abandonment of the relationship of parent and child; "normal relationship" is the substantial test of "living with" for the purposes of the section of the Act. The presence or absence of the relationship of parent and child must in my view itself be tested by the presence or absence of factors which normally constitute such a relationship of the case. The child in this case is not yet twelve months old, and the normal relationship between the child and its mother falls to be considered with this fact in mind. For such a child the mother's parental duties are constant, demanding and repetitive, both by day and by night; her prime obligation is to supervise, with an overall care, the basic requirements of infant life. These things, by arrangement with the grandmother, she does not do and never has done, and the grandmother has complete freedom of action. Such control as it may be necessary to exercise over the child is not exercised by the daughter, and in the matter of maintenance, the provision of food, heat, light, clothing and amenity she plays no part and has no responsibilities whatsoever. In this household, as far as the child is concerned, the grandmother acts as the child's mother in all aspects of the child's life, and it seems to me that the daughter can fairly be said to have relinquished or at least to have delegated all her maternal parental duties to the grandmother for an indefinite period and for twenty-four hours a day.

10. I have not overlooked the submission, that although care

and control of the child falls to a large extent on the grandmother, the daughter going out to work full time, this is not of itself sufficient to rebut the presumption. This may well be the situation where a working mother returns in the evening to reclaim her child and reassume responsibility for it from those at home who have had the child in daily, temporary care. But that is not the case.

11. It is true that the child has not been adopted by the grandparents. The grandmother has not taken any steps to that end because she wishes to leave the way open for her daughter to take her child if she ever marries the child's father. But whether this or any other marriage of the daughter will take place, and what will then occur cannot now be predicted. What is more certain is that if the grandparents move house (and they have removed 8 times in 18 years) the child will go with them, whether the daughter does or not. I do not find anything in Decision R(G) 4/62 which makes it incumbent upon the daughter to go to the length of consenting to an adoption of her child before it can be said that she has been relieved of her parental duties and obligations to such an extent that the normal relationship of parent and child no longer links them together. Having regard to what the grandmother does and the provision she makes for the child, there is, in the circumstances of this case, nothing left for the daughter to do in the exercise of parental responsibility, and nothing to which, in relation to parental duties and obligations, the normal relationship of parent and child can be attached. I do not regard the fact that the daughter may, if she wishes, recall and exercise the parental duties and obligations which she has relinquished, as affecting the *de facto* position. What the daughter retains is the power to exercise and fulfil her parental duties and obligations, if she chooses. She does not so choose. I am satisfied that the daughter has so far relinquished her parental duties and obligations that the normal relationship of parent and child does not exist. The local tribunal held themselves bound by Commissioner's Decision R(F) 3/63. In considering the question whether a child is "living with" the mother, the question of fact is to be determined in the light of all the circumstances of the case. No one case, decided on its own facts, can be binding on another case with different facts. On the present facts of this case I am satisfied, that, although the child lives in the same house as the daughter, she is not living with the daughter for the purposes of the Act.

. . . .

"contributing towards the cost of providing for"

R(F) 1/73

. . . .

2. The claimant and her husband had a family which included three children and a family allowance at the rate of £1 18s. 0d. was in payment in respect of that family. On 16th November, 1970 the claimant gave birth in hospital to a fourth child, a daughter to whom I will refer as N. The claimant claimed and was awarded and paid an increased allowance at the rate of £2 18s. 0d. on the basis that N. was included in her family. In fact however, on 27th November, 1970 before the date of the claim N. had been taken into the care of the local council direct from the hospital and had gone to live with foster parents. The intention at that time and for many months afterwards was that she should return to the claimant, but she was eventually adopted by the foster parents or one of them. Since leaving the hospital she has never lived with the claimant or her husband, and neither of them has contributed anything in money towards her support. They have however provided various articles mostly of clothing, and the substantial question for decision in this appeal is whether . . . the claimant and her husband have been entitled to include N. in their family . . . at any time during the period beginning on Tuesday 29th December, 1970. . . . . The effect of these provisions as to title is as follows. A child may be included in a family for family allowance purposes by virtue of residence ("living with") or maintenance. As to maintenance, if by a parent, it must be to the extent stated in section 3(2), at the relevant time 90p; if by anyone else, to the extent stated in the Schedule, paragraph 1. Temporary absence or interruption of contributions is disregarded, and what is treated as being temporary is governed by regulations (section 17(7)). Apart from special cases, absence and interruption cease to be temporary after four weeks (regulation 12) unless intended to be other than temporary (regulation 14).

Where a child qualifies for inclusion in the families of a parent and also a non-parent, the right of the parent prevails (Schedule, paragraph 2). Maintenance can be in kind; see section 18, where "providing for" a child means making available for the child food, clothing, lodging, education and all other things reasonably required for the child's benefit having regard to all the circumstances. The making available in kind of anything used for providing for a child is treated as a contribution equal to the value of it (section 18).

. . . .

4. The claimant's case is that on three occasions she has provided in kind articles coming within the description in section 18 of the Act.

. . . .

8. On the claimant's appeal to the Commissioner the case was helpfully and clearly discussed by the insurance officer in a submission dated 21st April, 1972 which quotes sufficient of the relevant statutory provisions. In this submission it was accepted that N. could be included in the claimant's family for certain weeks, though neither in this submission nor in the earlier proceedings does any effect seem to have been given to the provision of the canopy. The submission was based on the view that a contribution made on any date counts as a contribution during the week including that dàte and does not have to be "spread" forward in accordance with the life of the article or otherwise. In view of this I thought it right to raise the question whether this approach to the matter was consistent with Decision C.F. 6/62 (not reported). In that case as here the child was taken into care shortly after its birth. Its mother provided a layette of a value rather more than £5. The insurance officer submitted to the advantage of the claimant that the cost should be spread over a number of weeks at the required weekly rate (then 8s.) in accordance with the probable life of the article which was taken as 13 weeks. The Commissioner accepted this argument by the insurance officer in favour of the claimant.

9. In this case in a further written submission the insurance officer contented that if the costs of the various articles were spread forward, the claimant would not be entitled to have N. included in her family for any of the 17 weeks and this would operate harshly. He therefore submitted that having regard to the nature and cost of the articles it would be appropriate to treat their cost as a contribution for the week in which it was provided. At the hearing before me the insurance officer repeated and elaborated this contention, arguing that the rules must be applied so as to give the greatest possible advantage to the claimant, so that in effect she would be entitled to elect which of the two methods of calculation should be adopted. He said that this contention would apply even where there were conflicting claims. He contended in the claimant's favour that the pram canopy fell within the description of things contained in section 18, and with that contention I agree.

10. In my judgment however there is great difficulty in accepting the insurance officer's main contention, which could lead both to injustice as well as to great complication.

11. In many cases the person actually looking after the child has other children and would be able to receive an increased family allowance by including the child in question in her family. But she cannot do this for any week during which the mother can include the child in her family (paragraph 2 of the Schedule to the Act). This provision coupled with regulation 12 already operates in such a case seriously to the detriment of a foster parent. (No such question arises in this case since the foster parent has no children other than N.). It may be considered that it would be most unjust if a foster parent were deprived of her family allowance, though she was in fact entirely supporting the child, simply because the parent with or without her consent had bought the child an expensive article of clothing having a long life.

12. The complexities resulting from spreading forward are well illustrated by this case. The claimant's own evidence supports what seems to me obvious that the various articles concerned in this appeal have widely differing lives. She told me that plastic panties wear out quickly whilst some of the articles have a longer life, and she added that if they did not wear out they could be used again for a younger child. The shawl and pram canopy might well last for years. If in the present case one is to decide by means of the spreading method whether the claimant was entitled to include N. in her family for the last week with which we are concerned, including 20th April, 1971, it would be necessary to compile a fairly complicated schedule based on the cost and expected life of not merely the articles in bulk but each article separately. What would happen if one of them had been lost and was no longer available is a matter for speculation.

13. The questions arising under the three sections referred to in paragraph 2 above are largely questions of fact on which it would probably be wrong for me to attempt to lay down any hard and fast rules. I will therefore say no more than that I should not be in the least surprised if insurance officers in practice made the calculation as had been contended for by the insurance officer, namely treating the contribution as being made in the actual week when the article was provided, and regarding Decision C.F. 6/62 as applicable only in very exceptional circumstances. I think that such an approach to the problem would be perfectly proper. That is how I propose to treat this case. I do not accept the view that the claimant is entitled to elect which way the case should be treated, since that would mean that in most cases it would be necessary to do the complicated sort of calculation to which I have referred in order to see which basis was the more favourable to her and less favourable to anyone else concerned. The approach

to the matter which I adopt has the advantage of keeping payments in money and in kind so far as possible in line. If a parent thinks that her child living with a foster mother needs a winter coat and gives the foster mother some money to buy one, I have never heard it suggested that such a contribution should not be treated as a contribution during that week in the same manner as normally happens with money contributions.

Multiple Family Links

(See, now, the Child Benefit Act 1975, Sched. 2.).

R. v. Hoxton Local Tribunal, Ex p. Sinnott (Appendix to R(F) 1/74), (D.C.)

THE LORD CHIEF JUSTICE: Mr. Eric Michael Sinnott is the factual head of what appears to be a family comprising two children of his own by his wife from whom he is separated, a lady called Miss Windebank with whom he has been living for some time, and two further children born to Miss Windebank of whom Mr. Sinnott is the father.

. . . .

Section 3(3) contains a reference to the Schedule in the Act which is designed to deal with problems where a child may qualify to be in more than one family, and subsection (3) says this: "The provisions of the Schedule to this Act shall have effect as to the circumstances in which a man and his wife living together, or such a man or woman as is mentioned in subsection (1)(b) or (c) of this section, is to be treated as maintaining a child, and for determining as between parents and persons maintaining children, or as between one parent of a child and the other, in what family a child is to be treated as included."

It is to be observed in passing that the two children born to Miss Windebank are her issue, and she clearly could claim them as part of her family on that footing if she so desired. The latter sentence of section 3(3) brings into effect the provisions of the Schedule to the Act for determining as between parents and persons maintaining children or as between one parent of the child and the other in what family a child is to be treated as included.

Mr. Croft says that that subsection is intended solely for cases of dispute. I think he must mean acrimonious dispute, contention, because it is not necessary that the parent should be in any sense in acrimonious dispute in order to raise the question as to which family a child must be regarded as forming part of. After all those who have to administer this legislation have to form their own views as to its meaning, and if they take the view on an issue of this kind different from that taken by the parents then there is a question which has to be determined by somebody somewhere, and in my judgment there is no reason whatever for restricting section 3(3) to contentious disputes, or indeed beyond its natural terminology, being as I see it a section designed to point to the answer where the rules of thumb of section 3 would provide two or more conflicting solutions.

I should underline the fact that in Mr. Croft's submission we never get to the Schedule. He says in the absence of any dispute between the parents section 3 governs the situation and the Schedule, as I understand his argument, is not relevant at all.

In my judgment for the reasons I have already given it is highly relevant, and this is the relevant paragraph: "Where a child could otherwise be treated under section 3 of this Act as included at the same time in one family as being issue of his parents or either of them, and in another family as being maintained by a person other than his parents or either of them, the child shall be treated as then included in that family only in which he can be treated as included as being issue of the parents or parent."

I find that language crystal clear as intended to govern, and indeed governing, the facts of this case. What is it that it contemplates? It contemplates a situation in which a particular child might qualify in one family as being issue of his parent and in another as being maintained. That is exactly what the situation is in regard to the children in the instant case.

The children of Miss Windebank can be part of her family if one looks at the blood tie, but they cannot be part of Mr. Sinnott's family because they are illegitimate. On the other hand, since Mr. Sinnott maintains them they can be part of his family on the face of it on that score. You have a classic conflict which is intended to be cured by paragraph 2 of the Schedule, and the effect of paragraph 2 is that, given this conflict, the children of Miss Windebank must be treated as part of the family where the tie is blood and not as part of the family where the tie is maintenance. Since the tie of Mr. Sinnott is maintenance only for present purposes, it seems to me quite impossible that the children of Miss Windebank can form part of Mr. Sinnott's family for present purposes. It may be illogical, but if Parliament had intended that maintenance was to be the sole test it could easily have said so. It is quite obvious that Parliament did not intend maintenance to be the sole test, and construing the Act as we have to, I am left in no doubt that if this were a matter where an application for Certiorari was fit for consideration in the absence of other forms of appeal, I should nevertheless find it necessary to refuse the application because in my judgment the Tribunal below reached the right answer.

O'Connor and Goff J.J. concurred.

CHAPTER 10

SUPPLEMENTARY BENEFITS

PROVISION is made for payment of supplementary benefits by the Supplementary Benefit Act 1976. Benefit as of right (a supplementary pension in the case of a person over pensionable age, otherwise a supplementary allowance) is payable where the claimant, over the age of 16 and entitled to claim in his own right not being a dependant, has resources inadequate to meet his requirements. Requirements are determined by reference to statutory scale rates which vary according to whether the claimant is blind or sighted, newly on benefit or a long-term beneficiary, a householder or not, etc.

In certain cases (husband and wife, persons living together as husband and wife, or where "one person has to provide for the requirements of another person . . . . who is a member of the same household) requirements and resources must be aggregated.

In exceptional circumstances, the Supplementary Benefits Commission may increase (or, in the case of a supplementary allowance, reduce) the weekly benefit payable in its discretion. There is also discretion to make a single lump-sum payment to meet exceptional need.

R. v. West London Appeal Tribunal, Ex p. Clarke [1975] 3 All E.R. 513 (D.C.)

. . . .

The history of this matter begins some time in the year 1971 when the applicant, aged 72 and a citizen of India, lost her husband. Her daughter was married to Mr. Pitken and lived in High Wycombe. Both the daughter and the son-in-law earnestly requested her to come to England where they would look after her. After a good deal of persuasion she agreed, gave up her home in India and arrived in England on 23rd September, 1972.

She was permitted by the immigration officials to enter without any restrictions imposed on her stay. Prior to leaving India she had been issued with an entry certificate by the British High Commission in Madras. In accordance with the immigration rules she provided evidence that her son-in-law was able and willing to provide for her maintenance and accommodate her in his home. In due course she went to live with her son-in-law and his family. Things went reasonably well until 20th February, 1975, when owing to a family quarrel the son-in-law put her belongings outside the house and ordered her to leave.

The fact that an undertaking was given by the son-in-law to the immigration authorities to support the applicant is entirely irrelevant. It was clearly a genuine undertaking when given. It was not until a considerable time thereafter that a family dispute resulted in the ejection of the applicant from her son-in-law's home. She eventually went to live with her son and was taken into his home. She has tried many times to get in touch with her son-in-law, who she believes has the financial means to support her, but he has put the telephone down every time she has got in touch with him. Those are the brief facts.

The Supplementary Benefits Commission on 8th April 1975 had to do two things. It had to determine the applicant's requirements, which it did correctly according to the Act which is in force, namely the Supplementary Benefit Act 1966. It arrived at an amount of £9·65, and in addition there was a sum of 95p that had to be also taken into account by a non-householder claimant; so that the requirements of the applicant were assessed in total at the sum of £10·60.

It is the calculation of resources that has led, in my judgment, both the commission and the tribunal into error in this case. The commission and the tribunal correctly disregarded the sum of £1 in accordance with the terms of the 1966 Act. However, the resources were calculated on the basis of £11·60 by reference to "maintenance" and one can search in vain in the Act for any reference to maintenance by a son-in-law of his mother-in-law or by a son of his mother.

Section 4(1) of the 1966 Act provides:

> "Every person in Great Britain of or over the age of sixteen whose resources are insufficient to meet his requirements shall be entitled, subject to the provisions of this Act, to benefit as follows, that is to say,—(*a*) if he has attained pensionable age, to a supplementary pension . . . "

This applicant has in fact attained pensionable age.

Section 5(1) provides:

> "The question whether any person is entitled to benefit and the amount of any benefit shall, subject to the provisions of this Act as to appeals, be determined by the Commission and shall be so determined in accordance with the provisions of Schedule 2 to this Act and the other provisions of this Part of this Act and any regulations made by the Minister with the consent of the Treasury."

So one turns to Sch 2. That is divided into two parts which are relevant. One part deals with the calculation of requirements, and we are not concerned with that. Another part—in fact it is Part III—deals with calculation of resources, and nowhere in any paragraph of that schedule is there placed on anyone an obligation to support a mother-in-law.

One turns to s. 22 of the 1966 Act, which provides as follows:

"(1) For the purposes of this Act—(*a*) a man shall be liable to maintain his wife and his children, and (*b*) a woman shall be liable to maintain her husband and her children; and in this subsection the reference to a man's children includes a reference to children of whom he has been adjudged to be the putative father and the reference to a woman's children a reference to her illegitimate children."

There is no obligation at all on the part of either a son or son-in-law to maintain his mother or mother-in-law. Thus, the submissions made on behalf of the applicant are really these. The decision of the tribunal shows an error on the face of the record. The applicant has in fact no resources. She is accordingly entitled to benefit. For my part I entirely agree.

. . . .

Waller and Milmo JJ. concurred.

R. v. West London Appeal Tribunal, Ex p. Taylor [1975] 2 All E.R. 790 (D.C.)

MAY I read the first judgment at the invitation of Lord Widgery CJ: In these proceedings counsel for the applicant moves for orders of certiorari and mandamus in respect of a decision of the West London Supplementary Benefits Appeal Tribunal ("the appeal tribunal") dated 29th October, 1973.

The application arises in this way. The applicant has an illegitimate child born in December, 1963. She separated from the child's father in February, 1965 and was able for some time by working to maintain herself and the child. Eventually she found it impossible to provide for the family herself and accordingly on 7th February, 1972 she claimed a supplementary allowance under what was the Ministry of Social Security Act 1966. When the Supplementary Benefits Commission ("the Commission") were informed of her circumstances and realised that the father of the child was liable to contribute towards his maintenance, an agreement was made between the commission and the applicant whereby the commission would pursue the claim against the putative father on her behalf and she would repay to the commission part of the sums to be paid to her by way of benefit out of any moneys which might be obtained from the father.

There was in fact apparently a court order which had been made in 1966 but which had not been enforced, and the procedure which the commission was about to undertake on the applicant's behalf was the enforcement of that order.

These proceedings were successful and on 23rd June, 1973 a total of £958·75 was paid into court by the father. The commission deducted certain sums by way of recoupment of advances made by the commission before the money was paid, and there remained the sum of £704·75 of the funds recovered. A dispute then arose as to how this money should be applied having regard to the fact that the applicant was still claiming supplementary benefit.

On the applicant's side it seems to have been contended that the money should be treated as capital and, accordingly, should be dealt with under para 22 of Sch 2 to the Ministry of Social Security Act 1966 to which I must return for detailed consideration in a moment.

The contention of the commission on the other hand was that this sum was not capital but arrears of income, and that it was the commissioner's duty to have regard to this sum of £700 odd as a resource to which the applicant could turn for the maintenance of herself and her child. The commission said that this sum must be spread over an appropriate period and that the applicant's benefit would be reduced during that period by the weekly amount apportioned by the commission. In fact the commission directed that the sum of £704 should be spread over 44 weeks, which meant in practice that the applicant would be deprived of her supplementary benefit for about that period, and that the money would be absorbed in providing for her needs in the absence of any supplementary benefit. . . . there is no provision in Sch 2 which can in any way be said to give the commission the general over-riding discretion contended for by counsel for the respondent. As has been seen, para 1(*b*) of Sch 2 provides that the resources of a person are to be "calculated" in accordance with Part III. The use of the work "calculated" is I feel an indication that the draftsman intended that the amount of a person's resources was to be ascertainable arithmetically and not just arbitrarily.

. . . .

It is for the commission, therefore, to determine whether a given resource is capital or income. They decided that the £704 was income for the purposes of Sch 2, and the appeal tribunal agreed with them. In these circumstances I do not think that it is for this court to interfere with that conclusion. In my opinion this court should only so interfere if it could say that no tribunal properly directing itself on the evidence could come to this conclusion. Had I been deciding this point myself at first instance I might well have taken the view that the relevant sum was capital rather than income, but in all the circumstances I do think that one can say that the alternative view was one which could not properly be taken.

If, of course, the decision is that the money is to be treated as capital within Part III of Sch 2 to the Act, then the equivalent weekly amount attributable to the capital has to be calculated in accordance with para 22 of Sch 2.

Nevertheless, although for the reason I have given I do not think that this court should disturb the tribunal's decision that the £704 was income, as the tribunal have in their reasons indicated their approval of the way in which the commission proposed to deal with this resource, once having decided it was income, I think this court should consider whether such approval on the part of the tribunal was soundly based in law.

If an income resource found by the commission comprises current or future income, such as earnings or receipts under a court order, then it will be received periodically and its weekly equivalent will be a simple question of calculation.

The difficulty arises in this and similar cases where the found income resource comprises arrears of periodic payments. This is income which ought to have been received in the past. Not having been so received, how is it to be treated insofar as the future is concerned, in the necessary calculation of supplementary benefit under Sch 2?

I think that one can approach the probelm in two stages. Ex hypothesi the money under consideration is the aggregate of instalments of income which ought to have been received in a period of known length, in the present case one of 6½ years or thereabouts. Once again therefore the weekly equivalent of the aggregate sum is in my opinion merely a question of arithmetic. In the present case, as the arrears were of payments of a regular £2·50 per week which ought to have been made by the putative father under the affiliation order against him, the weekly equivalent of the arrears of £704 is clearly £2·50. As I have said, I cannot find any provision anywhere in the Act which gives the commission the arbitrary discretion, contended for by counsel for the respondent, to spread the aggregate sum over some other period, as the commission may think fair and reasonable.

The second question, however, is whether the aggregate arrears still determined to be income are to be referred not merely to a period of a given duration, thus producing a weekly equivalent *for the future* to be included as such in the claimant's resources, but to the actual period of that duration *in the past* over which the arrears in fact accrued, with the result that so long as the aggregate arrears, or whatever may remain unused of them, retain their quality of income, then they must be disregarded in the benefit calculations from time to time.

I do not think that there is anything in the Act which helps one to decide this question. Whichever answer is chosen gives rise to anomalies. If the arrears are attributed to the actual period during which they accrued, and so disregarded in the benefit calculation, it can be argued that the claimant will receive benefit out of central funds to a greater extent than his or her actual circumstances really warrant. If, on the other hand, the claimant has to give credit for the weekly equivalent on the basis that the arrears remain income, then it is difficult to dispute the logic of the argument that this must be given for the same period in the future as that in the past over which the arrears accrued, even though perhaps, for the very reason that the periodic payments were not made, the claimant was forced to incur debts which he or she would like to use the arrears in whole or in part to discharge.

Considerations such as these might well persuade the commission to conclude at quite an early stage that aggregate arrears like this should be considered to be capital, despite the income nature of their origin. Nevertheless for so long as the commission determine the arrears to retain the quality of income, as one obtains no assistance from the Act itself, in my opinion the more logical course is so to attribute the arrears to the actual period in the past over which they accrued and thus disregard them unless and until the commission conclude that they, or what remains of them, must be deemed to be capital.

. . . .

Lord Widgery C.J. and Ashworth J. concurred.

R. v. Preston Appeal Tribunal, Ex. p. Moore and Shine [1975] 2 All E.R. 807 (C.A.)

LORD DENNING M.R.: . . . In many cases the calculation of "requirements" and "resources" is simply an arithmetical exercise. First, find the applicant's weekly "requirements". Next find his weekly "resources". Then deduct the resources from the requirements. And you have the answer. It is the benefit to which he is entitled. But there is a special provision which says that "where there are exceptional circumstances" a greater amount may be awarded, or the allowance may be reduced or withheld, so as to take account of those circumstances . . .

Moore's case

John Moore was a student of engineering at Harris College, Preston, Lancashire. He was a married man aged 24 with a wife and two daughters, aged three and one. The Lancashire education authority awarded him a grant for the academic year 1971–72. It was his last year at the college. Though the last vacation ended on 31st August, 1972, the last term ended on 30th June, 1972. He could then be expected to get a job and earn his own living.

For this last year the education authority made him a grant of £850·40. It was made up of three parts:

	£
Student's own allowance for term time and travel	383·40
Student's maintenance allowance for vacation	42·00
Dependants' allowance for wife and two children	415·00
	840·40

This was paid to him in three instalments: £328·40 at the beginning of the autumn term, £267 at the beginning of the spring term, £245 at the beginning of the summer term. By the end of the summer term, on 30th June, 1972, he had spent all those sums and had nothing left. He registered for work at the Department of Employment. They had nothing to offer him. So on 3rd July, 1972, he claimed a supplementary allowance from the Supplementary Benefits Commission. They calculated the benefit payable to him at £4·10. It was arrived at as follows:

Requirements	£
Husband and wife	9·45
Two daughters	3·40
Rent allowance	2·05
	14·90

Resources	£
Vacation Grant	1·90
Dependant's Grant	7·98
Family Allowance	0·90
	10·78

Benefit £14·90 less £10·78 makes £4·12, rounded off to £4·10

Mr. Moore was dissatisfied with that award. He appealed to the Preston appeals tribunal. On 3rd August, 1972 they upheld the assessment of £4·10, but they made a special addition of £3·00 extra on the ground that there were exceptional circumstances: see para 4(1)(*a*) of Sch 2.

Mr. Moore moved the High Court for an order of certiorari to quash the decision of the tribunal. He made no complaint about the calculation of his "requirements". These came to £14·90. But he did complain about the calculation of his "resources". He was represented by Mr. Blom-Cooper QC, who made this submission on the meaning of "resources": he said that it meant his *actual* resources, that is the means which a man has presently available and to which he can resort to pay for his needs. On this meaning, counsel for Mr. Moore said that Mr. Moore had no "resources" on 30th June, 1972, because he had spent all of the grant and had nothing left. . . .

I cannot accept counsel for Mr. Moore's construction of the word "resources". It is not defined in the 1966 Act, but there are many indications that it refers to notional resources and not actual resources. Thus his capital resources are turned into a weekly income by means of a formula which may bear no resemblance whatever to the actual income: see Sch 2, para 22. He may have less or more than the formula provides. He may have spent it all or none. Nevertheless the income is to be calculated according to the formula. Again his earnings are to be calculated at a weekly sum, even though they are paid monthly or quarterly. Suppose he is paid monthly in advance. He may spend it all in the first day or two in buying a new stove or a suit of clothes. Yet his resources during the whole of that month are to be taken as the weekly equivalent. Suppose he is paid monthly in arrear, he has no acutal resources in the first month and he is not to be regarded as notionally having them; but thereafter he has resources which are to be calculated at a weekly sum and when he leaves at the end of the last month, he has a month's pay in hand as his resources for the following month.

So here when the grant for the wife and children was paid in advance for the period up to 31st August, 1972, his resources are to be taken ás £7·98 a week for that period. It is unfortunate that he was not aware of this and he spent it all long before. That was a reason for making him a special addition. But it does not make the calculation erroneous in point of law. Similarly in regard to the £1·90 a week for the vacation.

Shine's case

. . . . Malcolm Shine shared a flat with three other students. They were four joint tenants. Each of the four bore one-quarter of the rent and expenses. Each paid his one-quarter of the rent separately to the landlord every month. The gas and electricity bills were for convenience sent to one of them—Mr. Fairbairn—but each contributed his quarter share.

In assessing the "requirements", Mr. Shine claimed that he should be regarded as a householder within para 9(*b*) of 'Sch 2. There is a special provision which gives a higher benefit for a "person living alone or householder . . . who is directly responsible for household necessities and rent (if any)". The Supplementary Benefits Commission rejected Mr. Shine's claim that he was a "householder". On appeal the tribunal also rejected it. Their written reasons said:

> "Mr. Fairbairn receives gas and electricity accounts and therefore the others are in the same position as non-dependants contributing towards a householder's commitments."

Mr. Shine applied to the High Court for an order of certiorari. He said that being a joint tenant he was directly responsible for household necessities and rent and was, therefore, a "householder".

If this were to be regarded as a strict point of law, there is much to be said for Mr. Shine's contention. Under the Interpretation Act 1889, singular includes plural. So "householder who is" includes "householders who are". And these four students, being *jointly* responsible for household necessities and rent, are all four householders. It makes no difference in law that gas and electricity bills were sent in the name of one of them only. That was a mere matter of convenience which did not affect the responsibility of all four of them.

This seems to me a good instance where the High Court should not interfere with the tribunal's decision, even though it may be said to be erroneous in point of law. It cannot be supposed that each one of these four should each have the full allowance as if he was responsible for the whole, nor even that one of them—Mr.

Fairbairn—should have the full allowance. The better way of administering the Act is to hold that one of the four gets the allowance as being the householder, but that each should be regarded as a lodger contributing towards a householder's commitments. Each should get an allowance in respect of his contribution to the rent (see para 13) and each may be granted a special addition under para 4(1)(*a*) to take account of the exceptional circumstances. That is what the tribunal allowed to Mr. Shine. It was a reasonable way of administering the Act on a point which was not covered by the Schedule.

Principles on which the court should interfere

It is plain that Parliament indended that the Supplementary Benefit Act 1966 should be administered with as little technicality as possible. It should not become the happy hunting-ground for lawyers. The courts should hesitate long before interfering by certiorari with the decisions of the appeal tribunals. Otherwise the courts would become engulfed with streams of cases just as they did under the National Insurance (Industrial Injuries) Act 1965: see *R* v. *Industrial Injuries Commissioner, ex parte Amalgamated Engineering Union*. The courts should not enter into a meticulous discussion of the meaning of this or that word in the Act. They should leave the tribunals to interpret the Act in a broad reasonable way, according to the spirit and not to the letter, especially as Parliament has given them a way of alleviating any hardship. The court should only interfere when the decision of the tribunal is unreasonable in the sense that no tribunal acquainted with the ordinary use of language could reasonably reach that decision: see *Brutus* v. *Cozens*. Nevertheless, it must be realised that the Act has to be applied daily by thousands of officers of the commission and by 120 appeal tribunals. It is most important that cases raising the same points should be decided in the same way. There should be uniformity of decision, otherwise grievances are bound to arise. In order to ensure this, the courts should be ready to consider points of law of general application. Take these two cases. In Moore's case, counsel raised an important point on the meaning of the word "resources". Did it mean actual resources or notional resources? It applied to all students seeking education grants. It was very right for the High Court to give a ruling on it. In Shine's case, counsel raised an important point on the meaning of "householder" when there were two or more joint tenants. It applied to all students sharing a flat when all were directly responsible for expenses. Were all entitled to the householder's allowance or only one or none? It is very desirable for this point to be authoritatively decided. So we have decided it. But so far as Mr. Shine's £50 grant is concerned, that is of small importance though of general application. So the High Court should not be troubled with it, and his counsel did not press it before us. In short, the court should be ready to lay down the broad guide lines for tribunals, but no further. The courts should not be used as if there was an appeal to them. Individual cases of particular application must be left to the tribunals. And, of course, the courts will always be ready to interfere if the tribunals have exceeded their jurisdiction or acted contrary to natural justice. That goes without saying. I would dismiss this appeal.

Stephenson and Geoffrey Lane concurred.

K. v. J. M. P. Ltd. [1975] 1 All E.R. 1031 (C.A.)

CAIRNS L.J.: . . . the change in the mother's resources does not constitute a pecuniary loss to the children unless it can be shown, or inferred from the circumstances, that the care which the mother can give them is diminished by the loss of the father's support. This must depend on the extent to which she can be expected to be supported by supplementary benefit. She had been in receipt of such benefit for herself and the children from the date of death and the weekly payments at the time of the trial were at the rate of £19·25 a week. Now counsel for the children has maintained that once damages are awarded to the children to supply their own immediate needs in the way of food, lodging, clothing etc, the mother must lose her entitlement to benefit. He bases this on para 3(2) of Sch 2 to the Ministry of Social Security Act 1966 which provides:

"Where a person has to provide for the requirements of another person . . . who is a member of the same household, his requirements may be taken, and if that other person has not attained the age of sixteen shall be taken, to include requirements of that other person, and in that case their resources also shall be aggregated."

Counsel for the children says that the mother, as the only surviving parent of illegitmate children, is a person who has to provide for their requirements and therefore that the resources of the children (being the damages recovered by them and the interest thereon) will fall to be aggregated with the means of the mother, which would result in a family's resources being assessed at a figure which would rule out supplementary benefit. I am quite unable to accept that argument. It is not correct to say that the mother "has to provide for the requirements of the children". "Requirements" here must mean requirements in respect of payments for the necessaries of life and these are all provided for by the uncontested part of the damages awarded to the children. It therefore appears to me that the mother is entitled to supplementary benefit (or at least is likely to recieve it, because the payments are discretionary) at the normal rate for a single person, which at present is £10·40 a week. Consequently I consider that her estimated share of the housekeeping and holiday food money provided by the father, £334 a year, must be deducted from the figures arrived at by the judge in assessing the annual loss of the three children.

. . . .

Stephenson L.J. and Cairns J. concurred.

R. v. Barnsley Supplementary Benefits Appeal Tribunal, Ex p. Atkinson (1977) 3 All E.R. 1031 (C.A.)
JUDGMENT OF THE COURT DELIVERED BY BRIDGE L.J.:

. . . .

The real question which falls for decision on this part of the case, it seems to us, is whether voluntary payments can properly be treated as resources at all for the purpose of Sch 2 to the Act. The answer to that question in the handbook to which we have referred is in the affirmative. It is said in para 27:

" . . . the Commission under their discretionary powers normally ignore payments made by relatives, friends, or charities for, and provision in kind of, items regarded as not covered by supplementary benefit. [Examples are then given] . . . but regular and substantial provision in kind is normally taken into account."

The applicant submits that this is wrong and that no payment received by a claimant in cash or kind to which he is not entitled as of right ought to be treated as part of his resources. There is no definition of "resources" in the Act. Giving the word its ordinary English meaning, we think that it is clearly proper to treat a regular cash allowance from a parent to a student or the regular provision for him of maintenance in the family home during vacations as part of the resources of that student.

INDEX